A Madsen

The Loyal Orange Institution: Facts v. Fables

A rejoinder to the Rev. Father Cleary's book

A Madsen

The Loyal Orange Institution: Facts v. Fables
A rejoinder to the Rev. Father Cleary's book

ISBN/EAN: 9783744794084

Printed in Europe, USA, Canada, Australia, Japan

Cover: Foto ©Lupo / pixelio.de

More available books at **www.hansebooks.com**

THE
Loyal Orange Institution:

FACTS v. FABLES.

A Rejoinder to the Rev. Father Cleary's Book—
"THE ORANGE SOCIETY."

BY

REV. A MADSEN.

What he hit was—HISTORY;
What he missed was—MYSTERY.

Melbourne, 1898.

C. W. BURFORD, PRINTER AND PUBLISHER, 31 QUEEN STREET
AND AT 37-41 GORDON PLACE.

"I espied a little before me a cave where two giants, POPE and PAGAN, dwelt in old time; by whose power and tyranny the men whose bones, blood, ashes, etc., lay there were cruelly put to death. But by this place Christian went without much danger, whereat I somewhat wondered: but I have learned since that PAGAN has been dead many a day; and as for THE OTHER, though he be yet alive, he is by reason of age, and also of the many shrewd brushes that he met with in his younger days, grown so crazy and stiff in his joints, that he can now do little more than sit in his cave's mouth grinning at pilgrims as they go by, and biting his nails because he cannot come at them."   —JOHN BUNYAN in THE PILGRIM'S PROGRESS.

"It is a common error to suppose because Rome is unchangeable in her dogmas that she is unchangeable also in the forms of her logic. . . . . The creed of the Church of Rome is immutable: its logic is in perpetual flux: her policy is ever old as regards its ends: it is ever new as regards its phases."   —REV. J. A. WYLIE, LL.D.

"Catholicism, indeed, never can be looked upon merely as a religion. It is a great and highly-organised kingdom, recognising no geographical frontiers, governed by a foreign sovereign, pervading temporal politics, with its manifold influence attracting to itself much of the enthusiasm that would otherwise flow in national channels. The intimate correspondence between its priests in many lands, the discipline and unity of their political action, the almost absolute authority they exercise over large classes, and their usually almost complete detachment from purely national and patriotic interests have often, in critical times, proved a most serious political danger: and they have sometimes pursued a temporal policy, eminently aggressive, sanguinary, unscrupulous, and ambitious."   —MR. W. H. H. LECKY.

"The Church of Rome is a huge and intricate system of Government. . . . The papal government is a conspiracy of the subtlest and best individual minds against the fortunes and liberties of mankind. It has its agents in every land and nation: every priest, every monk, every member of this confraternity is an agent of its government."   —LORD ROBERT MONTAGUE.

"History has fared ill in many hands. But in no hands has she ever fared worse than in those of party leaders. When they engage her as their maid-of-all-work she sinks to the level of a very slattern. Truth in the hands of a casuist: morals in the hands of the proverbial Jesuit: facts in the hands of a special pleader: all these combined are but a feeble image of the fate of history when it is put to use by professional politicians."   —THE DUKE OF ARGYLL.

PREFACE.

THE ORANGE SOCIETY, by Rev. H. W. Cleary, done up in orange-coloured wrapper, with orange lilies and a medallion of William Prince of Orange, " FOURTH EDITION complete," price one shilling,[1] is before the public. Those who judge a book by its binding are probably appealed to in this way as a trick of the trade. The contents, however, speedily dispel any anticipation that the work is of Protestant origin ; for under an honest orange cover, the author makes a big attempt on the life of the Orange Association. Were it as successful as it is hoped to be, that organisation would now be sleeping "a hundred fathoms deep," with no prospect of a resurrection. But the unexpected often happens, and as "the best laid schemes o' mice and men gang aft agley," Mr. Cleary's work may contribute towards strengthening and lengthening the life he seeks to extinguish. One thing stands out conspicuously, and that is—that while the rev. gentleman may have prime qualifications for many things, he is by birth, tradition,[2] religion, and training, totally unfitted for writing an account of Orangeism which can reveal even a nodding

---

[1] An advance Circular of Mr. Cleary's Book came into my hand, published by Bernard King & Sons. In it the public are informed that his work "is published at *an absolute loss*, the kindness of a few friends encouraging the writer to place it before the public at the modest price of one shilling." Father O'Doherty, the proofreader, in a letter published in this Circular, remarks— " the patriotism of the Irish in Australia has been sadly over-rated if you do not dispose of the first Edition of the Book the week it is issued." Now, what does Father O'Doherty mean by the "patriotism of the Irish in Australia"?

On June 22, 1891, *The Age* observed—"The policy of the Catholic Church has always been to separate the faithful from the heretics by all possible means, and one of these has been the creation of a real or imaginary grievance." It criticises Dr. Carr's utterance on Irish Australians, and says :—" The Archbishop is singularly weak in relation to the question of whether Catholic Australians will be Australians first and Catholics afterwards, or the reverse. He seems to think that their local patriotism will be sufficiently shown by their desire for the disruption of the Empire, but it is not at all apparent even in this view they will be in accord with the bulk of their fellow countrymen."

[2] *Vide* his Book p. 299. Note: *John Cooney and the Author.*

acquaintance with impartiality on the subject. Every page of his book bears incontestable witness of his deep-rooted antipathy to the Orange Society, and all its works and ways. Father Cleary quotes Justin McCarthy, who quotes Lecky as saying of Froude's work—*The English in Ireland*—" His book has no more claim to impartiality than an election squib."[3] I present this to the author as a very accurate description of his own production. It reminds me of Dr. Mortimer Granville's revolt against the total abstainers who constantly preach from the text—" There is death in the cup." Dr. Granville made a spirited deliverance against them from the text " There is death in the *teapot*." The *English Alliance Record* serves him up in the following ditty :—

Tea, Coffee and Cocoa—those drinks of the devil—
Are bringing us down to a horrible level :
Men's courage is going—speak out they will not—
I only am left to attack the teapot.

Similarly Father Cleary has risen in his wrath against the *Orange* organisation. From the housetop, he proclaims that the rind is not only bitter, but that the juice is poisonous : death lurks in the pips, and the succulent pulp is a dreadful compound of iniquity. Beware of the Orange !

Wherever he finds one—be he noble, or be he simple —who entertains similar sentiments, he finds a man after his own heart : and every Protestant mouth which he has discovered during his pilgrimage through the Melbourne Public Library, uttering a good round curse upon Orangeism is immediately regarded as " distinguished." It is yet fresh in the public mind that, once upon a time, it was blazoned abroad that Mr. Parnell " had taken his coat off " for Ireland, and it is now clear that Father Cleary has followed the illustrious example. He did preliminary sparring in the Ararat press some years ago :[4] then I gather from reading his work that

---
3 p. 62 Note.
4 See *Ararat Advertiser* May 31, June 21, June 26, 1895.

he boxed even more vigorously recently in the columns of *The Advocate* ;[5] invigorated by these exploits and flattered by his friends, he now poses before the public as a "fighting" priest, throwing down the gauntlet to the Orange Society.

Candid minds are not likely to be influenced in their judgment by the nature of the attack, but the drift of his essay is well calculated to produce upon the Roman Catholic mind[6] at least, an impression that the Orange Society is a secret conspiracy against the peace and social well-being of the Roman Catholic section of the community. Orangeism is an union of Protestants without regard to denomination, and whilst pledged to observe the principles of toleration, is determined to resist, by all lawful means, papal encroachments on the glorious civil and religious liberty now enjoyed by all. Father Cleary, keenly aware how hopeless an attack would be on the *basis* of the Institution to which all its members are required to subscribe, like a skilful tactician, does not waste his energies in assailing the unassailable. It is difficult to resist the conviction, that the under-lying object of his publication is to produce an impression on the Roman Catholic mind of the nature already referred to, when we find him evading this lion in the path— which he is afraid to face—with the statement that the basis of the Orange Society and the general qualifications of its members serve "*to conceal the real aims* of the Institution."[7]

In this rejoinder I shall endeavour to point out a some-

---
5 p. ix.

6 In the publisher's Circular is printed Father O'Doherty's commendatory letter. It contains some interesting paragraphs—*e.g.*, he describes Mr. Cleary's book as—"simply epoch-making. It should *seal the doom* of Orangeism in the eyes of fair-minded men. . . . . Every Irishman who reads it will gather from it a firm determination to *put an end* to a system which has done unutterable evil to the dear old land . . . . and every honest man . . . . who reads your *true* story of Orangeism, must be the uncompromising foe of an organisation that has for its chief object the ruin and degredation of all who profess the Catholic faith." This glib writer also remarks—"every Irishman worth his salt will not only purchase a copy for himself but will also help to circulate the book amongst his non-catholic acquaintances."

7 p. 145.

what different complexion, and relate certain pregnant facts of history which he skilfully glosses over or completely ignores. I am conscious that my arguments could have been materially strengthened, had I been able to devote more time to the collection of data, and to an examination of literature contemporary with that frequently used by Mr. Cleary. Some works also referred to by Mr. Lecky are not accessible to me, though from the side of Orangeism they would doubtless be of the utmost service—notably a *Historical View of Orangeism* in the Stowe MSS. in the Irish Academy; Sir W. Verner's *Short History of the Battle of the Diamond; Orangeism—its Origin, Constitution and Objects*, by Richard Lilburn, 1866; Cupple's *Principles of the Orange Association*; Mortimer O'Sullivan's *Case of the Protestants of Ireland*. Without these documents a fulness of treatment in some directions is not to be expected. Still, much may be done with the materials to hand—sufficient indeed to more than render uncertain Father Cleary's gravest charges, and undermine his strongest positions. The reverend gentleman is, apparently, overwhelmed with astonishment at finding Protestants so wicked as to combine for the purpose of resisting the encroachments, and ascendency, of the Church of his choice. Evidently he fails to understand that Protestants resent the tone of superiority assumed by that Church, and see a menace to popular liberties should it again become a controlling ecclesiastical power, which it is considered by numbers scheming to become. In view of much in its past history the "infallible Church" should be humble, not arrogant: meek, not pretentious: apologetic, not assertive. Bellarmine depicts the true Catholic Church as consisting of those, and *those only*, who (1) profess the true faith: (2) partake of the true sacraments: and (3) subject themselves to the rule of the Pope of Rome as head of the Church, "even though they may be false, wicked and impious." This excludes from the pale of salvation all Protestants, and all Greek Catholics, no matter how good they are, while it includes the notoriously "false, wicked and impious." Nice elements in a Church, but surely not infallible characteristics of the true Church of the Redeemer? Submission to the Pope of Rome appears more important than character, according to Bellarmine. The Greek Catholics declare that "Peter's apostolic activity in Rome is unknown to History," but Leo I. in the fifth century *consigned to Hell* those who did not assent to the primacy of the Bishop of Rome. Archbishop Carr recently quoted as authoritative one of the canons of the Church of Rome as follows :—"If anyone say . . . that the Roman Pontiff is not the successor of Blessed Peter in the same primacy, let him be anathema." Dr. Rentoul forcefully says respecting the list of Pontiffs :—"They are, as a matter of historic fact, the successors of a long line of *despotic priestly politicians*, many of whom were amongst the worst figures in human history [8]" In the following pages the reader will find many evidences of the commanding power of the clergy over the Roman Catholic people in political matters, and in what directions that power is used. The Orange Society, so far as I can discover, has only become an active centre of political influence, when there has been a determined Roman Catholic combination for the purpose of forcing some measure, at the time, deemed to be injurious to the cause of civil and religious liberty. When no such movement was afoot, the Institution appears to have been but a passive or inert body—more of the sentinel than of any other type.

The form, which this work has taken, has been decided by the presumption that those who peruse it are acquainted with Father Cleary's strong statements. I disclaim all idea of creating religious or racial rancour in the community in compiling this reply : every historical allusion and argument which Roman Catholics deem offensive must be laid at the reverend father's

---

8 *The Early Church and the Roman Claim*, p. 28.

door. He quoted Mr. Lecky on Froude's History as follows :—" *The English in Ireland* 'is intended to blacken to the utmost the character of the Irish people, and especially of the Irish Catholics.' " (p. 62, note 25.) Another Catholic scribe has quoted Lecky on Froude to the following effect :—" A writer of English history who took the Newgate Calendar as the most faithful expression of English ideas, and English murderers as the typical representatives of their nation, would not be regarded with unqualified respect." *(The Maryborough Advertiser,* Sept. 7, 1896, letter by *Qui Vive.)* Now Father Cleary has done much the same thing with respect to Orangeism. Had he given his Orangemen the least semblance of common humanity or even of ordinary decency, he might have written twenty books without receiving any attention so far as I am concerned, but it would be ridiculous for the public to imagine that his production ranks as an unassailable repertory of truth —when it is simply a rubbish bin.

It may be of interest to the reader to know that Father Cleary publicly challenged me in 1895 to debate the question of Orangeism in the Ararat press, during a controversy between us, but as he assumed a position in the debate which tied one hand behind my back, I would not concede it ; so the challenge came to nothing. (See *Ararat Advertiser,* May 31, June 21, 28, July 2, 9, 12, 16, 19, 23, 30, &c. to Sept. 6, 1895.)

Had I followed my own preferences, readers would not have been confronted with so many quotations, but as Father Cleary made his book stand on *inverted commas,* I have adopted the method as being "the correct thing." This work will doubtless present many defects to the critical eye, but it should be borne in mind that it is a controversial piece of writing, and that it has been done in the spare hours of an active ministry which does not permit a large margin for personal leisure.

MELBOURNE, AUGUST, 1898.   A. MADSEN.

CONTENTS.

	PAGE.
PREFACE	1
CHAP. I.—COMMENT IN GENERAL	11
CHAP. II.—ORANGE PROCESSIONS IN MELBOURNE	34
CHAP. III.—THE PIVOTAL FACT OF ORANGE STORY	52
CHAP. IV.—MASSACRE OF 1641 : CROMWELL AND IRELAND	67
CHAP. V.—WILLIAM III. AND CLEARY'S CHARGES	77
CHAP. VI.—THE SOCIAL SETTING OF ORANGEISM	92
CHAP. VII.—THE EMERGENCE OF THE ORANGE SOCIETY	106
CHAP. VIII.—PETRELS OF 1798	125
CHAP. IX.—REBELLION OF 1798	145
CHAP. X.—THE ORANGEISM OF 1798	164
CHAP. XI.—"THE CUMBERLAND PLOT"	185
CHAP. XII.—SAMPLE COLLECTION OF CLEARY'S FABLES	204
CHAP. XIII.—SUPPLEMENTARY	255
APPENDIX A.—EARLIEST DECLARATION OF ORANGE SOCIETY	255
APPENDIX B.—FIRST OUTRAGE ON ORANGEMEN IN VICTORIA	257
APPENDIX C.—"THE LEGEND OF ULSTER'S PROSPERITY"	262
APPENDIX D.—THE POST OFFICE INQUIRY 1896	262

CHAPTER I.

COMMENT IN GENERAL.—CONCESSIONS TO ORANGEISM AND NOT FROM A FRIEND.—A NEW CURIOSITY SHOP.—AN EYE FOR EFFECT.—" RELIABLE INFORMATION."—A SCHOOLGIRL'S ACCOMPLISHMENT.—THE LINE OF CLEAVAGE —"A BIT HOT, THAT'S ALL!" —CAULD KAIL HET AGAIN.—" DISTINGUISHED " AUTHORITIES. —PRIVATE AND CONFIDENTIAL DOCUMENTS.

THE ORANGE SOCIETY is a fair subject for criticism, and provided such criticism be fairly conducted no ground of offence can be taken; on the contrary, only good can result. The Society has had a good deal of critical attention paid to it at one time or another, but so far as I am aware it has been reserved for the Rev. Father Cleary, of Ararat, to publish an Australian work devoted purely to a consideration of the subject. This writer, in feathering his shafts, has dwelt as lightly as possible upon, when he has not been the apologist for, contemporary events which light up the field of history exploited by the Orangemen as he represents, or rather mis-represents them. Mr. Cleary, I infer from certain turns of expression in his volume, hails from Ireland, and doubtless belongs to that class who are " handy wid the pen," of fragrant ballad memory ; and I am given to understand, by mutual acquaintances, that he is not prepared to abate one jot of the claims of the Roman Catholic denomination. If these two features regarding the author are correct, one can quite understand that the Orange Society, which should " by all LAWFUL means resist the ASCENDENCY of that Church, its ENCROACHMENTS, and the EXTENSION OF ITS POWER,"[1] is a vile thing meriting pious execration and forcible suppression. The Rev. Father starts off therefore on his narrative with this fixed assumption, and ransacks History, which to him is merely an arsenal, for appropriate weapons to sweep the Orange Society off the

---

[1] p. 145. The Nun of Kenmare writes :—" I can scarcely tell when I entertained the first idea of entering the Roman Catholic Church. My principal reason was the strong assurance which that Church gives that it has always taught and always will teach the same doctrine. But I have lived to see a stupendous change, which I know of my own knowledge *has shocked the moral sense*, if it has not offended the conscience even of many bishops. Instead of the Apostolic formula, It ' seems good to the Holy Ghost and to us,' the Roman Church has, ' It seems good to the Holy Ghost and to *me*.' The voice of the Church is practically lost in the voice of a single man."—(*The Nun of Kenmare*, pp. 16-17.)
This lady is a practical illustration of Dr. Pusey's good work for Rome.

face of the earth. There is room, however, for an exactly opposite conviction as a starting point of investigation; and in moving from it I repudiate the moonshine so elegantly enunciated as the policy of the Orange Society—" Lay low and say nuffin'."[2]

Mr. St. Loe Strachey in an article on "Ulster and Home Rule"[3] declares that—"A very large number of Ulster Protestants, before the growth of Parnellism made co-operation impossible, habitually worked with the Catholics on Liberal lines. The Liberals of Ulster *were brought up to hate* two things equally, Orangeism and Ribbonism;[4] and when the surrender of 1886 took the world by surprise, the Protestant Liberals and the Protestant Tories of the North found themselves, *for the first time in their lives*, with a common policy. Strange as it may seem, the Convention will even now be the first occasion on which many of the Orange and Liberal Leaders have ever met ......Nothing but *the gravest danger* would have united the Ulster Liberals and the Orangemen. With the Orangemen I do not desire to express much sympathy, for they have undoubtedly helped to keep alive the spirit of Religious intolerance in Ireland, and have abetted in this evil work the efforts of the more extreme Irish Roman Catholics. It must not be forgotten, however, that the Orange Organisation has suffered a good deal of *misrepresentation* in England, and that as a rule its *character is misunderstood.* Whether we like it or not as a whole, we must acknowledge that it has not a few redeeming features, and possesses a real hold on its members. It is, for example, a thoroughly democratic Institution. Class distinctions have no place in the Orange Lodges, and laborer and landlord are on an equality at their meetings. Again it is to be noted that though Orangeism and Episcopalianism usually go together, the Puritan spirit is still present. Every lodge opens its proceedings by a reading from the Bible." Here, then, we have sufficient, at any rate to hold our judgment on Mr. Cleary's "Orange Society" in suspense, until we are quite clear that he does not either misrepresent or misunderstand it. Mr. Strachey says:—"Whether we like it or not, as a whole, we must acknowledge that it has not a few redeeming features," and without endeavouring to set up

---

2 p. 3.   3 *The Nineteenth Century*, June, 1892.

4 W. Stuart Trench writing in 1869 on the subject of Ribbonism said : "I, myself, received a letter, illustrated with a coffin in flaring bloody red, and adorned with death's heads and cross bones, threatening the most frightful consequences to myself and family, if I did not continue to employ a young profligate carpenter whom I had discharged for idleness and vice." The writer then narrates a Ribbon murder, and the subsequent course of justice which nearly let the murderer escape.—(*Realities of Irish Life*, p. 49 &c. to 62.)

any claim that the Institution is monopolised by a set of infallibles [5] in the form of Orangemen, I so far find myself in agreement with that writer, as to believe, that Father Cleary builds men of straw for the pleasure of knocking them down again, thus gratifying the good old Irish propensity, which, it is said, dearly loves a fight—real or sham.

During my perusal of the work under consideration several first impressions occurred to me, which I may as a matter of order state at this stage, for subsequent critical examination has only confirmed them.

THE RELATION OF DETAIL TO EFFECT.

This struck me as being unique. The sources from which the Author has gathered his material : the paragraphic clippings : the ingenuity with which they are worked into narrative, and made to do duty for cumulative, and even supererogatory, evidence of Orange iniquities, stamp the work as a remarkable product of industry. The only parallel that occurs to me is, unfortunately, not of a literary character and therefore, for purposes of comparison, is likely to be below the mark, yet it will serve as *a parable*. There is a Curiosity House in Ballarat East which rivals the *Old Curiosity Shop* of Charles Dickens. It is a collection of outcast fragments worked up ingeniously. There are teapot lids, spouts and bowls of all colors and shapes. Jugs, urns and vases are arrayed in ranks and perched on pinnacles. Dolls' heads supply the element of tragedy—their glassy eyes stare from every angle and corner. Bits of mirror adorn the walls and shine brightly in the sun, but the visitor is not complimented by what he sees in them. Dilapidated toys, fragments of coloured glass, ruined china, broken bottles and crockery are there in endless profusion. In fact there is something of everything, plastered on the house, along the footpaths, and mounted on the fence walls. It is odd that this gorgeous show-house should come up in connection with a reading of Father Cleary's book. Doubtless it was the result of the law of association, and the two do not seem ill-matched. I find that pieces have been taken from the works of fully one hundred Authors, while the number of Government Publications, Newspapers, Periodicals, &c., made subject to the scissors and pastepot number 56. One of these latter has contributed 287 titbits ; a second 154 ; another 82 ; and yet another 60. While

---

[5] There is only *one* infallible Society upon the earth, to wit the Roman Catholic body—and its history is not sufficiently enticing for me to set up any rival.

of the former, one has furnished 406 extracts; a second 104; a third 63; a fourth 56; a fifth 54; and a sixth 46. Now in a Volume of the modest size and price as the one we are considering ten contributories have been levied upon for 1300 odd quotations in the aggregate, and according to the published figures at the back of the Book there are at least 146 others, who furnish bits of broken crockery or gory dolls' heads, as the case may be, for this new Curiosity shop. This of course secures variety in the ornamentation of the structure. In subsequent chapters the value of the contributions will be placed under examination, and in consequence need not be anticipated at this stage. I do not propose to follow the bad example set by Father Cleary and inflate the reading matter with "vain repetitions," but this much may be indicated, that the shocking massacres, in which his Orange Society indecently wallows, must be taken at a liberal discount—say $99\frac{3}{4}$ per cent.—for there is an atom of truth in some of them, but the majority have no more serious side than a row of dolls' heads exhibited under startling conditions, whilst his most thrilling narratives give no more accurate representation of the actual facts of the case, than a glance into the patched mirrors of the Ballarat House can be relied on, for giving a correct reflection of the person in front of them. It will be the business of this work to critically examine the most important, of the many, dramatic episodes with which Mr. Cleary has elaborately garnished his edifice of Orangeism, and where they are fragments ingeniously, but not ingenuously, pieced together to throw light upon the clever patchwork. My artistic sense will not prevent me from spoiling pages of the literary Mosaic, with which, and at great pains, the author has inlaid his story. But the general effect is the thing—the grand thing about this Book. The fragmentary prevails—all is in brilliant contrast—everything is aglow with colour—a skilful hand for grouping and posturing is at the back of the scene; quantity is displayed with lavish hand to hide the fact of a squalid quality: and the general effect is "stunning," as the boys say. Still, when once the parts are subjected to a close scrutiny, a suspicion arises in the mind. As the eye wanders over the Orangeism of Father Cleary, it is seen to be the work of an *Artist*, rather than that of an Historian—an Artist, too, in a literary sense, on a level with the decorator of the Ballarat Curiosity House—both at work on the same principle, viz.: to make use of the material to hand, rejecting nothing, no matter how commonplace, and all for the sake of the general effect.

Involved and Problematical.

A second aspect, which impressed me, was the involved and problematical character of its purpose. It opens with a view of the Melbourne Post Office Inquiry Board of 1896,[6] which appears the ostensible reason for the matter appearing in its present form,[7] and ends (if we exclude the Appendices) with that huge delusion, "the Cumberland Plot," in Great Britain, which is set down as occurring in 1835—some sixty years ago. All the way through, the author, pursuing the constructive principle for the sake of effect, moves from one end of a century to the other, and from one end of the earth to the other, with nonchalant ease. He can stride a century forward or backward in a paragraph, and pick up intermediate dates on the way—the direction or the duration does not trouble him in the slightest. With marvellous celerity he stands on Ulster soil in one line, on Canadian territory in a second, reaches Australia in a third, and is safe home again in Ireland by the next line. This peculiar feature of literary gymnastics renders it totally impossible to follow his movements in detail in a reply, and hence I have contented myself by dealing with periods and events in sections. Father Cleary says:—"The purpose of this Volume is not to give a set history of the Society, but to set before the reader certain broad features of the inner working and outward action of Orangeism, which embrace the greater portion of its annals, and which best explain its true aims, methods and character."[8]

---

[6] See Appendix D, which will indicate a present day parallel of the Mountain in travail, and the resultant mouse.

[7] In the Publishers' Circular, the inducing cause of Father Cleary's work is stated as follows :—" The attitude of the Society with regard to the Party Processions Act, the increasing violence and publicity of their Press and Platform attacks on a large section of their fellow-colonists, the spread of Orangeism in the Public Service, and especially in the Police Force, the revelations brought to light by the Melbourne Post Office Inquiry Board in the case of James Sullivan, as well as many other circumstances which are duly noted in the pages of this new volume, *constitute a menace* to the Catholic Body and to the peace of the whole colony. These, coupled with certain local circumstances, led the writer to study the subject of the Orange Society, as fully as his occupations would permit." One would think from this that Father Cleary was breaking new ground in his volume, but as far back as July 30th, 1895, he wrote in the *Ararat Advertiser* :— "In the course of my study of Orangeism, I have waded through the files of the *Victorian Standard* from its very first issue in December, 1884, to the 29th June, 1895." From his own account, he was a sort of howitzer *loaded to the muzzle* at that date, and was prepared to debate the subject with all comers. I observe that the Rev. Mr. Malyon has publicly challenged Father Cleary to discussion.

[8] p. 15 In the Circular by Bernard King and Sons, Publishers, an announcement is made of Mr. Cleary's work as follows :—This Book has been written with a view to throwing light on the aims, methods, secret workings and true spirit of the Orange Society." But the dead past is used much more than the living present

In the introduction to the first edition the author remarks: "They are now placed before the public, in the hope that they may supply in handy form, and as far as they go, RELIABLE INFORMATION as to the aims, methods, and tendency of a little-known, but active, Secret Society, which has kept a portion of the North of Ireland in a state of unhealthy ferment for over a century, and which for the past few years has been executing a forward movement in our midst."[9] Here, Mr. Cleary sets forth the "purpose," and indicates, in a measure, the plan of his work, vouching for it that he gives the public "reliable information" of the aims, methods and tendency of the Orange Society. We are aware that the Roman Catholic Church is accustomed to triumphantly and unanswerably prove the validity of the Scriptures, by the authority of the Church itself, and then to prove the authority of the Church from the Scriptures, thus giving a complete illustration of arguing in a circle.[10] This conclusive method of reasoning is not lost upon the reverend gentleman, who presents the "information," and then gives his personal assurance that it is "reliable."[11] We shall bear this—Father Cleary's headlight—in mind as we proceed. A marked feature in the Book is the tone it adopts towards English Administrations in their particular Irish policies. Any

for this purpose, and even " the tale of the dead " requires correction. Like the Irishman's gun the needed repairs amount to a new lock, stock and barrel.

9 p. x

10 In the Hammersmith Debate between Dr. John Cumming and Mr. Daniel French, the Rev. Doctor said of the Church of Rome :—"She proves her infallibility by the Bible, and the Bible by her infallibility : and yet, is it not a curious fact she has never yet *produced* an infallible interpretation of God's Word ?" Turning to his opponent, he said : "Your Church pretends to have an infallible exposition in her possession, somewhere or another of the whole of God's Word : and yet with the cruelty that is the characteristic of a Stepmother, not with that affection which is the characteristic of a Mother, she withholds that infallible exposition of God's Word from millions that implore it."—*Hammersmith Protestant Discussion* (New Edition, 1856), p. 469.

11 It may be objected that Father Cleary does not *explicitly* give his assurance that the "information" is "reliable," and that he only advances it *"in the hope"* that such is the case. Now (1) If he has no faith in the reliability of what he publishes at "an absolute loss," but is willing that it should be taken for what it is worth on the uncertain recommendation of his mere "hope," then I am most profoundly mistaken. (2) The *tone* of his book is altogether inconsistent with such a notion—it breathes assurance throughout respecting the truth of its narrative. (3) The most apparent intention of the statement is to give an *implicit* voucher for the reliability of the information set out. (4) If, however, neither explicit nor implicit guarantee is expressed in this language, then it is worth noticing that Mr. Cleary merely *hopes* that the thousand odd startling statements in his book are reliable. What a forlorn hope in contrast with his militant information ? Hope, as a term, always *implies uncertainty*, unless it is used, as it sometimes is in Scripture, to mean "assurance."

interference on their part with Roman Catholic aims, methods, and tendency, is splenetically resented, e.g.: "Lord Camden, the Viceroy who was sent over to Ireland in that year to superintend the work of *goading the people into insurrection*."[12] "The cruel policy of Pitt in *forcing the people into rebellion* for the purpose of depriving Ireland of her Legislature."[13] "Under the favoring smile of a friendly Government, the *worst crimes* of the 'Banditti of Plundering Ruffians' were either *connived at or openly encouraged* by Acts of Indemnity. Henceforth, till Pitt's policy was effected, the way to favor place and power lay through religious strife and persecution."[14] Naturally, from such a quarter we expect that Cromwell,[15] the idol of Carlyle, and William,[16] the pride of Hallam and Macaulay, will be both promptly and uncompromisingly condemned, but this merciless Iconoclast strikes down Disraeli,[17] and even Salisbury.[18]

One would think that Father Cleary had never heard the old oke, which says—the Scotch have all the money; the Irish all the billets; and the English what remains over, for, noting that a question (tendered to Police Witnesses in the Brunswick Riot Cases, 1897, as to whether these witnesses were members of the Orange Society) was objected to, he draws most astonishing and alarming inferences.[19] In the Preface to the Fourth Edition of his work, we find the following remarkable sentence:—" Since the lines on Orangeism in the Police Force (pp. 323-324) went through the press, incidents have occurred, arising out of disturbances at the Brunswick L.O.L. Procession, which are strongly calculated to increase the *growing distrust* of Catholics in the *administration of justice in this colony*.[20] This peculiar flavor —the open-handed buffet of English Administrations, and it is always pat or cuff with Father Cleary—the insinuation of corrupted justice on the slenderest and flimsiest of premises, is so

---

12 p. 23. 13 p. 26. 14 p. 63-64. 15 p. 80. 16 p. 173. 17 p. 338. 18 p. 330.

19 Father O'Doherty, in the Publisher's Circular previously referred to, ventures to say, "that Victoria is the only part of the world in which you will find Civil Servants—men supported out of the public taxes, contributed by Catholics as well as by Protestants—banded together in *sworn conspiracy* against their fellow men. Certainly, Victoria can claim this shameful pre-eminence. Her Police Force contributes largely, in men and money, to a Society that Parliament and the Judicial Bench have frequently pronounced illegal. The Post Office Inquiry reveals what is in store for Catholics, if Orangeism be allowed to work its own sweet will." One would like a *single instance* in which either Parliament or the Judicial Bench had pronounced the Orange Society to be *illegal*. Father Cleary does not give one. See Appendix D on the Post Office Inquiry Board.

20 p. xi.

marked in the book, that it is not the least aspect of its involved character and accentuates its bitterness.[21] Add to this taste of acrimony the fact that the author has been at pains to collect and parade, *ad nauseam*, every vigorous epithet which has been invented during the ages to describe Orangeism. Like some big school girl, who has been irritated, he finds gratification in pelting his opponents with " names," though no small part of his Essay is occupied with quotations of that sort of thing from Protestant publications ; and these furnish him with food for acid comment. Yet surely he is no mean type of his race and religion in returning the compliment. Mark with what majestic air he marshals out his battalions of abuse. What a dainty morsel is Grattan's " An atrocious Banditti !" though that fine old Irish choleric gentleman described the Roman Catholic priests, as " a band of prostituted men engaged in the service of the Government." How toothsome is Gosford's " lawless Banditti." With what unction does Killen's " Scum of the Earth "[22] stand in his columns ! Thomas Drummond's " Orange Demons " get into italics lest they should be unnoticed. But the " Banditti of plundering ruffians " fills the mouth best of all, and makes the bravest show. In Old Testament Scripture we read of one Balak—the Son of Zippor—who hired Balaam to curse a certain people for him. Father Cleary, with a fine scorn, quotes copiously from the *Victorian Standard*, to show the public what epithets

---

21 It is a favorite stroke with Mr. Cleary, as we shall have ample opportunities of seeing as we proceed, to make the casual and individual acts of alleged members of the Orange Society, the *responsible acts* of the Order itself ; and where this is not done, to draw an inference from the alleged acts of one or two as to the *general character of the body*. This, of course, is a very good plan to give force to a book, but is it in harmony with any canon of fairness, not to speak of good taste ? Perhaps the adage—" all is fair in love and war," is the working basis of the author.

22 Dr. Killen has a decided antipathy to the "*original* Orangemen ;" he says— " Nothing can be more evident than that the original Orangemen were the very scum of society and a disgrace to Protestantism." (Vol. ii. p. 359.) But he cannot resist the Presbyterian leaven, and hence a few pages afterwards he remarks—" About a year after its formation, the Orange System was placed on a more respectable footing. A considerable number of persons in the higher ranks of Society joined it . . . . and *some Presbyterians, not very warmly attached to their Church*, were induced to seek admission into the Lodges. At that time the whole Country was in a most alarming political condition, and not a few of the friends of the Government were disposed to employ the organisation of the Orange Body, to counteract the influence of another Association of a dangerous type, which had been recently established—the Society of United Irishmen." These grudging admissions surely indicate the Historian's attitude to Orangeism. (*Ecclesiastical Hist.*, vol ii., p. 365). On p. 366 Killen regarded the Orange Society as " a not unsuitable agency for the maintenance of Protestant ascendency," and on p. 367. he avers, "it reckoned among its members beneficed Clergymen and Barristers, Magistrates, Grand Jurors, and Peers of Parliament."

Orange Speakers forge when they launch their thunderbolts at Rome; but to avoid the edge of the old adage which speaks of "Satan rebuking sin," he would not sully the point of his pen by dipping it in such "gall and assafœtida:" not he—*he only quotes approvingly those who do*. But I find that the pure-quill knight also does a little business on his own account in this line; certainly not of the grossly vituperative type of the celebrated Biddy Moriarty—as is but natural, his original effort is much more refined. In the introductory remarks of the chapter, where he deals with what he pleasantly calls "Whiffs from Billingsgate," he refers to the "deformed Mokanna whose *soul was as black as his face was hideous*," and he points the allusion thus:—"*Secret Societies may be termed the Mokannas of our day*."[23] All these epithets go in with the "reliable information," and no extra charge is made for refreshers of this description—the price is still one shilling. A few years back, a Roman Catholic member of our Legislative Assembly referred to "those vermin who celebrate the 12th of July." This was a titbit Mr. Cleary missed, or more probably as it did not proceed from a Protestant mouth, it lacked credential and authority as abuse of the "right sort." The Political Exponents of the Orange Society, so he says, "have ever been notorious for their lack of ability, and are to this day known as 'the deadheads of Ulster.'" An instance is given of "their low level of mental capacity."[24] Moreover the association has been

---

23 p. 143.
24 p. 338. Professor Dicey gives us the following, and I recite it for the purpose of returning Father Cleary's compliment:—"For the last 20 years at least Ireland has been represented or misrepresented by eighty and more Politicians, nominated in the main by Mr. Parnell. No one supposes, for a moment that the Nationalist Leaders who appeared before, and were condemned by, the Special Commission, are fair samples of the Irish people. They are—take them at their best—reckless agitators. They are chosen by their patron, Mr. Parnell, not on account of their work or talent, but because they are apt instruments for carrying out a policy of Parliamentary intrigue, reinforced by a system of lawless oppression."—(*A Leap in the Dark*, p. 35-36.) He recognises that there are fine men in Ireland, "but they have been thrust out of politics by the talkers, the adventurers, the conspirators." (p. 36-37.) An even more crushing verdict is given by no less an authority than Mr. Michael Davitt. On July 7, 1879, this gentleman made a speech, Mr. Parnell being present, in which he said that the Irish people should depend upon themselves more than on the Irish Parliamentary Party. "As regarded that party he believed they could count *upon their fingers the honest men*."—(*The Work of the Irish Leagues*, p. 98.) Of Michael Davitt the *Edinburgh Review* says: "Michael Davitt and not Mr. Parnell is the true Author of the Land League and the real expositor of its policy and designs: and Michael Davitt is a convicted political character of the most dangerous type." Mr. Gladstone declared that Mr. John Dillon "was the apostle of a creed of force and oppression which tended to the destruction of all liberty, and to the erection of a despotism differing from every other despotism as being more detached from

suppressed, written down, exposed again and again, until after the Cumberland affair "the result was that the Irish Society was abandoned by all who gave it weight or respectability."[25] This is a favorite theme with the reverend gentleman. In a letter to the *Ararat Advertiser*, June 21st, 1895, he stated:— "It is as notorious there (Ulster) as it is in Victoria and in Ararat (Query—Where is Ararat? Out of Victoria?) that the great bulk of the membership of the L.O.L. is made up of the least enlightened portion of the Non-Catholic Community."[26] Further, this strange composite, *his* Orange Society, stained with blood, outrage, disloyalty &c., is under the peculiar patronage of those "roving agitators," the Orange Clergy, whose "inflammatory harangues" arouse the multitude of the rank and file of Orangemen to all kinds of demonism. It will be seen as we go on, that if the Orange Society is ankle deep in this sort of thing, the party it opposes is in it up to the chin.

When, therefore, one connects the acrimonious tone adopted by the Author with respect to English Parliamentary Admistrations deemed to be favorable to the Orangemen, and the pains he is at to indicate the wretched condition in point of morals, loyalty, capacity and respectability, of the whole body of Orangemen, clerical and lay, the conviction is irresistible—that as an exponent of Orangeism in any period, he is prejudiced to a degree, which, to say the least, is strong presumptive evidence —if not practical certainty—that his "reliable information" is anything but reliable, and must be taken *cum grano salis*—nay with copious doses of salt—provided it be taken at all.

SIGNIFICANT SILENCE.

Another feature is his all but profound silence on the attitude of Roman Catholics to Protestants and Protestant Institutions. He blandly prefaces the first edition of his work by assuring the public, that the Orange Society "has kept *a portion of the North of Ireland* in a state of unhealthy ferment for over a century." It is safe, therefore, to conclude on his own showing, that the multitudinous ferments in Ireland, outside the area which may be included in this "portion of the North of Ireland," are due to causes other than Orangeism, these other causes however are not hinted at, and the Rebellion of 1798

---

all law tradition, and restraint." The *Annual Register*, speaking of a six months' sentence given to Mr. Timothy Healy, remarked : "In making an example of him, the Executive only succeeded in raising Mr. Healy to the first rank among the politicians of the Parnellite Party."—(*Maxwell's Biographies of Celebrities.*)
25 p. 382.
26 Observe (p. 106) where Father Cleary dwells on the same theme.

is ascribed to the ferocities of Orangemen, and the policy of the Pitt administration, dictating to the Irish Parliament. An uncritical reader of his story might not note this clause in the introduction, and be led to imagine that the Orange Society was the chronic irritant of the Irish social organism. Father Cleary however assigns it only a limited sphere, viz., " a portion of the North of Ireland." It may not be amiss to point out, just here, what some Irish Presbyterians regard as the line of cleavage in that portion of the Empire, and as Dr. Killen appears to be high in his favour I will begin with him. In coming to the conclusion of his volumes Dr. Killen puts his finger upon the " open sore " of Ireland, and declares in vigorous terms—" For centuries Popery has kept Ireland in a state of chronic rebellion.[27] The Penal Laws have long since been abolished, but sedition is as rampant in some parts of the country as it was a hundred years ago. Do not these things point to the awkward conclusion that Popery in some way blunts the moral sense?[28] Another Presbyterian Divine speaks with equally dreadful plainness. "It is surely no wonder; that Irish Protestants dread the establishment of any Roman Ascendency in the country, when they know that on every single occasion since the Reformation, at which Popery has gained the upper hand in Ireland it has persecuted to the death."[29] Dr. Hamilton expresses a widely different view, it will be observed, from that which Father Cleary presents on

---

[27] In 1836 when O'Connell had reached his meridian of power in Ireland, he managed to eclipse the Orange Society, and transfer the ascendency of Ireland from the State, to the Roman Catholic Church, for the time being. But the violence of the Catholic party roused the Protestants thoroughly. "O'Connell and his allies—who, while continually declaiming that they only wanted Ireland for the Irish—entirely ignored any consideration for any of its inhabitants except *the members of their own creed."* The Rev. Dr. Cook, a Presbyterian Minister in Belfast, used his great powers with marvellous effect. Not only in the North but in Dublin and the adjacent counties "where people saw with alarm the fierce attacks made by the Catholics upon the Protestant Church, and *the evident readiness* of the Ministry, as far as the country would allow, *to give into them,"* political and religious debates were the order of the day. The Revs. Mortimer O'Sullivan, and Robert Maghee, of the Established Church were powerful debaters, and though in oratory the Roman Catholic apologists were outrivalled, the stream of political influence ran in their favor. A Protestant publication the *Achill Missionary Herald*, issued by the Rev. Mr. Nangle, was refused transmission by the Postmaster General, Lord Lichfield, but the *Post Circular* "a paper of *an opposite tendency*, was allowed *free* circulation on his Lordship's own authority, on the first application " The Government openly flirted with the Catholic Party; the Lord Lieutenant, the Earl of Mulgrave, publicly entertained Mr. O'Connell at a banquet and released prisoners in large numbers on a visit through the country. All these circumstances were ominous to Protestants.—(Wright's *History of Ireland*, vol. III. p. 542-543.)

[28] *Killen*, vol. II, p. 548.

[29] *Irish Presbyterian Church, Special Edition*, 1887. Dr. Hamilton.

the question of religious persecution in Ireland. We shall see too when we come to deal with this aspect specifically, that Dr. Killen and Lord Macaulay offer some livid facts which it suited our author to pass by in utter silence. During the great Unionist Demonstrations of 1893 against the passage of the Home Rule Bill, the Rev. Dr. Edgar, Moderator of the Irish Presbyterian Church, who had lived 29 years in Cork and in Dublin, told an English audience at the Albert Hall, on April 22nd, 1893, in unequivocal language :—" The cleavage in Ireland is mainly due to the policy of the Roman Catholic Priesthood, who do their best, as my Roman Catholic countrymen here to-day will acknowledge, to keep Protestants and Romanists apart. The claim of these Fathers in God is, that unless their flocks are kept apart in school and college, and even in the social circle, from the rest of us, *their religion will be endangered.*"[30] Even the Duke of Norfolk—unkindest cut of all—confessed :—"I am sadly conscious that the Meath elections, and many other events, show that among the dangers threatened by Home Rule, the attitude likely to be assumed by a large section of the (R.C.) Clergy will not be the least."[31] The Duke acknowledges this, while pointing out that the Pope had condemned the "Plan of Campaign," but we shall see something about *Nationalism plus Murder*[32] as we proceed. A

30 Father Godley examined before the Times-Parnell Commission said, to work the Land League properly "I include *keeping the people together, and keeping them as one body.*"—(*The Work of the Irish Leagues*, p. 715.)

31 *Corresp. between Duke of Norfolk and Col. Saunderson in The Times.* Letter dated March 16, 1893.

32 Sir Chas. Russell, speaking at the Times-Parnell Commission, confessed :— " It is no exaggeration to say that in Ireland th*e*re stood and stand *two powers*, the one the power of the Queen, constitutional, lawful, backed up by all the resources of the Crown and its great Imperial Executive, and yet comparatively a weak power, because it has not behind it, upholding and sustaining it, that moral sanction, that moral support which springs from a sense of benefit received and assent given, and protection afforded. . . . . The other a power extern of the law, unconstitutional by men who have comparatively little responsibility, because the law and the constitution do not put it upon them—moral responsibility I admit they have, but legal and constitutional responsibility is what I am speaking of, and yet a power, a real power in the land because their cause had got the *willing feeling and sanction and assent of the community.*" (*Ireland's Vindication*, Dublin, 1889, p. 4) In other words their stand two powers called *Loyalty* and *Disloyalty*. Father Cleary defines " loyalty " as follows :--

" 1. Devoted to the maintenance of the law : disposed to uphold the Constituted authority : faithful to the lawful Government.

2 Faithful to the Sovereign either as the maker of the law or as *the personal representative of the Government.*" Compare this definition with the admission made by Eminent Counsel on the state of Ireland. Father Cleary informs us that " *loyal submission to constituted authority is perhaps the most elemental condition of good citizenship. It is the partition wall which divides the law abiding subjects of the Crown from the criminal classes of the community.* Plain, unromantic, every-

manifesto by the Irish Presbyterian Church was issued when the Home Rule delirium was at its height. Parts of it are highly interesting and educating reading :—" In the light of the present crisis we speak in the name of nearly half-a-million Presbyterians, and possibly a million other Protestants and intelligent Roman Catholics in Ireland opposed to Home Rule. . . . . A Home Rule Parliament would injuriously affect the educational, social, and commercial progress of the whole community, whilst it would place in jeopardy the exceptional prosperity of Ulster and the Civil and Religious liberties of Irish Protestants. . . . . The Presbyterians of Ireland. . . . . determinedly refuse to have their interests placed at the mercy of a party which has shown itself to be as incapable of self-restraint as it has been regardless of the precepts of moral law." These Presbyterians are tolerably unanimous upon the question of "Popery" creating the line of cleavage between Protestants and "Romanists" in Ireland. Dr. Edgar, like a second Elijah, faces the Hierarchy declaring : " I have not troubled Israel, but thou and thy Father's House."

The reference in the Duke of Norfolk's letter to the Meath elections, bears on the fact that Mr. Michael Davitt was unseated on the ground of priestly influence. At an enquiry witnesses, under oath, declared that priests had, from the altar, refused absolution to any elector who voted for the other candidates, thus acting in downright rebellion against the law of the country and the ecclesiastical head of the Roman Catholic denomination. Mr. Michael Davitt, " father of the Land League,"[33] in an article on "The Priest in Politics,"[34] lets down both Dr. Nulty and the Priesthood as lightly as possible " for having resorted to undue spiritual influence, in what they believed to be a fight for moral and religious principles." He says, " I do not attempt to excuse the issuing of this Pastoral, nor to palliate the words or acts of those priests who were proved to have misused their sacerdotal positions for political ends."[35] Mr. Davitt enters into an

day citizens feel themselves bound to so much by the laws of God and man alike." While composing these sentences for the purpose of berating Orangeism, the Rev. gentleman is driving his knife into the very heart of Ireland up to the hilt, if we may accept the statements of Sir Charles Russell on the two powers, in what one humorist calls "the land of divilment and disthriss." (See Cleary pp. 242-244.)

33 *The Work of the Irish Leagues*, Sir Hy. James, p. 27.

34 *Nineteenth Century* Jan. 1893. A Lady Author, who ought to know, speaking of the parish priest, says, "He is the local pope and he knows it, and he takes care that everyone else shall know it also."—(*The Nun of Kenmare* [Hodder and Stoughton] p. 157.)

35 In 1872 at a Galway election contested by Captain Nolan and Captain Trench, the priests decided to support the former, and great feeling was occasioned

elaborate defence of the priest in politics, and excuses Irish defiance to the rescript of the Pope by advertising it as courage : —" the priest has not been afraid even to go against Rome, when Rome went wrong on Irish questions." Whether, therefore, Mr. Davitt, the Irish priest, or the Pope is right it is difficult to say, but evidently the latter has the two former against him when he goes "wrong on Irish questions," albeit the popular impression is that the Pope cannot err on this very troublesome topic. If, however, on Mr. Davitt's confession, a calamity of this nature should occur, it is within the range of probability that Father Cleary may also make a "blunder long drawn out" on the same subject. It will be observed that he has preserved a discreet silence on the line of cleavage, so that any one who happened to miss the limitation clause I have pointed out, would naturally conclude that the frequent epidemics of social disorder in Ireland arose from the petals of the Orange Lily, but no one, who has been a careful student of Irish History, can blink the stubborn fact set out by Dr. Edgar. Abundant evidence on the Irish priesthood will be furnished, in subsequent pages of this work, from many authorities, and we shall obtain a sufficiently clear type of ecclesiastic to identify him with the line of cleavage from reasons of religious policy.[36] There is a curious resemblance in Colonial

---

so that the episode became historic. During the course of the election Sir Thomas Burke, a Roman Catholic, was told by a priest that his " death knell was rung." On trial the priest explained that he meant the words in a political sense, but Judge Keogh, a Roman Catholic, said the " distinction was not likely to be much attended to by an Irish peasant." Lord Delvin, another Roman Catholic, had been so much insulted by the parish priest that he dared not go to Chapel for fear of being denounced. Other Roman Catholic gentry gave evidence to the same effect. Of course Nolan was elected by an overwhelming majority, but when the case was contested before Mr. Justice Keogh, Nolan was unseated. As might be expected, the Judge and the Roman Catholic opponents of the unseated candidates came in for abuse at the hands of their co-religionists. Cardinal Cullen took the initiative in the matter of fulmination, and the Judge reported to the House of commons "that the Archoishop of Tuam and other dignitaries of the Romish Church have been guilty of a violation of the law." —(*The True Catholic*, p. 112.)

On May, 17th, 1872, Captain Archdall presented a petition to the House of Commons from Roman Catholics at Kilkenny, in which they complained of the conduct of the pope's legate in Ireland. Father O'Keefe of Callan who had a dispute with Cardinal Cullen, in a letter to Lord James Butler said, "There is a real papal aggression this time . . . . Cardinal Cullen is in spirit an Italian monk." (*Ibid* p. 98.)

36 In *The Age*, October 20th, 1897, the Colac Correspondent says that " Mr. Baker, a Roman Catholic," standing in the Liberal interest at the recent Parliamentary elections, was defeated, and that his defeat is considered to be largely due to the religious factor and clerical influence." Mr. Baker declared "on the platform that he would allow *no interference with him on the Education question.*" Father P. McBride, in a press letter, accused Mr. Baker of " defying

life, where priestly influence operates to the kind of thing which Dr. Edgar depicts in Irish life. The State System of Education has long been a subject for attack by the periodic pastoral; and a formulated resolution, of Roman Catholics presided over by Archbishop Carr, spoke of "the *galling grievance* under which Catholics have labored, during the past quarter of a century, in the matter of primary education." Yet this "galling grievance" is merely eternal dissonance from the public policy, which has been steadily pursued in this Colony, of giving all children elementary secular instruction paid for from the public funds; and if the undenominational nature of the School System be regarded as a "galling grievance," it is to be observed, that in this respect, the Protestant majority suffer equally with the Roman Catholic minority. The Hierarchy, whilst denouncing the "godless system," and withdrawing children from the tuition of the State, to their own Denominational Schools, have been keenly on the alert, lest those children still remaining under that system should be "protestantised" by the introduction of the Irish National Scripture Lessons. They resolve, that such an innovation would have the effect of "destroying the undenominational character of the State Schools, ... of Protestantising the State Schools, and of subverting the principles of the Education Act." Thus the long and short of the matter amounts to this, that so far as it can be done, the Roman Catholic children will be separated from the Protestant children, and when it cannot be effected the State School System, godless as it is, must be maintained in its entirety, for there is less danger to be feared from a "godless system" than from a *Protestant one.*[37] There is no resisting the logic of the situation

his Church." (See McBride's letter, *The Age*, October 19th, 1897; and also E. McL. Forbes' letter, October 22nd, 1897.) Sir C. G. Duffy once felt sore over the same sort of thing. The priests were hand in glove with O'Connell, and the Young Ireland Party was as a consequence cold-shouldered. Dr. MacGennis, the parish priest of Clones, "*ordered*" a person "to write back to *The Nation* office to stop it." This was Duffy's paper. And he says on this action, "this was scarcely the liberty of which we had dreamed, or the justice and tolerance we had endeavoured to teach. It seemed doubtful to inconsiderate persons, whether the garrison law administered by Chief Justice Pennefather was much more arbitrary or unreasonable, than the patriarchal rule established in the parish of Clones or the diocese of Ardagh."—(*Four Years of Irish History*, p. 247.)

37 On the question of Roman Catholic policy towards Education in the Colonies, the reader may consult with advantage Cardinal Moran's *History of the Catholic Church in Australia*. Some peculiarities of this work, are the way it represents the first Protestant Church, in part paid for by rum—Justice corrupted—and Catholic children proselytised from the beginning of its history. The reader will note "the determined efforts made on the part of the Government to rob their (Catholic) children of their faith." (p. 12). The Governor enforced "the Protestant Religious observance throughout the settlement," under pain of lashes.

from the Roman Catholic standpoint, and hence in Victoria the line of cleavage is begun, as it is in Ireland, at the School.[38] Let it be observed that the Ecclesiastical policy withdraws its children from a "godless" education, but it never suggests that the State School Teachers belonging to that denomination, salaried under the Crown,[39] should for conscience' sake, or any other sake, deprive the State of their services; thus the withdrawal of the Roman Catholic children means an undiminished staff of Teachers in the payment of the Department. This policy of separation is so notorious, that to mention it is to state a truism which is in everybody's mouth. The following instances will serve to show the practical effects of that policy in other directions:—A young lady of my acquaintance had an intimate friend, a Roman Catholic by religion, whom she desired should act as Bridesmaid at her Wedding, but even the nuptial ceremony was found to be objectionable on account of its Protestantism, and the invitation was declined on the ground that the priest " would not permit it;" the priestly prohibition prevented an intimate friend from being even a spectator on this interesting occasion. Surely this is a safe-guarding policy run mad.[40] Another case—the accuracy of which is equally unimpeachable—was related to me by a member of my congregation. A relative of my informant had contracted marriage with a Roman Catholic—one of those mixed marriages which Father Cleary makes so much capital out of in his book. The children, who were the issue, attended a School of the R.C. denomination in one of the

(p. 39). It was either, attend a Protestant service or have flagellation. (p. 53.) Protestantism, in those days, appears to have been as bad as Orangeism is and always has been (?) to the Catholics. Archbishop Carr ascribes the growth of Catholicism in Australia to two causes, viz., "the distracted divisions of Protestantism, and the energy with which the Romish system of separate schools is maintained."—(*Review of Reviews*, December, 895, p. 561.)

38 Sir H. James speaking before the Times-Parnell Commission said : "I hope I shall not hurt anyone's feelings, if I say that I am under the impression, that the Roman Catholic Church has never made it its peculiar duty to bring education to the masses of the people whom it taught."—(*The Work of the Irish Leagues*, p. 25).

39. Dr. Pearson said that one-fourth of the public teachers in Victoria " are Roman Catholics, who are not deterred by their religion from teaching in our Schools, who rise to be Inspectors and to hold the highest places in the Department, and many of whom I know to be most cordially attached to the system.' —(Quote l Sir Chas. Dilke's *Problems of Greater Britain*," p. 577.)

40 In the cable messages from London under date October 26. is the following —" Much excitement has been caused throughout Canada, by the issue of a pastoral to the Roman Catholics of the Dominion by Archbishop Cleary, declaring it to be a *mortal* sin in any Roman Catholic to enter a Protestant Church, even for the purpose of attending a funeral service or a wedding ceremony."—(*The Age*, Oct. 27, 1897.)

Melbourne Suburbs. On one occasion my informant, visiting at the relative's residence, was invited to attend a festival in connection with the "breaking up" of the school for the holidays. The invitation was accepted. No less than half-a dozen priests were present; one of them launched out into a fiery speech dealing with the injustice of the State School System,[41] and warming to his subject, he urged his auditory to patience, in faith that their time would come and then they would "put their feet on the necks of the Protestants." After the proceedings had terminated the visitor inquired—"Do your Clergymen often talk to you like that?" And the excusing reply was made—"Oh! don't take any notice of him! He got a bit hot—that's all." Perhaps Father Cleary will compare this with some of the fervid, "exterminating" sentiments which he attributes to press reports of Orangeism. An American journal, *Harper's Weekly*, April 13th, 1872, contains an account from the pen of Mr. Eugene Lawrence of a murderous assault on a schoolmaster named Mr. E. C. Greene. From the account given, the priest *encouraged* if he did not direct the assassins. Several Protestants who sympathised with the mutilated teacher had to remove from the township, "lest they too may be assaulted, maimed, or murdered."—(*The True Catholic*, p. 100.)

It is hardly necessary, in dealing with this separative policy, to

---

41 Father Cleary has made reference to the Tammany ring of New York. In 1872 a New York letter described how it operated. "The leaders of the Ring were wise in their generation, and they perfectly understood the art of retaining a band of voters in their service which could always be depended upon, and for a moderate amount of pay. The Irish laborers in the city were completely under their control, and however other citizens might waver or revolt, the Irish could always be depended upon. But why, it may be asked, were the Irish voters more devoted to the cause of the Ring than their neighbors? We are informed that they were all brigaded together under the control of their priests : and if the priests could be secured to the service of the Ring, then the whole Irish vote was secured, the work was done, and the dishonest office-holders, secure in their Popish support, could afford to laugh at the denunciations of virtuous men." According to this letter the influence of the priests was procured by establishing what was called "Charity Schools," and the Ring voted "out of the public funds the sum of seven dollars a head to every scholar in attendance at them." The letter continues that the Public Schools are open to all, without respect to creed or color or circumstance, "but the Roman Catholic priests have determined that they will not allow the children of their Church to attend these schools, lest they come in contact with the free mind of American youth, and learn those notions of liberty which make Nations independent, and, of course, Protestant. These so-called Charity Schools are an organised warfare against the educational system of New York and the United States generally, and if sustained by either political party will result in the establishment of a Romanised system of public instruction. hostile to our Republican Institutions, and fitted and designed to perpetuate and spread the Romish despotism over the minds of the youth of this land."—(*The True Catholic*, Feb. 1872, p. 25-26.) The Orange Society materially helped to break up this ring.

mention the Papal injunction interdicting Roman Catholics from joining the Masonic fraternity.[42] One does not need to float a ship to find in which way a stream runs, when a straw will serve the purpose: these are more than straws on the current of Roman policy, and they furnish a striking clue to any investigator who seeks to penetrate the labyrinth of hierarchial action.

CAULD KAIL.

A large proportion of Father Cleary's book may be aptly described as "cauld kail het again." Cut out of it the "aged" matter and the "ancient history" and how much is left for present day purposes? Certainly not enough to justify that portentous attack on the Orange Society in Victoria, which is a miserable fiasco on its merits. With all the drapery of tragedy his case is purely farcical, and this is abundantly manifest when it is taken out of the theatre and stood on a plain platform of sheer hard fact. The Rev. gentleman appears to best advantage when serving up his Orangeism to-day with the sauces and flavorings made a century ago; and he presents quite a palatable dish for modern appetites, by the ingenuity he displays in putting sprigs of green amidst the dried-up morsels, thus giving his antiquated history a passably youthful appearance. He fights "the Battle of the Diamond" over again, and we seem to hear the crack of musketry. He re-enacts the Penal Code, and makes it live and move and have its being in modern life, though Orangeism had nothing to do with it, and the Diamond conflict was merely the social throe of the birth of the Orange Society. He pilots us through the Rebellion of 1798, and would have the world believe that ghastly epoch was an

---

42 Sir Chas. Dilke, indicating that Cardinal Moran has not "the broad, popular sympathies" of Roman Catholic dignitaries either in America or England, refers to the fact that "not only do the R C. authorities in Australia wage war upon what they style secret societies, as they do in Europe, but Cardinal Archbishop Moran has, according to a private circular which has been made public by the Ex-Attorney-General of New South Wales, Mr. Wise, pushed the prohibition further than it has been carried in England, by depriving of the services of the Church those who join the Oddfellows, Foresters, Good Templars, Rechabites, and all kindred societies. It is difficult indeed to draw a line as regards 'secrecy' which shall exclude the Good Templars or the Manchester Unity of Oddfellows from approval, and include the various Hibernian Lodges as worthy of recognition."—(*Problems of Greater Britain*, p. 590-591.)

He adds that such a circular is unwise in New South Wales "and can only be read as displaying the *intention to force the Roman Catholics out of the daily life of the Colonial State, and into close organisation as a separate community.*"—(Ibid.)

Father Cleary informs us—"Catholics are, moreover, forbidden to join *any* secret society, under serious Ecclesiastical penalties, which include that of Excommunication."—(p. 251.)

Orange Aceldama. He quickens our pulses by going over piecemeal, and constructing a Cumberland Plot, in which the Orangemen are represented as conspiring to interfere with the rightful succession to the British Throne. In short, he collects all the literary junk and juiceless morsels on record, to edify his readers and create a panic over the unhallowed existence of an Orange fraternity.

Father Cleary looks upon all anti-popery literature as nothing more serious than "shockers,"[43] but for the true "blood and thunder" of "the one shilling series," his volume is entitled to take a high place, and here is evidence of it:—"An Orange Oath of Blood."[44] "An Orange Reign of Terror."[45] "The Orange Inquisition."[46] "A Great System of Bribery."[47] "Sackfuls of Revolvers."[48] "Sniffing the Odour of Battle."[49] "Poisoning the Founts of Justice."[50] "Sword, Fire and Faggot."[51] "An Atrocious Banditti.'[52] "A Devil's Dance,"[53] and so on all through its pages. For placarding purposes, in the interests of sensational literature, the author would be hard to beat.

---

43 Father Cleary says the two characteristics of anti-popery literature delighted in by Orange readers are :—(a) "The crude style, or rather the complete want of style, which marks the schoolboy's 'penny dreadful': (b) A peculiarly fierce, and too frequently coarse, virulence against the Catholic Body." (page 150). The Rev. gentleman has a peculiar weakness for what he calls "an educated man;" facts appear to be only facts when uttered by men of certain educational attainments; and the significance of a fact appears to rise or fall in proportion to the altitude of mental culture in the author of the fact. It is peculiarly offensive to him that Orange speakers should refer to his church as "the Scarlet Woman of the Revelations." The gravamen of the offence appears to lie, not so much in the nature of the allegation, as in the source from whence it emanates, and he appears to think it is a sufficient refutation of what is urged to state, that the charges were made on Orange platforms. But most, if not all, of the multitude of accusations he quotes, are only the echo of what highly educated men have repeatedly affirmed. As an instance of this the late Dr. Christopher Wordsworth, Bishop of Lincoln, raises the question:—"Has then the Church of Rome ever stained herself with the blood of Christians?" He answers that question by reference to the "Holy Office of the Inquisition," the sufferings of the Piedmontese, and the St. Bartholomew's Day Massacre. Of the latter he says—her Pontiff went in a public procession to Church to return thanks to God for that savage and treacherous deed." She has inserted an oath in her Pontifical by which she requires all her Bishops to persecute and wage war against all whom she calls heretics. What would St. John have said to this? Would he not have justly *wondered with great admiration*. (Rev. xvii. 6) that such acts should be done under the auspices of one who calls himself the Vicar of Christ?" (Bishop Wordsworth's *Union with Rome. Is not the Church of Rome the Babylon of the Book of Revelation?*) An Essay, 8th edition London, Rivingtons, 1874. Noted by Dr. Wright. *Primer of Roman Catholicism*, (pp. 107-108) Most of the "educated" men have little to say in favor of the Roman Church. Prof. Mivart admits this on p. 989 of the *Ninteenth Century*, Dec. 1893.

44 p. 64.   45 p. 71.   46 p. 280.   47 p. 183.   48 p. 203.   49 p. 193.
50 Chap. xiv.   51 p. 57.   52 p. 61.   53 p. 155.

"DISTINGUISHED" AUTHORITIES.

One very amusing feature of Father Cleary's literary labor is its stately impressiveness upon the question of authorities. He has the happy knack of introducing the person, from whom he selects a quotation, with a high sounding adjective, in order that the reader may be duly conscious of the importance of the opinion about to be adduced. There is an exquisite illustration of the genuine Irish flavour in the author to be seen in this way. The national "blarney" comes out in its fulsome adulation of the authorities favorable to this view; and the national invective is strikingly displayed against those whose word is not as his. The following are samples:—
"The distinguished Statesman,"[54] "the well-known Protestant Journalist,"[55] "A Venerable Member,"[56] "The noted Protestant Historian,"[57] "the well-informed Contemporary,"[58] "the distinguished Presbyterian Journalist,"[59] "a high-minded and distinguished English Protestant,"[60] "this distinguished Witness,"[61] "An eminent Belfast Protestant Journalist,"[62] "the distinguished Under Secretary,"[63] "the distinguished Contemporary Statesman and Philanthropist,"[64]. "this Humane and distinguished Viceroy."[65] It is happily not the fate of many waifs on the ocean of literature to be so loaded, not to say bloated, with redundancy of compliment, but it may be set down to native Irish politeness, and taken as an integral portion of the "reliable information" which the rev. author certifies that his volume contains.

PRIVATE AND CONFIDENTIAL DOCUMENTS.

I have already referred to the fact that Father Cleary's work was written for effect, and it has already borne fruit. The following documents are put in as proofs:—

[Private.]

Hibernian Hall, Melbourne, 4th August 1897.

Dear Sir,—Recent events have brought about a crisis in the colony which demands that all who value *civil and religious rights* shall take action to defend the same. For nearly half a century the Party Procession Act has been enforced in Victoria, but now, on the advice of a Crown official, the act has been practically repealed by the Goverment without the authority of Parliament. This, combined with the revelations made at the Post Office Inquiry Board, shows that the liberties of citizens guaranteed them by the constitution are endangered,

---

54 p. 9. 55 p. 11. 56 p. 29. 57 p. 31. 58 p. 34. 59 p. 167. 60 p. 193.
61 p. 214. 62 p. 231. 63 p. 233. 64 p. 284. 65 p. 298.

and that it is the imperative duty of all who wish well to Victoria to safeguard such liberties.

With the *approval* of the Archbishop of Melbourne, it has been decided to form an association having for its object united action for the above purpose, particularly in view of the approaching general election.

A conference to establish such an organisation will be held in the Hibernian Hall on Tuesday evening next, at 8 o'clock, at which delegates from your district are invited, if possible to attend.—We remain yours truly,

    MORGAN P. JAGEURS, Provisional Chairman.
    F. J. TUCKER, B.L , Hon. Sec. pro tem.

P.S.—Should you or any other representative be unable to attend, a letter from you, expressing the feelings entertained in your district, would be very acceptable.[66]

A fortnight subsequent to the date of this, viz., on the 17th August, the following letter was sent out to the Clergy of the Roman Catholic Church, and speaks for itself.

  [Private and Confidential]
        Hibernian Hall,
        Melbourne, 17th August, 1897.

Rev. Sir,—I have been instructed by the executive council, elected by representatives from various parts of the colony, to bring under your notice the following resolutions that were enthusiastically and unanimously carried :—

1. That it is necessary to form an association for the purpose of ensuring to all inhabitants of this free colony of Victoria their *full and proper political, religious, civil and individual rights, as free men* under the constitution of this fair colony.

2. That all present form themselves into an association, to be called the Victorian Defence League, for the purpose of securing to every colonist the rights referred to in the first resolution. . . . .

The idea at the present moment is to obtain *privately*, an expression of opinion from candidates for Parliamentary honors on questions of the following nature, viz. :—

1. Are you opposed to any person in the public service, and particularly in the police force, being a member of the Orange Society? If yes, and elected, will you support a bill to attain that object?

2. Are you in favor of the appointment of a royal commission to inquire into the state of Orangeism in the public service?[67]

---

66 *The Age*, Sept. 15th, 1897.
67 " The complaint about Orange influence in the Civil Service is even more ridiculous, and will amaze and amuse the man in the street, who notices that

3. Are you, if elected, prepared to support a bill to remove all doubts concerning the illegality of members of the Loyal Orange Lodge marching in procession wearing the regalia of their order?

My committee desire me to inform you that this communication is strictly private, and would suggest that you should call together the leading parishioners of your district and lay before them this most important matter with the object of having a branch started in your locality, and for the purpose of ensuring concerted action.

In conclusion, my committee desire me to request you to be good enough to acknowledge the receipt of this letter and to report what success attends your efforts.—I am, rev. sir, yours faithfully,[68]

M. RYAN, Hon. Sec.

The grandiose wording of both circulars (upon which the idea of obtaining opinions from Parliamentary Candidates *"privately"* is a luminous commentary), simply means that this Association is to be an exclusively Roman Catholic one, and devoted to purely Roman Catholic interests. The approval of Archbishop Carr and the appeal to the Priesthood sufficiently indicate this. It may be not without significance, to recall the blighting Protest raised by 250 Protestant Clergymen and Laymen in Sydney, on the occasion of Cardinal Moran's Candidature for the Federal Convention.

That this meeting earnestly deprecates the candidature of Cardinal Moran for a seat on the Federal Convention, and resolves to use its influence to prevent his return for the following reasons. 1. The candidature of the Cardinal itself is unnecessary, the list of candidates comprising more than the required number of gentlemen eminently fitted by education, training and experience of public life to assist in the work that will devolve upon the convention, and who will approach the work unbiassed by prejudices and obligations that are contrary to the broad patriotic, truly British spirit. 2. It is impossible to separate the person of Francis Patrick Moran from the position occupied by him as a Roman Catholic Cardinal and Archbishop of Sydney. The entry

---

whenever his business brings him in contact with a Civil Servant, he invariably strikes an affable gentleman with a beautiful brogue. If there is Orange influence in the Service, all we can say is, that it must be *extremely beneficial to the Irish Catholic*, who flourishes in Government billets, like the green bay tree."—(*Melbourne Punch*, September 23, 1897). Mr. J. W. Ryan, Sec. to the Victorian Defence League, in a letter to *The Argus*, September 21, 1897, looks forward to an inquiry into Orangeism in the Public Service, and says:— "If such an inquiry be granted, *the main object* of the Victorian Defence League will have been accomplished." Mr. J. A. Baker, Grand Sec. of the Orange Institution, replied in the Oct. 1st, 1897, issue of *The Argus*, indicating the position of the Order, and what it would ask for in the event of such an inquiry being applied for. But this letter seemed to close the matter so far as the public press is concerned.

68 *The Age*, September 15, 1897.

of so high an ecclesiastic into the political arena necessarily means the stirring up of sectarian rancour, and the introduction of a most undesirable element into the federal elections. 3. Since his arrival in Australia Cardinal Moran has persistently played the part of the religious controversialist on every possible opportunity. He has assailed the religious faiths and practices of his Protestant fellow colonists; has championed the imperious and impossible claims of the Roman See to absolute supremacy; and has also resorted to statements which have been *proved to be untrue*, to discredit the apostolic labors of men and societies connected with the branches of Christendom which we represent. These statements when proved to be untrue *have not been withdrawn or apologised for.* The unprovoked character of these attacks shows the bias of the Cardinal's mind, and together with his unflinching advocacy of the intolerant claims of the papacy, unfit him in our judgment for the position of advocate of the rights of conscience and freedom of worship, as now announced by him. 4. Cardinal Moran is by virtue of his position a sworn soldier and servant of a foreign power. The claims of that power cover the whole field of life, secular and political, as well as moral and religious, and in any conflict of obligation that might arise the Cardinal would owe primary allegiance to the power that has invested him with the cardinalate. This his Eminence would be the first to acknowledge, and glory in. In the presence, therefore, of men who are in every way better qualified for the special work to be done by the approaching convention, we resolve to oppose the Cardinal's election, &c.[69]

Whatever recommendation, therefore, the approval of Archbishop Carr[70] may carry when applied to this projected Association, in the judgment of Roman Catholics, it is evident that even the patronage of high Ecclesiastical Dignitaries does not count for much with Protestants, when " civil and religious rights " is the theme. And this cannot be wondered at when the general attitude of the

---

69 The *Age*, February 17, 1897. Sydney Correspondent.

70 I observe, from the *Victorian Standard*, that Dr. Carr wrote a letter to the promoters of the Victorian Defence League, dated August 10, 1897, which commences—" In reply to your circular, I beg to state that I was surprised to find my name specially mentioned in it, in a way, that will seem to many to cast on me the responsibilities connected with the initiation, and future conduct of the proposed organisation. These responsibilities I am not prepared to assume. Up to *a recent time*, I have not favored the idea of any separate Irish or Catholic Political Association. I believed that it would be better for Irishmen and Catholics to throw in their lot with their fellow citizens in general. But recent events seem to demand some protective Association, &c." (*Victorian Standard*, September 31, 1897.) The Archbishop is *surprised* in one sentence, *refuses responsibility* in a second, *pats* the organisation on the back in the third, and then goes on to give *prudential directions*. Doubtless the "recent time," to which he refers as marking a change in his views, is the time at which the first edition of Father Cleary's work appeared. If this assumption be correct, then Father Cleary has landed a big fish—converted his Archbishop, no less.

Roman Hierarchy for ages is taken into account. The approval of the local Archbishop may be taken as a guarantee, that the "Victorian Defence League" will operate beneficially for the members of his Church solely.[71] But the defence idea is a hallucination, and is only put forward preferentially to stating its real object, which, beyond all question, is an organised attack on Orangeism, and Father Cleary is to be congratulated on the distinguished success of his labour of love.

CHAPTER II.

ORANGE PROCESSIONS AS SEEN IN MELBOURNE.—THE BE-
HAVIOUR OF THE GREEN.—HOOTING A FUNERAL.—GREEN
BRAVES AND WOMEN.—A STIRRING TIME WITH THE POLICE.
—JOURNALISM IN GREEN.—VINDICATING THE HONOR OF RE-
LIGION.—MR. GREEN AT CHURCH.—OUR MELBOURNE LETTER.
—A LOCAL GAUGE.—RUSTY FOR A BATING.—RHETORIC AND
BATHOS BY FATHER CLEARY.—SIR CHAS. DILKE'S VIEW OF
THE CATHOLICS IN THE COLONIES.

FATHER CLEARY has drawn such graphic pictures of Orangeism in its marchings through the century, that it may be as well to contrast the real with the pictorial—what we know in our own Colony with those kaleidoscopic views, which he serves up to us through the coloured media of "distinguished" authorities. The former, doubtless, are more prosaic than the racy reading he gives us at the expense of the Orange Society, but they are marked by greater fidelity to fact, though distinctly discredit-able to what he calls "the national colour." Before examining those historic pageants, which garnish his story, I shall revert to what is local history and of recent occurrence. In the year

---

71 The *Melbourne Punch*, which is not usually regarded as partial, thus comments: "The Documents, issued by the framers of the new Hibernian organi-sation, seem to imply the existence of some kind of Religious disability under which Catholics writhe. *This is absolutely ridiculous.* as the Anglican and the Catholic, the Hebrew and the Confucian, the Freethinker and the Spiritualist, live and labor under identical laws." (Sept. 23rd, 1897.)

1896[1] after obtaining the permission of the Mayor of Brunswick, the Orangemen held a Sabbath Service preceded by a procession. The Rev. Father Luby gave warning that the procession would probably be attended with disturbance, and sure enough it was. The days of the Prophets may be ended but the times of prophecy are not past. The *Argus* says :[2] " To cry aloud the danger is to create it. If any demonstration, however intrinsically harmless is magnified beforehand into a cause of affront, especially with people so high-spirited and quick to take fire as the Irish, the mischief is half done." The *Age*[3] remarked : " A year ago it was but a few words by Father Luby—but lo ! how great a fire a little spark kindleth." The Orange procession of 1896 at Brunswick was disastrous for the Orangemen. How fared it with them in 1897 at the same suburb ? I shall endeavour to tell the story, and it will corroborate Mr. Cleary's cautious statement, that " these demonstrations furnish year after year, at least, the *occasion* of many and serious breaches of the peace."[4] A Melbourne daily[5] gave the following description of the occurrence : " The permission to march had been granted by the local Mayor, Mr. J. H. Cook, M.L.A. The Chief Secretary, Mr. Peacock, when appealed to, consulted Mr. Finlayson, the Crown Prosecutor, and obtained from him advice that if no arms were carried, no party banners exhibited, and no factional tunes played, the march would be quite lawful. Mr. Peacock, therefore, would not intervene. Next came the 'solemn warning' by Mr. Murray, M.L.A., in the Assembly on Thursday, voicing as he affirmed, *the feeling of the Catholic Church,* that if the procession were permitted the northern Suburb would be deluged with blood." On Saturday night the rumor went like wildfire, that the procession was to be stopped at " any price " by some " wholly unauthorised horde." Dame Rumor spoke in a whisper, but firmly and with spirit. Some 20,000 or 30,000 people gathered along the line of march to witness 1500 Orangemen in procession, and as an indication of the spirit present in force it is recorded that—"a miserable looking Chinaman passed along, and gave the rowdies an

---

1 It is a remarkable coincidence that exactly fifty years before, viz.: July 13th, 1846, a savage outbreak took place in Melbourne against the Orangemen, who, with a tolerance that did them credit, refrained from a procession in order that no offence could possibly be taken at their celebration. But with or without procession the "Twelfth July " is notoriously objectionable to the people who sport green. I have related this wretched exhibition of Roman Catholic feeling, frenzy, or fanaticism, as drawn from the files of the *Argus* of 1846, in Appendix B.
2 July 19, 1897.   3 July 19, 1897.
4 p. 170.   5 The *Age*, July 19, 1897.

opportunity of relieving their pent up feelings by hooting at him, with all their lung power. *They did the same to a passing funeral.*⁶ The Police Authorities had so accurately gauged the feelings of the mob, that they took the precaution of having removed the heaps of road metal in proximity to the line of march, which would have furnished handy and dangerous missiles. "All being in readiness at 2.40 p.m. the foremost band struck up the National Anthem. Hats were doffed all along the processional line: the police officers sat or stood at the salute, and a *small* percentage of the onlookers uncovered their heads. Nevertheless it was an impressive spectacle, and as was but meet, 'God save the Queen,' was followed by loyal cheers from the Orangemen."⁷ Orange however was not the only colour on exhibition, for "men wearing green handkerchiefs round their necks, or shamrocks in their coats, were to be seen on every hand, and women wearing green were very numerous."⁸ This same Journal, commenting on the pacific nature and appearance of the procession, remarked— "how anyone could be inspired to attack one of them, or permit his blood to boil at the sight of the processionists, in such circumstances, is difficult to understand, unless under cover of the occasion certain persons satisfied old scores of personal enmity. Yet the marching hundreds, in yellow regalia, had not traversed 20 yards, when a man rushed out of the crowd from the southern side of the street, sprang into the midst of the procession, and, with a stick, struck one of the Orangemen a savage thwack on the head." Though several assaults had been made, upon the Orangemen, by both men and women, the procession had never been once checked in its progress by all the obstacles it had encountered. "Onward Christian Soldiers" its members sang, and as such passed onward, no matter who fell by the way.

THE BEHAVIOUR OF THE GREEN.

The newspaper, quoted previously, presented its readers with a graphic bit, descriptive of the passions at work among a portion of the spectators.

The scene as the procession wheeled into the church gates was intensely thrilling. While the Orangemen had been coming along the road a considerable body of young fellows, who meant mischief, accom-

---

6 *Ibid.*   7 *Ibid.*

8 Father Cleary says that Green is the *national* colour of Ireland. Mr. Davitt speaks of it in a different connection. In referring to a meeting at Milltown, at which 20,000 men were present, he represents them " with green ribbons, *green being one of the emblems of the Fenian meetings in the old time.*" Who is right— Father Cleary or Michael Davitt?—(*The Work of the Irish Leagues*, p 102.)

panied them and stationed themselves immediately opposite the church. The howls and yells were deafening. We have been told something of an awful execration of hate that pours from the spectators of an Irish eviction, and similar shrieks of concentrated venom were levelled at the parading Orangemen. Once an attempt was made to break into the street and scatter the whole order. Sticks were raised in angry menace, and with cries of " Down with them !" a dozen or more powerful roughs, screeching like maniacs, rushed forward. There was a brief instant when it looked as if the crisis that was dreaded had at length arrived, that the procession was going to be broken up, and that the traditional hatreds of two sections of the Irish race would stain with blood Australian soil. But happily the troopers were too strong. Out came the ugly black batons of the mounted and foot police, the horses charged forward with the heavy hoofs that never wait to argue the point, and, despite the daring blackguardism that caught hold of the reins and actually tried to drive the horses back into the roadway, the position was saved. It happened that Chief Commissioner Chomley was himself in evidence as the procession neared the gates, and he not only directed, but reined his horse into the howling mob, and assisted in checking the attempted rush. In the midst of the melee one trooper's horse slipped, and if he had absolutely come down all would have been confusion; but the horse was soon on his feet again, and his rider, who had his truncheon drawn, caught a fellow holding his reins a whack over the fingers that made him roar in pain.

Such a spectacle is not calculated to create respect for the main actors in it, but the worst has yet to be told of what the boys in green can do—that green which Father Cleary assures us is the National colour of Ireland.

It was after the services, and when almost everyone was homeward bound, confident that no further disturbances would occur, that the most disgraceful and exciting scene of the day took place. A mob of about 100 roughs, who were standing in the square opposite Parkstreet closely scrutinising everyone who passed, suddenly descried an orange-colored handkerchief peeping out of the coat pocket of a young man who, with a companion, was walking towards the city. Instantly there was an outcry. The mob began to close in upon the two, and cries of "Take it out !" were followed by " Down him ! Down him !" The young man, perceiving the cause of the fast increasing crowd's unrest, quickly dipped the handkerchief in his pocket well out of sight. But this was not enough. The colors were wanted. One young rough, more daring than the rest, rushed at the owner of the handkerchief and tried to take it from him. Others quickly followed, waving sticks and umbrellas; and in less time than it takes to record it the young men were in the centre of an infuriated mob. It was just at this critical moment that Sub-Inspector Irvine and half a dozen troopers, hearing the wild shouts, and divining what was happening, charged down upon the crowd, scattering it all directions, and succeeded in putting the two on a tram, although not before they had been somewhat roughly handled. Robbed of their "sport," the crowd, which was largely of the larrikin class, looked round for fresh objects on which to vent their vengeance. They had not long to wait. The troopers had scarcely returned to the square when a man, accompanied by a young woman of about 25, and another about 18, each of the ladies wearing some orange-colored trimmings in their hats, passed by in the direction of the city. This was enough. The roughs, whose appetites for riotous behavior had now been whetted, quickly turned their attention to them. In a moment the were surrounded, and cries of " Tear the colors out !" " Take it out !" were heard on every hand. Scared beyond measure by the menacing mob, the two young women clung to the arms of their male companion. The latter shielded them as best he could, but their strength was as nothing pitted against the brutal mob bent on tearing away the women's head dress. Some two or three more gallant than the rest rushed forward to assist them, but they were struck with sticks and umbrellas, and carried from one side of the road to the other by the oncoming crowd, which had now become almost frantic with excitement. It seemed as if the hapless women would be trampled under foot, when suddenly Sub-Inspector Irvine and his half-dozen troopers charged down on the cowardly crowd. But this time the work of rescue was not so easily accomplished. Sticks were thrown at the troopers, and one great fellow aimed a blow at Sub-Inspector Irvine with a piece of blackthorn, which whizzed by, perilously close to his head. Amid a perfect hurricane of boohooing, the troopers worked their way to the spot where the two young women still struggled to escape, and, forming a solid phalanx, carried them across to the fence surrounding the triangular-shaped enclosure at the corner of Sydney and Royal Park roads. There one of them fainted. The sight was greeted with derisive laughter by many in the attacking party. " They're frightened ! They're frightened !" they shrieked, and again they made a move as if to renew the attack, but were speedily driven back by the troopers. The lady having recovered, an attempt was made to put her and her friends on a tram ; but the cars were crowded. There was not an inch of standing room even, on the footboards of the first which passed, and three others followed in quick succession, each as closely packed. Finding it impossible to put them on a tram, the mounted men escorted the party along the road in the direction of the city, and then it was that for the first time during the day that stones were thrown. One struck a trooper on the helmet, but fortunately did no harm, and the others were happily badly aimed, and, so far as is known, did not reach their intended mark. Again and again the infuriated mob tried to break through the cordon of police which shielded the women from their wrath, but each time they were repulsed, and after 250 yards had been traversed. a cab was found, into which the still half-fainting woman and her girl companion were hurried and driven off. Then before the crowd had realised what had happened, Sub-inspector Irvine wheeled his horse round, and charging down upon them, seized a young rough who had been conspicuous in the stone-throwing incident. "That's the man!" two or three other troopers exclaimed in a breath, and before anyone had time to interfere the prisoner had been handcuffed, and was being marched off towards the Royal Park police station.

For a few moments the crowd fell back. Suddenly a man, who was wearing a large green rosette in his coat, called on his companions to rescue the prisoner. The cry was taken up by others, and a determined rush was made. The police, however, stuck to their man, and hurried him off at a trot. The crowd followed at the double. Men and boys surged round on every side, and suddenly the cry of "Stone them!" was raised. In an instant the air was thick with sticks and stones. It seemed that serious injury would be done, but fortunately the outbreak was quickly quelled by a smart movement on the part of the troopers, who throughout had been acting splendidly. They were seven in number, and at a signal from their officer four of them unexpectedly wheeled round and charged the mob, scattering it in all directions. Just at that stage another cab drove up, and into this the prisoner was bundled and hurried off to the watch house in charge of a foot constable. Hardly had they rid themselves of their man than the mob was alongside again, and the police seized another young rough, who had been singled out as one of the ringleaders in the disturbance. He, too, was put in a cab. The crowd, dashing through the mud and slush which covered the track between the main road and Princes Park, sought to get by the police and reach the cab, but once more they were outwitted by the troopers and driven back. This happened again and again, until finding their efforts futile, the mob gradually retreated, and after a most exciting battle the troopers were left on the field victorious.[9]

It need hardly be said that all the arrested were Roman

---

[9] The *Age*, July 19, 1897. It argues a good deal of hardihood in Father Cleary, that with the secular press accounts of these occurrences before him he should quote the *Argus* as attributing "the freedom from *grave* disturbances mainly to the pacific admonitions of the Catholic Clergy of Melbourne." He points his allusion by remarking "on all hands serious riots were anticipated, but the forebodings were happily not fulfilled." With a wondrous command of euphemism he serenely veils the futile efforts of desperadoes in green (p. 218). At the Police Court proceedings, Brunswick, when the question of the legality of the Orange processions was being tested, Mr. Cook, M.L.A, was asked by Mr. Purves—"Do you think that the Police repressed the riot or did Archbishop Carr and his priests avert it by their influence, as Mr. Smyth has suggested?" The reply was—"*I think that the police prevented it.*"—(The *Age*, Feb. 10th, 1898.) The *Argus* reported the question and answer: "Do you think it was the police or the priests who were most instrumental in stopping a riot in 1897? There were very few inclined to riot, but I think *the police were most instrumental.*"—(The *Argus*, Feb. 10th, 1898.)

Catholics. The newspaper of the denomination, the *Advocate*, with its usual regard for veracity, and to put its readers in possession of the facts relating to this affair, gave the following lucid and unhysteric account of it: "Two young women, wearing Orange ribbons in their dress and accompanied by a male friend, were set upon by *two* or *three* young men. One of the assailants made a grab at the Orange decorations[10] . . . . one of the girls, either through the jostling she received, or from fright, fainted and had to be carried off the road."[11] Not a word of condemnation is uttered, not a sign of regret is published.

SOME FEATS OF R.C. JOURNALISM.

According to the Press Organ of the Roman Church,[12] which worked itself up into a black fury over this procession, it was made to appear a monstrous injustice to their "religion and nationality." The secular press of the city had given prominence and publicity to the considerable, and by no means costless, efforts of the Roman Catholic party to *prevent* the Orange parade from taking place. They had appealed to the Government, and to Eminent Counsel, and having secured favorable opinions from their Counsel, they again besieged the Cabinet Minister, but all to no purpose. The Religious Journal therefore felt itself free to bestow its favors all round, and to do it justice it omitted nothing in the way of emphatic phraseology. It commenced an account of the proceedings with the headline "AN ORANGE OUTRAGE." One would naturally imagine, that the processionists had fallen foul of the men in green and brutally maltreated them, but, the *Advocate,* while liberally covering the Orangemen with epithets of this description, in its rancour, so overshot its aim, as to clearly show how harmless and unaggressive the spectacle really was. The following extracts will serve to indicate, how impartial that journal was in meting out censure to those who acted, in a manner, hostile to its cherished notions.

---

10 Lest it should be thought that the omitted clauses contribute materially to the account I insert them here : " The man accompanying the girls defended them, and in this way the riot spread, for others of both parties came up and there was soon a general melee. On the police running up the youth who is said to have started the disturbance was arrested, and "—This paper minimised the occurrence by remarking—" a commotion took place in the middle of the tram track, leading to a further, though *not very serious*, disturbance."—(The *Advocate*. July 24, 1897, p. 7.)

11 The *Advocate*, July 24, 1897.

12 Archbishop Carr, in his controversy with the Rev. Dr. Rentoul, virtually acknowledged the *Advocate* as the press organ of his Church.—(*The Early Church and the Roman Claim*, p. 208.)

It is necessary to reproduce these accounts, because Father Cleary has made out such a strong case against Orange processions in distant lands at by-gone dates, that by comparing them with one we know something about, with a reasonable degree of certainty, and seeing how a party newspaper distorts the facts to suit its own ends, we are put in possession of a critical standard, to measure the worth of his strong points on Orange processions generally. Hear the *Advocate* speak for itself:—"The *entire blame* of last Sunday's Orange outrage rests upon the Government." This appears to be a very candid and remarkable exoneration of the Orangemen, but in effect, it is merely an instance of the paper in its spleen over-reaching itself, for it intended nothing of the sort. With uncommon candour, it confesses to the wisdom of the Police Authorities who had removed the heaps of road metal "lest an indignant people should be tempted to use it in vindication of their outraged Religion and Nationality." This is corroborative of the estimate, which the police rightly made, concerning the stuff of which Irish Catholics consist, and is an involuntary compliment to their insight upon this occasion. This journal is trenchant and outspoken in its comment on the attitude of the police. "The form of the Chief Commissioner as he threw up his head, and tried to put on a military bearing worthy of the high and honorable duty he was about to perform, viz.: to bring the recalcitrant to their bearings by a blow of the baton, formed a somewhat striking picture." With amusing partisanship, the paper sums up the inoffensive attitude of the participants in the "Orange Outrage," in this style, utterly unconscious of its *reductio ad absurdum*. The Orangemen formed in processional array, "looking about them in a scared and uneasy manner as if expecting a foe on every side, they donned their uniform (?) and made a lame attempt to look steady and cheerful." Again—"the procession of law breakers . . . . . quaking with fear, and visibly dreading lest their guilty heads should be made to bear a *just retribution*." It also quoted the *Age* with approval saying : "if the Orangemen had been under a solemn oath not to have molested any person, they could not have been more lamblike in their demeanour." Such terms as "abject terror" and "craven fear" are also used to depict the Orangemen. One would think, from this account, that the hated colour-bearers were more deserving of public commiseration, than of being styled perpetrators of "an Orange Outrage." Perhaps, however, this aspect can be accounted for, by studying the repressive measures put on the gallant operations of the green boys, for it is remarked that "conspicuous among them (the sightseers) were numbers of men, women, and children, displaying the 'green immortal shamrock,' and here and there were to be seen parties of stalwart Irish lads, who were evidently 'out for the day' *to do honour to the national colour.*[13] The Orange lads and lasses displayed their party rags, but with much evident trepidation." To evince what the "Irish lads who were evidently out for the day" were capable of, it is stated that " the immense sea of humanity surged round the Orange procession, and were it not for the mounted troopers and foot police, who speedily came to the aid of the threatened law-breakers, the Orange demonstration would have been utterly routed before it had moved a step forward." Doubtless this is the "*outrage*" so bitterly complained of—the muzzling of procession-smashers; but what a comment it is on Father Cleary's encomiastic handling of the affair.

HOW CATHOLICS HONOR THEIR RELIGION.

In vainglorious delight over the wrathful ebullition produced by this procession, the *Advocate* becomes responsible for the the statement, that "*a large proportion of men, prepared to vindicate the honor of their Religion and nationality,*" were in the crowd.[14] It may not be strictly just to take the denomina-

---

It is argued by the Hibernian party, that the arguments, which stand good against Orange demonstrations, do not stand good against St. Patrick's day celebrations and processions, on the ground that Orangeism is a party, while St. Patrick's represents the national, sentiment. In that case, therefore, it is to be presumed that any Irishman, whether Protestant or Roman Catholic, is qualified by the fact, of his *nationality* for membership in the organisations which celebrate the 17th March. The Australian Natives' Association only bars from its ranks candidates that are not native born : it raises no question of Religious belief. Is this the law of the Hibernian Societies, which claim the right to march on the ground that they are national, and not party, organisations ? If so, I should like to know how many *Irish Protestants* are in the membership, and demand the right of procession as against the Orangemen ? I am informed by one who has perused the Rules of the Hibernian Society, that before a man is qualified for admission into the order, he must produce a recommendation from the parish priest vouching for the fact of his *active* communion with the Roman Catholic Church.

At the Brunswick Police Court when the legality of Orange processions was being tested, Mr. Denehy, a Roman Catholic, was asked :—" You think that Roman Catholics should carry whatever symbols or colors they please? Yes ! in their case they're not intended to give offence.—Oh ! supposing a banner of Robert Emmett is carried through the streets? It might give offence, but I cannot understand why it should.—Supposing an address is drawn up alluding to the rule of the English people as a foreign despotism ? No reasonable man could regard English rule in Ireland as anything else."—The *Argus*, Feb. 12th, 1898.

14. The *Advocate* loves to deal with Orangeism in strong and slashing statements, but it can be "puss in gloves" as well, as the following extracts will show :— Father Cleary refers to the Publisher of the *Victorian Standard* being compelled to publish a "correction" of a report on a certain convent (p. 161). This is how the *Advocate* refers to the matter :—"*An Orange lie nailed.*" The paper goes on—" It was a question of money or grovelling in the dust, and naturally

tional organ too seriously on this matter, but Father Cleary has paraded, and commented on, every casual sentiment which he has found in Orange papers, and on his principle, which of course is unexceptionable, one may conclude that a Religion which requires what the *Advocate* vouches as having taken place, in order to vindicate its honor, is like Bret Harte's heathen Chinee, something "peculiar." It is not without significance that the violent, the turbulent, and the blatant, are all regarded as heroic by this Catholic journal, and their performances entitled to praise in its columns. " Scarcely had the Orange ranks advanced a dozen yards, when a *brave* fellow made an attack on the procession, and after administering a sharp thrashing to a couple of the 'yellow pups,' was seized by the police." Another assailant was panegyrised—Mr. Mulcahy did his best to impress the Orangemen with his disapproval of the whole proceedings by the aid of a stick, but the ubiquitous policeman placed the "fine old Irish gentleman under arrest," with heart-breaking callousness. Others did nobly, according to this Catholic paper, in well meant efforts to "vindicate the honor of their religion," but they were all abortive, and so far from vindicating their religion, they merely made mock martyrs of themselves for the prosaic offence of assaulting citizens, who had obtained the sanction of the authorities for their parade.

The green braves who were "out for the day" in vindication of "the honour of their religion," did as well as possible under their severely limited opportunities, and are liberally rewarded for their *intentions* by the laudatory drivel published in their particular paper. They are seen to be all "*brave*" in this print,

---

the *Standard* grovelled." The opening paragraph of the correction was said to be as follows :—" In our January issue we reprinted from one of our Exchanges a report of an alleged scandal, &c. The report was stated to have previously appeared in the *New York Staats Zeitung* of 8th November, and from such we acknowledged it," &c. (The *Advocate*, 13th July, 1895, p. 8.) About the same time, Cardinal Moran uttered his sensational strictures on Protestant Missions. This is what the same paper had to say on this matter :—" Spiritual Cargo. Cardinal Moran's *little joke*. Under these headings, the *Sydney Evening News* of Thursday, 11th inst., had the following :—' Although Cardinal Moran got his laugh at the Guild Hall on Tuesday evening easily enough, by reading the 'John Williams grog manifest,' the cream of the joke is that his Eminence obtained his information from the occasionally amusing, and always respectable, *Sydney Morning Herald*. . . . . Cardinal Moran, had he wished, especially as it is fair to assume he *never saw* the two line *correction* which appeared in the *Herald* two days later, might have made more fun out of the thing than he did,' " &c. . (The *Advocate*. 20th July, 1895, p. 6.) The printing of a libel on a R C. Convent, where the correction has not been previously seen, is *an Orange lie*. The uttering of a libel by a Cardinal of the Church on Protestant Missions, though a correction was inserted in the paper previous to the utterance is a *little joke*. This is how the *Advocate* represents the two incidents at any rate.

and if the Roman Catholic Religion feels itself vindicated or honoured by this kind of heroism, it is not for me to detract from such kudos.

The following fragments will suffice to illustrate the feeling of the Papal organ in regard to what occurred. It condemns the police, who only did their duty in preventing rioters from committing serious mischief, and accusingly says—they spurred "their horses recklessly into the crowd, drew their batons, and laid about them in an unnecessarily ferocious manner." Contrast with this the *Argus* comment: "The Jubilee week gave much practice in dealing with big crowds, and the police handled that of yesterday in a fashion which was *worthy of the highest praise.* They were good-tempered and cool, refused to take notice of mere youthful folly, such as 'hootings and cat-calls, but were swift to act when anything in the nature of physical force was employed. The first few moments were the worst. They were the psychical moments, and the determined action of the police in quelling the demonstration then made, won the day in the interest of law and order."[15]

ORANGE WORSHIP SEEN BY MR. GREEN.

I extract the following from the fair and impartial (?) account given of the service and its environment by the party press, in order that the sort of stuff served up to Catholic subscribers may be observed.[16] If they believe this kind of thing one can hardly wonder at their fanatical outburst against the Orange Society: and the blame must be shifted from them to their educators.

"The architecture of the Wesley Conventicle suited to a T the miserable, quaking gathering within its four walls. Of a heavy, sombre style, the Chapel[17] resembles a prison, and if justice had had her rights last Sunday, its congregation should now be in durance vile. The women were trembling like leaves, and the men, young and old, looked ashy pale, and ill at

---

15 The *Argus*, July 19, 1897. At the Consecration Procession of St. Patrick's Cathedral in Melbourne, on Sunday, Oct. 31, 1897, there were present 120 policemen. Were these there as a guard of honour or for the purpose of keeping the public peace ?—(The *Age*, Nov. 1, 1897.)

16 The singularly discriminating writer in the *Advocate* says :—" As soon as the bedraggled Orangemen and women, numbering 250, reached the Wesleyan Chapel, they ran pell mell into the building as if the *Father of Lies was at their heels.*" He might have added " on press duty "—and not been far out.

17 The Wesleyan Church, Brunswick.

ease. . . . . Near a fourth-rate organ were a score of lads and lasses in white surplices, who vainly tried to put a little life into the miserably depressed spirits of the congregation by shouting 'Onward, Christian Soldiers.'" I am just a trifle incredulous about the accuracy of this description, and had I read it anywhere, save in the columns of the immaculate Catholic Journal, I should instantly conclude that Mr. Green felt so out of place in a Protestant assemblage, that he succumbed to a bilious attack of a peculiarly bitter nature on the spot.

Letters appeared in the *Advocate* of this date, one of which, headed "Privileged Ruffians," ventures to describe the present administration as the "Orange Government," though Mr. Duffy, a well-known Roman Catholic, holds the portfolio of Postmaster-General in the Cabinet[18]. From what the paper itself has to say about the Orangemen in procession, and at Church it is difficult to perceive how the element of ruffianism was present except as opposed to them, but then it is to be remembered that the "brave" Irish lads gave their opposition under religious inspiration—it was, so the paper stated, to "vindicate the honour of their Religion." Another letter declared: "No one is more disappointed at the *absence of disorder* (sic) at Brunswick than the average Orangeman and his semi-veiled press supporter, the *Age*." Take the procession from the standpoint of the Catholic press, and it was terribly disappointing in that quarter as well: it regards the Roman Catholic Community as too tolerant altogether, for it spiritedly refers to that section as "their *too-forbearing* fellow Colonists;" and laments the fact of the Orange worshippers leaving the Church so inoffensively as to disappoint the cherished hope, that "their friends outside might *after all* get satisfaction." Hence it is clearly manifest, if the *Advocate* has any influence in the Colony, that the reputed "good old Orange procession" will be revived with a vengeance."[19] Father

---

[18] This Writer concludes his letter thus—"It remains to be seen whether the only Catholic in the Ministry will deem it right under present circumstances to retire from it."—(*Advocate*, July 24, 1897, p. 8.) The "only Catholic" evidently sees matters in a different light from this heated correspondent, for up to date of publication he has not withdrawn from the Ministry, probably because he does not "deem it right" to do so, and thus adds another injustice to the Bill of Wrongs drawn up by the *Advocate*.

[19] Journalism which uses language of the following description is certainly exceeding the limits allowed to party accounts. Speaking of the Orangemen retiring from the Wesleyan Church it is stated, "They were careful however to conceal the Orange Regalia, and came out looking thoroughly cowed." (p. 7.) "Mr. Tregear, anticipating that his brethren had that day held their last Orange procession in this Colony, announced that they did not intend to hold any more

Cleary's book will doubtless lend a hand in promoting this good work, while carefully deprecating it in phrases which may be read two ways, according to the sympathy of the reader. He uses language of this sort: Orange displays are "not merely impolitic but in a sense *criminal*." They commemorate events which brought triumph and ascendency to a "small minority of the population; defeat, humiliation, social and political degradation to the Catholic majority."[20] He urges that "the methods of conducting the celebrations are highly calculated to arouse sectarian feeling, to provoke resistance, and thus imperil the public peace." He speaks of "the always offensive and frequently inflammatory character of the platform attacks on the Catholic Church and its members."[21] Another of his assertions is that "Orange Anniversaries, Processions, &c., have as a matter of fact been traditionally made the occasion of studied insult, menace, intimidation, outrage and too often of strife which has at times almost reached the dimensions of civil war in portions of Ulster."[22] Now all this is very nice and beautifully maintains the sublime ignorance, real or simulated, of the author on the contributory causes which made Orangeism a necessity. There are two ways open to a writer on party lines to make a good thing out of the business in hand—he may either delineate a feeling which is in existence towards an antagonistic institution, carefully refraining from hinting at culpability on his own side, or else he may depict what *ought* to

---

gatherings of the kind—at least on Sunday." (p. 7.) "The parsons at the Wesleyan and Presbyterian gatherings advised their brethren to take off their regalia lest their friends outside might after all get satisfaction. The Orangemen required no pressing. Every sash and collar was at once consigned to oblivion. Cautiously the Williamites emerged into Sydney Road, and stole quietly away, apparently very glad to escape observation." (p. 7.) Jibes of this nature are plentifully sprinkled through the account, and though Orangemen have better sense than to treat them with anything more than contempt, yet, such comments exceed even the allowed license of party writings; and if the Orangemen generally were half as intolerant and inflammable as Father Cleary represents them, such statements would fairly provoke them. As it is, they merely laugh at the harmless fit of sulks taken by the *Advocate*.

20 p. 170. On p. 236 Father Cleary says:—"The reader will bear in mind that *I am not defending* these expressions of Catholic discontent. My purpose is to give a record of warning incidents which deserve to be more widely known, in the hope that these new lands may be spared some of the heart-burnings which have been the bane of Ulster ever since 1795." I have looked in vain for any expression of condemnation on the Catholics in his pages, and if he does not defend, he endeavours to extenuate by parading the Orangemen as the chief offenders in all cases of collision, and accusing them on the statements of others of wanton and bloody cruelties." Note the paragraphs immediately following on "a losing Battle" and "Counter Associations." (pp. 236-237.)

21 p. 170. 22 p. 171.

be the prevalent feeling in those whose cause he advocates, in order to create it.[23] The principle laid down by the *Argus* is one, in this connection, which cannot be set aside as a merely casual newspaper platitude:—"*To cry aloud the danger is to create it.*"[24] Another paper most pertinently remarks in a review of the proceedings at Brunswick in 1897: "Such processions are common to most places in the Colony, but trouble is never dreamed of except at Brunswick. A fortnight ago there was a demonstration of the kind at Prahran, and there was no disturbance, although there were drawn swords at the head of the procession. Again last Monday in Melbourne itself a regiment of Irish Protestants marched to the Town Hall and no one thought of interfering. How then is it that the Northern Suburb of Brunswick should be the only place in the whole Colony where parties are spoiling for a faction fight?"[25]. Is there any reasonable explanation of this very penetrating question? The pungent Pictorial Censor known as *Punch* observes: "As for the Orange procession, that small function occurs once a year, and has a significance now in the popular mind not due to the Procession at all, but springing entirely from the opposition offered by the Hibernian Party. Whilst the latter kept away from Brunswick, the Orange Procession there was a peaceable and comparatively unimportant business, as it will be again, if the processionists receive no more opposition than is offered to the Hibernian Society when they parade the town."[26] This journal offers the above as a comment on the newly-formed "Defence League."

---

23 When the test case on the legality of Orange processions was being heard at Brunswick the following evidence was given by Senior Constable Nolan. He had described an Orange Celebration as equivalent to the enquiry—"How do you like the thrashing my father gave your father?" The cross-examining Counsel, desiring to test the Historical knowledge of the Witness, asked:—"How does this Orange color record a beating?" The reply eventually came, "I only know from what I've read."

"Where did you read it?"—"I never did read much of history."

"Where did you read it?"—"I could not tell you."

Further on he was asked: "You made certain statements as to the effect certain colors had on your co-religionists. Where did you get that information? *I refuse to say.*" This witness, while admitting that he was color-blind, thought that Orange badges would have the same effect on the minds of the Roman Catholics as they had on his own, which was "tantamount to holding a red rag to a bull."—(The *Age*, Feb. 12th, 1898.)

24 The *Argus* July 19, 1897.

25 The *Age* July 19, 1897.

26 *Melbourne Punch*, Sept. 23, 1897.

Our Melbourne Letter.[27]

I have endeavoured to get all possible light upon this particular Orange procession, and as will be observed have availed myself of every paper which came under my observation that treated of it. Through many lenses one ought to get a view which, if not absolutely conclusive, will, at any rate, allow the reader to note which way testimony preponderates. And in a conflict of witnesses, sampling the evidence is perhaps the best method for obtaining a correct judgment. The following paragraphs will therefore be of interest, as the writer appears, in Father Cleary's hackneyed phrase, " well-informed."

The second battle of Brunswick, fought A.D. 1897, was a very poor affair indeed, and must not be regarded as being in any sense an historical parallel to the famous conflict which immortalised the Boyne. Something, of course, may be urged as to the denominational distinctions (to use a modern phrase) of the combatants, to the antagonistic principles contended for, and to the issue in both cases, but in all other respects comparisons are odious. The representatives of British freedom acted with the calmness, dignity and unmistakable determination of men who had a sacred duty to perform, and which they were resolved to go through, come what might. Their opponents were a heterogeneous collection of fortuitous units without organisation, discipline or leaders, and directed simply by the blind and unreasoning instincts of religious bigotry. What purpose could be served by the howls and outrageous violence of a crowd without a single element of cohesion, and with the police authorities resolved to maintain the public peace? That the incident should have resulted as it did in a miserable exhibition of childish fraptuousness, shame and discomfiture was only to be expected. It is no reflection on respectable Catholics to write so. Not one possessed of ordinary intelligence but will condemn the conduct of these co-religionists on the occasion, no matter what may be their opinion as to the legality of the procession held by the Orangemen. Even upon this point it must be conceded that authority was given to march, and that the legal question should have been referred to the law courts.

This Writer also sends a shaft of light athwart Mr. Cleary's remark on " the growing distrust of Catholics in the administration of justice in this Colony,"[28] because a question addressed to

---

27 *Stawell Times*, July 26, 1897.

28 The charge of corrupting the administration of justice, repeatedly made by Roman Catholics against Orangeism, is one of the *most favourite*; as it is one of the *most ancient*. On June 25. 1823, Mr. Brougham presented a petition to the House of Commons, signed by 2000 Catholics, "complaining of the partial administration of justice in Ireland." He moved for an inquiry and " concluded with a sweeping denunciation of the whole magistracy of the land. This charge was loudly and sternly repudiated by the whole of the Irish members. Mr.

Police witnesses was objected to, which produces a curious effect. The Rev. gentleman in that light appears a trifle hysterical.

In connection with last Sunday's proceedings an order was issued by the Chief Commissioner directing all members of the police force not to appear outside their stations, officers or quarters from 1 p,m. till 8 p m. on Sunday, 18th July, unless in uniform, and notifying that any member departing from the instructions thus given would be severely dealt with. What do you suppose was the reason of this? Simply because last year some of the police were reported to have sided with the rioters, and escaped observation except in a few cases by appearing in civilian's clothes. Evidence could be adduced to show that several of the police on duty, and in uniform, turned their backs when the roughs upset the trap in which four Orangemen were seated, and assaulted the occupants, remarking "Let them give it to the b———."

A LOCAL GAUGE.

This procession is one, with the particulars of which we are well acquainted, and hence I erect it into a standard of criticism, by which Father Cleary's entertaining and blood-curdling accounts may be judged. There can hardly be two opinions respecting the actual facts of the case, even though the *Advocate* does its little best to make the wielders of the blackthorn martyrs for the Church and the Nation. The incidents which transpired on the occasion under review at Brunswick as well as the documents "private and confidential," previously mentioned are regarded in many quarters as the stormy petrels[29] of a Roman Catholic party intent on combatting the Orange Society in order

---

Daly, especially, denounced the whole affair as a mere job, and asserted that the petition was not signed by a *single nobleman, gentleman, or man of known respectability in Ireland.*" The Commons indicated their sense of the " job " by declining to grant the inquiry ; only 59 members voting in favour, and those 59 would probably have voted for a motion to expel every Orangeman from Ireland without inquiry.—(Wright's *History of Ireland*, Vol. iii. p. 470.)

In 1834 O'Connell attacked the impartiality of Baron Smith, one of the judges of the Court of Exchequer in Dublin. "It is almost needless to say," after a Special Committee had inquired into O'Connell's charges, " that the judge was honorably acquitted."—(*Ibid*, p. 536.)

29 In the *Age* of Oct. 14, 1897, are three letters signed respectively "Roman Catholic"—"John Farrell"—and "Elector," protesting against the action of the Defence League in politics, and revealing some of its methods, declaring it also unrepresentative of Catholic opinion. But in the issue of October 16, 1897 is a notice a portion of which reads :—" In connection with the Parliamentary Election for East Bourke Boroughs two letters were published in the *Age* on Thursday, exposing and deprecating a sectarian movement in that constituency. These letters seem to have been as gall and wormwood to one section of the Brunswick electors, who are said to be now scouring round to find and scalp the authors."—(Vide the *Age*, Oct. 16, 1897, " Religion and Politics at Brunswick. ")

to produce a public opinion hostile to it. An old Irishman in a quiet place once observed that he was

"RUSTY FOR WANT OF A BATING."

The Jovial Journal[30] of Melbourne tells the following story and moralises in the following fashion : "'Ah! Pat, I see Gladstone is going to rob you of your grievances.' 'Is he then,' replied Pat fiercely. 'Down wid him! Down wid him!'" This is a very good joke because the essence of truth is in it. It is not a peculiarly Irish characteristic, but the love of something to fight for is a strongly marked trait of the Irish character, and it happens occasionally that when the good fighting blood of the race is not otherwise engaged, it creates a grievance, and shows itself as ready to fight for the imaginary wrong as for a real infliction, and to fight just as fiercely. *Punch* has an idea that the recently-established organisation which aims to suppress Orange processions in the interests of Catholicism, is founded entirely on an *imaginary* grievance, and is due, not to any existing injustice one way or the other, but to the fact that there are a number of good Hibernians in our midst, whose fighting instincts, having been too long smothered, are now breaking out. The formers of the new order are rusty for an oratorical Donnybrook, and we have no doubt but that wordy knocks will be exchanged before matters simmer down again."

Father Cleary either does not read the *Advocate*—which is a ridiculous assumption, seeing that he confesses himself a contributor to its columns—or else the significant side thrusts of that Journal at the Orange processions, the daring charges it openly makes or insinuates in connection therewith, and the premium it puts on the gallant conduct of rowdies in green, representing them as it does in extravagant terms of laudation, have been wasted on him. This latter assumption, however, would be as ridiculous as the former, in view of the keen way in which he has pressed his case against Orangeism. I am therefore compelled to believe that the following paragraph from the Rev. gentleman's pen is a fine bit of purest bathos and rhetorical gush :—" The Brunswick (Melbourne) L.O.L. Demonstration of Sunday, July 19, 1896, the displays which took place in 1897 at the same place and at Prahran, Walhalla, and elsewhere, all prove that the Orange question is looming up in Victoria. We have in our midst, fully organised and preparing, the forces which with pious phrase and in Christ's sweet name, have

---

30 *Melbourne Punch*, Sept. 23, 1897.

crimsoned the streets of Belfast, Derry, Toronto, and so many other places, with the blood of the very fellow Christians whom they call Brethren."[31] The author and the Catholic organ are as far as the poles asunder in sentimental address, but then one wrote for Protestant or "non-Catholic" readers, and the other for Roman Catholic subscribers—this little fact doubtless accounts for the bifurcation of sentiment. Sir Chas. Dilke, commenting on the disturbance in Queensland over the appointment of Sir Henry Blake as Governor, in which the Roman Catholic Irish element made itself felt, remarked—" It must be remembered that in the Colonies, the Roman Catholic party is, as a rule, *the best organised of parties*, and the only one which has the advantage of possessing a *never-changing policy*—the defence of Roman Catholic interests by securing support from the public Treasury for the education of Roman Catholic Children in Roman Catholic schools under the general direction of priests."[32] Apart, however, from the question of the organisation of party, there has also to be remembered the grip that religion maintains on the political conscience of the Roman Catholic. Mr. Denehy gave his testimony on this point at the Brunswick Police Court when the legality of Orange processions was being tested. This gentleman was asked—" Supposing you were ordered by the Pope to walk in procession, and by a Police Magistrate not to do so, who would you obey?—The Pope has no power to order me to do anything of the kind. According to the circumstances I'd please myself. If I was bound by the law of the land I must obey it, *providing it was not against my conscience*, in which case *I would disobey the law*." He was further asked—" Would you disobey the law if it was against your religious belief?—*Most assuredly*. But you are assuming impossible things. I have always voted according to my conscience. I have often voted for Protestants."[33] I only urge this evidence because the *Advocate* is peculiarly bitter against Orangeism on the ground of violating law, though that law has not yet been judicially interpreted. This is regarded as a peculiarly aggravated offence. But if the principle

---

31 p. 169. A culprit, arrested at Brunswick in July, 1898, when *no* Orange procession took place, said :—" He was the leader of 500 men on the borders of Brunswick, waiting to flood the streets of the town with blood, if the Orangemen marched along." The constable deposed that this gentleman was under liberal spirituous influence when he made the statement. But if he had been an Orange man, what a shriek would have gone up about the "qualifications," &c.—(The *Age*, July 19, 1898.)

32 *Problems of Greater Britain*, p. 202, Ed. 1890.

33 The *Argus*, Feb. 12, 1893.

affirmed by Mr. Denehy is a valid and admissible one, that a law which is against his conscience may be disobeyed, why should not a similar privilege be extended to the Orangemen ? The same witness in reply to further questions said—"He had spoken to many Catholics about the demonstration at Brunswick. There was no pre-arranged organisation to disturb the procession, but *it was understood a good many would be there.* He spoke to Mr. Winter of the *Advocate* about it, but only in a casual way."[34]

CHAPTER III.

BLOWS FROM LECKY'S CLUB.—PESTLE AND MORTAR.—DUFFY ON MITCHEL.—TORTUOUS HISTORY.—JUNCTURE OF ORANGEMEN AND CATHOLICS.—" ORANGE CATHOLICS."—THE PIVOTAL FACT OF ORANGE STORY.—THE MYTH OF IRISH NATIONALISM. —ARGYLL ON THE REFORMATION.—WHEN THE IRISH BECAME " ARDENT CATHOLICS."—THE RELIGIOUS FINGER IN THE POLITICAL PIE.

FATHER CLEARY has aimed to discredit Mr. Froude as an authority on events in Ireland by specially recording whatever adverse criticisms he had discovered on that writer.[1] Mr. Lecky

---

34 *Ibid.*

1 In order to show Froude's " deep seated antipathy to Catholics," Cleary puts in evidence that he states :—" The rebels on their march to Arklow in 1798 ' *halted at every mile* to hear mass.'" (p. 62. *Note* 25.) If Froude said this, I presume he got it from the following source. Lord Castlereagh's letter, dated June 12, 1798, remarks that England should decide the struggle raging in Ireland, because the Irish Government was most likely to favor a party in the strife, inasmuch as it was " exasperated by the religious persecution to which the Protestants in Wexford have been exposed. In that country it is perfectly a religious frenzy. The priests lead the rebels to battle : on their march they kneel down and pray, and show the most desperate resolution in their attack. They put such Protestants as are *reported* to be Orangemen to death, saving others *upon condition of their embracing the Catholic faith*"—(Wright's *History of Ireland*, vol. iii. p. 111.) (Hassencamp's *History of Ireland*, p. 303.)

I presume the phrase relating to the "*halting at every mile* " is the evidence relied on to show Froude's antipathy. Gordon, whom Wright says " was by no means a partisan of the Irish Government of that time " (vol. iii. p 38), describes the march of the Catholics under Father Roche towards Ross. " In their march

was the principal critic appealed to for this purpose. In working up his case against Orangeism, the Rev. gentleman quoted from authors favourable to his project, on whom Lecky had also passed strictures which he must have seen. With a discretion, for which the father should take out a patent, he makes his extracts and never so much as hints that his "authorities" are scouted by the Member for Dublin University. As I have no false modesty on this score, I shall take the liberty of putting in Mr. Lecky's "pillory" some of Father Cleary's favourite writers, who supply the "reliable information" which is the gold of his book.

BLOWS FROM LECKY'S CLUB.

The Orange Society's Critic prides himself on the fact that much of his work is based on "Protestant testimony,"[2] a matter also which affords Father O'Doherty, his proof-reader, unspeakable gratification. It is assumed that, to cite certain adverse opinions on the Orange Society given by Protestant writers, is ample proof of their validity: it is equivalent to "Rome has spoken: the cause is ended." Under the influence of this peculiar delusion the Father proudly parades a whole regiment of authors to trample upon Orangeism. Mr. Lecky is the "Protestant" Hercules of the group, and his club is wielded—with due deference to the time-honoured principle of tactics—by Father Cleary to deal 406 strokes. The reader will note as he proceeds, that Lecky's club, like the Boomerang, has the awkward propensity of re-acting on the user; and some rather painful "back-cuts" come from this weapon. The Rev. gentleman is in this plight —having used Lecky's stick to trounce the Orange Society, he cannot object to his own castigation from the same source. (Psalm vii. 15-16.) When Froude strikes, it is with the hammer of Thor, but Lecky is no mean hand in swinging the literary shillaleh.

---

great numbers of the rebels under Roche exhibited much reluctance, and they halted so frequently to kneel and pray and receive *Benedictions of the Clergy*, that at length Father Roche lost his patience, and swearing violently, asked them if they thought they had come there for nothing but to pray, and whether they intended to fight or not."—(Wright's *History of Ireland*, vol. iii. p 72.)

Father Cleary has not been able to show that any critic accuses Froude of undue partiality to Orangeism.

2 Dr. Rentoul describes the peculiar characteristic "of all Roman Catholic advocates" as being "to shun actual facts of history and to pile together (under the Romanist notion of the impressiveness of '*authority*' and *names*) a mass of odd 'quotations' from 'Fathers' and from 'Protestant' testimony."—(*The Early Church and the Roman Claim*, p. 8.)

Sampson's *Memoirs*[3] from which Cleary has made three extracts is disposed of by Lecky in these terms:—"The Book appears to me very *mendacious and incredible*."[4] Madden's *United Irishmen* has furnished the Father with twenty-nine choice tit-bits, but Lecky says—"Madden on this, as on *all other matters* connected with the United Irishmen, writes as *the most furious partisan*."[5] Hay's *History of the Wexford Rebellion* has done good service for Mr. Cleary. The twenty-five quotations taken from it were needed to properly garnish his story: but then, as in the case of Madden, this writer is a Roman Catholic, and there is no "Protestant testimony" in corroboration. Lecky sums him up as "*a violent partisan of the rebels*,"[6] and accuses him of "malevolently" misrepresenting "the strong resolutions of the Magistrates under the presidency of Lord Gosford."[7] Froude is equally severe upon Hay[8]:—"He confesses only what he cannot deny, and leaves half of what is undeniable unmentioned. . . . For what purpose all Ireland had for two years turned itself into an arsenal, and every village into a place of drill, he does not care to enquire. He passes over in silence the correspondence with France, and the series of savage murders which made necessary the Insurrection Act. The Assassination Committee, the plots for the murder of

---

3 This Sampson is quoted by Father Cleary (p. 66, Note 38) as giving an amended Orange Oath of a highly grotesque and blood-coloured nature, ending as follows:—
"Can you write your name?—I can.
" With what sort of a pen?—With the spear of life or Aaron's Rod that buds, blossoms, and bears almonds in one night.
" With what sort of ink?—*Papist blood*."
Father Cleary has the italics in his account of this tawdry and transparent forgery. Another part of the bogus oath, which is also in italics, runs that if a Roman Catholic shall offend an Orangeman, "then I will use my endeavours to *shed the last drop of his blood*." This is a very liberal sort of forgery, for it actually contemplates a Catholic giving the offence to the Orangeman. *O sancta simplicitas!* Mr. Cleary has seen Lecky's criticism of Sampson, doubtless, but this rubbish was too good to omit from his "*reliable* information."

4 *Ireland in the 18th Century*, vol. iv. p. 16, Note.

5 *Ibid*, p. 316, *Note*.

6 *Ibid*, p. 343, *Note*.

7 *Vol*. iii. p. 444.

8 Hay's treatment of the Scullabogue Barn atrocity is touched by Froude with this piece of caustic: "Mr. Hay claims more than the permitted license of a partisan, when he explains what happened *at nine in the morning* at Scullabogue, as the *result* of the behaviour of the troops at Ross *at three in the afternoon*." —(*Ireland*, Vol. iii. p. 470.)
Wright remarks of Hay's book that it is a work—"Written with strong party feeling and in many of the statements in which we cannot place much confidence."—(*Ireland*, Vol. iii. p. 68.)

the Council, are events too insignificant for him to notice : nor does he touch on the combination of treachery and ferocity which distinguished the performances in Kildare on the night of the 23rd of May. He assumes that when the Irish took arms, and used them in the manner which has been described, they were entitled to the courtesies of war; and that when punished as incendiaries and murderers they were within their rights when they retaliated in kind."[9] Byrne's *Memoirs* have also been handy to Father Cleary inasmuch as he makes use of them 11 times. Lecky has a word of depreciation for this writer, however. " Byrne *naturally* minimises the number of murders by the rebels. . . . . He dishonestly calls Gordon 'the Orange Historian.' "[10] Mr. Lecky also gives us his impression of Mr. Gordon's narrative of the Rebellion. "He was a writer of little ability and no great research, but he had admirable opportunities of knowing the truth, and no one who reads his history can doubt that he was a most excellent, truthful, moderate and humane man . . . but yet with an occasional, and very pardonable, *bias towards the weaker side*."[11] In noticing this author, Froude said, he " wrote with the same desire to soothe the wounded feelings of the Catholic party."[12] Probably this sympathetic strain in the writer induced the Father to extract 21 allusions from his History to adorn the pages of the " reliable information."

PESTLE AND MORTAR.

There is no monopoly granted to Messrs. Lecky and Froude, to pound in their literary mortars the authors whom they abhor. Other authorities handle the critical pestle and batter "historic reliability." Mr. Mitchel has been a much needed friend to the Orange Society's latest critic—he is the handy "Protestant;" he openly flouted the authority of Froude ; he also wrote or quoted a lurid description of an Orange procession, gratefully incorporated in Father Cleary's production.[13] Altogether, therefore, Mitchel has been a strong pillar to him, and 56 extracts represent his worth to the good cause. Justin McCarthy glowingly depicts Mitchel as "the *one formidable man amongst the rebels* of '48 : the one man who distinctly knew what he

---

9 *English in Ireland*, Vol. iii. p. 426.
10 *Ireland*, vol. iv. pp. 443, 444, *Note*.
11 *Ibid*, p. 354.
12 *Ireland*, vol. iii. p. 426.
13 pp. 229, 230.

wanted, and was prepared *to run any risk* to get it."[14] This is a capital recommendation—from a certain point of view. Sir Charles Gavan Duffy says a great deal about Mitchel, and he knew him well. The following samples must serve the reader —" During the period of negotiation, Mitchel tried my patience sorely by *defending negro slavery*, and denouncing the emancipation of the Jews as *an unpardonable sin.*"[15] Mitchel " is not a generous critic *on his friends.*"[16] What must he be to his opponents ? Lalor accused Mitchel of "appropriating his ideas."[17] Duffy speaks of a debate leaving " Mr. Mitchel profoundly discredited for judgment and capacity."[18] On another occasion he says :—" Mitchel's theories proved to be gaseous."[19] Sir Charles very candidly exposes what he conceived to be the error of Mitchel's policy, and which by forcing projects unripe burst up the young Ireland movement, and turned it into a fatal burlesque.[20] Of the personal relations between Duffy and Mitchel the former speaks reluctantly, preferring to " suffer injustice " rather than to " criticise the dead."[21] In a pregnant passage, is summed up the patriotism of Mitchel as compared with Davis. " Davis loved Ireland : Mitchel hated England." Mitchel proposed nothing " during his whole lifetime " which would affect England " more than the prick of a pin. Yet he continued to be loved by multitudes of Irishmen, because it was certain beyond all doubt that he execrated England. He was not a guide whom it was possible to follow : in the main he pointed to no road which led anywhere: but he was a constant trumpet of resistance to England and *that was enough.*"[22] This, then, is the windy Mr. Mitchel described by two Roman Catholic writers. We may be sure Duffy does not put the worst side out, with respect to his one-time friend and co-worker ; but what he does say is amply sufficient to account for Mitchel's versatile acquaintance with Orangeism, and is an X Ray upon his inner motive of hostility towards it. (See pp. 755, 756 Duffy on Mitchel's imagination as an author.)

Father Cleary refers to Plowden and Madden as " valued Standard Catholic Authorities."[23]. We have already seen Lecky's opinion of Dr. Madden. The Duke of Argyll regards Plowden as " one of the most prejudiced and clamourous of Irish writers."[24] Another author passes the following stricture

---
14 Hon. Emily Lawless' *Ireland*, p. 393.
15 *Four Years' Irish History*, p. 500.
16 *Ibid*, p. 666. 17 *Ibid*, p. 522. 18 *Ibid*, p. 523. 19 *Ibid*, p. 526.
20 *Ibid*, p. 559. 21 *Ibid*, p. 583. 22 *Ibid*, pp. 585, 586. 23 p. 15.
24 *Irish Nationalism*, p. 123.

on the "valued Standard Catholic" authority:—"Plowden's *History of Ireland* like its predecessor which treats of the *History of the Union*, is little better than a political pamphlet of the most bitter and prejudiced character."[25] Mr. Banks in his *History of the Orange Order*, 1898, remarks that Plowden had to pay a fine of £5000 "for libelling certain parties in his unreliable *History of Ireland.*"—(p. 22.) But the Father, like Gallio, "cares for none of these things," and treats his readers to 104 quotations from this source.

The *History of Orangeism* by M.P. has supplied 63 quotations, but this anonymous scribe is acknowledged by Mr Cleary to be a Roman Catholic. I have an idea that many of the incidents attributed to newspaper reports have been filtered through pamphlets — political and partisan — either from Nationalist or Roman Catholic pens. To the careful reader it will be apparent that in the Rev. gentleman's work, the most serious and tragical episodes rest almost exclusively upon *Roman Catholic authority*: and that the "Protestant testimony" is considerably the less important part of it. Exclude Roman Catholic authorities, such as Messrs Plowden, Hay, McNevin, Healy, Madden, and M.P., and the element of tragedy is drained from Father Cleary's *Orange Society*: except in cases where Roman Catholics have made fierce attacks upon Orangemen.

Tortuous History.

The foregoing criticisms have been inserted here to show that, apart from the actual facts of Irish History, the political or religious view of the Historian has to be considered. It is not the lot of many men to chronicle movements and events which mould the life of a Nation, and eliminate from their story the writer's personal convictions. The Historian has yet to be born who can do it. It is quite natural that an author, having abundant material before him, will, however fairly disposed, select that which renders his work most forceful.[26] Thus it sometimes happens that a subsequent author, seeing the same occurrences from a different level, finds in the unused matter a refutation of the aspect formerly paraded. On this principle Father Cleary promptly dismisses Mr. Froude as an

---

25 Browne's *Narratives of State Trials in the Nineteenth Century*, vol. i.

26 Sir Henry James, speaking of Sir Charles Russell's defence of Parnell, said: "I am sure my friend only did what any of us would have done: he read such portion of an authority as he deemed to be of assistance to the argument which he was using."—(*The Work of the Irish Leagues*, p. 12.)

authority on Irish affairs, and peremptorily excludes his History from consideration in his work. But it is a poor rule that only holds good in the case of one writer. I have shown how the Father's exclusive method acts on his own authorities, and we shall see that several other "distinguished" authorities, high in his favor, have been adversely criticised as we go on. It is notorious that accóunts of movements in Ireland are of the most involved and complicated character. This occurs of course in histories of other countries, but not so persistently and peculiarly. It is an aspect that any writer or speaker on Irish matters must reckon with. The reverend critic of Orangeism has not made sufficient allowance for this peculiarity.[27]

The Father tells us in mild accents :—" My purpose is to give a record of warning incidents which deserve to be more widely known, in the hope that these new lands may be spared some of the heartburnings which have been the bane of Ulster ever since 1795." (p. 236). When it is remembered that this writer represents the Orange Society *almost solely* as "the bane of Ulster" from that period, and carefully picks his quotations for that purpose, the statement savours of Cant. Naturally, as the exponent of broad and tolerant feeling, Mr. Cleary tries every phase of his Orangeism by present day standards, and holds up his highly coloured pictures of it for judgment in the political atmosphere of Victoria. He stands in the wrong pulpit, however, to make it a pronounced success. Still, it is good policy on his part, for he can trade on a modern conscience possibly uninformed in the whole history of the subject. The cradle of Orangeism is in Ulster. Now what stands at the back of that? Let us lift the curtain and see. A colony of English and Scotch Protestants have been planted in Ireland—(rightly or wrongly need not now be argued, but this is the starting point if we would understand the Orange question)—and though England has often acted the part of the proverbial stepmother, these Colonists have desperately clung to her skirts in the main all these years.[28] Now and again they have passionately ventilated

---

27 Sir Charles Russell defending Parnell speaks of the "many qualities of a noble kind" possessed by the Irish ; he admits that they are "disgraced by crime of one particular kind," but warns the Times-Parnell commissioners against concluding " because there is this black record of crime in the past, that therefore the Irish people are to be branded as a nation of criminals "—(*Ireland's Vindication*, p. 19.) I think we will observe crimes in Ireland which have not on the wedding garment of Sir Charles Russell's proposition.

28 Hall, while not enamoured of the Orange Symbols, says :—"England is certainly indebted to the Orange Societies for having retained Ireland as part and parcel of the dominions of Great Britain, for assuredly if there had been no

their grievances, and have seriously thought of setting up housekeeping for themselves, but on every occasion, while they were aided and abetted by their fellow countrymen in the majority, it was soon seen that in the new national house the priest was meant to be a chief factor, and they ultimately chose the lesser evil of abiding by England than of mating their Protestantism with Romanism to found a nation under the domination of the latter religion. Mr. Gladstone lent the sanction of his great name and powerful political influence to the "inflated fable" of seven centuries of English misgovernment in Ireland, and by his Home Rule scheme endeavoured to settle the Irish question, but that crisis brought long forgotten facts to light, and evoked an expression of feeling which it is not desirable to produce often.[29] One of the most incongruous features of that political cataclysm was

The Fusion of Loyalists—Orange and Green.

Mr. St. Loe Strachey has called attention to the union of the Ulster Liberals with the Orangemen, on grounds of public policy, in spite of traditional hatreds. The danger must have been extremely critical to merge into one, political parties so essentially opposite; but Roman Catholics and Orangemen in political embrace is nothing short of miraculous. That such a thing could occur in Ulster within *the last fifteen years*, is a criticism of Father Cleary's book more startling than a volume of the most acute refutatory argument. Such a criticism takes on a razorlike edge, when it is remembered that the juncture of Northern Catholics with Orangemen has been made the occasion of bitter and sneering denunciation by their co-religionists. The following paragraphs from *The Times' Articles and Letters* will reveal a state of things in Ireland not usually known in this country. A letter by "J.P.," December 21st, 1885, states that the writer "acted (as a volunteer) as sub-agent for two of the loyalist candidates, so can speak with authority on the subject. For several Sundays previous to the days of polling, the Roman Catholic Clergy gave directions to the un-

---

Union of the Irish Protestants acting together, and in concert, between the years 1793 and 1800, Ireland would have become for a time at least a province of France."—(*Ireland : Its Scenery, Character, &c.*, vol. ii. p. 468.)

29 The *Nineteenth Century*, July, 1892, publishes ten short articles with the common title "Why I shall vote for the Unionists." The Dean of St. Paul's, Prof. Butcher, Dr. Dallinger, Prof. Romanes, Mr. Allies a Roman Catholic, and Aubrey de Vere are amongst the writers: their opinions show a political temper with which it is dangerous to trifle, and emanating outside political circles they are the more forceful.

fortunate voters, as to how they were to exercise the franchise, and used every description of clerical intimidation to coerce them to vote for the Nationalist candidate. In one case the Curate of the parish used the following expression: 'Let me see, will one single member of my congregation dare vote for the *Orange Catholic* Candidate. These Orange Catholics are the curse of our country.' .... An Orange Catholic is supposed to mean a loyal independent Catholic, who uses the intelligence nature gives him for himself, and refuses to obey the dictates of the priest in political matters."³⁰ This correspondent also adds, "the Roman Catholic priests are disloyal to a man, and are well paid for supporting the Nationalists." Another writer later on in the course of events observes that— "Some members of the Irish Roman Episcopacy have taken occasion to launch bitter sarcasms at some of those men, who at the late elections for a political and honest purpose, joined their conservative and in some instances *their Orange Countrymen :* but those dignitaries must have known at the time they designated them 'Orange Catholics' that they associated with Orangemen for no Orange purpose : they stood forward in the face of obloquy showered upon them with no niggard hand, to avoid the alternative of joining the National Land League, or of forfeiting their property, their rights and their liberties."³¹ Surely irony can go no further than this! Father Cleary has made the Orangeman appear to be a coward, a hypocrite, a concentrated and venomous bigot, and everything that is odious and detestable : he has made it appear that Orangeism has been the curse—the torture chamber—the malign vendetta of Irish Catholic story, and yet here it is avowed that Irish Catholics, from fear or distrust of the large body of those professing the same Religious faith, united with the Orangemen, to prevent the forfeiture of "*their property, their rights, and their liberties.*" Let it be allowed that this union took place on but a moderate scale, and for one political transaction only, and let it be further

---

30 *Home Rule*, p. 43.
31 *Ibid.* p. 510-511. Sir Chas. G. Duffy mentions the position of a sympathiser—Mr. John Martin, subsequently Home Rule member for Meath. "As a Protestant of Ulster, he declared that the present condition of the Association was ruining the cause of Repeal among his class. Their chief objection to Repeal was a dread of Catholic ascendency : they feared that freedom of speech and civil and religious liberty would be at the mercy of O'Connell and the Catholic Clergy." Martin stated his opinions in a letter to the (misnamed) *Freeman*, but that Journal "declined to publish this letter."— (*Four Years of Irish History*, p. 251.)
The peculiar methods by which Martin was gagged are described by Duffy (p. 253).

allowed that this fear or mistrust was utterly mistaken, still its significance is truly phenomenal. I do not wish to unduly magnify it, I only adduce it as an indication of the multiplex whole which the Irish Question presents when its inner working is examined, and it has its meaning when one comes to examine the forces awork to make Ireland, and Irish history, a conundrum to all students.

Protestant Ulster is the plantation of English Government, and the Orangeism Father Cleary attacks sprang up in Protestant Ulster. This is the pivotal fact of Orange story—to lose sight of it is to miss the luminous land mark of its existence. Mr. Prendergast relates the early English connection with Ireland in this way: "Now the 'Irish Enemy' was no nation in the modern sense of the word, but a race divided into many nations or tribes, separately defending their lands from the English barons in their immediate neighbourhood. There had been no ancient national government displaced, no national dynasty overthrown. *The Irish had no national flag*, nor any capital city as the metropolis of their common country, nor any common administration of the law: nor did they ever give a combined opposition to the English. The English, coming in the name of the Pope, with the aid of the Irish Bishops, and with a superior national organisation which the Irish easily recognised, were accepted by the Irish."[33] The best friends of Ireland succeed in bringing out the fact that the destructive powers which inhered in the native population far outrivalled their constructive forces with regard to nation making. They "*accepted*" English rule, says Mr Prendergast, and Prof. Richey relates—that when King Brian had an opportunity, and did establish a native government, its very excellence was the prime cause of its being overturned—"a truly National Government of this description found its bitterest enemies among the provincial chiefs, who longed to restore anarchy, and were willing to league with the foreigner for that purpose."[34] The Duke of Argyll presents us with a companion picture of the native Irish Church: "Its organisation was unlike anything that existed elsewhere in any part of the Christian world. It had no parochial clergy—it had no territorial Bishops. Its, so called, Monastic bodies had none of the characteristics we are accustomed to associate with the name. . . . . It may well seem incredible, but it stands on the firmest historical evidence,

---

33 *Cromwellian Settlement of Ireland*, 1870, p. 28.
34 Richey's *Short History*, p. 110.

that *more than two hundred years after* St. Patrick had established the Celtic Church in Ireland,[35] its so called clergy were regularly bound by the customs of the country to take part *in all the wars* of the chief or tribe under which they lived. And when we consider what these wars were. . . . . *wars of mere plunder, slaughter, and devastation,* we may conceive what the degradation must have been, and how completely in this form it was divorced from all the influences which elsewhere in Europe made it the precious seed bed of Civilisation."[36] Prof. Stokes speaks of the Church in the 13th Century, after the reforming work done by the Roman See in the 12th, in this fashion :—" The Monasteries were as completely tribal institutions, bound up with certain septs, and hated by other hostile septs, as they were in the seventh and eighth centuries. . . . . The tribes venerated—sometimes but not always—the Monasteries belonging to their own patron saint or their own tribe. But the monasteries of a hostile tribe, or of a different saint, were regarded as fair game for murder, plunder, and arson."[37] One by one pleasing illusions fade away as we face past records ; Prendergast makes early Ireland a ragged regiment of aboriginal tribes engaged in internecine strife: Richey reveals order and organisation shattered by jealous chieftains: Argyll shocks us with a militant and gory Church ; and Stokes accentuates the Duke's picture, indeed, he goes beyond it and ascribes " the comparative indifference of the Irish to the sacredness of human life " to an hereditary survival of the taint which was conspicuous in all the centuries of which he wrote.[38] Prof. Richey sums up in graphic phrase Ireland in the 16th Century—" At the commencement of the 16th Century there remained no tradition of national Unity—no trace of an organisation by which they could be united into one people. The separate tribes had been disorganised by civil wars, and the original tribesmen were suppressed and supplanted by the

---

35 Cardinal Moran said at the opening of the Melbourne Roman Catholic Cathedral (St. Patrick's)--" When St. Patrick landed in Ireland it was yet a pagan wilderness. When he went to plead for his people in Heaven it had become *God's garden.*" In the same sermon the Cardinal panegyrised Ireland thus—" A lamp of civilisation, a garden of sanctity, a hive of missionaries, a home of sages, *an island of saints.*" Evidently the Cardinal does not stick at trifles when he eulogises.—(The *Age,* Nov. 1st, 1897.)

Arch Deacon O'Sullivan, the parish priest of Kenmare, in a letter, mentions the murders of Lord Cavendish and Mr. Burke, and asks—" Will Ireland ever outlive the *villainy of her own sons* ? "—(*The Nun of Kenmare,* p. 80.)

36 *Irish Nationalism,* pp. 26-27.
37 *Anglo-Norman Church,* p. 363.
38 *Celtic Church,* p. 200.

mercenary followers of the several rivals for the chieftaincies."³⁹ From this brief and necessarily condensed sketch, it will be seen that the political and religious forces, which should have moulded life into organised strength and evolved order out of anarchic elements, acted detrimentally to both the national and religious spirit: for instead of order being brought out of chaos, the original chaotic causes remained practically unchanged.

The Myth of Irish Nationalism.

All through his work Father Cleary cherishes the National idea of Ireland—for instance, he speaks of Green as being the "National colour." I omit argument with respect to this on account of the limitations of subject and space, and it is sufficient to say that "Irish Nationalism" is looked upon by some eminent writers as a myth. Prof. Goldwin Smith says:— "Ireland has a distinct boundary, but she can hardly be said to have *any other element of a separate Nationality*." And Sir Geo. Baden-Powell in his recent volume, *The Saving of Ireland*, published 1898, remarks on this same subject:—"To those who are acquainted either with Irish History or with Ireland, it does seem *past comprehension* how there can be any vitality or reality in the cry of Irish Nationalism." (p. 50.) The Duke of Argyll deals at large with the whole matter in his work on *Irish Nationalism*, from which I quote in this Chapter.

The Duke of Argyll on the Reformation.

In 1534 Henry VIII. had finally broken with the Roman Pontiff, and in the midst of this had quarrels with Germany, France, and Spain. England's position was supremely critical: a great conspiracy of the Catholic Continental Kings was entered into, to humble the country, and write *hic jacet* on the tomb of her reformed Religion.⁴⁰ For 200 years this dream

---

39 *Short History*, p. 238.

40 Dr. Döllinger in a lecture on the English Reformation related the history of the Papal Bull dethroning Elizabeth and excommunicating every Englishman who should regard her as Queen : he then came down to James I. and indicated that the temper of Rome had not improved, He said :—"It was stated to the Pope that the idea of a murder committed in the interests of Religion being deserving of praise, was much diffused abroad : that it was hurtful and degrading to the (Roman) Catholic Religion : that this false doctrine had even been defended in the writings of the Jesuits : and it was pressingly requested that the Pope should openly and solemnly condemn this error. But Rome *remained dumb*. Not even could they obtain this concession that the *worst* of the Jesuit writings which recommended the murder of the king *should be placed on the list of forbidden books*." The Doctor after thus plainly describing the intolerant spirit of the Roman See of that day, denounced the "new dogma of absolute Papal Supremacy " as "a production of *imposture and falsehood*, and a source of ruin to Church and State.—(The *True Catholic*, May 1872, p. 84.)

captivated the continent in one form or another. Ireland geographically was the tactical ground for operation, and even Prof. Richey admits that only one course of action was open to England, in self-preservation, especially when Ireland was intriguing with the foreign foes of Britain, which then lay under the Papal ban. Richey, strange to say, has the warmest praise for the Statesmanship of Henry VIII. and his Ministers at this national crisis: "His own subjects understood him better than his historians. He was all through supported by the masses of the people. The violent and despotic acts of which he was accused, were done by a Monarch who had no standing army, scarcely even a body guard, and who resided close beside, almost within, the powerful and turbulent city of London. As regards his Irish policy his State papers disclose a moderation, a conciliating spirit, a respect for the feelings of the Celtic population, a sympathy with the poor which no subsequent English ruler has ever displayed."[41] In 1542 Henry VIII. summoned a parliament "professing to represent the whole of Ireland," which changed the old feudal title "Lord of Ireland" into that of King. This date, however, does not really give what may be termed the initial subjugation of Ireland to English rule, which occurred in 1603, in the reign of Queen Elizabeth. The following points are emphasised by the Duke of Argyll. (1) That the Roman Catholic Church—wholly in the 16th and 17th, and partially even in the 18th, Century—" was not a mere religious body or communion, but was more or less actively one great political organisation of the most formidable kind."[42] He does not admit the doctrine of religious freedom and toleration until religion is reduced to definition, and contends if a man "tells us that it is part of his religion to acknowledge the supremacy, over his conduct, of some priest, whether at home or abroad, he must be told that we shall not allow him to translate his belief into act, if it leads him to transgress one iota of our laws. If another man tells us that it is part of his religion to obey a Spiritual Potentate who pretends, or inherits the tradition of

---

41 *Short History*, p. 268.

42 *Irish Nationalism*, p 161.

Dr. Wylie refers to the proceedings of a Roman Catholic Provincial Synod at at St. Mary's, Ascot, in Aug., 1852. "In this Synod we have the first instance since the Reformation of a body of Popish Ecclesiastics meeting together in Great Britain, to make laws which, when they have received the assent of a Foreign Prince, are to be binding, are to possess authority, and are to be enforced. Here in short we have a Parliament framing laws, claiming jurisdiction over all Her Majesty's subjects, and exercising that jurisdiction over a large body of them, by enforcing obedience to its laws."—(*Rome and Civil Liberty*, p. 132.)

pretending, to influence his allegiance to our laws, he must be told that we will hold him in perpetual suspicion, and take all necessary precautions against him, until we have good reason to believe that his doctrine has been either formally abandoned or has died a natural death."[43] At this period he regards the Roman Catholic Church over the whole of Europe as "*one great standing conspiracy against the English Monarchy and the liberties of England.*" (2) The native Irish, and the Celtic Church, so far as the one had solidarity, and the other cohesion, "resented the original papal gift of the Lordship over Ireland to the English Sovereign, and had not very long before addressed a laboured remonstrance to the Holy See against its legitimacy and justice." (3) It should not be forgotten by Irish Catholics even now—"that whatever share they may be disposed to claim for their share in its (the Church's) influence over the Irish people, was a share due to *the continued support and patronage of the English Kings* against the anarchial, and even degrading influences, which had been long exercised by their own native Ecclesiastical organisation." (4) The rebellion of the Geraldines, which Henry VIII. had to suppress, was marked by a significant feature, which clearly enough showed the hostility of the original Celtic, to the Anglo-Norman Church. One of the first performances of the Geraldines was to murder the Archbishop of Dublin and his Chaplains.[44] (5) The Irish surrender is declared by Prof. Richey in the following terms:— "*The renunciation of the Pope's pretensions was made a necessary article in the submission of the local rulers. None of them seem to have had any hesitation upon this subject. The instruments still remaining are such as to forbid our considering this arrangement less than universal.*"[45] (6) The religious aspect of this conquest of Ireland did not become acute for half a century afterwards, because the native Irish "*did not become ardent Catholics, until an intimate connection with Spain at*

---

43 *Irish Nationalism*, pp. 161-2.

Argyll's contention is in harmony with the maxims of Locke, and, indeed, of common sense. Tolerance must have its limits, for it cannot tolerate intolerance. Locke says "That Church can have no right to be tolerated by the Magistrate which is constituted on such a bottom, that all those who enter into it do thereby, *ipso facto*, deliver themselves up to the protection and service of another Prince. For by this means the Magistrate would give way to the settling of a foreign jurisdiction in his own country, and suffer his own people to be listed, as it were, for soldiers against his own Government."—(Vide *Rome and Civil Liberty*, Dr. Wylie, pp. 146-147.) If, Wylie says, "the right to toleration rest on the fact of being subjects, verily the right of the Romanist to toleration is somewhat ambiguous."—(*Ibid*, p. 151.)

44 Richey's *Short History*, p. 304.   45 *Ibid*, p. 363.

E

the end of the 16th century, taught them that the cause of Celtic independence, in order to be successful, must be united with the Catholic Church." But the Latin Church in Ireland, when the native population became "ardent Catholics," does not shine out in any transcendently creditable colours, for an historian passes this cutting verdict on it—" Its condition in the 16th resembled more that of the 12th than that even of the 14th Century."[46] It maintained no learning : it kept up no piety : it promoted no culture, and coming to particulars:—" In an age of lawlessness and violence they never came forward to protest, as Christian Priests, against the tyranny, robbery, and murder rife around them : their Bishops to a great extent were agents of the English Government : and the mass of the Clergy were split into hostile parties, and *participators in the national animosities and lawless violence of those times.*"[47] If the past is the father of the present, then we may expect to discern on the face of the present, with the necessary evolutional modifications, the lineaments broad and clear of the paternal countenance.

Ulster was planted by England, and Orangeism arose in Ulster. The handful of Protestant Colonists were set down among a people whose religious and political history I have been briefly sketching up to the year 1600. One might predict the massacre of 1641 from such data, especially when the religious rancour and strife of the 17th Century in Europe fill out the back-ground. Grattan is credited with inventing the maxim that "England's extremity was Ireland's opportunity," and there is incontestable evidence of this scattered throughout the pages of History. When England had her hands full with hereditary and Catholic foes, then Ireland indulged in some little speculations of massacre or rebellion, which always took on a religious aspect no matter what ostensible cause lay at the root. Age after age she has maintained the axiom of being " agin the government," and impregnated her politics with the priestly presence. Nothing can be less deniable in Irish History than the fact, that sooner or later in its organised movements, the shadow of the Church is seen, and the finger of the religious is inserted into the political pie, even though a Protestant should wear the Cook's apron. Sir Chas. Russell, in eulogising the leaders of Irish public opinion, could not overlook this patent proposition, and lamented the absence of " unsectarianism " in Irish political projects. He states that the sectarian spirit " had too often blighted and corrupted the Irish movements."[48]

---

46 *Short History*, p. 297.   47 *Ibid*, p. 295.   48 *Ireland's Vindication*, p. 13.

CHAPTER IV.

MASSACRE OF 1641.—SCENES IN ARMAGH.—A CATHOLIC CONFEDERACY.—SAY MASS IN ALL CHURCHES.—CATHOLIC JURIES WILL NOT CONVICT.—MURDER OF 40 PROTESTANTS.—OLIVER CROMWELL.—"THE INNOCENT BLOOD."—SCHEME OF SETTLEMENT.—WHY THE POPE COUNSELLED "HUMANITY AND MODERATION."

MR. LECKY, commenting on 1641, says:—"Irish writers have very often injured their cause by overstatement: either absurdly denying the misdeeds of their countrymen, or adopting the dishonest and disingenuous method of recounting only the crimes of their enemies." Father Cleary, in mentioning 1641, endeavours to discount its legacy to Irish Protestantism, by partially assuming Lecky's mantle. He charges popular accounts with being "enormous palpable exaggerations"— "grossly, absurdly and mendaciously exaggerated"—"grossly and malignantly represented," &c.[1] I cannot allow this outrage to pass off in such mist. For Mr. Lecky also says, "It is equally impossible to doubt that murders occurred on a large scale, with appalling frequency, and often with atrocious circumstances of aggravation."[2] Again, "there can be no real question that the rebellion in Ulster was extremely horrible, and was accompanied by great numbers of atrocious murders."[3] This heritage put a deposit of suspicion and conservatism into the Protestant colonists not easily eliminated, and which subsequent events frequently rendered acute.

The Conspiracy[4] originated with Rory or Roger O'Moore, Sir Phelim O'Neill, Lord Maguire, Hugh McMahon, the Bishop of Clogher and a few others. "They were to seize Dublin Castle, which was known to be weakly defended; get out the arms and powder, and re-distribute them to the disbanded troops; and at the same time seize all the forts and garrison towns in the North; turn all the Protestant settlers adrift—though it was first stipulated without killing or otherwise injuring them; take

---

1 p. 18, Note. 2 *Ireland in the 18th Century*, vol. i. p. 61. 3 *Ibid*, p. 60.

4 Mr. Green remarks:—"A conspiracy, organised with wonderful power and secrecy, burst forth in Ulster. . . . . Dublin was saved by a mere chance; but in the open country the work of murder went on unchecked."—(*History of the English People*, p. 524.)

possession of all the country houses, and make all who declined to join in the rising, prisoners."[5] A Presbyterian, named Conolly, overheard the conspirators, and caught the drift of their plot. He gave information, and was only tardily credited, but wise counsels prevailed, and Lord Maguire and Hugh McMahon were arrested. This timely action saved Dublin Castle. But in other parts—Armagh and Tyrone—the Protestants were "suddenly set upon by a horde of armed or half-armed men, dragged out of their houses, stripped to the skin, and driven naked and defenceless into the cold . . . . . hundreds perished within the first few days of exposure, or fell dead by the roadside of famine and exhaustion."[6] Sir Phelim, though defeated in several of his schemes, was roused to demoniacal fury; as the Hon. Emily Lawless puts it, he was "mad with excitement, and intoxicated with the sudden-sense of power," and this blood-stained monster[7] "hounded on his excited and undisciplined followers to commit every conceivable act of cruelty and atrocity. . . . . . Some hundreds of the inhabitants of Armagh who had surrendered on promise of their lives were *murdered in cold blood*. As for the more irregular murders committed in the open field upon helpless terrified creatures powerless to defend themselves, they are too numerous to relate, and there is happily no purpose to be gained in repeating the harrowing details."[8] We are left to speculate how the people of Dublin felt when they saw the survivors in this piteous state—"spent, worn out, frozen with cold, creeping along on hands and knees, and all but at the point of death."[9] When Cromwell came to Ireland, he spoke sternly. The opening message of the grim Protector was—" We are come to ask an account of the *innocent blood* that hath been shed, and to endeavour to bring to an account all who by appearing in arms shall justify the same."[10] The words were solemn and portentous, and the man who announced them was one not to be trifled with. His vengeance was a terrible one, and

---

5 *Ireland*—Hon. Emily Lawless, p. 242.   6 *Ibid*, p. 242.

7 Lecky confesses "There is no doubt that crimes of the most hideous description were committed, and that all the hatred of *race and creed were let loose*."— (Vol. i. p. 68.)

8 Lawless'*Ireland*, p. 243.   9 *Ibid*, p. 244.

"Tales of horror and outrage, such as maddened our own England when they reached us from Cawnpore, came day after day over the Irish Channel. Sworn depositions told how husbands were cut to pieces in presence of their wives, their children's brains dashed out before their faces, their daughters brutally violated and driven out naked to perish frozen in the woods."—(*History of the English People*, p. 524.)

10 Lawless' *Ireland*, p. 261.

judged by the ethics of our times overlapped a just retribution. The writer, whose account of the transaction I have been following, takes note of the exaggerations with regard to numbering the slain of the massacre, and remarks, " 4000 murdered, swelled to 40,000 ; and 8000, who died of exposure, to 80,000. . . . . Take it, however, at the very lowest, it is still a horrible one. Let us shut our eyes and pass on."[11]   Thomas Carlyle said of it, in his massive way :—" Not a picture, but a huge blot : an indiscriminate blackness, one which the human memory cannot willingly charge itself with."[12]   I have already adverted to the peculiarity which strikes the student of Irish History, that whatever primary cause generates some wild wanton act, whether it be organised or not, it is not long before we find the shadow of the Church being projected upon it.   The Hon. Emily Lawless notes this peculiarity, for she records that in October, 1642, a meeting of over " 200 Roman Catholic Deputies, nearly all the Irish Roman Catholic Bishops, many of the clergy, and some 14 peers," was convened at Kilkenny, famous or infamous for its cats, by the way.   The result was that " a council was formed, of which Lord Mountgarrett was appointed President. . . . . The war was declared to be *a Catholic one*, to be known henceforward as the Catholic Confederacy, and between old Irish and Anglo-Irish there was to be no difference."[13]   This author regarded the massacre as arising from agrarian causes, while affirming—" It was a rising unquestionably of a native Roman Catholic community against an introduced Protestant one, and the Religious element counted for something, though it is not easy to say for how much, in the matter."[14]   In the English mind, this treatment of their fellow-protestants, on Irish soil, was simply a new edition of St. Bartholomew, an atrocity " which the very amplest and bloodiest vengeance would still come far short of expiating."[15]   The Catholic Confederacy, which had declared the war a religious one, formulated their demand— " The free exercise of the Catholic Religion ; an Independent Irish Parliament ; a general pardon, and a reversal of all attainders, were amongst their conditions, and *they would not take less*."[16] A supplemental demand laid it down that, " *Mass was to be said in all the Churches.*"[17]   Charles had a plan of his own for treating with the Catholic negotiators.   He despatched Edward Somerset, Earl of Glamorgan, to make terms with the Confederates,

---

11 Lawless' *Ireland*, p. 245.   12 Carlyle's *Cromwell*, vol. ii. p. 40.
13 Lawless' *Ireland*, p. 249.   14 *Ibid* p. 252.
15 *Ibid*, p. 253. 16 *Ibid*, p. 253. 17 *Ibid*, p. 254.

behind the back of the Duke of Ormond, the nation's representative. Glamorgan promised everything they asked for[18] — he would have given them the moon on a promissory note if they had thought to demand it—and they agreed to despatch a large force to England to assist the needy King; in the meantime they blazed away at Ormond with sham requests and proposals. But the Duke was wide-awake, and had a suspicion which was turned to certainty when that doughty warrior, the Roman Catholic Archbishop of Tuam, fell at Sligo in October, 1645, for a copy of the secret treaty was found upon his person. Ormond sent it to the English Parliament, but the perfidious Charles stoutly repudiated it: few, however, believed his denial, and certainly none of the Irish Confederacy.[19] It killed the Royalist cause. To help matters along, the Pontiff Innocent X. sent over Rinuinci,[20] Archbishop of Fermo, as his Nuncio. His policy, however, was not one likely to succeed in Puritan times. The situation "to him narrowed itself to one point. The moment, he felt, had come for the re-establishment of the Catholic Religion in Ireland, and, if possible, for its union with one of the Catholic powers of Europe."[21] Mr. Jervis in his history draws attention to the fact that "the Roman Catholic Religion had become a bond of union, and enactments against Roman Catholics could not be enforced for *juries would not convict.*"[22] Such was the feeling amongst English Parliamentarians, that "on the 2nd December, 1641, after a solemn debate," it was resolved, "by the Lords and Commons, that they would never consent to any toleration of the Popish religion in Ireland, or in any other of his Majesty's dominions."[23] This, beyond all possibility of denial, is a lurid comment on the nature of the massacre from the standpoint of the British Government. Mr. Martin declares that, in Ireland, there have been "50 Rebellions of hatred against England," and he does not hesitate to say, with a frank-

---

18 "The seizure of his (Charles') papers at Naseby had hardly disclosed his intrigues with the Irish Catholics, when the Parliament was able to reveal to England a fresh treaty with them, which purchased no longer their neutrality, but their aid, by *the simple concession of every demand they had made.*"—(Green's *History of the English People*, p. 541.)

19 Walpole says:—Ormond "recalled Glamorgan from Kilkenny and flung him into prison on a charge of treason in exceeding his instructions. Charles, prompted by Lord Digby . . . boldly denied his authority to Glamorgan." To save Charles, Glamorgan even denied that what he had done was at the instigation of the King.—(*Short History of the Kingdom of Ireland*, p. 254.)

20 Jervis calls him "A vain meddling Italian Priest," p. 171. Lecky also refers to his "disastrous influence." Vol. i. p. 101.

21 Lawless' *Ireland*, p. 245.   22 *Ireland Under British Rule*, p. 142.

23 Rushworth's *Hist. Collect.*, vol. i. p. 456.

ness, that reminds one of the outspokenness of Mr. Froude, "the rebellion of 1641 was a rebellion of hostility to England and to the Protestant faith."[24] Mr. Lecky, while defending the Roman Catholics from unjust imputations of cruelty, does not exonerate the priesthood from complicity in the brutal work of the period, for he says: "A priest, named Maguire, is said to have been the leading agent in the treacherous murder of 40 Protestants, to which I have already referred, who had abjured their faith. The Bible was sometimes torn and trampled on by the infuriate mob. Protestant Churches were occasionally wrecked, and several Protestant Ministers were murdered. Priests undoubtedly supported the Rebellion from the pulpit, and even by the sentence of excommunication; and they were accused, though on much more doubtful authority, of forbidding any Catholic to give shelter to the fugitives."[25] In this passage is another reminder that *Chapel wrecking* by the Catholic mobs was a portion of the legacy left to Ulster by the Rebellion of 1641.

COUNTING THE DEAD.

Other authorities may be consulted on this Rebellion, such as Mr. Jervis' *Ireland under British Rule*, pp. 142, 155, 169, 170, 171. Green's *History of the English People*, pp. 524, 525. Lord Macaulay's *History of England*, vol. 1, p. 52. Dr. Ingram's *England and Rome*, pp. 380-430. Godkin's *Religious History of Ireland*, &c.

On the question of the numbers slain, the following may be indicated :—Mr. Lecky quotes Father Walshe, "The slaughtered must be about 8,000."[26] He, however, admits that this estimate differs widely from that of Temple (Master of the Rolls), Lord Clarendon, Milton, and Hume.[27] Green says, "50,000 English people perished in a few days, and rumour doubled and trebled the number."[28] Walpole inclines to Dr. Warner's figures, who gives "between four and five thousand as murdered in cold blood, and eight thousand as victims to exposure and ill-usage."[29] Jervis follows Sir William Petty's account, which speaks of 37,000 English being killed "during the first year of the Rebellion."[30] Lord Clarendon, quoted by Mr. Lecky, asserted that "There were 40,000 or 50,000 of the English Protestants murdered before they

---

24 *Ireland Before and After the Union*, p. 21.
25 *Ireland in the 18th Century*, vol. i. p 96.   26 *Ireland*, vol i. p. 79.
27 *Ibid*, p. 80.   28 *History English People*, p. 524.
29 *Short History of Ireland*, p. 235.   30 *Ireland under British Rule*, p. 161.

suspected themselves to be in any danger, or could provide for their defence."[31] The frightful nature of the strife may be appreciated from the following figures:—The population of Ireland, in 1641, was nearly 1,500,000; in 1649 it was considerably under 1,000,000. "More than a third, therefore, of the entire population had disappeared bodily." Of the number remaining, "about 300,000 were Protestants."[32] The Father passes over this matter in its details in a way that recalls Matthew Arnold's pithy saying on the Irish as "eternal rebels against the despotism of fact."[33] The Duke of Argyll remarked concerning the Penal Laws that they had their origin "entirely in political dangers and political apprehensions. . . . The Catholics were held down, not because of their theological opinions, but because of their supposed political designs. They were persecuted, not because they believed in transubstantiation, but because they believed, or were held to do so, in the Pope's power to absolve subjects from their allegiance. They were held to be, presumably, always in league with the great conspiracy of the Catholic Monarchies on the continent against the laws and liberties of the British people. We can hardly realise now, how burnt this impression was into the hearts and minds of that people, and *especially into the hearts and minds of the Protestants of Ireland.*"[34] In *Irish Nationalism* the same writer deals with this subject more extendedly. To rake up the Penal Laws in modern times is simply to take advantage of the public conscience which has been trained in religious toleration in spite of, and not by, the papal religion. As Mr. Lecky shows, when the time came to modify and abolish those laws, Romanism had been shorn of much of its political influence. In 1770, "the general aspect of Catholicism both in Europe and America greatly strengthened the case. Probably at no period, since the days of Constantine, was Catholicism so free from domineering and aggressive tendencies, as during the pontificates of Benedict XIV. and his three successors. The spirit of Ultramontanism seemed to have almost evaporated even in Italian counsels, and in Western Europe the prevailing type of theology was studiously moderate."[35] In 1774, the Irish Catholic prelates formally "repudiated the opinion that heretics might be lawfully murdered, that faith need not be kept with them, and that excommunicated sovereigns may be deposed or murdered, and

---

31 *Ireland*, vol. i p. 46.   32 Lawless' *Ireland*, pp. 266-277.

33 *Ibid*, p. 415.   34 *Nineteenth Century*, May, 1890, p. 754.

35 *Ireland*, vol. ii. p. 203.

denied that the Pope *had, or ought to have, any temporal or civil jurisdiction*, power, superiority, or pre-eminence, *directly or indirectly* with the realm."[36] A few years previous to this, De Burgo, the Bishop of Ossory, "had strongly asserted the unlawfulness of a similar oath." Father Cleary may bid for public sympathy by pleading for "the proscribed creed," but facts are too strong to make it go down with students of history. The Duke of Argyll contends—that not till the 17th Century had the Catholics sufficient cohesion to rely upon their power. " But besides and in addition to the close alliance of the Irish Catholic party with those foreign governments who were pre-eminently persecutors, when at the Revolution, a moment did come, when the Irish Catholics gained a complete ascendency, then their disposition towards religious persecution blazed forth in overt acts of the utmost violence and injustice." His Grace says, Lecky pleads provocation for the Irish massacre of 1641-2, but let him apply that principle all round, and " it remains *undeniable* that the doctrines of religious persecution were then the doctrines of the Catholic party, and its practice too, *whenever it got the power*."[37] The Rev. Dr. Wylie remarks, " The Penal Statutes against Popery were abolished in 1778. They were framed by our fathers, not to oppress papists, but to protect their own liberties against popish machinations.. They were extremely mild, when we consider that when they were framed, the gibbets, on which the Protestants had been hanged, were but newly taken down, and the ashes of the fires, in which they had been burned, were yet scarce cold : mild especially, when when we compare them with the statute, '*De Comburendo Heretico*,' framed in the time of Henry IV., and always acted upon so long as the Government was in the hands of papists." In thorough agreement with Argyll, this writer affirms, " The Church of Rome was not so much a religious Society as a political confederation, hostile to the liberties of this country."[38] Lecky and Richey both admit that the Penal Statutes were but the echo and rejoinder of Protestant England against the abundant persecuting Catholic laws.

CROMWELL IN IRELAND.

Mr. Green remarks :—" No greater moral change ever passed over a nation than passed over England during the years which parted the middle of the reign of Elizabeth, from the meeting of the Long Parliament. England became the people of a book,

---

36 *Ibid*, p. 196.   37 *Irish Nationalism*, pp. 197-8.
38 *Rome and Civil Liberty*, pp. 30-31.

and that book was the Bible."[39] This period is known in History as the Puritan Age, and Puritanism included "three-fourths of the Protestants of England." It arose when England, aided by its "Divine Friends"—the wind and the sea—sent a crippled fragment of the proud Armada back to Spain, and made the Papal Power but a dead hand. James I., "the wisest fool in Christendom," as Henry IV. styled him, reversed the Spanish policy of Elizabeth. The Queen's policy had humbled Spain; his policy sought alliance with it. When the champion of the Papacy made war upon German Protestantism, the English Ministers advised James to declare war with Spain, but they were *promptly dismissed*. The King, however, had to reckon with "the two-handed engine at the door, ready to smite once and smite no more," as Milton put it. Parliament, in its session, repeated the demand of the dismissed Ministers. James re-resented this interference with what he regarded as his exclusive right, and Parliament rose to the occasion. It formulated a spirited protest against the King's despotic claim: whereupon the King sent for the Journals of the House, and with his own hand tore out the pages upon which the "Protestation" was recorded, saying—"*I will govern according to the common weal, but not according to the common will.*"[40] This lusty defiance was followed by a dissolution of Parliament. The Spanish ambassador gleefully wrote his Chief—"It is the best thing that has happened in the interests of Spain and of the Catholic Religion since Luther began preaching."[41] He was mistaken. The King's act shook the blind faith of the nation in his theory of the Divine right of Kings and Bishops. Charles on his accession completed the work his father began, and in his famous reply to the demands of Parliament for constitutional government—"if I granted your demands I should be no more than the mere phantom of a King"[42]—he gave the signal for the war between King and Parliament, which brought Oliver Cromwell on the stage of British politics in behalf of popular liberties, Father Cleary has a fling at the Orangemen, because, as he asserts, "they have a warm corner in their hearts for Oliver Cromwell, who, after William of Orange, did most to impoverish, persecute, and degrade their Catholic fellow-countrymen."[43] But he does not hint at Cromwell's enquiry as to the "innocent blood" that had been shed. It may be information that the Protector challenged his enemies to give "an instance of one

---

39 *History of the English People*, p. 447. 40 *Ibid*, p. 478. 41 *Ibid*, p. 478.
42 *Ibid*, p. 530. 43 pp. 79-80.

man, since my coming into Ireland, *not in arms*, massacred, destroyed, or burnt." In one of his despatches he says, "I am persuaded that this is a righteous judgment of God upon those barbarous wretches who have imbrued their hands in so much innocent blood, and that it will tend to prevent the effusion of blood for the future."[44] Carlyle has lifted the "wreck and dead ashes of some six unbelieving generations," from the face of Cromwell. Let us read his reply to the charges of impoverishing, &c., laid by the Father. The Sage of Chelsea quickly disposes of them by outlining his scheme of settlement—or the "settling and healing." From this document "all husbandmen, ploughmen, labourers, artificers and others of the meaner sort," in the Irish nation are to be *not exterminated*, " but rendered *exempt* from punishment and question as to these eight years of blood and misery now ended."[45] As to the ringleaders, the rebellious landlords and papist Aristocracy, "there is a carefully graduated scale of punishments established, that *punishment* and *guilt* may in some measure correspond: All that can be proved to have been concerned in the Massacre of forty-one: for these and for certain other portions of the turncoat species, whose names are given, there shall be no pardon: extermination, actual death on the gallows or perpetual banishment and confiscation for these: but not without *legal inquiry and due trial first had, for these or for anyone.* Then certain others who have been in arms at certain dates against the Parliament, but not concerned in the massacre: these are declared to have forfeited their estates, but lands to the value of one-third of the same as a modicum to live upon shall be assigned them, where the Parliament think safest—in the moorlands of Connaught as it turned out. Then another class who are open popists, and have not manifested their good affection to the Parliament: these are to forfeit one-third of their estates; and continue quiet at their peril."[46] Under these new conditions of national life the mass of the people ploughed, delved, and hammered, with their wages punctually paid to them, "with the truth spoken to

---

44 Green's *History of the English People*, p. 550.   45 Carlyle's *Cromwell*, p. 83.
46 *Ibid.* Sir William Petty, in his *Political Anatomy of Ireland*, speaking of England's pacification of Ireland after Cromwell had settled the matter, says: —"That of the Irish who pretended innocency seven out of eight had their claims allowed: that those who under this plea or under special favour of the Crown were restored, received their estates again enlarged by a fifth, as a compensation for their losses: that by forged feofments of what was more than their own they obtained an additional third; and finally of those adjudged innocent not one in twenty was really so." This is the glorious *Restoration*.—(Noted in Froude's *English in Ireland*, vol. I.)

them and the truth done to them so as they had *never before seen it since they were a nation.*" Lord Clarendon admitted that Ireland flourished to an unexampled extent under this arrangement. Another thing that Cromwell's Administration had done for Ireland was to give 30 seats to its representatives in the general parliament,[47] and to put English and Irish commerce on an equal footing.[48] Father Cleary may find occasion to grumble at the Puritan Protector's method of treating Ireland, but others looking at things from a different standpoint are not at all disposed to second him in his grievances. He asserts the Orangemen cherish a remarkable veneration for the memory of Oliver Cromwell, but if they err in so doing, they at least have the merit of erring in good company. Macaulay points out the reason why the name of Cromwell is hated all over the Roman Catholic world:—"After half a century, during which England had been of scarcely more weight in European Politics than Venice or Saxony, she at once became *the most formidable power in the world*, dictated terms of peace to the United Provinces, avenged the common injuries of Christendom on the pirates of Barbary vanquished the Spaniards by land and sea, seized one of the finest West Indian Islands, and acquired on the Flemish coast a fortress, which consoled the national pride for the loss of Calais. She was supreme on the ocean. She was the head of the Protestant interest. All the Reformed Churches scattered over Roman Catholic Kingdoms acknowledged Cromwell as their guardian. The Hugenots of Languedoc, the shepherds, who, in the hamlets of the Alps, professed a Protestantism older than that of Augsburg, were secured from oppression by the mere terror of his great name. The Pope himself was forced to preach humanity and moderation to Popish Princes. For a voice which seldom threatened in vain had declared that, unless favor were shown to the people of God the English guns should be heard in the Castle of St. Angelo."[49] I see in this every justification for Father Cleary's hatred to him and all his ways; but it will not strengthen his case against the Orange Society, in the sight of Protestants outside the order. He may utter "the curse of Cromwell" on the Orangemen, but like Balaam, when he strives to curse, he will only bless them more abundantly.

---

47 Green's *Hist.*, p. 573. 48 Lawless' *Ireland*, p. 308. Walpole, p. 352.
49 *History of England*, vol. i. p. 69.

CHAPTER V.

ORANGE ASSOCIATIONS BEFORE THE DIAMOND.—THE "TOLERANCE" OF JAMES.—CHEAP MONEY.—WILLIAM PRINCE OF ORANGE.—THE LIMERICK TREATY.—THE PENAL STATUTES.— THE WOOLLEN INDUSTRY.

THE idea of forming Protestant associations, in which politics and religion were blended, appears to have originated amongst British Protestant Refugees in Holland. The House of Orange had fought the fight of faith in religious toleration, and Holland was full of fugitives from Roman Catholic persecutors. On September 30, 1688, an Orange association in England, after "long and careful deliberation" decided to invite William Prince of Orange to accept the Throne. The invitation was signed by the Earls of Shrewsbury, Danby, and Devonshire, Lord Lumley Bishop of London, Dr. Sydney Herbert, and Admiral Russell. The last-named took it to the Hague and presented the memorial to the Prince. On the 11th November, 1688, the first religious service under the House of Orange was held in Exeter Cathedral, and there was no one to silence or tune the pulpit. At the suggestion of Sir Ed. Seymour, Dr. Burnett undertook to form a permanent Orange association. The first declaration or "engagement" ran in the terms of the times :—"We do engage to Almighty God, to his Highness the Prince of Orange, and with one another to stick firm to this cause and to one another in defence of it, until our religion, laws and liberties, are so far secured to us in a Free Parliament that we shall no more be in danger of falling under popery and slavery," &c.[1] In 1695, the Commons and Lords drew up declarations couched in similar terms, and these with the original document were lodged by the King himself in the Tower of London for safe custody at the request of Parliament. The Commons also passed a resolution in which it was set forth that—"whosoever should by word or writing affirm that the association was illegal should be deemed a promoter of the late King James and an enemy to the laws and liberties of the kingdom." In Ireland, on June 27th, 1696, a similar resolution was passed, and but one member, Robert Saunderson, refused to sign it.[2] This Orange Association soon em-

---

1 *History of the Orange Order*, Wm. Banks, p. 4.   2 *Ibid*, p. 5.

braced the chief Protestants of England, Ireland and Scotland and the public declarations of those times are faithfully reflected in the Obligations and Qualifications of two hundred years later. In 1689 the Antrim Association issued an official address, portion of which ran — "Though at present we will admit none but Protestants into our Association, yet we will, to our power, protect Papists from violence, whilst their behaviour amongst us is peaceable and quiet." The Sligo address is in much the same strain. Down, Derry, Donegal, Tyrone, Armagh, and Monaghan, were soon in line with their fellow Protestants. In 1689, Capt. Leighton carried the message of the Irish Orangemen to William III., in London The reply of the King, on January 10th, said, "We are resolved to employ the most speedy and effectual means in our power in rescuing you from the oppressions and terrors you lie under." He also indicated his approval of their method of association.[3] Mr. Banks, of Toronto, in the work from which I quote, has given a compendious history of Orangeism, not, of course, of a controversial nature, and he presents a number of valuable documents, to which the reader is referred for further information.

THE "TOLERATION" OF JAMES.

On James it may be as well for the reader to consult the following authorities. Lord Macaulay's *History of England*, vol. i. p. 216, 217, 390, 393, 405. Dr. Killen's *Ecclesiastical History*, vol. ii. pp. 166, 167, 168, 176. Green's *History of the English People*, pp. 646, 649, 651, 652, 663, 672. Hon. Emily Lawless' *Ireland*, pp. 280, 281, 287. Walpole's *Short History of Ireland*, p. 302, and Prof. Seeley's *Growth of British Policy*, vol. ii., article—William III. As Father Cleary had the good sense to denounce James as "worthless," he saves me the trouble of proving it generally. But as he clings to the notion of this Sovereign's "tolerance," I shall offer a few remarks upon that subject. Lord Macaulay points to the freedom from penal restriction enjoyed by the Irish Catholics. The Statute Book which was subsequently "polluted" by barbarous intolerance, "then contained *scarcely a single enactment and not a single stringent enactment*, imposing any penalty on Papists as such. . . . The Sacramental test and the declaration against Transubstantiation were unknown: nor was either House of Parliament closed by law against any religious sect."[4] He, however, indicates the inherent difference between the Protestant and Catholic inhabitants. "The English settlers seem to have

---

3 *Ibid*, p. 9. 4 *History of England*, vol. i. p. 390.

been in knowledge, energy, and perseverance rather above than below the average level of the population of the Mother Country. The aboriginal peasantry on the contrary were in an almost savage state."[5] Elsewhere he observes that "whatever evils the Roman Catholics suffered in England were the effect of harsh legislation, and might have been remedied by more liberal legislation. But between the two populations which inhabited Ireland, there was an inequality which legislation had not caused, and could not remove. The dominion which one of those populations exercised over the other, was the dominion of wealth over poverty, of knowledge over ignorance, of civilised over uncivilised man."[6] The fact of the religious tolerance enjoyed in Ireland, in 1686, is not *an immaterial one to the student of Irish history*, it is a deeply significant one, and the policy of James is accentuated by it. Tyrconnell, in carrying out the King's plan, showed a degree of thoroughness which created the utmost alarm and consternation amongst the British Colonists. Reports of "a general massacre, one which was to surpass the massacre of '41, flew through the land."[7] Macaulay thinks that there were good grounds for this terror. Houses were burnt, and cattle were stolen with impunity. " The new soldiers roamed the country, pillaging, insulting, ravishing, maiming, tossing one Protestant in a blanket, tying up another by the hair and scourging him; that to appeal to the law was vain; that *Irish Judges, Sheriffs, Juries, and Witnesses were all in a league to save Irish criminals.*"[8] Once more, therefore, a fell legacy drops to the Ulster group, a legacy of corrupted justice, of hand joining hand to save the guilty, of persecuting madness, and Protestants are the sufferers. Dr. Killen, whose account I summarise for brevity's sake, explains the acts of rigour with which James and his Irish Parliament of 10 weeks' session, intended to convert Ireland into a Roman Catholic Kingdom. (1) The Acts of Settlement and Explanation were repealed and the landed proprietors were virtually outlawed. James had avowed again and again to uphold what he afterwards upset, now he gave the owners no redress. (2) By another Act, 2400 persons,[9] " Peers, Baronets Knights, Clergy, Gentry, and Yeomanry," unless they surrendered within a certain period were adjudged guilty of treason, and

5 *Ibid*, p. 391. 6 *Ibid*, p. 393. 7 Lawless'*Ireland*, p. 281. Green's *History*, p. 663. Walpole's *Ireland*, p. 302. 8 *History of England*, vol. 1. p. 405.

9 Mr. Green says:—" 3000 Protestants of name and fortune were massed together in the hugest Bill of Attainder which the world has seen."—(*Hist. of the English People*, p. 672.)

sentenced to death. A clause in this Act prevented the King, had he been so disposed, from exercising the usual Royal prerogative, after the first day of the following November. (3) This gracious Act was *concealed, and no Protestant was allowed to see it, until the time for granting pardons had been passed by four months*. Lord Macaulay makes this matter even blacker than Killen :—" Some Protestants who still adhered to the cause of James, but who were anxious to know whether any of their friends or relations had been proscribed, tried hard to obtain a sight of the list, but *solicitation, remonstrance, even bribery*, proved vain. Not a single copy got abroad till it was too late for any of the thousands who had been condemned without a trial, to obtain a pardon."[10] This is "toleration" from a Catholic Sovereign with a vengeance, but by a hardly singular perversity his Protestant subjects failed to see it, even though as Father Cleary tells us "all classes had sworn allegiance" to him. The test was too severe for flesh and blood. The Presbyterians were driven from the country to America and Scotland, and others got behind the historic walls of Derry. The Episcopal Clergy in many districts were threatened with starvation; their places of worship were wrested from them by "Popish Priests ;" attendance at the public services of the Sanctuary was virtually forbidden ; an order was issued that *not more than five Protestants should meet together even at Church on pain of death*."[11] One requires a microscope to discern any traces of the tolerance so confidently affirmed to exist during the short reign of James.[12] Dr. Killen inexorably holds us to the pitiless logic of facts respecting the brief triumph of "the second Stuart Tyranny," for he says that in the time of William of Orange a law was passed for *abolishing the burning of heretics which had been revived in the Irish Parliament of James II*.[13] This should dispose of any lingering doubt and banish all argument in favor of the asserted tolerance.

10 *Hist. of England*, Vol. i. p. 763.   11 *Eccl. History*, vol. ii. pp. 166-8.

12 Mr. Green, while affirming that the "one aim" of the Irish Parliament of James " was the ruin of the English settlers," says that when the French Envoy "the Count of Avaux dared to propose a general massacre of the Protestants who still lingered in the districts which had submitted to James," the King shrank " horror struck from the proposal. 'I cannot be so cruel,' he said, 'as to cut their throats while they live peaceably under my government.' ' Mercy to Protestants,' was the cold reply, 'is cruelty to Catholics.'"—(*History of the English People*, p. 672.) This is merely a characteristic statement of the Religious inveteracy of those times, and in judging of laws and movements of that period we must take into account the prevalent bigotry which dominated the Roman Catholic Religion. (See also Macaulay's *History of England*, vol. ii. p. 85.)

13 *Eccl. History*, vol. ii. p. 176. There were *six* Protestants in this Parliament.—(Lawless' *Ireland*, p. 287.)

Father Cleary condemns strongly, and indeed justly, the Penal Statutes against Catholics, but we have already seen that the Irish Statute Book was singularly free from laws of disability upon any sect. Naturally we want to know how they came as a sad blot upon that Book ? We are learning, and we now know *the original fingers which held the pen of proscription*. Macaulay, while admitting that the Colonists in their hour of victory indulged in unjust and tyrannical legislation, has to say—" But it is not less true that they never quite came up to the *atrocious example* set by their vanquished enemy during his short tenure of power." While James was loudly boasting that he had passed "an Act granting *entire liberty of Conscience* to all sects, a persecution as cruel as that of Languedoc was raging through all the provinces which owned his authority."[14] The Jacobites defended James and his policy with audacious partyism, and put forward every plea which they imagined would have the smallest weight, but James " refuted these pamphlets far more effectually than all the ablest and most eloquent Whig writers united could have done. Every week came the news that he had passed some new act for robbing or murdering Protestants. Every Colonist who succeeded in stealing across the sea . . . . brought fearful reports of the tyranny under which his brethren groaned. What impression these reports made on the Protestants of our Island may be easily inferred from the fact that they moved the indignation of Ronquillo, a Spaniard and a bigoted member of the Church of Rome. He informed his Court that though the English laws against Popery might seem severe, they were so much mitigated by the prudence and humanity of the Government, that they caused no annoyance to quiet people : and he took upon himself to assure the Holy See that what a Roman Catholic suffered in London was nothing when compared with what a Protestant suffered in Ireland."[15] This tolerant Sovereign was a capital financier for hard times, and settled the question of " cheap money," which has bothered the Victorian parliament so greatly in less than no time. " A mortgage for £1000 was cleared off by a bag of counters made out of old kettles,"[16] " Any man who belonged to the caste now dominant, might walk into a shop, lay on the counter a bit of brass worth threepence, and carry off goods to the value of half-a-guinea. Legal redress was out of the question."[17] What happy fiscal inventions for people in debt ! Of course, Protestant trades-

---

14 *History of England*, vol. i. p. 763.   15 *Ibid*, p. 765.
16 *Ibid*, p. 760.   17 *Ibid*, p. 761.

men were the sufferers under this system of coinage. I have advanced sufficient to depict the Second Stuart, and the condition of Ireland under his government; and as the story of his defeat is so well known, there is no need to relate it here. The Hon. Emily Lawless, however, tells this good anecdote. After the battle of the Boyne "James arrived in Dublin, foaming and almost convulsed with rage. 'Madam, your countrymen have run away,' was his gracious address to Lady Tyrconnel. 'If they have, Sire, your Majesty seems to have won the race,' was that lady's ready retort."[18]

WILLIAM, PRINCE OF ORANGE.

Father Cleary has several complaints to make against the Prince of Orange. 1st. The violation of the Treaty of Limerick.[19] 2nd. The Penal Laws which began in his reign.[20] 3rd. The destruction of the Irish woollen industry.[21] As far as possible, his reverence endeavours to make these charges personal, for following Lecky, he says, " whatever may have been his personal ideas of religious toleration, he certainly ' never offered any serious or determined opposition to the Anti-Catholic laws which began in his reign.' This is all the more remarkable since he possessed 'the Royal Veto which could have arrested any portion of the Penal Code.'" As a set-off against this, the Father also quotes Lecky, in his *Leaders of Public Opinion*, thus—" The ceaseless exertions of the extreme Protestant party have made him (William) far more odious in the eyes of the people than he deserves to be; for he was personally far more tolerant than the majority of his contemporaries."[22] This may be regarded as a saving clause, for any writer attacking the Prince of Orange to-day, on his merits, must be either miraculously ignorant or invincibly prejudiced. Hallam, vindicating the memory of William III., points out that, "By the opposition party he was rancorously hated, and their malignant calumnies still sully the stream of history."[23] This veteran historian goes on to tell us that "It must ever be an honor to the English Crown that it has been worn by so great a man." " He was in truth too great not for the times wherein he was called to action, but for the peculiar conditions of a King of England after the Revolution. . . . His reign is no doubt one of the most important in our Constitutional History, both on account of its general character . . . and of those beneficial alterations in our law to which it gave rise."[24] He was almost " the

18 *Ireland*, p. 289. 19 p. 174. 20 p. 175. 21 p. 182. 22 Note 26, p. 175.
23 *Hist. of England*, Vol. iii. p. 147 24 *Ibid*, p. 148.

only consistent friend of toleration in his kingdom, at least among public men."²⁵ See Lord Macaulay's fine conception of the attitude of the Prince of Orange, which he has expressed in his best style. The noble passage ends thus:—"His clemency was peculiar to himself. It was not the clemency of an ostentatious man, or of a sentimental man, or of an easy tempered man. It was cold, unconciliating, inflexible. It produced no fine stage effects. It drew on him the savage invectives of those whose malevolent passions he refused to satisfy. It won for him no gratitude from those who owed to him fortune, liberty and life. . . But none of these things moved him. He had done well. He had risked his popularity with men who had been his warmest admirers, in order to give repose and security to men by whom his name was never mentioned without a curse. . . If his people did not justly appreciate his policy, so much for the worse for them. He had discharged his duty by them. He feared no obloquy: and he wanted no thanks."²⁶ Mr. Green remarks that "the religious results of the Revolution were hardly less weighty than the political," and that active persecution had now become impossible because "the passing of a Toleration Act in 1689 practically secured freedom of worship."²⁷ Walpole, in his *Short History of the Kingdom of Ireland*, p. 318, says that "Ere the new campaign began, William, not only anxious in his own interest to close the war, but by nature tolerant, and 'touched,' as Sir Charles Wogan says, 'by the fate of a gallant nation that had made itself the victim of French promises,' offered the Irish Roman Catholics the free exercise of their Religion, half the Churches in the Kingdom, and the moiety of their ancient possessions. But the Irish *were still sanguine* . . . . *and no response was made.*"

The Limerick Treaty.

The Hon. Emily Lawless, in referring to the disputed clause,²⁸ says that it was "in the first draft is admitted; that it was not in the document itself is equally certain. Had it been intentionally or accidentally excluded? is the question. William's own words were that it had been 'casually omitted by the writer.'"²⁹ This author further remarks that some historians have questioned the King's accuracy, but "that his own mind was clear on the point there can be little doubt, seeing that he made the most

---

25 *Ibid*, p. 336. 26 *Hist. of England*, Vol. ii. pp. 164-165.
27 *Hist. English People*, p. 674. Godkin's *Religious Hist. of Ireland*, p. 214.
28 The full text of the Articles of Limerick will be found in Wright's *History of Ireland*, vol ii. p. 263.

honorable efforts to get the clause in question carried into effect. In this he failed. Public opinion in England ran furiously against the Roman Catholics, and the Parliament absolutely refused to ratify it."[30] Lord Macaulay has no doubts upon the subject, and treats minutely of its history. Both the Commons and the Lords had no objection to the "absurd and cruel rule" which excluded Roman Catholics from the liberal professions. At a Conference between the two Houses, "Rochester, in the Painted Chamber, delivered to the Managers of the Lower House a copy of the Treaty of Limerick, and earnestly represented the importance of preserving the public faith inviolate. This appeal was one which no honest man, though inflamed by national and religious animosity, could resist." The Bill became law. "It attracted, at the time, little notice, but was, after the lapse of several generations, the subject of a very acrimonious controversy. . . . . It may be doubted whether any dispute has produced stranger perversions of history. The whole past was falsified for the sake of the present."[31] Macaulay asks very pertinently, on the supposition that the English Parliament violated the Limerick Treaty, how is it that no voice was raised in any part of the world against such wickedness? that the Court of St. Germains and the Court of Versailles were profoundly silent? that no Irish exile, no English malcontent ever uttered a murmur in protest? that not a word of invective or sarcasm on so inviting a subject was to be found in the whole compass of the Jacobite literature? and that it was reserved for *Politicians of the Nineteenth Century to discover that a treaty made in the Seventeenth Century had, a few weeks after it had been signed, been outrageously violated* in the sight of all Europe.[32] Macaulay further says that at a later period, an Irish Parliament violated the Treaty. Seven years after a law was passed "for banishing the Catholic Bishops, dignitaries, and regular clergy." He quotes the Abbé MacGeoghegan to a similar effect, and argues that such complaints are only proofs that Stat. 3, W. and M.C. 2 was not a violation of the Limerick Articles.[33] Wright relates in what spirit the Irish Parliament met. "The Irish Protestants were in general irritated against the Articles of Limerick,[34] and their temper was not mended when they understood that among the Bills transmitted from England to be laid before the House of Commons were two money bills, in direct violation of the

---

29 *Ireland*, p. 296. 30 *Ibid*, p. 296. 31 *History of England*, vol. ii. p. 300.
32 *Ibid*, p. 301. 33 *Ibid*, Note, p. 301.
34 Macaulay's *History of England*, vol. ii. p. 417.

privilege the Irish Commons claimed of determining in the first instance both the sum and the manner of raising every supply granted to the Crown."[35] Viscount Sydney arrived in Ireland on the 25th August, 1692, as Lord Lieutenant, and Parliament was called together on October 5th. On the 20th of that month, the Commons "expressed their animosity against the Catholics in a resolution—that the continuing Papists in the army, or suffering them to have serviceable horses or arms, was at this juncture of dangerous consequence to the Kingdom."[36] The defiant tone assumed by Parliament caused Sydney to suddenly prorogue the sittings on November 3rd until April 6th, 1693, but it never again met for business, and was dissolved on the 5th September, 1693. The friends of the Irish Parliament in England took the matter up, and a warm debate on Irish affairs occurred in the Commons on February 24, 1693, which resulted in an address[37] being presented to the King on the 19th of March. The grievances of the Parliament in Ireland were set out :—"(1) In exposing his Protestant subjects to the misery of free quarter and the licentiousness of the soldiers, to the great oppression of the people there: which they conceived had been chiefly occasioned by the want of that pay which they did hope they had fully provided for. (2) In recruiting his Majesty's troops with Irish Papists and such persons as were in open rebellion against his Majesty, to the great endangering and discouraging of his Majesty's good and loyal subjects in that Kingdom. (3) In granting protections to Irish Papists, whereby Protestants were hindered from the legal remedies and the course of law was stopped. (4) In reversing outlawries for high treason against several rebels in that Kingdom (not within the Articles of Limerick) to the great discontent of his Protestant subjects there. . . . (7) In the addition made to the Articles of Limerick after the same were finally agreed to, signed, and thereupon the town surrendered, which had been a great encouragement to the Irish Papists, and a weakening of the English interest there."[38] After humbly requesting the King to redress these abuses they added that the additional Article to the Treaty opened "wide a passage to the Irish Papists to come in and repossess themselves of the estates which they had forfeited by their rebellion: they also besought his Majesty that the Articles of Limerick, with the said addition, be laid before the Commons in Parliament that the manner of obtaining the same might be inquired into." This address was by no means to the mind of

[35] Wright, vol. ii. p. 271.   [36] Macaulay, vol. ii. p. 418.
[37] Macaulay, vol. ii. p. 419.   [38] Wright, Vol. ii. p. 273.

William. A new Parliament met at Dublin on August 27th, 1695, which passed acts contrary "to the letter as well as the spirit of the Treaty of Limerick."[89] The author adds that William, "tolerant by inclination," had not the power "to stem the current of intolerance into which his Protestant subjects hurried in the moment of triumph."[40] Dr. Killen uses the Penal Code as an argument against the Irish Episcopalians, by passing this stricture upon them :—" The representatives of the Anglo-Irish Colony acted most ingloriously when they compelled their deliverer to break faith with their fallen foes, and when they refused to supplement a treaty which *he had accepted* as proper and equitable."[41] He also shows how William treated a Clerical dignitary for intolerance. " Dopping, the Protestant Bishop of Meath, a divine whose own career had been so inconsistent, was so imprudent as to assert that 'the peace ought not to be observed with a people so perfidious . . . and that those articles which were intended for a security would prove a snare.'" In a note the author adds :—" William was so displeased with the conduct of Dopping that he ordered him to be dismissed from the Privy Council."[42]

THE PENAL LAWS.

The Duke of Argyll dealing with the general question of reactionary legislation against the Roman Catholics, remarks :—" How thoroughly justified the English Government'

---

39 *Ibid*, p. 274.

40 *Ibid*, p. 279. Father Cleary, while quoting Walpole on the "perjured Roman Senate," omitted to show that Walpole also said :—" The Treaty was subsequently confirmed by William by Letters Patent. The unscrupulous Irish Parliament of 1697, consisting wholly of the new Protestant interest passed an Act which professed to confirm it, but in fact so mutilated it as to cut out all parts which were vital to the interests of the Roman Catholics, and left an empty husk which afforded them no protection !"—(*Short Hist. of Ireland*, pp. 323-324.)

Further on Walpole adds :—" William was *kindly disposed* towards the beaten nation : he was anxious to treat the Irish with all moderation and clemency. He accordingly restored to the old landholders over a fourth of the confiscated land, either under the Treaties of Limerick and Galway, or by Royal favour, or by the granting of pardons."—(pp. 326-327.) Father Cleary absolutely refuses to mention this. It would not be in harmony with his tactics.

41 *Eccl. Hist.*, Vol. ii. p. 180.

42 *Ibid*, p. 176. See also Harris's *Life of William* III., p. 372.

Mr. Justin McCarthy quotes the statement of Bishop Dopping and remarks: —" The violation of the Treaty of Limerick had justified his utterance." But though McCarthy saddles William with the blame of this saying :—" If William were unable to make his ministers respect the royal honour, he could have respected it himself and resigned his sceptre ; " he most unfairly gives the King not the slightest credit for doing anything, and does not even mention the dismissal of Dopping. —(*Ireland since the Union*, pp. 9-10)

was in its Penal Statutes "comes out in a strong light indeed from a discovery which Mr. Lecky tells us has been made in documents recently brought to light. For from these documents it appears not only that all the Catholic Priests in Ireland were in sentiment and opinion adherents of the Pretender, but that *he* actually held from the Pope the personal privilege, during the whole of his life, of appointing his own nominees to the Catholic Bishoprics in Ireland."[43] I have already quoted the address delivered by the English Commons to the King for the redress of existing abuses in Ireland, and I have also called attention to the fact of James, and his brief Parliament, making regulations for the comfort and security of his Protestant citizens—these things, with the existing laws in Catholic Kingdoms, imposing great disabilities on Protestants, account for the penal restrictions on Roman Catholics.[44] It is true that the people in power followed a vicious example; but *what party first established the precedent?* Father Cleary hardly does well to be silent on this matter, for history is not in any conspiracy of silence. This legislation, seen in the light of to-day, is hideous—seen in the light of its advisers, it was prudential and self-protective.[45] But the true way, after all, is to judge it by laws of a similar class contemporary with it. This only is a fair comparison, and if it is found to be worse than existing ones, modern criticism may mercilessly castigate it. How does the Penal Code stand when weighed in these balances? The Hon. Emily Lawless remarks:—" As compared with some of the enactments passed against Protestants in Catholic countries it was not, it must be said—sanguinary."[46] This Lady also adds: —" To the credit of the Irish Protestants it may be said, that once the first violence of fanaticism had died out there was little attempt to enforce the legal enactments in all their hideous ferocity." After recounting the laws against the Roman Catholic Clergy, we are told—" As a matter of fact, however, they came with very little hindrance, and the succession was steadily kept up from the Continent."[47] We have seen that the Treaty of Limerick was not violated in English law, and that about seven years after its being drawn up, the Irish Legislature

---

[43] Lecky, vol. i. pp. 168, 169 Note. See Wright's *History of Ireland*, vol. ii. p. 282. [44] See also Macaulay's *History of England*, vol. ii. pp. 425-8.
[45] Walpole remarks—" Though the country was utterly reduced and nominally quiet, the English inhabitants found their ricks burnt, their cattle houghed, and their houses broken into by gangs of men with blackened faces, who beat and otherwise maltreated them."—*Short History*, p. 330.
[46] *Ireland*, p 301.   [47] *Ibid*, p. 303-304.

infringed it, to the great displeasure of William, and thus all Father Cleary's ingenious attempts to saddle the Prince of Orange with a dishonorable violation of that Treaty and the subsequent Penal Statutes fall to the ground.[48] Whilst maintaining a profound silence on William's attitude in this matter, he revels at large in the iniquities of the laws against Catholics, yet his references indicate that the bulk of those laws was enacted at a period subsequent to the King's death. It is notorious, as he admits himself,[49] when quoting Walpole that the severest acts of the Penal Code were placed on the Statute Book in the reign of Queen Anne.[50] Wright points out that in the Session of the Irish Parliament of 1703 under the Lord Lieutenancy of the Duke of Ormond[51] a Bill was introduced for preventing the further growth of Popery—the most severe and oppressive Statute in the Irish Penal Code. " It assumed that the Roman Catholics of Ireland, universally, were the natural and inveterate enemies of the State, and placed them under restrictions and regulations which it was calculated would render them incapable of any kind of hostility."[52] When the measure was carried, the Catholic party applied for and obtained leave to appear at the bar of the House of Commons before the final committal of the Bill after its being received from the English

---

48 Lord Grenville presented a Catholic Petition to Parliament, on March 25, 1805, after the Union between England and Ireland. Speaking in favor of it on May 10, of the same year, he referred to the Penal laws :—"*In justice to the memory of one of the greatest Princes that ever existed on the face of the globe, and one of the warmest friends of liberty and toleration*, let me say, that it is *not to the memory of King William we must attribute the measures that were taken afterwards.* We may confidently say, they were measures forming no part of any system that could have obtained his approbation or concurrence."—(Wright's *Ireland*, vol. iii. p. 302.) Sir Hercules Langrishe spoke to the same effect when supporting Grattan's Catholic Relief Bill.—(*Ibid*, vol. ii. p. 584.)

49 p. 176.

50 On consulting Walpole, I find that he ascribes the Penal Acts, passed in the reign of William, to the " English Colony and the English Government, which had suffered so much in maintaining its ascendency." (p. 332.) And he adds— " At the commencement of Queen Anne's reign it was found that, like every other severe and unjust law, the Penal Acts were *largely evaded*, and the ' Protestant Ascendency ' believed that the mischief which they sought to counteract, could be overcome by fiercer statutes." (p. 338.) But Father Cleary never mentions this. Oh, no !

Godkin says :--" Manifestly there was no cruelty which these Protestants embodied in Acts of Parliament, and carried out in their subsequent policy, which could not be justified by an appeal to the conduct of James's Parliament in Dublin, and the vindictive tyranny of the Catholic Government of that day." —(*Religious History of Ireland*, p, 207.)

51 The Duke of Ormond, and many of the people in power, " Were secret favorers of the Pretender's cause, and did all in their power to pave the way for his return."—(Wright's *History of Ireland*, vol. ii. p. 282.)

52 *History of Ireland*, vol. ii. p. 291.

Parliament. On the 22nd February, 1704, Sir Theobald Butler, Counsellor Malone, and Sir Stephen Rice with others stated their reasons for appealing against the Bill. Their principal arguments were — (1) The general infraction of the Articles of Limerick implied in this measure: (2) The robbery of their estates by placing them at the mercy of designing relatives : (3) The Sacramental Test was unnecessary, as it related to offices which the Catholics could not hope for under the present accession : (4) The suffering of the Dissenters, who though loyal were under disqualification. The Commons, however, were not deterred by this appeal, and the Appellants appeared before the Lords to arrest its final stage. Their main argument was " To make any law that shall single any particular part of the people out from the rest, and take from them what had been confirmed to and entailed upon them, will be *an apparent violation of the original institution of all right, and an ill precedent* to any that *hereafter* might dislike either the present, or any other settlement, which it should be in their power to alter : the consequence of which is hard to imagine."[53]

During the session of the House which passed " the Popery Act,"[54] a Member stated that " the Irish Papists in the County of Limerick had begun to form themselves into bodies, to plunder the Protestants of their arms and money and to maintain a correspondence with the disaffected in England. At this moment an attempt in favor of the Pretender was apprehended, and the Irish House of Commons came to a hasty resolution that—' The Papists of this Kingdom still retained hopes of the accession of the person known by the name of the Prince of Wales in the lifetime of the late King James, and now by the name of James III.'."[55] Under circumstances of this nature the Penal Statutes were passed, and neither the Irish Lords nor Commons, from all that I can learn, had the slightest qualms of conscience in passing the severest restrictions. William of

---

53 Wright's *Ireland*, vol. ii. pp. 293, 294.
54 Lord Sidmouth (Ex-Premier Addington) speaking on Catholic Relief in 1812, *i.e.*, after the Union, quoted Mr. Burke saying of the operation of the Penal Laws that they had by " a sort of vicious perfection a tendency to degrade and impoverish the people : but at the same time they were *manifestly and indispensably necessary.* Ireland had smarted under Roman-Catholic Parliaments, which had by the exertion of their priests, virtually repealed the Act of Settlement, which secured all the Protestant property and the Act of Henry VIII. which annexed the Crown to that of England, and a rapine succeeded to the Acts of those Parliaments which formed one of the foulest stains in the history of that Country. The Protestants followed in violence with a proportionate vigour to give themselves a perfect system of security."—(Wright's *Ireland*, vol. iii. pp. 370, 371.)   55 Wright, vol. ii. p. 294.

Orange appears to be the only public man, Protestant or Catholic, in Great Britain that exhibited a disposition to tolerance during the troubles of the Revolution.

THE WOOLLEN INDUSTRY.

Mr. Lecky quoted by Father Cleary says:—" William III. is *identified* in Ireland with the humiliation of the Boyne, with the destruction of Irish trade, and with the broken treaty of Limerick." Upon the question of the pretended identification, Father Cleary reminds me of the ruse of the Irish orator who disposed of a difficulty by saying—" *We will look it in the face and pass on.*" I have shown how King William was connected with the Limerick Articles—his conduct in respect to them was dignified and honorable. I have also shown how he treated the overture of the British House when it presented an address virtually requesting the imposition of Penal Laws.[56] It remains now to examine his connection with the "destruction of Irish trade." King William's relation to this matter appears to me to be no subject for censure. The Woollen Trade restrictions arose out of a dispute between the two Legislatures.[57] The Irish Parliament had a disposition to assert its independence of the English House, which was intensified by a book published in 1698 by Mr. Molyneux, one of the members for the University of Dublin; this book was entitled "*The Case of Ireland's being bound by Acts of Parliament in England stated.*" Macaulay ridicules the position of Molyneux, saying:—" No Colony had owed so much to England. No Colony stood in such need of the support of England. Twice within the memory of men then living the natives had attempted to throw off the alien yoke: twice the intruders had been in imminent danger of extirpation: twice England had come to the rescue, and had put down the Celtic population under the feet of her own progeny. Millions of

---

[56] M'Carthy reviles "Capel's Parliament" in strong terms, and says—"Capel and his creatures had done their best, but their work appeared clumsy and half-hearted to the Statesmen of Queen Anne."—(*Ireland Since the Union*, p. 9.) See also Wright's *History of Ireland*, vol. ii. p. 274.

[57] Walpole urges that the English Government was guilty of crippling the *Protestants* of Ireland. "England had done her best to ruin her Protestant Colony in Ireland. She had starved its manufactures, destroyed its trade, made a farce of its Legislature, billeted all her disreputable dependents upon its revenues; and in order to maintain her grasp she had shamefully plundered it and spent the money in corrupting the guardians of its interests"—(*Short History*, p. 388.) If these charges are true and due to the Prince of Orange surely the Protestants of Ireland should curse the memory of William III. rather than reverence it; but the opposite is the course pursued. Either therefore they are drivelling idiots or Father Cleary's charges against him fall under Hallam's stricture of the " malignant calumnies that still sully the stream of history."

English money had been expended in the struggle. English blood had flowed at the Boyne and at Athlone, at Aghrim and at Limerick. The graves of thousands of English soldiers had been dug in the pestilential morass of Dundalk."[58] He also quotes a paper, written in 1711, on "*The Case of the Roman Catholic Nation of Ireland,*" in which "the tyranny of the Parliament at Dublin" is appealed against, and the Irish "apply themselves to the present Parliament of Great Britain, as a Parliament of nice honor and staunch justice." The writer accuses the Irish Parliament of encroaching on the supreme authority of the English Parliament. With some asperity, and, in order to assert itself, the English Legislature petitioned the King to "enforce the Acts which had been passed for the protection of the Woollen manufactures of England, and to direct the industry and capital of Ireland into the channel of the Linen Trade, a trade which might grow and flourish in Leinster and Ulster without exciting the smallest jealousy at Norwich or at Halifax."[59] Macaulay adds "The Irish Woollen manufacture languished and disappeared, as it would, in all probability have languished and disappeared if it had been left to itself."[60] The Hon. Emily Lawless points out that this Act was directed as much against Protestant as against Catholic : "the worst was that this arbitrary Act directed, it must be repeated, by England not against the *Irish natives* but against *her own colonists,* done, too, without there being an opportunity for the country to be heard in its own defence, struck at the very root of all enterprise, and produced a widespread feeling of helplessnesss and despair."[61] Mr. Wright gives the proceedings with some fulness of treatment. When the English House addressed the King to maintain the supremacy of its Legislature over that of the Irish House he replied coldly that "he would take care that what was complained of might be prevented and redressed as the Commons desired." The English Parliament determined "on showing their power, and they seized the opportunity of some complaints, that the then staple trade of England was prejudiced by the woollen manufacture carried on in Ireland, to bring forward a Bill to restrict the Irish Trade."[62] This Bill

---
58 *Hist. England,* vol. ii. p. 660.   59 *Hist. England,* vol. ii. p. 661.
60 Dr. Grimshaw in his report says :—"No doubt Irish industries were interfered with by hostile tariffs and legislation of a restrictive character : but so were industries all over the world and in every country, but so far as I can find the only industry which suffered materially in this way was the wool industry, which could scarcely have grown into a serious competition with England after the introduction of steam machinery."—(Quoted Sir Hy. James' *Work of the Irish Leagues,* p. 11.)
61 *Ireland,* p. 310.   62 *History of Ireland,* vol ii. p. 277.

was eventually laid aside, and another address was made to the King in which he was requested to "enjoin all those he employed in Ireland to use their utmost diligence to hinder the exportation of wool from Ireland (except to be imported hither), and for the discouraging the woollen manufactures and encouraging the linen manufactures in Ireland, to which the Commons in England should always be ready to give their utmost assistance." The existing Act in this direction was strengthened,[63] "which excited considerable jealousy in Ireland." When the Lords Justices impressed the English view upon the Irish Commons, in September, 1698, they replied that they would endeavour to establish the linen manufacture, and make it profitable to both England and Ireland, and "they hoped to so regulate their woollen trade that it should not be injurious to England."[64] It is thus seen that King William's connection with the destruction of the Irish woollen trade was purely the accident of his being King at the period when the two Legislatures were in a mood to quarrel over a Constitutional question. Father Cleary is as wise in silence as in speech; what he does not know in this respect is hardly worth learning. He loudly reminds Roman Catholics of the "humiliation of the Boyne," but suppresses matters which would have most weight with rational people.

CHAPTER VI.

A TALE OF THE DEAD.—THE LOST CHORD.—THE POLICY OF TOLERATION.—LITERARY DEFENCE OF CATHOLICS PAID FOR.— THE VOLUNTEERS OF 1778.—THE PEEP OF DAY BOYS.— CLEARY'S METHODS OF IDENTIFICATION.—THE DEFENDER MOVEMENT.—MORE LEGACIES TO ULSTER PROTESTANTS.

SIR CHAS. RUSSELL in his famous speech called "Ireland's Vindication," related what Sir Henry James termed, "the tale of the

---

63 "England did to Ireland but little more than she had done to America and Scotland, and she acted in accordance with commercial principles that then governed all her Colonial Policy."—(Lecky's *History of England in the 18th Century*, vol. ii., quoted by Sir Henry James in *The Irish Leagues*, p. 10.)

64 Wright's *Ireland*, vol. ii., vide proceedings pp. 275-277.

dead." His positions were condensed by the latter as follows:—
"The causes of discontent and crime were (1) The restriction on the commerce and manufactures of Ireland (away back in 1663, 1665, 1680). (2) The Penal Code, or as he afterwards by his reference explained the meaning of that phrase—religious disability and inequality. (3) The power of the landlord over the tenant. And (4) the mistrust of the government of Great Britain as he termed it."[1] These come in very handy, it will be noted, for a defence of Ireland in the mouth of Sir Charles Russell, and for an impeachment of Orangeism by the pen of Father Cleary. In fact it is difficult to determine how many ends these ancient episodes may serve. Lecky however tells us that "before the middle of the 18th century the laws against Catholic worship were virtually obsolete."[2] The critic of the Orange Society produces sweet melody from his harp as to Roman Catholic tolerance, the union of hearts,[3] and similar music, all of which goes to show the happy blending of racial and religious differences in the Irish house until Orangeism arose with its fierce discord and turned Ireland into a pandemonium. Then bigotry roused passion and hearts were torn, and his song changes to a dirge. Every softening feeling is lost, the sun is quenched and naught but Orange meets the Father's jaundiced eye. Orange waves aloft while gory streams flow over the green. I will examine Mr. Lecky whom he quotes so copiously, to correct this lachrymose ballad and restore "the lost chord."

Religious Asperity Dying—A Policy.

In 1760 "Traditional antipathies and distinctions, though they had lost their old vitality, passed languidly and passively into the mind, but they were only slightly and remotely connected with Religion, and as Arthur Young truly said the Penal Laws were now directed much more against *the property* than against *the creed* of the Catholics. . . . Even in Ulster, where the spirit of intolerance was much stronger than in other provinces, sumptuous Mass Houses were everywhere arising, and Bishops and Monks as well as ordinary Priests and Schoolmasters lived in the country without concealment or difficulty."[4] Henry Brooks, writing in defence of the Catholics in 1762, declared that there are Penal Laws which if put in execution would not suffer a single Papist to breathe beyond the bars of a jail in Ireland. But though those

---

1 *The Work of the Irish Leagues*, pp. 9, 12.   *Ireland's Vindication*, p. 15.
2 *Ireland*, vol. i. p. 301.   3 pp. 17, 19.   4 Lecky, vol. ii. p. 182.

laws are still in force it is long since they have been in action. They hang—like a sword—by a thread over the heads of those people, and Papists walk under it in peace and security.⁵ The Catholic Association founded in 1759 was the "first important effort to create an independent Catholic opinion."⁶ Henry Brooks, who wrote for Catholics, is said to have received *money* as well as information from the Catholic Leaders, for his brilliant advocacy, while Mr Plowden admits that the Catholic Association employed "the most leading literary men of the day to write in favor of the Catholic claims."⁷ Mr Lecky says:—That in 1746 Brooks' writings were very *Anti-Catholic.* Commenting on this the Historian remarks—"If he accepted money for writing, even in a cause in which he sincerely believed, this fact weakens his authority."⁸ It is a very memorable and well attested fact, that the Irish Catholics for a long time before 1778 looked upon the Government not as their oppressors but as their protectors, and sympathised much more strongly with their English Rulers than with their native Parliament. At the end of 1767 or the beginning of 1768 prayers for the King and Royal Family were offered up in the Catholic Churches *for the first time* since the Revolution.⁹ In 1774 a measure was passed which enabled the Catholics to show their loyalty by taking the Oath of Allegiance. The Catholics who subscribed to this declaration "solemnly renounced all allegiance to the Stuarts, repudiated the opinion that heretics might be lawfully murdered, that faith need not be kept with them, and that excommunicated Sovereigns may be deposed or murdered, and denied that the Pope had or ought to have any temporal or civil jurisdiction, power, superiority, or pre-eminence directly or indirectly with the realm.¹⁰ It is worthy of notice that a few years before De Burgo, the Bishop of Ossory, in his *Hibernica Dominicana* had strongly asserted the *unlawfulness of a similar oath*, but now the Bishops of Munster, without even consulting Rome, met at Cork and unanimously agreed that the oath contained nothing contrary to their faith, and they took the same occasion of condemning the treatise of the Bishop of Ossory, and of proclaiming their emphatic loyalty to George III. The congregation *De Propaganda Fide* afterwards mildly censured them for expressing their opinion without consulting Rome: they stated that the oath, though not contrary to orthodoxy, appeared to them liable to misconstruction : and in the Ultramontane Seminaries on the

---

5 *Ibid*, Note p. 183.   6 *Ibid*, p. 183.   7 *Ibid*, p. 185.
8 *Ibid*, Note p. 185.   9 *Ibid*, p. 195.
10 Consult Dr. Wylie's *Rome and Civil Liberty*, pp. 170, 171, 173.

Continent it was much condemned, but in Ireland both Ecclesiastics and laymen accepted it with alacrity. It was powerfully defended by O'Leary, and it contributed much to lighten the position of the Catholics, and to allay the fears of those who saw in the rebellion of the Whiteboys against tithes the symptoms of a Papist rebellion."[11] It is easy to trace, as we now look back, the policy of Religious toleration, especially in Ireland. The Irish Protestants had grown indolent and good natured with respect to the security of the Protestant Faith.[12] They were in political power, and during disputes abroad the Catholics at home had been quiet. The fierce wave of persecution and religious proscription that had swept over Europe to quench the Reformation had become either a spent force, or was seen by Rome to be now impolitic. Reactionary measures had brought about the most dreadful conditions, and the Papal power was steadily receding. Lecky points out the new policy started by Benedict XIV., and carried on by his three successors. Ultramontanism was muzzled for the time being, and the type of theology was "studiously moderate."[13] In Ireland the Catholic party were defeated; they had suffered as much for the crimes of their Church as for their own sins. But now a favorable moment had come. Contention had ceased, and Protestant opinion, through a sense of security, sank down to normal point. The policy of conciliation and toleration must be enacted. The Catholic Association is formed in 1759. The best literary men have retaining fees to write up the Catholics. The prelates solemnly renounce, without consulting Rome, the sanguinary dogma of assassination in the name of Religion. The Catholic Association issue a Declaration of Principles—"drawn up by O'Keefe, the Bishop of Kildare—in which they abjured in the strongest terms the doctrine that any ecclesiastical power in the Church had the right of deposing Sovereigns, absolving subjects from their oaths, making war upon heretics as such, exercising any temporal power or jurisdiction in Ireland, or committing any act which is in its own nature immoral. They denied with much truth that the infallibility of the Pope was an Article of the Catholic Creed."[14]

---

11 Lecky, vol. ii. p. 196.

12 The Hon. Emily Lawless remarks:—"The Eighteenth Century with its *easy-going indifferentism* had passed away, and one of the effects of this new Revival was unhappily to re-awaken in many conscientious breasts much of the old and half extinct horror of Popery."—(*Ireland*, p. 385.)

13 Lecky, vol. ii. p. 203.

14 *Ibid*, p. 203. Döllinger in his inaugural address as the Rector of Munich University remarked—"On the 18th of July, 1870, Rome, the second metropolis of Latinism, declared war against German science and German intellect. 547

Mr. Walpole points out another item in the policy—excusable probably, but by no means elevating to morals :—"By the year 1738 as many as a thousand Roman Catholic families of rank had nominally joined the Established Church; and no scruple was felt in taking the oaths when perjury could be atoned for, as it constantly was, by a small penance, which purchased absolution from the priest." In this manner "sham conversions" were common. (*Short History of Ireland*, p. 372.) This is certainly one way to keep the faith, but what a facile faith it must have been !

An Awkward Fact.

One of the strange things which Father Cleary has not thought it worth his while to mention, far less attempt to explain, is the fact that amidst the toleration which streamed across Ireland according to his account, nearly all the Protestant leaders of public opinion who advocated the legislative repeal and extinction of the Penal laws against Catholics, were singularly unanimous in opposing the grant of political power to persons of that faith. Lecky certainly remarks on the "decadence of sectarian bigotry,"[15] and that "politics had begun to dominate over theology :"[16] he also quotes Lord Sheffield in 1785 :—" It is curious to observe one-fifth or one-sixth of a nation in possession of the power and property of the Country eager to communicate

---

Bishops proclaimed the Infallibity of the Pope. Witnesses of authority have shown that this dogma, the dangerous character of which had never been mistaken, was promulgated only to checkmate the Germans. and to serve, so to speak, as an antidote against inconvenient German investigations. For more than 20 years the Roman Hierarchy has banished the old Theological handbooks from the Seminaries and Colleges, and introduced new ones full of misstatements and falsifications, thus endeavoring to gain over the younger Clergy to the cause of the Ecclesiastical revolution in favor of Papal Absolutism," etc.—(*The True Catholic*, 1872, p. 30.) See also Griesinger's *History of the Jesuits*.

15 Lecky, vol. ii. p. 506. Dr. Wylie says:—"A Papal Bull is no matter of Religious profession—it is a matter of *civil obedience*. . . . ' France concedes no such power to the Pope. No rescript from Rome can be published in that country without permission of the Government. It is the same in Spain and Austria : indeed in every country of Continental Europe, Protestant and Popish. But in Great Britain this Statute was repealed in 1846 so far as regards the penalties attached to the 13th of Elizabeth, prohibiting the introduction of Letters Apostolic from Rome. As regards the order Statutes, in especial that of Richard II., Government has declared that it will not prosecute upon them, so that the abolition of these prohibitory enactments, is virtually total." (*Rome and Civil Liberty*, p. 31.) The Pope's Edict to England in 1850 wound up with decreeing " that all which may be done to the contrary by *anyone, whoever he may be, knowing or ignorant, in the name of any authority whatever, shall be without force.*" This is very sweeping language—what does it mean? (*Ibid*, pp. 34-5.)

16 Lecky, vol. ii. p. 510.

that power to the remaining four-fifths, which would in effect entirely transfer it from themselves."[17] This shows how quickly Protestant opinion had toned down and how *generous* in act that opinion had disposed the people who had power to be. Lecky further cites from a document — "*Thoughts on the Volunteers*"—written in 1784.[18] He does not wish to mislead, for he carefully says:—" It would, however, be *easy to exaggerate* the extent of the change. The elements of turbulence in the country were very numerous, and little provocation was needed to fan them into a flame."[19] There can be little doubt, I think, that the general conservatism of the Irish Protestants, in sharing political power with the Roman Catholics, was dictated by prudence rather than from intolerance of their religion. It is certain that public men whose names are held in honor by the Catholics,[20] were decidedly adverse to anything more than religious toleration to the people of that denomination. Sir James Cauldwell never dreamed of their political equality.[21] Flood was " inflexibly opposed " to giving them any measure of political power.[22] In 1782 he said the penal laws " were not laws of persecution but of political necessity."[23] Lord Charlemont " expressed his full approbation of the Penal Code."[24] Walpole bitterly complained of concessions to them in 1776.[25] Dean Swift " looked upon the existing penal proscription under which Catholics lay as not merely desirable but indispensable."[26] Mr. Lecky quotes a pamphlet published in Dublin in 1787, on the question of Catholic education which concluded, " It would be the greatest solecism that ever was thought of in politics, to give them (Roman Catholics) either votes in Parliament or liberty to carry arms."[27] Even Grattan, "the warmest and most unflinching advocate of the Catholics," replying to an address from Dublin citizens in 1792 said he loved the Roman Catholic. " I am the friend of his liberty, but it is only in as much as his liberty is entirely consistent with your ascendency, and an addition to the strength and freedom of the Protestant community. These being my principles and the Protestant interest my first object, you may judge that I will never assent to any measure tending to shake the security of property in this kingdom or *to subvert the Protestant ascendency.*"[28] Ed-

---

17 *Ibid*, p. 510.   18 *Ibid*, Note p. 510.   19 *Ibid*, p. 510.
20 McCarthy speaks approvingly of them in *Ireland since the Union*.
21 Lecky's *Ireland*, vol. ii. p. 206.   22 *Ibid*, p. 207   23 *Ibid*. p. 208, Note.
24 *Ibid*, p. 207.   25 *Ibid*, p. 210, Note.
26 Lawless' *Ireland*, p. 315. See Macaulay's *History of England*, vol. ii. pp. 296-7.
27 Lecky's *Ireland*, vol. ii. p. 513, Note.   28 *Ibid*, p. 97, Note.

mund Burke in 1760-65 wrote that the exclusion of Catholics "from all offices in Church and State" was "a just and necessary provision." In 1796—"I doubt whether the privileges they now seek, or have lately sought, are compassable."[29] In 1792 George Ponsonby said: "I confess I do not think that it would be wise to extend to them the elective franchise at this time."[30] Grattan went so far in his advocacy of the Catholic claims as to assert that the Protestant Religion *"will become the religion of the Catholics* if severity does not prevent them. . . . Gentlemen who speak of the enormities committed by Catholics . . . . do not take into account the enlightening and softening of men's minds by toleration."[31] Mr. Lecky comments on Grattan's soft cooing— "*Experience has not verified* Grattan's anticipations of the results that would follow from bringing Catholics within the pale of the Constitution, but those anticipations appeared extremely probable in the state of Religious thought prevailing *before the great convulsions of the French Revolution.*"[32] In this passage it strikes me that Mr. Lecky has disclosed the root cause of the strife which shook Ireland, both previous and subsequent to the Rebellion of 1798, from a religious point of view. The Catholic Religion was a diminishing quantity—it might have been absorbed altogether. Father Cleary phrases his view of it prettily. It reads well. "The demon of Religious discord was being laid by the fast gathering spirit of friendly toleration. It was evoked by the results that followed upon the midnight raids of the rude, ragged, and illiterate Peep-o'-day Boys. It shakes its gory locks in Ulster to this day."[33]

The Volunteer Movement.

This famous movement, the outcome of the American War of Independence, was a force which Ireland raised for her own defence in the year 1778, which year is also memorable for the modifications which took place in the commercial code and the

---

29 Arnold's *Burke on Irish Affairs* pp. 13 and 434
30 Wright's *Ireland*, vol. ii. p. 563. 31 Lecky's *Ireland*, vol. ii. p. 314.
32 *Ibid* p. 313.
33 p. 33. The reader will see how hysterical this bit of rhetoric is as he proceeds with the narrative; he will find evidence that the Peep of Day Boys were merely a local combination of Protestants against a well organised body of Catholics called Defenders, and that the latter ultimately terrorised thirteen counties in Ireland. If the mere handful of Peep of Day Boys could evoke "religious discord," how much more effective for that end were the numerous and well organised Deenders? It is to be noted that the Peep of Day Boys were not *exclusively Protestant* either in their *origin.*

popery laws.³⁴ The volunteers soon included 40,000 men,³⁵ and all of them loyal Protestants. In 1782, backed by this force, the Irish Parliament demanded and received its Independence. But, as Mr Lecky shows, the local legislature was threatened with the danger of becoming the slave of the movement which gave it power.³⁶ Father Cleary tells us, such was the tolerance of the period, that the "volunteers of the north (where the Orange Society arose) admitted Catholics to their ranks. At their Convention they turned out and presented arms to Father O'Leary."³⁷ Now Mr. Fitzpatrick says that in 1784 the Government desired to secure the services of Father O'Leary. He quotes Musgrave—" A corps, called the Irish Brigade, was raised in Dublin, of which nineteen out of twenty were Roman Catholics, and they appointed Father O'Leary *to be their chaplain.*"³⁸ When the volunteers had survived their usefulness they gradually disbanded, but during their decline the corrupting influence of the Catholic element which had crept in was manifest. For example—The Earl of Meath's "Liberty corps" thought fit, without consulting any other Volunteers, "to advertise for recruits and enlisted about 200 of the lowest class, who were chiefly Roman Catholics. Such a proceeding was wholly contrary to the wishes of Charlemont, to the general custom of the Volunteers, and *to the law which forbade Catholics to carry arms without license*: and at a time when the spirit of outrage was so rife in Dublin it was peculiarly dangerous. The other corps of the Volunteers marked their disapprobation by refusing to join the 'liberty corps' at their exercises."³⁹ Again he says this change which was taking place in the Volunteers was especially alarming. "The original Volunteers had consisted of the flower of the Protestant Yeomanry commanded by the gentry of Ireland. . . . But after the signature of peace and again after the dissolution of the Volunteer Convention, a great portion of the more respectable men connected with the movement considered their work done, and *retired from the ranks, and they were being replaced by another and wholly*

34 Lecky, vol. ii. p. 218.   35 *Ibid*, p. 242.   36 *Ibid*, p. 319.

37 p. 19. See a document quoted by Lecky—"Thoughts on the Volunteers," 1784 —in which it is stated—" To permit the use of arms to all Catholics would have been madness."—(*Ireland*, vol. ii. p. 510 Note.) The current Irish Protestant conception of the Penal Laws in 1810 is given in Dr. Duigenan's book—*Demands of the Irish Roman Catholics, &c.* This is his reply to *A Statement of, and Comments on the Penal Statutes*, put forward in Roman Catholic interests. Duigenan had been a Roman Catholic in his youth, and was educated for the Priesthood.— (Barry O'Brien's *Fifty Years' Concessions*, vol. i. p. 332.)

38 *Secret Service under Pitt*, p. 222.   39 Lecky, vol. ii. p. 394.

different class." Grattan was "one of the first to denounce the change."[40] The debates of this year furnish many illustrations of the growing evil.[41] "The law forbidding Catholics to carry arms without license had hitherto been enforced, and it was regarded *even by the Catholic gentry* as of vital importance to the peace of the country, for while the more respectable Catholics readily obtained licenses, it gave the Government the power of restraining, in a very lawless and turbulent country, the great mass of the rabble from the possession of arms. But now, under the colour of Volunteering, and in direct defiance not only of the letter of the law, but also of the wishes of the Commander of the Volunteers, *an extensive and indiscriminate arming of the Catholics was going on.*"[42] In an endeavour to extort the approval of Parliament for the Volunteers as latterly constituted, a motion was tabled based on previous votes of thanks. Gardiner moved an amendment, strongly supported by Grattan, and carried by a great majority—*"expressing high approbation of those who since the conclusion of the war had returned to cultivate the blessing of peace."*[43] This was a direct snub for the Volunteers on their irregular and deleterious practices. Mr. Grattan, in his usually intense way, said—*"*That great and honorable body of men, the *primitive* Volunteers, deserved much of their country, but I am free to say that they who now assume the name have much degenerated. There is *a cankered part of the dregs of the people* that has been armed. Let no gentleman give such men countenance or pretend to join them with the original Volunteers."[44] This is Grattan's denunciation of the hybridised Volunteers in 1785. Orde, in his letter to Nepean, January 26, 1785, wrote—Grattan had exposed the fact that "Roman Catholics were admitted, and the lowest and most riotous of the people were armed." This letter describes the debate on the question in the House.[45] So much therefore for the mixture of Catholics with Protestants in the famous Volunteers.

THE PEEP OF DAY BOYS.

Father Cleary quotes Lecky's *Leaders of Public Opinion* on the Peep of Day Boys and the Defenders, and says a similar account of the origin of the two associations is given in the same writer's *Ireland in the 18th Century*. The extent of the quotation is—" The Defenders were professedly as their name imports a purely defensive body."[46] After showing how superficial was

40 *Ibid*, p. 395. 41 *Ibid*, p. 396. 42 *Ibid*, p. 397. 43 *Ibid*, p. 398.
44 *Ibid*, p. 426. 45 *Ibid*, p. 427. 46 p. 31, *Note* 80.

the character of the toleration growing up in Ireland, or at least the intense caution which pervaded it, Mr Lecky calls attention to the dangerous sectarian elements then in combination :—" The contests between the Peep of Day Boys and the Defenders in Ulster are said to have originated in a private quarrel unconnected with Religion, but they speedily assumed the character of a Religious war.[47] The former, who were exclusively Protestants, and *mainly, Presbyterians*, professed a determination to enforce the law disarming papists, and they were accustomed to enter their cottages in early morning to search for and to seize arms. The Defenders were exclusively Catholics, and were professedly as their name imports, a purely defensive body. In truth, however, both sides were animated by a furious hatred, and both sides committed many acts of violence and aggression. The disturbances began in the year 1785, but they continued for several years, and the Peep of Day Boys ultimately merged into Orangemen, and the Defenders into United Irishmen. Bodies of several hundreds of men of the lowest class on more than one occasion came into collision : several lives were lost : a reign of terror prevailed in Ulster, and it led to a new enrolment of Protestant Volunteers to maintain the peace." Lecky then lays it down that the Peep of Day Boys were " mainly Presbyterian." Father Cleary insists that the " early " Orangemen were of " the Religion of the State." Dr. Killen will only admit that about a year after the Orange Society began was it put on " a more respectable " basis, and a few Presbyterians not very warmly attached to their church joined it. The Father also contends that the Peep of Day Boys constitute " the pre-lodge phase "[48] of the Orange Association, facts to the contrary notwithstanding. He says:—"The whole history of the Peep of Day Boys utterly forbids the supposition that *this early phase* of Orangeism ever adopted what were in later years, (and still are), alleged to be the groundwork principles of the Society, namely, the defence of the Protestant Religion, the maintenance of the laws, and the cultivation of virtue. The stigma of illegality and of disregard of both human and divine law, attaches to that organisation from the day that the first oathbound (*sic*)

---

[47] Walpole agrees with Lecky on the "religious war" and accounts for it thus:— "Originating in a quarrel between two Presbyterian peasants, one of whom was joined by a Roman Catholic, the feud grew into a village brawl, which rapidly spread in the surrounding country until the Counties of Armagh and Louth were divided into two contending camps."—(*Short History of the Kingdom of Ireland*, p. 421.) This is corroborated by Sir Rich. Musgrave, and Wright.—(Wright's *History of Ireland*, vol. ii. p. 489.)   [48] p. 30, 31, Note 76.

'crowd of miscreants' sallied forth under cover of darkness to do what, under the title of Orangemen, they were soon to carry out on a wider scale, and in the face of day, namely, to plunder and wreck the homes of the Catholic minority who lived amongst them. In the first of these midnight raids lies the *fons et origo* of the Orangeism of our day."[49] Let us analyse the evidence on which this gaudy passage rests. (1) The Peep of Day Boys are said by the Father to have been *bound by oath*. On this point so far as I am aware he does not offer one solitary proof, but the inference is that the Peep of Day Boys formed a compact and secretly organised body. I cannot find anything to support this. Evidence tends to regard them as casual and local associations. One writer remarks :—" The Peep of Day Boys had *no regular system of union*, while their adversaries (the Defenders) formed a perfectly organised combination with signs and passwords. The latter therefore in a short time became a most powerful body, not confined to the North but extending over a large portion of the Kingdom."[50] (2) The question of *religious sect*. The Father quotes Dr. Killen as saying the first Peep of Day Boys were Protestants of the Established Church. Wright says that in 1784 both Defenders and Peep of Day Boys were named " Fleets," and that these antagonistic " fleets " comprised mixtures of Papists and Presbyterians from local reasons. "From the inveterate hatred which has ever existed between the two sects, they soon began to separate, and to enlist under the banners of religion, and as the Roman Catholics showed uncommon eagerness to collect arms, the Presbyterians began to disarm them. The former assumed the appellation of Defenders, and the latter were known by the title of the Peep of Day Boys."[51] Musgrave says that the country gentlemen for " electioneering purposes " patronised the party squabbles, and upheld one side or the other as they had "Popish or Presbyterian tenants."[52] Commenting on the conflicts between the two factions he remarks :—"A detail of their battles would be as uninteresting as that of the kites and the crows." He further says : " The Protestants of the Established Church were in no way connected with their disputes at the time " (1788).[53] On the collapse of the volunteer convention, Walpole observes— " Faction fights took place in the North between the Roman Catholics and the Presbyterians." This was subsequent to

---

49 p. 35.   50 Hall's *Ireland*, vol. ii. p. 463.
51 Hist. *Ireland*, vol. ii. pp. 489-490.   52 *Memoirs*, vol. i. p. 54.
53 *Ibid*, pp. 54, 55, 56.

Nov. 1783.⁵⁴ In the *Charlemont Correspondence* several letters represent the blame as attaching to the Roman Catholics. What Mr. Lecky terms a "very honorable letter" from Fitzgibbon (Lord Clare), asks advice from Lord Charlemont "about a report from Armagh that 500 Catholics were in arms." In the Irish State paper office there is a letter from Newry, dated July 17, 1789, "giving a detailed and very graphic picture of the terrorism which a mob of Presbyterians, under the name of Break of Day Boys, were exercising over the poor Catholics of that district."⁵⁵ I do not find any corroboration of Dr. Killen's statement as quoted by Father Cleary. Musgrave, Wright, Walpole, and Lecky are all against it. Mr Cleary's mode of argument on the connection between the Peep of Day Boys and the Orangemen, is the good old one of producing muddled and conflicting testimony, and therefrom quietly stealing the inference that a specific issue has been settled in his favor.

One statement the Father advances on Tone's authority, it is this :—" The Presbyterians who had become Peep of Day Boys were *reconciled to the* Defenders in the middle of 1792, more than three years before the Battle of the Diamond."⁵⁶ Walpole says—" The antagonism between the Defenders and the Peep of Day Boys was a great trouble to Tone, whose plan had been to unite Protestant with Roman Catholic in one common cause. He endeavoured to induce them to accept the teaching of the United Irishmen, but *only with the result that many of the Defenders* joined that Society, and so connected it with the *party of violence.*"⁵⁷ Wright supports this view and quotes the *Memoir* by Emmett, O'Connor, and M'Nevin, in which it is affirmed that the United Irishmen went amongst both factions, " but particularly the Defenders " and " melted them down into the United Irish Body."⁵⁸ Musgrave credits the Presbyterians with doing splendid service against the Defenders' frightful outrages in 1793. In this year the Defenders attacked the Presbyterians on the borders of Cavan. About 150 got into ambush when they learned the Scots were approaching, and fired upon them, but happily without much damage: on their opponents returning the fire they ran away.⁵⁹ Now if the Presbyterians were reconciled to the Defenders in 1792, as Tone, quoted by Father Cleary, says they were, how does it happen that we find them in conflict in 1793 ? This is *two years before* the Diamond.

54 *Short History of Ireland*, p. 409.   55 Lecky's *Ireland*, vol. ii. p. 511.
56 p. 61, Note 21.   57 *Short History*, pp. 442, 443.
58 *Ireland*, vol. ii. pp. 574, 575.   59 *Ibid*, p. 568.

Catholic Societies in Ireland.

There is not the slightest doubt that secret combinations amongst Catholic peasantry were, without exception, renowned for diabolical outrages. (See Lecky, vol. ii. pp. 46, 51.)

(1) *The Whiteboys.* These usually met in R.C. Chapels, and during their reign the law was powerless. Walpole says:— " When the judges came round on Circuit no juries would convict, and no evidence could be procured."[60] Musgrave says the clergy appeared "deeply concerned in encouraging and fomenting them in the commission of outrages."[61] Wright gives a description of their horrible deeds in 1784. Munster and Leinster were under their scourge. Protestants were "robbed of their arms, stripped naked, and in this condition dragged over the country on horseback, and finally buried in the earth up to the chin, with dreadful threats against anybody who should relieve them before the noon of the next day. Sometimes they had their ears cut off and were otherwise mutilated."[62] The Archbishop of Cashel and the Bishop of Ossory strongly denounced them.[63] The Whiteboy Act of 1787 contemplated originally, so Mr. Lecky says, where it could be proved that their oath had been given in a papist chapel, the building should be destroyed. This part, however, was omitted in the passing of the measure.[64]

(2) *The Defenders.* This terrible and disgraceful combination is one of the greatest blots upon the history of the Catholic people in Ireland. The Catholic Committee were compelled to take some action both to repudiate and moderate their atrocities.[65] In 1788 a volunteer corps had to be organised to put them down.[66] They challenged the volunteers in Armagh.[67] The House of Lords appointed a Secret Committee which discovered alarming secrets in connection with the movement.[68] In 1793 they were the terror of the country. "They assembled in large bodies by night and went through military evolutions

---

60 *Short History*, p. 376. 61 *Memoirs*, vol. i. p. 32.
62 *Ireland*, vol. ii. p. 488.

63 Bishop Moriarty spoke of the Fenian atrocities in forcible terms. "Hell is not hot enough, or eternity long enough to punish their crimes." This did not make the Bishop popular.—(*The Nun of Kenmare*, pp. 56, 57.) The Archbishop of Tuam wrote a denunciatory letter on the Land League. Sir Henry James quoting it said that when "called to Mr. Parnell's attention," there was a denial that the Rev. Dr. McHale wrote the letter. It made a difference when the letter was put in as evidence against the League.—(*The Work of the Irish Leagues*, p. 98.) 64 Lecky, vol. ii. p. 457.

65 Wright's *History of Ireland*, vol. ii. pp. 573, 574.
66 *Ibid*, p. 529. 67 *Ibid*, pp. 529, 530. 68 *Ibid*, p. 572.

under their captains, mostly infamous individuals who were obliged to conceal themselves from the laws of their country. As their necessities increased they indulged in every sort of crime," &c.[69] On October 25, 1793, the Rev. Mr. Butler, chaplain of the Bishop of Meath, was shot from behind a hedge near Ardbraccan. He had been active in putting down defenderism about Navan. Walpole gives a short account of their savage exploits.[70] Musgrave observes that when a judicial enquiry was made concerning a Riot in Tanderagee in 1786, it was discovered that the Defenders had offered £5 *for the head of a Protestant*.[71] In 1789 a magistrate found on one of the Defender leaders named Sharky, one of their plans or constitutions showing that he belonged to Lodge No. 18. This discovery was made in Armagh, and it was dated April 24, 1789, Drumbanagher. " One *essential* required in a member of the order *was to be possessed of a musket and a bayonet.*" Musgrave also refers to a Defender Lodge certificate issued to Michael Moor, recommending him to the committee at Carrickarnan No. 1 Louth.[72] Fitzgibbon (Lord Clare), speaking on the Union, said—" My unalterable opinion is that so long as human nature and the popish religion continue to be what I know they are, a conscientious popish ecclesiastic never will become a well attached subject to a Protestant state, and that the popish clergy must always have a commanding influence on every member of that communion."[73] If this be a clean-cut truth that does not know the ways of the " circumlocution office," these secret societies were even more significant than their acts were alarming. Father Cleary would have us believe that the Defenders were only a defensive league. Much depends upon a name in his book. The Orangemen were persecutors. The Defenders were what their name imports. The case is as plain as a pikestaff. Argument is wasted against the importance of an association label. The truth is, the Defenders, were a formidable organisation carrying terror and dismay along their course : and the Peep of Day Boys—whether they belonged to the Presbyterian or Anglican Church—did good service in resisting their terrible depredations. The point which I wish to emphasise, in showing the many forms of secret combination in Ireland during this period, is that the Orange Society having its origin in such a state of things was under the necessity of borrowing from its foes methods which helped it to defeat them.

---

69 *Ibid*, pp. 576, 577. 70 *Short History*, pp. 441, 442.
71 *Memoirs*, vol. i. p. 55. 72 *Ibid*, p. 57.
73 Lecky's *Ireland*, vol ii. p. 419.

Its cradle was set in a country where the common classes of Protestants were daily threatened by secret ruffians, whose movements could not be timed, and who were so leagued together, that common law, destitute of a police force, could give no adequate protection to the individual or family, and whose outrages for the same reason could not be punished. The legacies left to the Protestants of the North of massacre, assassination, and defeated justice were so vivid and awful, that both memory and environment suggested a form of self-protection which expressed itself. in the Boyne Society, or as it became later, the Orange Society. The Physician usually treats his patient according to the symptoms developed, and we may, on this principle, regard the association as a treatment of the racial and religious symptoms prevalent in Irish society at the time of its emergence.

CHAPTER VII.

THE ORIGIN OF MODERN ORANGEISM.—THE CONFLICT OF THE DIAMOND.—DEFENDERS AT THE OLD GAME.—THE BERKELEY OUTRAGE.—THE FIRST ORANGE LODGE.—THE "ORANGE REIGN OF TERROR."—AN INFANT SOCIETY EXPELLING HALF A COUNTY.

I HAVE already indicated certain notable features in Irish life, which will explain the cleavage of the two populations close up to the commencement of the present century. The periodic convulsions from which the country suffered were in the main the result of difference in race and religion ; to this was added the occasionally strong-handed government of the minority over the majority, and the ferocious rebellions of the latter against the ascendency of the former. Towards the close of the last century, however, on wholly Protestant instance remedial measures for chronic asperities were brought into existence. The result was not all that could be desired, though from the more enlightened Catholics a gratifying spirit of loyalty to the Empire was manifested. But the feeling of that people generally was indicated by the tone of the addresses poured in upon Lord Fitzwilliam: these displayed not so much a gratitude for past ameliorations as a hope for future extensions of power and favor. In 1782 two Relief Bills were passed. The first related to the private ownership of land and was conditioned by the oath of allegiance.[1] The second gave Catholic schoolmasters the liberty of teaching, and repealed the statutes relating to the guardianship of children.[2] In 1792 Sir Hercules Langrishe's Bill became law. This opened the legal profession to the Catholics, and repealed statutes against the intermarriage of Catholics and Protestants.[3] In 1793 Mr. Secretary Hobart's measure was carried which gave the right of voting to Catholic forty-shilling freeholders—admitted them to Dublin University, and to most of the civil and military offices, &c.[4] Tone exulted "over the pressure notoriously exerted upon it (the Irish legislature) by the Cabinet of London" to procure its passage. He did not hesitate to bestow his "hypocritical laudations on the great minister (Pitt) whom . . . . he so cordially hated."[5] This does not support Father Cleary's accusations of goading the Irish into rebellion.

Despite these concessions[6] Lord Fitzwilliam, upon whom the Catholics of Ireland relied as their emancipator, wrote the Duke of Portland in 1795—" Not to grant *cheerfully all the Catholics wish* will not only be exceedingly impolitic, but perhaps dangerous."[7] He also intimated that the *"disaffection among the lower orders is universal,* though the violences now committing are not from political causes but the *outrages of banditti."* Mr. Lecky gives us his opinion of Ireland at this time. "The real obstacles to material prosperity were now much more *moral* than political."[8] Under such conditions, therefore, the Orange Society came into being in Ireland. Father Cleary has occupied himself with depicting very different circumstances.

1 21, 22 Geo. III. c. 24.   2 21, 22 Geo. III. c. 62.   3 32 Geo. III. c. 21.
4 33 Geo. III. c. 21.   5 The *Nineteenth Century,* June, 1890. Argyll p. 1002.
6 " The Penal Statutes against the Roman Catholics had been repealed : they held their land on the like terms with the Protestants : they enjoyed in short every right and franchise in common with the former, saving only the Offices of State, and the privilege of sitting in Parliament. These exceptions, however, were viewed in the light of persecutions for difference of Religion. . . . . but the Protestants, dreading the consequences of putting themselves in the power of the Roman Catholics, whose disposition they still considered unaltered, maintained *the propriety of these restrictions," and they " resolved on no account to permit a participation in the power they enjoyed to men who undisguisedly stigmatised them as intruders."—(*The Annual Register,* 1798, vol. 40, p. 153.)
7 Walpole's *Short. Hist.,* p. 443   8 *Ireland,* Vol. ii. p. 504.

THE CONFLICT OF THE DIAMOND.

The recall of Earl Fitzwilliam was the signal for loud and angry discontent on the part of the Roman Catholics. Dublin soon became a scene of riot, which continued for some length of time. When the new Viceroy, Lord Camden, was sworn in, on the 31st of March, 1795, both himself and the Protestant Archbishop of Armagh were attacked by the mob; their carriages were assailed with a bombardment of stones; and Camden had his head laid open by a missile. Other mobs endeavoured to impress Lord Claudius Beresford and certain obnoxious public individuals with a sense of their supreme displeasure by attacking their houses. " The same spirit extended into the provinces and the Defenders became everywhere more numerous and outrageous. In some counties, every gentleman was obliged to keep a constant military guard in his house as a protection against plunder and assassination, and, dreadful as had been the state of the country during the preceding two years, it became this summer considerably worse."[9] Froude's description of " the Defenders " in this year is dreadful. " First in Connaught and then gradually in all parts of Ireland, bodies of men who seemed to have started out of the earth, were out at night on the prowl like wild beasts. Houses were burned, cattle were houghed with the peculiar ferocity which characterises the Irish peasant when roused to violence: the udders of the cows belonging to Protestants were sliced off. When arms were demanded and were not delivered, death was the punishment. Barracks were surprised in the darkness. Parties of militia were attacked even in open day with desperate courage: and by whom these deeds were done remained for the most part a mystery."[10] In some parts of the country these depredators called themselves Masons, especially about Loughal, Charlemont, Richhill, Portadown, Lurgan, and the Ban-foot, and Blackwaterfoot, " where they were very active in robbing Protestants of their arms."[11] In the month of September they assembled in arms in broad daylight, and marched into the parish of Tentaraghan, in the County of Armagh, where they fired into the houses of the Protestants.[12] Lecky says the year 1795 is "very memorable" in Irish history, as the year of the formation of the Orange Society. Recognising the attempts which have been so zealously made to blacken the Orange Association by party writers, he speaks carefully:

---

9 Wright's *Ireland*, vol. ii. p. 592.
10 Froude's *Ireland*, vol. iii Ed. 1887, p. 186.
11 Wright's *Ireland*, vol. ii. p. 592.   12 *Ibid*, p. 592.

—" It is with a feeling of unfeigned diffidence that I enter upon this branch of my narrative. Our authentic materials are so scanty, and so steeped in party and sectarian animosity, that a writer who has done his utmost to clear his mind from prejudice, and bring together with impartiality the conflicting statements of partisans, will still, if he is a wise man, always doubt whether he has succeeded in painting with perfect fidelity, the delicate gradations of provocation, palliation and guilt."[13] Mr. Lecky, with all his vast stores of information, is modest; his modesty sits becomingly on his ability and crowns it. Father Cleary has no such modesty; he is not troubled with any of this squeamishness. Like the famous parrot, he has only one answer to all questions:—" There is no doubt about it." When treating of the old popular feud between the lower ranks of Papists and Presbyterians in the Northern Counties, Mr Lecky says:—" The Catholic and Protestant tenants came into a new competition, and the demeanour of Catholics towards Protestants *was sensibly changed.* There were boasts in taverns and at fairs that the Protestants would speedily be swept away from the land, the descendants of the old proprietors restored, and it was soon known that Catholics *all over the country were forming themselves into committees or societies,* and were electing representatives for a great Catholic Convention at Dublin."[14] In the year 1787 a gentleman named Jackson died at Dundalk, leaving considerable property for the purpose of educating a number of children of the Established Church as weavers or in other trades. " The object was to plant a nucleus of industry and order in the midst of a savage, bigoted, idle, and entirely lawless population, who seem to have been allowed for many years to live and to multiply without any kind of interference, guidance, or control."[15] The expedient was not appreciated, and the result was that the Catholics " assembled the Defenders from all parts of the country and struck such horror that none of these Protestants but half a dozen ever appeared here afterwards."[16] The School, however, continued until in the beginning of 1791, a long series of outrages culminated in " one of those ghastly crimes which make men's blood boil in their veins."[17] A Protestant schoolmaster named Berkeley[18] was

---

13 Lecky's *Ireland*, vol. iii. p. 421.   14 *Ibid*, p. 422.
15 *Ibid*, p. 423.   Wright's *Ireland*, vol. ii. p. 556.
16 Lecky, vol. iii. p. 424.   Wright's *Ireland*, vol. ii. p. 556.
17 Lecky, vol. iii. p. 424.
18 Wright spells the name as pronounced—Alexander Barclay; whom he describes

attacked in his house by a party of 40 or 50 men. "They stabbed him in several places. They cut out his tongue, and they cut off several of his fingers. They mangled his wife in the same way, and in other ways also, and they then proceeded to mutilate hideously a boy of thirteen." After plundering the butchered man's house they marched along triumphantly with lighted torches. Lecky says "*The feeling of the neighbourhood was indisputably with them.* Only one of the culprits was brought to justice : he would give no evidence against his accomplices, and he went to the gallows attended by the priest and maintaining, it is said, *all the demeanour of a martyr.*"[19] Dean Warburton wrote in 1798 to urge the expediency of arresting "two priests of infamous character." The Dean mentioned that one of them "had been parish priest at Forkhill and was reproved by his Bishop as he was supposed to have been concerned in the outrage on the schoolmaster there."[20] Whilst the historian calls attention to the fact of retaliation in outrage by the Protestants he shows that the violent alternation of hope and despondency that followed the appointment and recall of Lord Fitzwilliam : " the constant rumors of rebellion and invasion, and the great extension of the Defender movement through Ireland contributed to aggravate the situation."[21] In the midst of all this the Defenders in Armagh who had been serenading the Protestants in broad daylight with their guns, were confronted by a body who were not disposed to tamely yield to the marauders.[22] Each party camped on an eminence and blazed away at each other during the day, without, however, doing serious damage. On the 18th September some magistrates living in the neighbourhood interfered and "persuaded the leaders of both parties to meet at the house of a man named Winter, near Portadown, where they were persuaded to lay aside their

---

as "*a Scottish Presbyterian.*" After detailing the fearful barbarity of the occurrence, he says: "This outrage produced *a great sensation among the Presbyterians* of the North, and the report that the treatment of the Barclays had been approved by the Popish Priests in the vicinity served to exasperate the two religious parties against each other." This was in 1791. It is not likely that in 1792 the Presbyterians would have forgotten all about it and become "*reconciled*" to the Defenders as Tone quoted by Father Cleary says they were. The Presbyterians are not characterised by short memories.—(Wright's *Ireland*, vol. ii. pp. 556-7.)

19 Lecky, vol. iii. pp. 424-5.   20 *Ibid*, Note p. 425.   21 *Ibid*, p. 425.

22 Walpole declares that " Tone's plans for uniting the Protestants and Roman Catholics had *not resulted in the reconciliation of the two Religious factions in Armagh.* There the disgraceful civil strife was unabated. The authorities appeared content to permit the two fanatical parties to fight it out."—(*Short Hist.* p. 456.)

animosity, and sign articles by which they bound themselves to keep the peace towards each other.[23] This pacification was, it appears, of very short duration, for one of the Protestant leaders was waylaid and fired at on his return from signing it, and this so excited both parties that they were in arms again next day. *Each party now threatened the other with extermination.* The Catholics are said to have been much more numerous than their opponents, and elated with this circumstance, having received reinforcements from the mountains of Pomeroy and Ballygawly, in the County of Tyrone, they proceeded to attack the Protestants in the neighbourhood of a village called the Diamond. The Protestants of the surrounding country, ever on the watch, collected in arms on the point where the attack had commenced, and a severe conflict took place, in which the Defenders were beaten with a loss of 48 killed and a great number wounded. This engagement, which took place on the 21st of September, 1795, was long celebrated as the battle of the Diamond."[24] Mr. Lecky says—" The Catholics on this occasion were certainly the *aggressors*, and they appear to have considerably outnumbered their antagonists, but the Protestants were better posted, better armed, and better organised."[25] Father Cleary's account of the Defenders leads us to suppose that they were armed with such primitive weapons as pitchforks, &c., but, probably through an inadvertence, he quotes Plowden as saying —" The Defenders remained *under arms for three days* successively, challenging their opponents to fight it out," &c. (p. 50). The Father, with all his selected stores of information, could only ascertain that the aggressors had "pitchforks and swords and things of that sort." Musgrave says—" The Defenders were in the proportion of six to one of the Protestants," and that "the former had been supplied clandestinely with large quantities of arms and ammunition from Dublin."[26] The Father's citation from Plowden tends to give this statement very strong support. I have already quoted the "qualifications" of a Defender—he must be possessed of *a musket and a bayonet*.[27] Mr. Banks, of Toronto, in his account, says that the Defenders were better equipped than Mr. Cleary would have us believe. They had

---

23 Musgrave says the recognisance of each side was a sum of £50, and that *two priests* signed the agreement on behalf of the Defenders.—(*Memoirs*, vol. i. p. 67.)

24 Wright's *Ireland*, vol. ii. p. 592. See Froude's account, *Ireland*, vol. iii. p. 154, and Walpole's *Short History*, p. 456.

25 *Ireland*, vol. iii. p. 426.

26 *Memoirs*, vol. i. p. 68.   27 *Ibid*, p. 57.

"a good sized brass gun, almost a cannon," and it was under the special charge and control of a priest—Father Quigley. This writer also says that there were 1200 Defenders and about 200 Protestants engaged in the encounter.[28] This accounts for their peculiarly persistent "challenging," as related by Mr Plowden. Among the many virtuous reflections indulged in by the Father upon this doleful business, in which as might be expected, he maintains the utter innocence of the Defenders,[29] occur the following :—(1) "The suspicious one-sidedness of the encounter has led many persons to refer to it as the 'massacre' of the Diamond." (p. 55.) When a party means to assert that black is white, there is nothing like doing it thoroughly. The louder the assertion and the more audacious, the better is its chance of being heard and believed by somebody. I judge that this is the axiom upon which the "many persons" act when they refer to the Diamond in these terms. Their names are not given, but we may take it for granted they are of the first consequence and famous for their veracity. Father Cleary has a happy knack of cloaking an unfortunate phrase which he desires to turn to some account. For instance, he refers to Molesworth's *History of England*, in which, he says, is admitted " a somewhat extensive belief, *among certain classes* at the time, in the existence of the Orange conspiracy." (p. 382, 383 Note.) Now Molesworth's words are : "Though all well-informed persons saw that these suspicions were destitute of foundation, they were nevertheless extensively believed by *the very ignorant.*"[30] The Father does not let his case suffer by under-statement when a reference can be " dressed." (2) The next reflection I note is that the Diamond conflict was not fought for the "defence of the Protestant religion, nor for an open Bible, nor for the maintenance of the laws or constitution, nor for any of the principles set forth in the basis of the Orange Society." (p. 56) It was not. There is no disputing the point. Those 200 Protestants scandalously delayed drawing up any charter of principles, and went at the business of fighting in astounding obedience to the first law of nature, commonly known as self-preservation. As the Father says, and I quite agree with him, these principles " were after-

---

28 *History of the Orange Order*, p. 19.

29 It is true that on pp. 22, 23 he says that Defenderism was obnoxious to the Catholic Church, but he does not anywhere admit that it was *aggressive against Protestants*, and he certainly acts as the apologist for the Defenders in his account of the Diamond. Observe the quotations from M'Nevin and Plowden, both of whom are Catholic writers and virulently opposed to the Orange Society.

30 *History of England*, vol. i. p. 378.

thoughts." But I do not think the Orange Society should be charged with putting up a wrong signboard—it has never pretended an existence prior to the battle of the Diamond, and but for that battle it probably would never have been organised at all. Father Cleary is the only one, that I know of, who has attempted to make the Orange Society exist before it began. He instances a number of authorities to say that the Peep of Day Boys were " the pre-lodge phase " of Orangeism. When his quotations are analysed we see that his idea is an import—that *creation*, and not continuity, is the essence of them. He quotes *Chambers' Encyclopedia* to illustrate his scheme of identity. But the Chambers' declare that the Peep of Day Boys " *made way* for the rich and influential organisation of the Orange Society, which having *its first origin in the same obscure district* which had long been the scene of agrarian violence," &c. The idea of this is clearly that a separate organisation, with a superior nature, and a different origin has displaced the Peep of Day Boys. The phrase—" made way"—is certainly not used in the sense of *preparing* the way, which, however, is the construction put upon it by the Father. However, not to wrangle over the meaning of a phrase, let us refer to a letter written by Arthur O'Connor, dated December 24, 1796. This letter was intercepted at the instance of the Government. It describes the United Irishmen, then the Defenders, and finally the Orangemen. Speaking of the Defenders, O'Connor says—" But their opponents in Armagh are of a *new description*. They have an oath which binds them to support the Protestant ascendency."[31] Had they been the old and well-known Peep of Day Boys surely O'Connor would have known it. The Father's ingenious theory has hardly a feather left to fly with. (3) He refers to Lieutenant Col. Verner being " sternly reprimanded by Under-Secretary Drummond, and dismissed from the magistracy[32] for having com-

---

31 Lecky's *Ireland*, vol. iii. p. 488.

32 " Sir Wm. Verner, if Mr. Disraeli's memory served him, had been deprived of some of the honors he possessed for toasting the ' Battle of the Diamond ' at an obscure local dinner. Was this ' more outrageous, more incendiary, than the allusion of *the Queen's representative* to the ' glories of Vinegar Hill ' ? " (p. 15.) In this speech Mr. Disraeli referred to the state of Ireland as follows :—" Landlords were shot down like game ; respectable farmers were beaten to death with sticks by masked men ; bailiffs were shot in the back ; policemen were stabbed ; the High Sheriff of a county, going to swear in the Grand Jury, was fired at in his carriage and dangerously wounded ; households were blown up, and firearms surreptitiously obtained. All this time the Government *would not move*." (p. 16.) —(*The Annual Register*, 1870) On pp. 80, 81 the Father gives what he calls the " charter toast " of Orangeism on Barrington's authority. But that writer said the toast " existed *before* the foundations of Orangeism." The " insulting

memorated such 'a lawless and most disgraceful conflict.'" (p. 56.) Drummond was no doubt quite right in denouncing the conflict as "lawless and disgraceful," provided he put stigma on the right shoulders, which, however, when those shoulders happened to be Catholic ones, he had no disposition to do. As one writer observed, the Diamond affair was aggravated "by the unaccountable negligence of government which left the attacked party *to defend themselves.*"[33] Mr. Under Secretary Drummond did not please all the Irish citizens by his conduct in office, even though he gives unqualified satisfaction to Father Cleary and his next friend, Barry O'Brien. There is a fly in the ointment of his reign in Ireland. On the 1st day of January, 1839, Lord Norbury was shot, and he died on the 3rd of the month from the assassin's bullet. At an assembly of magistrates, Lord Oxmantown, the Lord Lieutenant of the county, said: "The cause of the lamentable event which had brought them together, was to be sought for in a far-spread conspiracy (Ribandism) for wresting the property out of the hands of the proprietors by the abolition of rent, with the determination of effecting, by association, what they were unable to extort by open rebellion." The magistrates came to several conclusions, amongst which are the following:— "Resolved—That it appears to this meeting that the answer conveyed to the magistrates of Tipperary by Mr. Under Secretary Drummond has had the effect of *increasing the animosities* contained against the owners of the soil, and has emboldened the disturbers of the peace. That, finding from the circumstances mentioned in the former resolutions, that there is *little room to hope for a successful appeal to the Irish executive,* we feel it a duty to apply to the people of England, the Legislature and the Throne for protection. That the magistrates here assembled are determined to co-operate with the Government in any manner pointed out by Her Majesty's Ministers, which may give the slightest hope of restoring tranquillity in this distracted country."[33a] There was something wrong with the

---

distich" quoted from Lecky was also *prior* to the Orange Society. Cleary mentions that in the charter toast an allusion is made to Bishop Browne, who wrote against "toasting the dead" in the year 1715!!! Did said Bishop say anything about *praying* to the dead? The *Encyclopedia Britannica* (vol. xvii. ninth edition) gives the Orange toast as follows: "The glorious pious and immortal memory of the great and good King William who saved us from popery, slavery, knavery, brass money, and wooden shoes." This toast was not made any secret of, and it ended with any grotesque additions invented by the proposer. Those who have read Barrington will readily understand his version of the toast. He was an inveterate joker. .

33 Wright's *Ireland,* vol. ii. p. 592.   33a *Annual Register,* 1839, pp. 39, 40.

state of Ireland even under a rule so happy and glorious as Mr. Drummond's, and one can guess why he regarded Orangemen as "demons." The House of Lords appointed a commission for enquiring into crimes in Ireland chiefly in relation to Riband Societies about this time, and I may be pardoned for disposing of Judge Fletcher's famous deliverance in this connection. Sir Charles Russell quotes Baron Fletcher as pointing out "that the Ribandism which then began to show its head was a product of oppression."[34] Father Cleary wishes it to be understood that the Judge's strictures on Orangeism are from an impartial source, but the impartiality is jeopardised when we find him *excusing* Ribandism. Baron Fletcher's address was a political one, and comprised an extraordinary medley of themes. It is given in full in the *Annual Register* for the year 1814. The Judge deals with the Currency question—Orange Societies—Acts of Parliament, &c. He tells the Grand Jury he has been absent from Wexford for twelve years, and liberally uses what Sam Slick calls "soft sawder": but what relation all his topics had to the legal question before the Grand Jury, I cannot in the least determine. Charles Phillips remarks—"The ultra-liberalism of a charge which he (Baron Fletcher) delivered to the Wexford Grand Jury, threw all Ireland into a flame, and well nigh invoked on him the vengeance of the Government. . . . It is curious to observe how perfectly innocuous the discussion of the topics contained in that celebrated charge would appear in our day: yet at the time it was considered *little short of treason*. . . . Without discussing the soundness of these opinions which is quite apart from the purport of this work, there can be no doubt that the Bench of Justice was not a fitting place for their enunciation."[35] The learned Judge's address would have been in order at a pleasant Sunday afternoon. Phillips also gives an insight into the Baron's peculiarities which may act as a commentary on his charge. Our critic has quoted Judge Fletcher again and again, and he is the *only* Judge whose remarks I have been able to scrutinise, the references given in the other cases alleged, being of *no possible service* to the reader for this purpose.—(See Cleary p. 330.)

THE ORANGE SOCIETY.

We are told the "later Orangemen generally" were "ashamed of the undoubted connection of their Society with the Peep of

---

34 *Ireland's Vindication*, pp. 23-4.
35 *Curran and his Contemporaries*, pp. 427-8.

Day movement."[36] But the writer has not proved the "undoubted connection." His idea of fusion is akin to confusion, in which he proclaims a genuine marriage, and takes it for granted that a mere time order in the existence of the two societies establishes the union. What the Orange Society repudiates is the accusation—that it expelled Catholics from Armagh, by gratuitous and malevolent persecution. Mr. Lecky says on the evening of the day on which the battle of the Diamond was fought, September 21, 1795, the Orange Society was formed. " It was *at first a league of mutual defence*, binding its members to maintain the laws and the peace of the country, and also the Protestant Constitution." It was bound to defend the King and his heirs " so long as he or they support the Protestant ascendency."[37] In a note the author adds —"The conditional oath of allegiance was exchanged about 1821 for the ordinary oath, and that was abolished in 1825."[38] The fearful excesses and rampant cruelties of the Defenders had taught the Protestants the necessity of secret combination, while the inadequacy of civil protection and the negligence of Government, threw them upon their own resources.

(1). *The First Lodge.* Mr. Banks informs us that this was formed at Dian on June 24, 1794. A Mr. James Wilson, member of the Freemason's Society, being present on an occasion when some Protestants were assaulted by the Defenders, called upon his brother Masons to deliver the unfortunates out of the hands of their persecutors, but with no result. He then said he would light a flame in Ireland that would outrival the Masonic fraternity : and to realise it started a lodge at Dian.[39] This was

---

36 Cleary, pp. 54, 55, Note. Sir R. Musgrave depicts the Orange Society at its beginning thus :—"They were merely a society of loyal Protestants, associated and bound together solely for the purpose of maintaining and defending the Constitution in Church and State as established by the Prince of Orange at the glorious Revolution, which they regarded as a solemn and sacred duty."— (*Memoirs*, vol. i. p. 70.)

37 *Ireland*, vol. iii. p. 426. Wright's *Ireland*, vol. ii. p. 592.

38 Lecky, *Ibid*, p. 426, Note.

39 *History Orange Order*, p. 17. Robert Young's verses on No. 1 Lodge present this view—'Twas then a few good men and true
At Dian in Tyrone—
Resolved to stand for life and land,
The Bible and the Throne.
—(Ulsterman's *Rise and Progress of Orangeism*, p. 5.)
A writer, commenting on the Diamond, observes that " the more correct account was that Orangeism began at Dian or Dyan, on Lord Caledon's estate in Tyrone. " The Lodge consisted merely of yeomen and a few respectable farmers of the middling rank of life, little imagining that it was to be the germ of so numerous and mighty a body, as the Orange Institution afterwards became."—(Hall's *Ireland*, vol. ii. p. 464.)

known as No. 1, and such names as Isaac Jelf, John and Abraham Dill, are associated with it. In Orange circles it was regarded as the parent Orange Boys Society. A little later, No. 2 Derryscollop was formed from the same source.[40]

(2) *The Orangeism of the Diamond.* The victors in the conflict met in James Sloan's hotel at Loughgall, and formed a very elementary association; the first numbers and the names of those who received them are, as far as are now known, given by Mr. Banks. We are told that the lodge met regularly in this hotel, until the Grand Lodge passed the resolution prohibiting hotels as lodgerooms.[41] "When the lodge was launched at Loughgall, it was necessarily the crudest possible form of organisation, and the only means of general consultation was that of a casual meeting of the officers and members on the occasions of Portadown fairs and markets." All the evidence accessible to us concurs in showing that the movement originated with the small Protestant farmers and tenantry. These sturdy sons of the soil refused to be overawed by the ruffianly bands that sought to terrorise and drive them from their holdings. As Sir Richard Musgrave put it, their union was highly creditable to them, inasmuch as they were "unsupported and unprotected by the great and the powerful, to whom their motives were misrepresented by traitors, who knew that the institution would form a firm barrier against their nefarious machinations."[42] The delegate from Canada to Ireland in 1897, said that Orangeism had taken hold of the Canadian community and was developing rapidly: "the very best people in the community belonged to these Orange Associations. . . . . The backbone of the Orange Association there, however, was the working men." The Hon. N. Clarke Wallace, another Canadian delegate, declared that "he came representing 2000 Orange Lodges and 150,000 stalwart Orangemen."[43] Mr. Froude tells us that the union of Ulster Protestants was engendered through "fear and exasperation."[44] He relates it thus —"Threatened now with a general Catholic insurrection, with the executive authority powerless, and determined at all events not to offer the throats of themselves, and their families, to the Catholic knife, they formed into a volunteer police to prevent murder."[45]

"THE ORANGE REIGN OF TERROR."

Father Cleary, in knitting up his Catholic theory of the identity of the Peep of Day Boys with Orangeism, steers pretty

---

40 *Ibid*, p. 18.   41 *Ibid*, p. 20.   42 *Memoirs*, vol. i. p. 70.
43 *Belfast Weekly*, July 17, 1897.   44 *Ireland*, vol. iii. p. 176.   45 *Ibid*, p. 177.

clear of our mutual friend Mr Lecky. A few loose statements made by that writer are carefully culled, which, however, do not substantially represent his opinion. The following quotations will more fairly, as well as more fully, indicate his position. (1) "The title of Orangeman was probably assumed by *numbers who had never joined the organisation*, who were simply Peep of Day Boys *taking a new name*, and whose conduct was certainly not such as those who instituted the Society *had intended*."[46] (2) He quotes a magistrate writing from Waringstown, in which he urged that a "distinction must be drawn between the Orangemen, who were simply *a loyal body enlisted for self defence*, and the depredators who had assumed the name."[47] (3) Lecky says the refugees in County Kerry avowed that they left for "fear of being destroyed by *the Presbyterians*."[48] Father Cleary, it will be remembered, holds the view that the original Orangemen were all of the Established Church. (4) Lecky quotes Mr. Cuffe's list as being "a very candid and temperate estimate" of the causes which led to the exodus of Catholics from the North to his locality. This magistrate judged that the exiles had been Defenders, and that their opponents, the Peep of Day Boys, had "become too powerful for them, and they therefore thought they would be happier in any other County."[49] (5) "The Catholics and the Presbyterians in the North had long confronted each other as two distinct and dissimilar nations, and the low standard of comfort which accompanied the inferior civilisation of the Catholics, enabling them to offer higher rents than the Protestants, gave them the advantage in the competition for farms. There had been, as I have already noticed, *a great displacement* of the Protestant, by the Catholic, element owing to this cause, and although it was not the immediate and direct motive of the disturbances, it no doubt intensified the animosity which difference of religion, difference of race, and great difference of civilisation had already produced."[50] (6) Lecky

---

46 *Ireland*, vol. iii. p, 428.   47 *Ibid*, pp. 435, 436.   48 *Ibid*, p. 442, Note.

49 *Ibid*, pp. 443, 444. Mr. Cuffe also remarked :—"Many of them owned to me candidly, that they had been *in fault in the beginning*."—(*Ibid*, p. 444.) Musgrave says concerning the Defenders who were expelled, "Their protectors had reason to repent of the reception which they gave them."—(*Memoirs*, vol. i. p. 68.)

50 *Ibid*, p. 445. Judge Morris is totally opposed to Father Cleary on the alleged Orange reign of terror. "Presbyterians and Catholics in Ireland had been at feud for ages wherever the populations had been intermixed. At this very period, two large factions—the *Presbyterian* Peep of Day Boys and the Catholic Defenders—were distracting whole counties by furious discord." He further says—"Hundreds, nay thousands, of the *Defenders* were driven from their homes and fled out of Ulster." In ascribing the expulsion to the Orange

takes the view that what he terms " Protestant retaliation " was carried on by Orangemen or by persons *assuming* that title, and by the dissenters—principally Presbyterians. Lord Camden spoke of the commotion as the "ill-conduct of the dissenters in Armagh." Again he wrote, a "party of dissenters, called Orangemen, keep up a system of terror at least, if not of outrage, in Armagh."[51] (7) Father Cleary presents what I have characterised as loose statements from Lecky. His quotations are three in number. One of them runs—"In another part of the same work, he (Lecky) states that the 'Orange disturbances' in Ulster in 1795 and 1796 'were a continuation, or revival, of the war between the Peep of Day Boys and the Defenders.'"[52] In this extract the Father's selective principle is applied. What Lecky says is this:—" It is plain I think that these disturbances, considered as a whole, cannot be regarded as *unprovoked*. They were a continuation or revival of the war between the Peep of Day Boys and the Defenders, which had raged furiously in Ulster for many years before the Orange Society was founded. The Defender movement had *long ceased to be a mere league for self defence*. It was distinctly treasonable, for it was intended to assist and provoke a French invasion : it was accompanied *by numerous and horrible outrages*, and in 1795 it had spread over 12 counties, or *more than a third part of Ireland*. It is also true that in the battle of the Diamond, which was *the immediate cause* of the Orange outbreak, *the Catholics were the aggressors.*"[53] I am obliged to Mr. Cleary for calling attention to this. The extracts I have advanced are indubitably more representative of the historian's real opinions, than the meagre three which the Rev. gentleman offers his readers as "reliable information." In a note, Mr. Lecky remarks:—" The later Orangemen have been extremely anxious to disclaim all connection with the outrages of 1795 and 1796, which they attribute wholly to the Peep of Day Boys. . . . . *It seems clear that the Society was originally founded with a defensive object*. On the other hand, the depredators called themselves, and were called by others— Orangemen, and the Peep of Day Boys rapidly merged into

---

men, he admits that they "*were backed by the great majority.*" Mr Morris is a County Court judge, and I think a Roman Catholic.—(*Ireland from '98 to '98*, pp. 17, 26.)

51 *Ireland*, vol. iii. pp. 445, 447, 448.   52 p. 60.

53 *Ireland*, vol. iii. p. 445. Musgrave informs us that the Defenders in Armagh County became so terrible, that the Protestants in Sego in 1795, afraid of being murdered, " would not venture to go to the market towns of Lurgan or Portadown unless they were well armed and in considerable numbers."—(*Memoirs*, vol. i. p. 69.)

Orangemen and ceased to exist as a separate body."[54] Father Cleary renders this in the following fashion: "He (Lecky) points out that 'the later Orangemen have been extremely anxious to disclaim all connection with the outrages of 1795 and 1796, which they attribute to the Peep o' Day Boys,' but, he adds, 'on the other hand, the depredators called themselves, and were called by others, Orangemen, and the Peep o' Day Boys rapidly merged into Orangemen and ceased to exist as a separate body.'"[55] In this passage Father Cleary deftly, if not honestly, cuts out the sentence—"*It seems clear that the Society was originally founded with a defensive object.*" Why this excision when the writer pointedly refers to the reliability of the information he gives? But I find that the Rev. gentleman saves his credit by a reservation; his chapters, "*as far as they go,*"[56] it is hoped, supply "reliable information." His omissions, therefore, are above comment, or beneath it.

In returning to the general question of the "Orange Reign of Terror," I wish to call attention to certain points in Father Cleary's account of it. (1) "What has come to be known as the Orange Reign of Terror began with the foundation of the first lodge in 1795."[57] (2) He quotes Lecky as saying that "a terrible persecution of the Catholics immediately followed the battle of the Diamond."[58] (3) On the 28th December, 1795, "about three months after" this battle, Lord Gosford's famous report of the Orange proscription was tendered in the presence of some "thirty of the leading Magistrates and Grand Jurors of the County of Armagh."[59] (4) Among the signatures to this report "are the names of those pioneers of Orangeism, James Verner, Stewart Blacker, and William Blacker."[60] (5) A letter from Lord Gosford to Secretary Pelham is put in by Father Cleary, in which the writer says that the Protestants declare "a fixed intention to exterminate their opponents." The father explains that Gosford is referring to the month of October, 1795—but a few weeks after the formation of the first Orange Lodge.[61] It appears to me that Mr. Cleary proves *too much*. In his anxiety to fasten certain characteristics upon the Orange Society, he destroys that plausibility which is the essential merit of his work. We are agreed on the point that the Orange Society was formed on the evening of September 21, 1795. In the nature of things—(1) The organisation was very primitive in its nature.[62]

54 *Ireland*, vol iii. pp. 428, 429. 55 p. 60. 56 p. x. 57 p. 71.
58 p. 71. 59 p. 72. 60 p. 73. 61 p. 66.
62 Hall tells us : —" In a short time several Lodges were formed with a regular

(2) The number of members, being largely known by name even yet, was small. (3) The opportunities for securing cohesion and extension were few. These points have been already shown. When, therefore, we consider the abilities of the people amongst whom the idea of association originated : the necessity of caution in enrolling members living in the midst of conspirators and Defenders : the work of unifying a people in secrecy, and spreading the lodge sentiment from its local centre to neighbouring towns and villages : the difficulty of producing a one-mindedness amongst a variety of persons at varying distances, and of bringing them into line for concerted and connected action—it will be seen that more than ordinary doubt attaches to the famous letter of Lord Gosford so far as the Orange Society is concerned. I select the following passages from Father Cleary's quotation :—
" It would be extremely painful and surely unnecessary to detail all the horrors that attended the execution of so wide and tremendous a proscription that certainly exceeds in the comparative number of those it consigns to ruin and misery, *every example that ancient and modern history can afford.* For where have we heard, and in what history of human cruelties have we read, of *more than half* the inhabitants of a populous county being deprived *at one blow* of the means as well as the fruits of their industry, and driven, in the midst of an inclement winter, to seek a shelter for themselves and their helpless families where chance may guide them."[63] This is Lord Gosford's picture on December 28, 1795, *three months* after the battle of the Diamond. Let us treat the account by analysis, and see how it works out. (1) Gosford says—"*More than half* the inhabitants of a populous county" (Armagh) were expelled. But the Father argues frequently, and it is such an important matter that he prints it in one place in italics, that the Catholics were a "*minority of the population* of Armagh County."[64] This is hobble No. 1. Gosford and Cleary cannot both be right, for they contradict each other. It is manifest that the Catholics could not, at the same time, constitute " more than half " the population of Armagh, and yet be in the "minority."

system of rules for their guidance. They consisted chiefly of persons in the humble ranks of life. . . . As none but Protestants were admitted, and most of these were *Presbyterians*, the Institution partook considerably of the religious character of that sect. United in a cause which they believed to be a holy one, they always commenced and concluded their meetings with Prayer, a custom which continued to be universally observed ever afterwards, though their other rules were, of course, modified and altered, when the management of the Institution came into the hands of more enlightened men."—(*Ireland*, vol. ii. p. 464.) It would puzzle the " Philadelphia lawyer " to reconcile all the floating theories of early Orangeism.

63 p. 72. 64 p. 71.

(2) Father Cleary says that the Catholics were an "*unresisting* minority." But Judge Morris and other writers, as I have already indicated, refer to those expelled as *Defenders*. From what has been advanced concerning these gentry, we can quite understand their peaceable nature. This is hobble No. 2. Are we not told by Mr. Cleary on the authority of Plowden, that three short months before the Defenders were under arms for three days challenging the Protestants to fight it out? But now the scene has changed, and we are asked to believe that these valiant warriors have become "unresisting" lambs. (3) If Gosford's picture is aimed at the Orange Society, as the Father evidently understands it to be, then we are to infer that a Society, only three months old, has grown into a formidable force, sweeping out the bulk of the people in the county where it arose, not by degrees, but "*at one blow.*" This is hobble No. 3. Allowing a liberal scale of increase in the Association, it is still difficult to conceive how "so wide and tremendous a proscription," as the expulsion "of more than half the inhabitants of a populous county," could have been effected by what must have been at biggest but a mere *fraction* of the whole. (4) With a curious disregard of probability the Father mentions that Lord Gosford's report is signed by those "pioneers of Orangeism James Verner, Stewart Blacker, and William Blacker." Surely the fact of these signatures prick the bubble so far as the Orange Society is concerned? Is it in reason to suppose (if this Report pointed at their Society) they would foul their own nest, and sign a document to put a blot upon Orangeism at its very origin? As a matter of fact Verner defended the Society in Parliament from the attacks of Grattan and Curran. Mr. Banks says that Gen. Sir Thomas Molyneux, who was in charge of the troops stationed at Armagh at the time, wrote a letter to the press about 1835, challenging proof that the disturbances were caused by the Orangemen. It is significant that nobody undertook the demonstration. The letter was never answered.[65] Only when the Society became a distinct obstruction to the designs of a powerful and truculent body, was it found convenient to attack its character by accusations of the description quoted by Father Cleary. Sir Richard Musgrave puts the case keenly when he says: "I have observed that the disaffected who arraigned with the utmost severity the Orange Society *never uttered any censure* on the committees of assassination to which so many loyal men fell a sacrifice."[66] He offers as a

---

65 *Hist. Orange Order*, p. 22, 23.   66 *Memoirs* vol. i. p. 70.

reason for the abuse showered upon the Orangemen, the fact that the Lodge was "resisting the progress and contributing to defeat the aims of confederated traitors."[67] Musgrave also shows how the organisation as it grew was protected from degenerating into a squalid faction :—" Lest its members, roused by wanton and unprovoked outrages, might have been stimulated to retaliate, and from retaliation to committing excesses, gentlemen highly respectable not only by birth and fortune, but by moral excellence put themselves at its head to regulate its methods, whose characters alone were sufficient to refute the many falsehoods and calumnies uttered against the Institution."[68] It is further contended by the same writer (" that the Orange Association should not be confused, as it has often invidiously been, with the mutual and disgraceful outrages which prevailed in the County of Armagh many years preceding, between the lowest class of Presbyterians under the denomination of Peep of Day Boys, and the Roman Catholics as Defenders : for it was not instituted till the Defenders manifested their hostile designs against Protestants *of every description in most parts of the kingdom.*"[69] Mr. Lecky in noticing the outbreak of hostilities coincident with the founding of the Orange Lodge accounts for it in this way :—" The animosities between the lower orders burst out afresh, and after the battle of the Diamond the *Protestant rabble* of the County of Armagh, and of parts of the adjoining Counties determined by continuous outrages to drive the Catholics from the country."[70] And in summarising the cause of the disturbances as I have already mentioned he declares :—" *It is plain I think that these disturbances considered as a whole cannot be regarded as unprovoked.* They were a continuation or revival of the war between the Peep of Day Boys and the Defenders, which had raged fiercely in Ulster for *many years before* the Orange Society was founded."[71] Froude's narrative of this matter is, as usual, powerfully put. His paragraphs are not pleasant reading for those who imagine that the Defenders were an inoffensive body of Catholics. "The massacre of 1641 had not yet been resolved into legend by steady lying and sentimental credulity. It reminaed in the memory of every Irish Protestant a definite and dreadful fact which might recur if opportunity served: in Armagh and Antrim especially the small Protestant farmers combined in fear and exasperation to disarm the Catholics settled among them-

---

67 *Ibid*, p. 71. 68 *Ibid*, p. 71. 69 *Ibid*, p. 73. 70 Vol. iii. p. 429. 71 *Ibid*, p. 445.

selves: and at last when nothing else would serve—to expel them out of Ulster, and force them to return to the South.[72] The friends of liberty made the air ring with eloquent shrieks. Protestant girls might be ravished. Protestant farmers and gentry might be murdered. No matter. It was but punishment overtaking tyranny. When a Catholic was injured by a Protestant, the very heart of humanity was invited to bleed. To such persons it did not occur to inquire why the Catholics who were forbidden to possess arms were in such haste to obtain them. But the question occurred very strongly to the Protestants in the midst of whom these persons were living. When they found that they were confronted with a conspiracy which was enveloping the Island, they resolved naturally that they would not be caught sleeping a second time. If they were rough, violent, and unscrupulous the blame lay most with those who had brought Ireland into incipient rebellion."[73] In bringing this chapter to a close, I am not bringing the matters of which it treats to a conclusion. More has to be said in the succeeding one when the Rebellion of 1798 is under consideration. Whatever part the Orange Society played in the Armagh displacement of Roman Catholics in 1796, it is pretty certain that for the last three months of 1795, when it was in its swaddling clothes, it would be incapable of doing the terrific damage ascribed to it. Let those who think otherwise pause and consider the matter. On what hypothesis can it be conceived that an organisation in its birth hour, would possess the power to do the mischief set out in Lord Gosford's report—a mischief said to outrival "*every example that ancient and modern history can afford*"? Either this is a bit of rhetoric, or we must conjecture that the expulsion was due to a sympathetic combination of Protestants, of all sects, harassed by the Defenders, and exasperated by conspirators, rather than to a wanton persecution of Catholics by an abnormal infant called the Orange Society.

---

72 Walpole says the Protestants "set on foot a counter-organisation to Defenderism forming themselves into associations called Orange Lodges, and demanding an oath of secrecy from all who were enrolled. . . . It declared war against the Defenders and *openly professed* as its object the complete expulsion of all Roman Catholics from Ulster."—(*Short Hist.*, p. 456.)

Walpole evidently does not favor the view that Orangeism is the *development* of Peep of Day Boyism; neither does he represent Defenderism at this stage as a *defensive* league. There is not any documentary declaration extant to support his statement that the Orange Lodge "*openly professed* as its object the complete expulsion of *all* Roman Catholics from Ulster," that I know of, and Father Cleary does not know of any or else he would have had it in his book: I am disposed to think that Walpole is here repeating the old legend.

Ireland, vol. iii. p. 176-177.

CHAPTER VIII.

THE REBELLION OF 1798.—THE TAIL OF THE ARMAGH TROUBLES.
—JUSTIN M'CARTHY V. FATHER CLEARY.—A CLOUD ON IRELAND.—TONE ON THE POPE AND IRISH PRIESTS.—THE DEEPENING OF THE CLOUD.—WHAT MERVYN ARCHDALL SAID.—COMMITTEE OF ASSASSINATION.—HOW THE ORANGEMEN CAME IN.
—THE BOGUS OATH OF EXTERMINATION.—LYING RUMOURS.—
CAMDEN AND THE ORANGEMEN, MARCH, 1798.

THE Attorney-General, introducing a measure in 1796 to the Irish Parliament for the repression of conspiracy to murder, said—" Assassination had become as familiar as fowling."[1] In the debate upon this Coercion Bill Mr. Grattan's oft quoted speech was made. Froude described it in this way—" More prudent, more plausible than Fitzgerald, Mr. Grattan made a counter-attack upon the Orangemen."[2] In this celebrated utterance, Grattan admitted that the Attorney-General " did indeed expatiate very fully and justly on the offences of the Defenders, but with respect to another description of insurgents . . . . he had observed a complete silence." With respect to the outrages in Armagh, Grattan had *heard* that their object " was the extermination of all the Catholics of that County : it was a persecution conceived in the bitterness of bigotry, carried on with the most ferocious barbarity, by a banditti, who being of the Religion of the State, had committed, with the greater audacity and confidence, the most horrid murders," &c.[3] The speaker added that these insurgents called themselves " Orange Boys or Protestant Boys."[4] Mr. Vandeleur wished "some allusion had been made

---

1 Froude's *Ireland*, vol. iii. p. 194. The Attorney-General would not, he said, go back any further in Defender atrocities than the year 1790. "The object of the Defenders then was to plunder the peaceable inhabitants in that County (Meath) of their firearms : they associated together and bound themselves by the solemn tie of an oath. The Defenders, it had since appeared, had their Committee Men and their Captains, whom they were bound to obey, and their object was to overthrow the established order of Government. . . . To repress these disturbances the efforts of Government were exerted in 1790, 1791, and 1792. . . . . These wretches associated together by night for the purpose of plunder, murder, and devastation. To prevent witnesses appearing against them on trial they had adopted a system of assassination." Grattan admitted that he "had heard the Right Honorable gentleman's statement, and *did not suppose it to be inflamed.*"—(Wright's *Ireland*, vol. ii. pp. 596, 597.)

2 Froude's *Ireland*, vol. iii. p. 194.   3 Wright's *Ireland*, vol. ii. p. 597.
4 *Ibid*, p. 598.

to the outrages of the Peep o' Day Boys, which were certainly as reprehensible as those of the Defenders."⁵ Froude says Curran followed "clamoring that 1400 Catholic families had been expelled from their homes in Armagh."⁶ There appears to be, even in 1796, some confusion about the identity of the Armagh party of expulsion, among public men. Grattan calls them—Orange Boys or Protestant Boys: and Vandeleur—Peep o' Day Boys. Mr. Verner, presumably the same Magistrate who had signed Lord Gosford's Report in 1795, related the position of the Orange Society in reply to Grattan and Curran. He said:—"The number of the expelled had been enormously exaggerated: that the Orangemen were a very loyal body, and that the outrages they had no doubt committed (sic) had been committed under great provocation. The Catholics in 1795 had systematically attempted to deprive the Protestants of their arms: *they had assembled together in their own language 'to destroy man, woman and child of them'*: they had treacherously attacked them in the battle of the Diamond, and they had been beaten in open fight. Many, he said, who fled had been active in the Defender disturbances : and others had gone with the idea of getting cheap land in the West. These persons sold the interests of their farms at a high price, and emigrated to the West at the instance of persons who had large tracts of waste land, and employed agents to invite people to take farms from them."⁷ The confusion of names for existing

---

5 *Ibid*, p. 597.

6 *Ireland*, vol. iii. p. 195.

Lecky also says—"According to some reports, which were no doubt *grossly exaggerated*, no less than 1400 families, or about 7000 persons, were driven out of the County of Armagh alone. Another and *much more probable account* spoke of 700 families." He quotes a paper by Mr. Alexander, of Boragh, dated November, 1896, which contended that the alleged outrages "had been grossly exaggerated, and he believed that the number of families driven from the County of Armagh was less than 200 : that the stories of rapes and mutilations perpetrated by Protestants were totally untrue ; and that exclusive of those who fell in the battle of the Diamond only about six lives had been lost." He substantially corroborates Mr. Verner's statement, and adds—"The name of Orangeman had been frequently assumed by a plundering banditti, composed of all denominations, whose sole object was robbery." Mr. Lecky, however, says that Mr. Alexander's paper cannot compete with the authority of Lord Gosford and other Magistrates, but it appears to me impossible to reconcile Lecky's view that the "*much more probable account* spoke of 70C families" being driven out of Armagh County alone, and Lord Gosford's statement about the depopulation of "*more than half the inhabitants of a populous county.*"—(*Ireland in the 18th Century*, vol. iii. pp. 428, 432, &c.)

7 *Ireland*, vol. iii. p. 438.

Froude in his third volume supplements Lecky's report of Verner's address. "In some instances they (Orangemen) had acted improperly, but not till they had been *goaded beyond the forbearance of human nature.*"(—*Irish Debates*, 1796.)

organisations is one chief feature in the historical records to which we have access at this time. The generic term, Orangeman, was applied indiscriminately to all Protestant bodies which actively opposed Catholic combinations; and in this way the Boyne Society, that arose on the night of the battle of the Diamond, and was subsequently called the Orange Society, is saddled with all the floating odium attaching to the name of Orangeman, in party documents and newspapers, during the troubled period in which it emerged. Mr. Lecky tells us that the battle of the Boyne had been annually celebrated by Irish people "long before the Orange Society existed."[8] Mr. Froude is in agreement with this:—"The name of Orangemen had long existed. It had been used by loyal Protestants to designate those who adhered most faithfully to the principles of 1688."[9] Mr. Lecky in a passage of remarkable clearness separates loose designation and explicit organisation, and in leaving the Armagh "reign of terror," I commend it to Father Cleary as a model of discrimination in the use of terms for the purpose of identification. "The terror inspired by the Orangemen was extreme. As the Armagh *depredators had taken that name,* their outrages were naturally regarded as *the deliberate acts of the Society*, which was now said to be intended for the extermination of the Catholics, and to have embodied this object in its secret oath. *Of this charge no evidence has been adduced. The Society in its first conception was essentially defensive,* and at a later period when many respectable country gentlemen joined *they solemnly declared that no such oath had been taken by its members.* But the *false report* had struck too deep a root to be eradicated, and the United Irishmen very skilfully put themselves forward as the champions of the oppressed."[10] This is the explanation of the whole matter. Some reason has to be invented to account for the Roman Catholics—priests and people—joining the United Irishmen movement with its low and negative Religious tone, and some excuse discovered for the conspicuous part which that denomination took in "the 53rd Rebellion of hatred to England."[11] It is found in the determined attempt to blacken and villify the Orange Society. Every rancorous calumny afloat, every exaggerated rumour,

---

These no doubt are Verner's own words which Mr. Lecky has made to read— "That the outrages they had no doubt committed, had been committed under great provocation."

8 *Ireland*, vol. iii. p. 427. 9 *Ireland*, vol. iii. p. 177.
10 *Ireland*, vol. iii. pp. 448-449. (See letters of Gosford and Knox, p. 437.)
11 Martin's *Ireland before and after the Union*, p. 27.

every malicious fiction, every confusion in party names—is caught up, passed into printed form, and made the heritage and storehouse for future generations to draw upon when attacking Orangeism. Looking up certain information in the Melbourne Public Library I picked out a volume of pamphlets called *The Anti-Union*, published in the interests of the Irish Legislature. In one of these, dated December 27, 1798, under the title "*Lies of the Week*," occurs the following: " The Orangemen attacked the Catholics in Clarendon-st. Chapel on Christmas Day." In the following number, December 27, 1798, "*A Query for Casuists*," is a conundrum which indicates the state of opinion in the year of the Rebellion. " Dr. McKenna's pamphlet argues that an Union is necessary to protect *the Catholics from the Orangemen*. The pamphlet ' Union or Not,' by an Orangeman, argues that an Union is necessary to protect *the Orangemen from the Catholics*. The pamphlet attributed to the Editor argues that an Union is necessary for *both the above purposes*. Query—which of the th ree arguments is true ?" If, therefore, during the commotion of the time such conflicting views prevailed, how much greater di fficulty lies now in the way of obtaining a satisfactory account of all phases of the question ? However, if Mr. Justin McCarthy m y be regarded as of any authority on the question of the extent and power of the Orange Society, during the period when it was supposed by Father Cleary to be expelling " more than half the inhabitants of a populous County," and generally revelling in an Orange carnival or " Reign of Terror "—then Mr. McCarthy simply *extinguishes* Cleary. After recounting the institution of the Lodge, Mr. McCarthy goes on to say—"*For some time the Society made but little progress, and it was not until after the passing of the Act of Union* (1800) *that it began to make sensible advances in number and in influence.*"[12] According to this account, Orangeism as an organisation, was nothing of consequence as a practical factor in Irish life and politics, until some *five* years after its institution. But then Mr. McCarthy had not read Father Cleary's book.

A Cloud on Ireland.

Cardinal Moran has styled Ireland the "Island of Saints." Its historians have recorded events which to say the least indicate that the "Saints" are not so numerous as to jostle one another, and that sufficient room is left for a considerable deposit of

---

12 *Ireland since the Union*, p. 78.

sinners, whose deeds rather overshadow the gorgeous panegyric which the Cardinal scatters broadcast. The memory of 1798 is not one to commend this idealistic view to Protestants, though it may have added some names to what Mr Froude calls "the roll of Irish Martyrology." The rebellion has been attributed to various causes. Father Cleary with exceptional cleverness discovers it was all due to Pitt's policy and the Orange Society. Whatever dubiousness may be entertained with respect to Mr. Pitt, he allows no uncertainty respecting the Orangemen. "The Lords Justices of 1641," remarked Mr. Froude, "were accused of having permitted the Rebellion to break out when they foresaw it coming, as an excuse for spoliation and confiscation. Lord Camden was accused of provoking the Rebellion of 1798 by using force to disarm a population who were preparing, *without concealment*, for open insurrection."[13] There is no satisfying some people. Mr Lecky notices that the revolutionary movement of the United Irishmen in its earlier stages existed mainly among the Protestants of the North, and that "the Belfast principle" was largely Presbyterian, but he points out that "the fierce revival of Religious animosity was a fatal obstacle to that co-operation of Protestants and Catholics for the purposes of revolution which it was the object of the United Irishmen to produce." The Defender organisation "owed its origin to religious animosities, and consisted exclusively of the most ignorant Catholics."[14] When a union was compassed by the United Irishmen with the Defenders, Lecky declares that "great bodies took the oath, and were incorporated. . . . The most turbulent Catholic element in Ireland thus passed into it, and its introduction into the Catholic *militia* regiments was greatly facilitated."[15] The Presbyterians, however, were soon seen to be opposed to the schemes of the United Irish party, which had absorbed the forces of Defenderism. A letter by Mr. Buchanan in 1796 brings out this fact. He mentions that after Divine Service he had been addressing a meeting of nearly 2000 Presbyterians on the necessity of forming Volunteer Corps, in order to resist the French, and also the Belfast principle. "The strongest spirit of loyalty, he says, prevailed among them : hatred of the Roman Catholics

---

13 *Ireland*, vol. iii. p. 272.   14 *Ireland*, vol. iii. p. 486.

15 *Ibid*, p. 486. The Bishop of Killala gives evidence that the landing of the French at Castlebar had been promoted by "treason" in the *militia*. He mentioned that 53 men from the Longford militia came in "with their coats turned," and it was reported that 80 more deserted from the Longford and Kilkenny militia. He also shows how the rebels kept the Protestants in constant terror.— (Wright's *History of Ireland*, vol. iii. pp. 131, 132.)

is very great, so much so that should one be admitted in any corps they declared they never would join with them, as a *spirit of Defenderism and revenge* exists in that body against administration. This violent change has been wrought within the year—a change fraught with the best consequences to our King and Constitution."[16] The avowed religious sentiments of Wolfe Tone, the founder of the United Irishmen movement, were of such a character that whilst extreme Protestants—Orangemen for instance—might have united with him; it would be thought that the traditional veneration of the Irish Catholics for their religion would have been thereby repelled. In 1796 he said respecting the Pope—" I am heartily glad that old priest is at last laid under contribution in his turn. Many a long century he and his predecessors have been fleecing all Europe, but the day of retribution is come at last, and I am strongly tempted to hope that this is but the beginning of his sorrows."[17] This was his expression when the Pontiff was conquered by the armies of the Revolution. It was Tone also who spoke of " the Irish properly so called " as being " trained from their infancy in an hereditary hatred and abhorrence of the English name."[18] He declared of the Irish Catholics that " their own priests fleece them."[19] And yet he was keen enough, whilst professing such sentiments, to see the open door through which the Catholics would enter the revolutionary movement. " The Defender organisation has

16 Lecky's *Ireland*, vol. iii. pp. 439, 440. This is enough to discredit Tone's assertion of *reconciliation* between Presbyterian Peep of Day Boys and Defenders. Herr Venedey, referring to the displacement of Presbyterian tenants by Roman Catholic ones, because of the latter offering higher rents, remarks :—" The immediate consequence was that a very considerable number of the Presbyterian farmers and tenantry, who had been ' United Irishmen,' deserted that body and joined the Orangemen. It was as such that they took part against the insurgents in 1798 and 1803, and from *that time to the present* have participated in all the Orange festivals, and in every conflict between the Orangemen and the Catholics. With the progress of time they have estranged themselves still more and more from the exertions and feelings of the Irish." He also adds that this union with Orangeism was proved beyond a doubt in the enquiry of 1835, and indicates the evidence of Sharman Crawford and others as furnishing the necessary demonstration.—(*Ireland and the Irish*, 1843, pp. 300, 301.) Father Cleary on p. 89 informs his readers " that the Presbyterians as a body have *never been in sympathy* with the Orange movement in Ireland."

17 Lecky, vol. iii. p. 512.   18 *Ibid*, p. 513.

19 *Ibid*, p. 514. In December, 1792, Tone went to London "with the celebrated deputation which the Catholic Committee had sent direct to the Sovereign, in order to mark most effectually *their distrust and hatred* of the Irish Administration." At the *end of that year* the United Irishmen were organised "into an armed body, and they had called it the *National Guard*." The Catholic Relief Act of 1793 was "*part of a series of precautionary measures* " to meet this imminent danger.—(The Duke of Argyll in *The Nineteenth Century*, June 1890, p. 1003.)

already prepared the way: it includes the great body of the Catholic peasantry in Ulster, Leinster, and Connaught, and is spreading through Munster."[20] Father Cleary has given too little credit to the conspicuous success of Defenderism in Ireland ; he has made it appear that they were a milk and water body. whose only merit consisted in being what their name implies But facts are too strong to be resisted. They called into existence the Orange Society with all its power for good or ill ; they alienated the great body of the Presbyterians from the United Ireland movement; and they put into that movement the most powerful Catholic element of turbulence when they joined it. Mr. Lecky, besides these facts, shows how corrupting their influence was on justice. In 1796 the crimes of the United Irishmen and Defenders multiplied alarmingly—especially the murder of informers. Cooke sent Pelham two long lists of the most recent on July 27th of this year. "A Derry jury, adds Cooke, in terminating the dismal catalogue, acquitted a man clearly proved guilty of administering oaths. The other Crown prosecutions in Derry are put off."[21] On August 24th a magistrate wrote from Tyrone,—since the Derry Assizes, "where all the United Irishmen were tried and acquitted, everyone that will not instantly join that set is threatened with destruction. God knows how and when this will terminate. No man will pay a penny of debt so sure are they of an immediate rising."[22] And yet another magistrate wrote from Dromore—"The Protestants about me bordering on the County of Antrim are in a most horrid panic about those United people rising. They absolutely dare hardly go to bed at night and never without a watch. They tell me plainly that they expect every night to be murdered."[23] Lord Castlereagh after a journey through Ulster expressed his horror at the "infernal system" which prevailed of "murdering witnesses." If the Orange Society had not learned the secrets of partyism thoroughly, all blame might be lifted from the Defenders and the United Irishmen. Father Cleary accuses Orangeism of corrupting justice, screening the guilty &c., but he did not say one word of the abundant object lessons in this kind of thing which thronged round its cradle, and amazed the eyes of its babyhood. Strange too, that the Rev. gentleman with all his apparent candour, does not allow even a hint to escape him, that such shocking depravities were common occurrences at the time Orangeism was cutting its first tooth. I will not do him the injustice to suppose he was unconscious that this was

---

20 Lecky, vol. iii. p. 214. 21 *Ibid*, p 457. 22 *Ibid*, p. 464. 23 *Ibid*, p. 465.

the case ; a man who quotes over 100 different authorities and many of them Protestant ones, could hardly fail to be impressed with this prominent feature. To be sure he was writing down the Orange Society, but some measure of fairness would not have weakened his essay : it would have rather strengthened its plausibility. His Orangemen are a set of malignants, whose conduct is so utterly unexplainable within the covers of his book, that one must go further afield to discover that they have sentiments and feelings in common with the human species : and that they are not, as represented, a class illustrative of spontaneous devilism, or continuous imbecility. Lord Camden was advised to deal gently with the powers conferred upon him by the Insurrection Act, and the unhappy Administrator replied—" How *without* severity " he was to deal with murders, threats of murder, plundering and sacking houses, waylaying and wounding soldiers, &c., he was for his " part at a loss to comprehend."[24] The Orange Society, cradled in this atmosphere, was, under necessity, induced to act at times determinedly, but to represent strong defensive measures as typical of Orangeism in a normal state, is as misleading as to judge the general humanity of our soldiers by depicting their actions under the stress of war. Acts must be taken in connection with their circumstances, if a sound judgment is to be formed upon them. Mr. Froude gives the following extracts from a letter posted on the door of a *Catholic Chapel* at Nenagh, November 1st, 1797, which Lord Camden sent over to the Duke of Portland. They will serve to show how the Orange Society was malignantly misrepresented so that the purposes of the United Irishmen might be advanced. " While the honest United Irishmen were grasped with the iron hand of ferocity and cruelty, the infamous Orangemen who thirsted after blood and murder, were caressed and encouraged by the heavenly Government." " That the Orangemen had sworn to be true to the King and Government, and to destroy the Catholics of Ireland." " That an Orangeman had invented a toast—' That the skins of the Papists should be drumheads for the yeomanry,' and that the framer of that toast had been appointed secretary at the Castle."[25] These stories were accepted as truth, says Froude, " reported in the papers, and gained credit even in England." In a letter to Mr. Pitt, the distracted Pelham expressed himself as inclined to proceed to England to drag " before the English Parliament the situation in which the Castle was placed. He was deterred by fear of exasperating further the bitterness be-

---

24 Froude's *Ireland*, vol. iii. p. 217.   25 *Ibid*, p. 314.

tween the two Countries." Lord Camden said that only "*dreary familiarity* with the details of outrage and cruelty prevented every one of his despatches from being filled with accounts of murders of magistrates, assassinations of informers and yeomen, and conspiracies against persons of rank."[26] These letters are dated November 2nd and November 15th respectively.

THE DEEPENING OF THE CLOUD.

In 1796, after Grattan and Ponsonby on conciliatory measures towards the Roman Catholics had been heavily defeated, the former by 149 votes to 12, and the latter by 137 to 7, out of a house of 161 members, Mervyn Archdall said :—" It has come to this: in 1793 the Catholics were to be eternally grateful for admission to the franchise: they say now, 'admit us to Parliament, and we will not thank you, refuse and we will rebel.' "[27] Though the United Irish movement originally contemplated a purely political strife, and endeavoured to unite Protestant and Catholic in one combination to procure it, yet in Parliamentary circles the conviction had early obtained footing that the struggle would be speedily distinguished by religious prejudices. Edmund Burke regarded the United Irish movement as one of the " greatest calamities " that could have befallen the country : he declared that "Great Britain would be ruined by the separation of Ireland : but as there are degrees even in ruin it would fall the most heavily on Ireland. By such a separation Ireland would be the most completely undone country in the world: the most wretched, the most distracted, and in the end the most desolate part of the habitable globe."[28] Without raising the question of separation, Burke's view of the movement in itself receives ample confirmation from the pages of Lecky's work. A letter from Camden to Portland on March 9th, 1798 is termed " a very important letter to the Government in England." In this despatch the Viceroy says " the most outrageous and systematic murders have been committed in the Counties of Down and Donegal. A farmer had been murdered for having joined the Yeomanry and many others had been obliged by terror to resign their posts in that body. He mentioned the murder of Dr. Hamilton and added that it was the system of the United Irishmen to prevent the Magistrates from acting and the yeomen from assembling. Several districts, on the requisition of the Magistrates, had been placed under the Insurrection Act, and there was almost an unanimous voice in the country that no

---

26 *Ibid*, p. 315.   27 *Ibid*, p. 209.   28 Lecky's *Ireland*, vol. iv. p. 164.

mild measures could eradicate the disease. . . . . If, he adds, the urgency of the case demands a conduct beyond that which can be sanctioned by the law, the general has orders from me not to suffer the cause of justice to be frustrated by the delicacy which might possibly have actuated the magistracy."[29] But previous to this the Viceroy had said in the month of January, 1797 — "A system of terror had been established" in Ulster. "The Orangemen had been severely checked in deference to Grattan's clamors. The disaffected peasants and artisans had gathered courage from the suppression of the only body whom they really feared, and assassination became the law of the province. Murder had followed murder."[30] Froude gives us an awfully vivid picture of the murders of Dr. Hamilton, the crippled Mr. Waller and his brave wife, to which Lord Camden made reference in his letter above quoted. The alarming state of the country was indicated in the official letter of instructions written by Pelham on March 3rd for the guidance of General Lake. In this letter it was pointed out that secret treasonable associations existed in the Counties Down, Antrim, Derry, and Donegal " attempting to defeat by terror the exertions of the well disposed, and threatening the lives of all who gave any evidence against the seditious." There was a constant succession of meetings and drillings by night : peaceable inhabitants were disarmed : the magistrates were openly defied : many kinds of outrage were practised. Vast stores of arms had been collected and stored in convenient places : numbers of trees had been cut down for making the formidable pike : lead in great quantities had been stolen for bullets : and many men had been prevented by intimidation from joining the Yeomanry. They boycotted those who would not be intimidated, and "they not only threaten but ill-treat the persons of the Yeomanry, and even attack their homes by night and proceed to the barbarous extremity of deliberate and shocking murder, and they profess a resolution to assist the enemies of his majesty if they should be enabled to land in this Kingdom."[31] Dean Warburton wrote about this time—"The game is nearly up in the North. No juries, no prosecutions, no evidence against any person under the denomination of a United Man : the men of property and Clergy

---

29 *Ibid*, p. 18. 30 Froude's *Ireland*, vol. iii. p. 268.

It is related that the Down insurgents commanded by Dr. Jackson beside other outrages—" set fire to the house of a farmer named McKee, who had been an informer of treasonable meetings, and burnt his family of eleven persons, with circumstances of great cruelty."—(Wright's *History of Ireland*, vol. iii. p. 91.)

31 Lecky's *Ireland*, vol. iv. p. 19.

completely alarmed, and instead of residence are flying away
into garrison towns; the mobs plundering every gentleman's
house. . . . Threatening letters especially breathing vengeance against any juryman who convicted a United Irishman,
were industriously circulated, and they were completely successful. Neither in Monaghan nor in Armagh would any jury in
such cases convict. A system of terror was triumphant. It is
impossible to give you an idea of how ferociously savage the
people have become in these parts."[32] A Magistrate wrote—
" You can have no idea of the terror that pervades the whole
country." In the district where Dr. Hamilton was butchered,
the insurgents were everywhere, " but no evidence could be procured. The fear of assassination has so thoroughly got possession of the minds of the people."[33] These are only samples of
what generally prevailed. I need not multiply cases of the
kind. A rumor gained currency that by a certain date no
further members would be admitted to the United Irish ranks,
and all who were outside the body on that date would be summarily disposed of; this brought multitudes of hesitating souls
speedily in. There were persistent stories of a French Invasion,
and these evidently inspired and believed by the leaders of the
movement. In the letters of the Bishop of Clogher it is stated
--" The insurgents now go about in numerous gangs, swearing,
plundering, burning, maiming. . . . Well meaning people,
more especially those of the Established Church, [are] literally
dragooned into revolt. . . . Nor can anyone form an adequate idea of the wanton violence, outrage, and brutality which
prevail. Every morning a fresh list of outrages is reported.
. . The seduction of the military was steadily pursued, and
there were great doubts about the loyalty of the Yeomanry."[34]
Mr. Lecky says—" Disarming had plainly become a matter of
the first necessity at a time when a great portion of the population were organising, at the command of a seditious conspiracy
for the purpose of co-operating with an expected French invasion, and it could hardly be carried out in Ireland without exces-
sive violence." Whilst the historian has animadverted upon the
harsh measures employed to prevent the insurrection by taking
arms from those suspected of intending to use them disloyally,
and has condemned the military excesses which operated in
carrying this plan into effect, he thinks there is much which
explains and largely palliates these misdeeds, and at least divides
the blame.[35] The correspondence of Brigadier General Knox is

---
32 *Ibid.* pp. 31, 32.   33 *Ibid*, p 33.   34 *Ibid*, pp. 34, 35.   35 *Ibid*, p. 39.

drawn upon by Mr. Lecky for the purpose of giving "the judgment of an honest and very able man about the state of feeling in Ulster." Knox wrote that in Down, Antrim, Derry, and parts of Donegal and Tyrone the whole people were ill-disposed and should be disarmed: but in Armagh, Cavan, Monaghan, Fermanagh and part of Tyrone "a proportion of the people are hostile to the United Irishmen, particularly those calling themselves Orangemen."[36] Knox seemed to have a rather good opinion of this class, for he says—"Were the Orangemen disarmed or put down, or were they coalesced with the other party, the whole of Ulster would be as bad as Down and Antrim." He writes again that Mr. Verner could enrol a considerable number of men as "supplementary yeomen, to be attached to his corps *without pay*, if Government would give them arms. They would consist of staunch Orangemen, *the only description of men in the North of Ireland who can be relied upon.* He reckons upon two or three hundred."[37] Pelham was advised from other quarters to make use of the Orangemen. It was urged, says Mr. Lecky, that "the Armagh Orangemen might be organised into a new Fencible Corps: that their loyalty was incontestable: and that if they were not armed they would be in much danger in case of an insurrection."[38] Gen. Lake's testimony at this time was somewhat brief, but very much to the point—"The system of terror practised by the United Irishmen had completely destroyed all ideas of exertion in most of the magistrates and gentry throughout the country."[39] There was doubtless some force, therefore, in the representations of those who desired to interpose the Orangemen as a buffer between the terrorists and the Government, but the administration hardly knew in whom to place its trust. Its militia was corrupted, so was its yeomanry: and Grattan's fierce invectives had prejudiced the name of Orangemen. The authorities, upon the information of an informer named Newell, seized two whole committees of the United Irishmen at Belfast, consisting of about 40 persons. A number of important papers was discovered which disclosed the organisation, objects, and extent of the Society. 72,000 were enrolled in Ulster. Newell told more than was made public through Parliament. "His most startling statement was that he had himself been one of a secret committee of 12 members, which was formed for the purpose of assassinating members of the Society who were suspected of having betrayed it to the Government. . . . Newell mentioned that he had known of the

---

36 *Ibid*, p. 51.   37 *Ibid*, p. 52.   38 *Ibid*, p. 53.   39 *Ibid*, p. 60.

assassination of several persons, and had himself been present when a soldier was first made drunk and then flung over a bridge near Belfast with weights in his pockets." Dr. Madden questions the information given by Newell, but Mr. Lecky declares—" It is certain that assassinations and threats of assassination constantly accompanied the United Irish movement, but it was *pretended* that these were isolated instances of private vengeance, provoked by the severities of the troops and of the Government."[40]

How the Orangemen came in.

We have already been made acquainted with the outrages which brought the Orange Society into existence to meet a desperate confederation. Since its rise there were stirring events in connection with the United Irish movement which made the Lodge as a loyal centre more and more an object for destruction ; and if open violence did not destroy it, then shameless and profligate lying should swear away its character. It was attacked by the midnight assassin with knife and bludgeon, but it was also assailed by the stiletto of calumny ; one danger can be met and its danger passes with the occasion, but the other lives on and gains strength with the progress of the years. It is thus that Father Cleary is so profuse concerning the Orange Society in its alleged relation to provoking, quelling, and finally stamping out the embers of the rebellion. Still, Lecky has much to advance which, with all his copiousness of quotation from this source, my Rev. friend carefully avoids : whatever admissions are made, are made grudgingly and belittled.

Mr. Froude tells us that the small Protestant farmers of the North formed into a Volunteer police " to prevent murder, to see the law put in force which forbade the Catholics to be armed ; and to awe into submission the roving bands of assassins, who were scaring sleep from the bedside of every Protestant household. They became the abhorrence of traitors whose designs they thwarted. The Government looked askance at a body of men who interfered with the time honored policy of overcoming sedition by tenderness and soft speech. But the Lodges grew and multiplied. Honest men of all ranks sought admission to them as into spontaneous Vigilance Committees, to supply the place of the constabulary which ought to have existed, but did not, and if they did their work with some roughness and irregularity, the work nevertheless was done. In 1797 they could

---

40 *Ibid*, pp. 79, 80.

place 20,000 men at the disposition of the authorities. In 1798 they filled the ranks of the Yeomanry: beyond all other influences the Orange Organisation counteracted and thwarted the progress of the United Irishmen in Ulster, and when the moment of danger arrived *it had broken the right arm of insurrection.*"[41] Mr. Lecky, however, deals with the subject more in detail, and perhaps as Mr. Cleary is generally enamoured of him, it may be more congenial to have treatment from his pen rather than from that of the detested Froude, who he tells us is "a fashionable preacher gone wrong." Lecky, in noticing the growing importance of the Orange movement, does not in this as clearly depict the difference between the nebulous Orangeism of the North and that of the Orange Society freshly organised, as he does in some passages: and his statements here must be taken in the light of numerous discriminating expositions in other portions of his work. He refers to Orangeism as a form of outrage—" The Protestant side of a faction fight, which had long been raging in certain counties of the North among the tenants and laborers of the two religions ; and the Protestants in Armagh being considerably stronger that the Catholics, Orangeism in that County had assumed the character of a most formidable persecution.[42] . . . As, however, it was the main object of the United Irishmen to form an alliance between the Presbyterians and the Catholics : as in pursuance of this policy they constituted themselves the champions of the Catholics who had been persecuted by Orangemen :[43] and as the Defenders steadily gravitated to the ranks of the United Irishmen, the Orangemen by a natural and inevitable process became a great counterpoise to the United Irishmen, and the civil war which raged between the two sects was a great advantage to the Government. The successful efforts of the United Irishmen to *prevent their party* from enlisting in the Yeomanry resulted in that force being largely composed of men with Orange sympathies : and when

---

41 *Ireland*, vol. iii. pp. 177-8-9.

42 Rolleston wrote a letter dated October 26, 1797, in which he detailed the frightful barbarities committed by Defenders, and says—"I am well assured the Defenders' oath goes to a general massacre of all Protestants."—(Froude's *Ireland*, vol. iii. p. 313.)

43 Dr. Killen in his strictures on the original Orangemen is largely influenced by the view which prevailed amongst the United Irishmen previous to the period when the Catholics got hold of the movement and dominated it. It will be observed that Dr. Killen bases a great deal of his opposition to Orangeism on the authority of the Catholic historian, Mr. Plowden. I have counted as many as *14 quotations in 7 successive pages* of Killen's work from this source.—(*Vide Eccl. History*, vol. ii. pp. 359-366.) The noted discretion of the amiable Father Cleary preven s him from giving this fact publicity.

the outrages of the Defenders and United Irishmen multiplied, and when the probability of invasion became very great, several considerable country gentlemen in Ulster changed their policy, placed themselves at the head of their Orange tenantry, and began to organise them into societies. . . . The country gentlemen who now took the name of Orangemen were mainly or exclusively strong opponents to the admission of Catholics to Parliament, though some of them were of the school of Flood and desired a Parliamentary reform upon a Protestant basis. The society as organised by them, *emphatically disclaimed all sympathy with outrage*, and all desire to persecute. It was intended to be a loyal society for the defence of Ulster and the Kingdom, against the United Irishmen and against the French, and for maintaining the constitution on an exclusively Protestant basis, but it included in its ranks all the most intolerant and fanatical Protestantism in the province, and it inherited from its earlier stage traditions and habits of violence and outrage which its new leaders could not wholly repress, and which *the anarchy of the times* was well fitted to encourage."[44] I have quoted at length in order to give Mr. Lecky fair expression in his drastic passages, and I will now go on to show the development either in his thought of the Orange Society or of the Society itself. He extracts General Knox's view which advised the arming of the Orangemen. "If I am permitted," wrote the General, "as I am inclined to encourage the Orangemen, I think I shall be able to put down the United Irishmen in Armagh, Monaghan, Cavan and part of Tyrone." He forwarded to Pelham a series of resolutions which had just been carried at Armagh by the Masters of the different Orange Lodges of Ulster in which it was manifest that the organisation was "a legitimate political Association." In these resolutions Lecky observes, "The organisation expressed warm loyalty to the Crown, detestation to rebels of all descriptions, and determination to support, at risk of their lives, the existing Constitution of Church and

---

44 *Ireland*, vol. iv. pp. 48, 49.
Cleary on pp. 273, 274 of his work quotes Capt. Giffard's letter accusing the *Ancient Britons* of a terrible outrage. The humanity of that letter must be credited to Orangeism, for the writer held " several appointments under the Government, edited a newspaper, and is *furiously abused* by Dr. Madden as *a persecuting Orangeman.*" In this light it is curious to note the Father calling the Ancient Britons on Catholic authority "*mostly* Orangemen." This, however, can be explained by reference to Cooke's letter, which runs—" The Popish spirit has been set up against the Protestants by representing every Protestant as an Orangeman, and by inculcating that every Orangeman has sworn to extirpate the Papists : to these *fictions* are added the real pressure of high rents, &c."—(Lecky's *Ireland*, vol. iv. p. 41 *Note* and p. 237.)

State, dwelling especially on the Protestant ascendency. They recommended the gentlemen of the country to remain on their estates, offered to form themselves into different corps under their guidance and invited subscriptions for the necessary expenses. They also declared that the object of the Orange Association was to defend themselves, their properties, the peace of the country and the Protestant Constitution, and they *solemnly and authoritatively denied* that they had sworn to extirpate the Catholics. The loyal, well-behaved men, they said, let their religion be what it may, need fear no injury from us."[45] Declaratory resolutions when made by the Orangemen find small favor with Father Cleary, though how they could do more than express their strongest repudiation and denial of the calumnious whispers raised against them it is difficult to understand. Whether, however, Father Cleary is satisfied or not is a matter of no consequence, for men of more weight on his side have not raised any cavil or cast suspicion upon the truth of this denial. Justin McCarthy tells us that Francis Plowden, the renowned Catholic author of two veracious histories, declared: " It has been asserted by *well-informed* though *anonymous* authors "—this is always a safe and impressive phrase to use, when the authority is questionable or bad—" that the original obligation or oath of Orangeism was to the following effect: ' I, A. B., do swear that I will be true to King and Government, and that I will exterminate the Catholics of Ireland so far as in my power lies.'" McCarthy adds : "*This oath, it must be admitted, has been denied by the Orange Lodges,*" and he apparently accepts the denial in good faith.[46] One has to understand the peculiar methods of Irish warfare, political, social and literary, to adequately conceive the malignant misrepresentation to which the Orange Society has been subject. One method is to lie an objectionable thing out of existence. A plentiful crop of illustrations to prove this policy will be found in these pages. Mr. Lecky mentions that a " Book of Rules and Regulations

---

45 *Ibid*, p. 53-4.

A general meeting of the lodges was held informally on July 12, 1796, for the purpose of forming a Grand Lodge, but nothing was done until July 12, 1797, when a meeting took place at Portadown. On the same day General Lake reviewed the Orangemen at three centres—Belfast, Lisburn, and Lurgan. (p. 27.) On March 8, 1798, Dublin desired a better organisation. After settling a few preliminaries the meeting adjourned to April 9th. On its meeting then it further adjourned to Nov. 30th, 1798. (p. 28.) On this date the new rules were issued. Mr. Banks says that 'fabricated rules had been spread by the rebels. He speaks of "the usual frauds" and tells us that " many Catholics of those days voluntarily testified to their falseness." (p. 30)—.(*Hist. Orange Order,* 1898.)

46 *Ireland since the Union*, p. 78.

was drawn up and circulated amongst the Orangemen, which clearly showed the desire of its leaders to give the Society a character not only of loyalty but of *high moral excellence.*" From the description furnished by the historian, it would appear that the original qualifications were substantially the same as they are to-day—if not the *ipsissima verba* of the obligations of an Orangeman. He was " expected to have a sincere love and veneration for his Maker, and a firm belief in the sole Mediatorship of Christ. He must be humane and courteous, an enemy to all brutality and cruelty, zealous to promote the honor of his King and country. He must abstain from cursing, swearing, and intemperance, and he must carefully observe the Sabbath." The writer goes on to say that—" The Society was exclusively Protestant, and it was based upon the idea of Protestant ascendency, but it was intended also to be actively loyal, and to combat the forces of Atheism and Anarchy. Like the Freemasons, the Orangemen had secret signs and passwords, but the only object of these was to prevent traitors from mixing with them to betray them, and also to recommend each Orangeman to the attention and kindness of his brethren."[47] Lord Blayney wrote from Castleblaney, in the county of Monaghan, complaining of Orange outrages, and asking Secretary Pelham to punish the evil doers. The reply was that "the Government did not wish to favor one party more than another, but to do equal justice to all." On this Lord Blayney answered that "Orangemen ought certainly to be shown some countenance," but he intimated that "under that cloak (Orangeism) *robbers and assassins would shelter themselves,* and the most conspicuous who countenance them will be held forward as their leaders."[48] This is an aspect which should be borne in mind. The respectable term of Orangeman was tainted by the infamy of individuals who assumed it as a cloak of decency, beneath which they practised the most brutal enormities. Another feature of the times is explained by Mr. Lecky—anonymous letters were circulated " accusing the Orangemen of concealing arms in the houses of Catholics in order to have a pretext for burning them." Still another device was the industrious spread of a report that " the Orangeman had sworn an oath to extirpate Catholics," and although it had been " *explicitly and solemnly denied by the heads of all the Orange Lodges it was persistently repeated and readily believed.*" There were rumours " that the Orangemen were about to massacre the Catholics." Amidst this ferment in which

---

47 *Ireland*, vol. iv. p. 54.   48 *Ibid*, pp. 89, 90, 91.

every report was invented that was calculated to heat the blood and inflame the passions of men, other rumours gained currency: "That not a Protestant would be left alive in Ireland in the following March, and there were vague disquieting reports of great movements of religious fanaticism agitating the Catholic masses."[49] On December 23, 1797, Cooke's letter to Pelham affirmed that *the Committee of secrecy* had printed an example of the "*pretended Orange Rules which were fabricated for the purpose of exciting the passions of the Catholics.*"[50] Mr. Lecky says that "in the Orange Society as organised by the Ulster gentry there was no oath even distantly resembling what was alleged; and the Masters of all the Orange Lodges in Ulster had, as we have seen, most emphatically disclaimed any wish to persecute the Catholics."[51] One thing he notices as a "curious fact," that the fear of the Orangemen "appears to have been most operative upon populations who came *in no direct contact* with them." Has not Father Cleary been struck with this when working himself up on this question? It is pointed out that as the rebellion was on the eve of taking the field of open action— "Loyalty in Ireland was beginning more and more to rally round *the Orange Standard,* and to derive a new energy and courage from religious passion."[52] Notwithstanding the loyalty of the Orangemen, Lord Camden the Viceroy was morbidly nervous on the question of creating religious antipathies, and refused to avail himself of their proffered services. Froude, in commenting upon this, declares that "the English mind had been so poisoned against the name of Orangemen, by stupid and lying declamation, that the Viceroy was afraid to employ them, but felt himself compelled to repress their demonstrations, while the insurgent leaders, though each one of them was known, were allowed to pursue their machinations unharmed."[53] Again Camden had been "reproached with encouraging the Orangemen. He had been cold and hostile to them."[54] The Duke

---

49 *Ibid*, p. 98.   50 *Ibid*, p. 126, Note.   51 *Ibid*, p. 126.
52 *Ibid*, p. 237. "It has been a matter of doubt whether the designs of this great Association (United Irishmen) terminated as given out in a reform of Parliament, &c. . . . . Certain it is that the shrewdest members of the Irish Parliament considered the real object of those who contended for a Parliamentary reform and a Catholic Emancipation, to be finally an entire disjunction from the sister Kingdoms. On this conviction, the zealous friends of their permanent Union, firmly persuaded that its only security depended on supporting the Protestant cause uninjured, and upon its established footing of superiority entered into formal Associations everywhere for this purpose. They assumed the name of Orangemen in honor and remembrance of King William, to whom the Protestants in Ireland acknowledged themselves indebted for their deliverance from the oppression of the Roman Catholics."—(*The Annual Register*, 1798, vol. 40 p. 153.)
53 *Ireland*, vol. iii. p. 350.   54 *Ibid*, p. 372.

of Portland considered that a body which the United Irishmen confessedly feared was not to be lightly flung away in the day of danger, and he wrote Lord Camden March 24, 1798—" I heard yesterday that the Orange Associations in Ulster had been joined by all the principal gentry and well affected persons of property in that province for the purpose of protecting themselves against the United Irishmen. . . . Exertions of this kind may do more than all the military force you could apply towards the establishment of order. . . . The sense of danger and the proper spirit which has prompted this combination may dispose those who have entered into it to allow your Excellency . . . to employ their zeal to the best advantage."[55] Lecky quoting this letter says that Portland had heard from two quarters that the Orange Society "consists already of 170,000 persons," but Camden in his reply clearly reveals his attitude to the Orangemen by saying their numbers had been exaggerated:— "There were perhaps 40,000 men enrolled in it;" he was not certain that it would be wise to employ them until "the disorders in this country should take *a still more serious turn.*"[56] Father Cleary, after his manner, passes over in silence the policy of Camden towards the Orange Society. In his story the Government are aiding, abetting, winking at, and possibly inspiring the Orangemen to do all sorts of wicked things, whilst this correspondence reveals Lord Camden as combating the suggestion of the English Minister, and definitely refusing to use the Orangemen until the country is in a more serious state, and this in March, 1798, *the year of the rebellion itself.* Well might Mr. Froude exclaim—" Had Camden's Administration been actuated by the fanatical spirit of Protestant ascendency which it is usually said to have represented, the Viceroy would have caught at a permission to accept assistance which would have relieved him of all anxiety for the possible success of the rebellion. He had shrunk from the Orangemen, and he shrank from them still, because he held it inconsistent . . . to arm Protestants against Catholics."[57] Froude regards this

---

55 *Ibid*, pp. 372, 373. 56 *Ireland*, vol. iv. p. 248.

Camden's policy towards the Catholics which induced him to cold-shoulder the Orangemen was indicated by the Viceroy himself in a letter to Portland dated Aug. 6th, 1796—" I will not conceal from your Grace that *political considerations influenced my opinion.*"—(Froude's *Ireland,* vol. iii. p. 171.)

In March, 1798, " two magistrates were killed in open day in Kildare. In the body of one of them was found the bayonet of a *militiaman.* . . . The Orange Lodges offered their services and organised for their own defence. . . . The House of Commons was indignant at what it called the timidity of the Government, and clamored for the reimposition of the Penal Laws."—(*Ibid*, p. 306.) (Lecky, vol. iv. p. 231.) 57 *Ireland*, vol. iii. p. 373.

forbearance on the part of Camden as creditable to him, for he had cause to know that "Catholic loyalty, even when most loudly professed, was from the lips outwards." This writer also supplements Lecky's account of Camden's reply to Portland. He admitted that the Orangemen were "*very respectable persons*," and that they were likely to increase. Many of them, he believed, would enter "either the Yeomanry or the Militia." With an involuntary compliment he added they are the persons most to be trusted with arms in either Kingdom.[58] Father Cleary has some very hard words for Lord Camden in his pamphlet. He accuses him of carrying out "the policy of forcing the people into insurrection,"[59] and yet he quotes him saying of the Orangemen, "they justly irritated the Catholics, and gave a pretence to the disaffected."[60] Froude commenting on Plowden's statement that the Government "had permitted and encouraged the rebellion," says —"Lord Camden's letters form *a conclusive answer* to the charge of encouragement. . . . His attempts to prevent the rebellion were described as the gratuitous provocation of an innocent people."[61] It might have been happier for England and for Ireland, if Camden had taken Portland's advice and frankly adopted the Orange Boys; he had already confessed that of all subjects of the Crown they were the most to be relied upon—so says Froude.[62] But not until danger had become imminent were the Orangemen called to arms. This fact sweeps aside many tragic paragraphs of Father Cleary's work.

---

58 *Ibid*, p. 374

59 p. 263. Joseph Holt's narrative shows how Orangemen were treated. He says—"I had 960 men, *all Wicklow men*, under my command at this period." While sacking the house of Mr. Hynes, a respected J.P., "a man was found hiding in a potato garden, and was brought to the party: they made short work of him: he was tried and shot. . . . I was not at his trial: it was short and probably an unjust one. *His hiding was considered evidence enough of being guilty of Orangeism.*" (p. 99.) In another part of this narrative Holt speaks of his band capturing three prisoners, of whom "two were found guilty of being Orangemen, and were shortly after put to death. . . . My people alleged that they were in the habit of *informing against United Irishmen* and procuring their destruction." (p. 146.)—(Wright's *History of Ireland*, vol. iii.)

60 p. 213. 61 *Ireland*, vol. iii. p. 402.

Lord Camden, on April 11th, 1800, wrote a letter to Lord Castlereagh. This was nearly two years *after* he had resigned his position to Lord Cornwallis. In this letter he says—"I am convinced that Lord Cornwallis came into Ireland with a *bad opinion of all the old advisers* of Government and a determination to *estrange himself from them*. . . . The insinuation thrown out *against the Yeomanry*, an institution founded *by me*, could not be otherwise construed by the friends of that institution, than as a disapprobation of that conduct they had been suffered to pursue before."—(Wright's *Ireland*, vol. iii. pp. 249, 250.)

62 *Ireland*, vol. iii. p. 388.

CHAPTER IX.

THE REBELLION OF 1798.—HOW THE CATHOLICS CAME IN.—LIBELLING ORANGEISM TO SCARE CATHOLICS.—THE PRESBYTERIANS DISGUSTED. — LORD MOIRA. — THE METHODS OF UNITED IRISHMEN.—SOME PECULIARITIES OF LEADERS.—THE DEFENDER SUPPLEMENT.—WHEEDLING THE LOYALTY OUT OF SOLDIERS.—ALARMING THE CATHOLICS.—THE YEOMANRY.—WHAT A YEOMAN HAD TO EXPECT.—FATHER CLEARY MINDS HIS STOPS.—TO BE CONTINUED.

THE Duke of Argyll remarks that "the loyal behaviour of the Catholics of Ireland, generally, in the Rebellion was a very reassuring fact, although, of course, their loyalty was not severely tested by a rebellion in the interests of Jacobins, whose attitude to all Religion was that of an envenomed paganism."[1] The reassuring fact to which the Duke here makes reference must be qualified : doubtless his thought is directed more to the Roman Catholic *gentry* than to the Roman Catholic *multitude* : for there is no disputing the fact that the peasantry of that denomination, as well as numerous priests, were terribly in evidence,[2] and that in the South of Ireland the Rebellion was exclusively a Roman Catholic one. Indeed, it was this feature which largely caused the defection of the Protestants of the North from the movement. Mr. Froude shows that in 1798 the Catholic and Presbyterian alliance so ardently aimed at " proved incapable of realisation. The county population of Ulster became year after year more and more Orange, the party of insurrection more and more Catholic. . , . The Catholics were four-fifths of the population, and they were sworn into the confederacy almost to a man."[3] . He also says—" The massacre of Scullabogue

---

[1] *Irish Nationalism*, p. 262.

[2] Dr. M'Nevin, a Roman Catholic, informed the French authorities :—" The Catholic Priests are no longer alarmed at the calumnies diffused about the irreligion of the French : *they have adopted the principles of the people on whom they depend* : they are in general good republicans : they have done good service by propogating with a *discreet zeal* the system of Union, and they have *persuaded the people to take the oath* (of allegiance) *imposed on them by force without in any respect renouncing their principles and their projects.*"—(Lecky's *Ireland*, vol. iv. p. 146.) Father Cleary never quoted from M'Nevin this eulogy on the priesthood, in which they were commended for encouraging perjury and fraud amongst their people.

[3] *Ireland*, vol. iii. p. 405.

K

was worth 50 regiments for the pacification of Ulster. It was not for an Irish nationality headed by the priests: for another 1641 : for a war of creeds and races in which the Catholics of the South were to pike, and shoot, and burn, till every Protestant had been destroyed out of the land, that the Presbyterians of the North had formed in a conspiracy for Irish independence. Thousands who had hung back and hesitated now joined the Orange ranks. . . . Rebellion in Ulster drifted away to its special home and nursery, the estate of Lord Moira, at Ballinahinch."[4] Father Cleary has made good use of Lord Moira; he is one of the handy Protestants rung in to strengthen the story against Orangeism, but we shall meet him further on. For the present I must call attention to the peculiar feature which I have previously remarked—that public movements in Ireland which are aimed against England, no matter with whom they originate, are certain before their course is spent to be dominated by the Church of Rome or her constituents. The Rebellion of 1798 is one more addition to the list. Lest, however, it should be said that this is only one of Froude's falsifications, I shall proceed to put in the unexceptionable authority of Mr. Lecky to the same effect.

How the Catholics came in.

General Knox made the sweeping allegation that "the loyalty of every Irishman who is unconnected with property is artificial."[5] This view renders the loyalty of the peasantry as very doubtful indeed, even though it should be accepted in a modified form. Lord Camden, however, wrote that he had heard and was inclined to believe that Archbishop Troy with six priests had been sworn into the ranks of the United Irishmen. Mr. Lecky does not altogether agree with the Viceroy, and thinks that the report, so far as the Archbishop is concerned, may be "most confidently discredited." But there is little doubt, he goes on, "that many priests were in the conspiracy. Higgins (a Government spy) expressed his belief that there were not 20 loyal priests in Dublin. The Catholic Clergy, M'Nally wrote in April, are to a man with the people . . . the lower clergy were among the most active organisers of sedition."[6] In his treatment of the

---

4 *Ibid*, pp. 484, 485. The Rev. Dr. Reid says :—" When the Northern Rebels heard of the cruelties perpetrated on their Protestant brethren in other parts of Ireland by the Roman Catholic Insurgents they threw down their arms in disgust and indignation."—(*History Presbyterian Church*, vol. iii. p. 426.)

5 Lecky, vol. iv. p. 57. 6 *Ibid*, pp. 77, 78.

identification of the Roman Catholics with the insurrection Mr. Lecky describes what he terms "the true motives which agitated the great Catholic masses."[7] For the sake of brevity and convenient statement, I arrange them in the following order, and refer the reader who desires more complete information to the volume itself at the pages indicated. (1.) The Catholics came into the rising *not on the ground of Catholic Emancipation*:—" To the overwhelming majority of Catholic people in Ireland it was a matter of *utter indifference.*"[8] (2) The reason was *not to force the question of Parliamentary Reform,*[9] which was one of the planks of the United Irishmen in their early agitation. (3.) It was the matter of the *abolition of tithes* which brought the Catholics into the Rebellion. " The tithe grievance was now the *chief political bond* between the Presbyterians of the north and the Catholics of the south, and the fact that the French had begun their Revolution by abolishing tithes was one of the chief motives put forward for welcoming a French invasion."[10] (4.) After tithes—"but after it at a considerable distance—came the question of Rent."[11] (5.) Another factor which had some influence "was *a vague feeling of separate nationality* which was thrilling powerfully through the Catholic masses."[12] (6.) A concluding item, in the sum total of influences contributing to work up the Catholics to the requisite pitch of fury, was the circulation of prophecies attributed to St. Columkill pointing to the reinstatement of the old race, and the expulsion of the stranger. These musty traditions had gone the round of Irish cabins during the great troubles of 1641. " They were now once more passing from lip to lip and vague, wild hopes of a great coming change were rapidly spreading."[13] A letter from Cooke to Pelham, dated Dec. 23, 1797, contains the information that—" Reports are propagated among the lower Roman Catholics that the Orangemen are to rise and murder them: other reports that not a Protestant is to be left in Ireland by the 25th March. Confraternities of Carmelites are establishing near Dublin by the priests, and some old silly prophecy of Columkill is circulated among them, which gives Ireland this year to the Spaniards."[14] It was asserted by the newspapers of the United Irishmen, says Mr. Lecky, and it was *taught and believed in every quarter of Ireland* that the secret

---

7 In another part of the same work Lecky gives a synthetic account of the Rebellion from the side of the Catholics.—(Vol. iv. p. 290.)

8 *Ibid*, p. 120.   9 *Ibid*, p. 121.   10 *Ibid*, p. 122.   11 *Ibid*, p. 123.

12 *Ibid*, p. 123.   13 *Ibid*, p. 125.   14 *Ibid*, p. 126 Note.

oath sworn by every Orangeman was—" I will be true to the King and Government, and I will exterminate, as far as I am able, the Catholics of Ireland."[15] He explicitly affirms that the representations of extermination by the Orangemen on the one hand, and by the Catholics on the other were " essentially false." Lecky also expressly observes—" In the Orange Society as organised by the Ulster gentry, there was no oath *even distantly* resembling what was alleged, and the Masters of all the Orange Lodges in Ulster had, as we have seen, most emphatically disclaimed any wish to persecute the Catholics. But the seed had been already scattered among an *ignorant, credulous, and suspicious* peasantry. *The United Irishmen persistently represented the Orange Society as a Society created for the extermination of the Catholics, by men high in rank and office, and under the direct patronage of the Government,*† and they were accustomed to contrast its *pretended* oath with that of the United Irishman, which bound him only to endeavour to form a Brotherhood of affection among Irishmen of every religious persuasion, &c. This was probably their *most successful mode of propagandism,* and *the panic which it created* had, as we shall see, a great part in producing the horrors that followed. It is, however, a curious fact that the *fear of the Orangemen appears to have been most operative upon populations who came in no direct contact with them.* The worst scenes of the Insurrection were in Wexford where the Society had never penetrated: *while in Ulster, and in Connaught, which was full of fugitives from Ulster, the rebellion assumed a far milder form.*"[16] I could overlook Father Cleary's revolt against the Orange Society had he not quoted so copiously from Mr. Lecky's writings. Had he confined himself to the narratives of Catholic historians for the period of the Rebellion, I could have pardoned, though I deplored his onesidedness, but since he has explored every nook and cranny of *Ireland in the 18th Century,* and travelled over every inch of its territory, and must therefore have seen the lengthy passage I have just quoted, it is hardly decent that he should have ignored these pregnant matters, and yet called attention to his book as presenting " *reliable* information." In pointing out the tran-

---

15 *Ibid,* p. 126.

†Readers of Father Cleary's book will be struck with the similarity between his theory of the Orange Society and this statement from Mr. Lecky. One cannot entertain much doubt as to where Father Cleary got his idea from—it is a wholesale absorption of the falsehood propagated by the United Irishmen.

16 *Ibid,* pp. 126, 127. See also Lecky on Grattan, pp. 69-71, for the causes of Rebellion in the North.

sition of the rising from the political to the religious stage, Mr. Lecky says that an evidence of the change was the "persistent efforts of the *United Irishmen to goad the Catholic masses into rebellion, by representing the Orange Society as a conspiracy to massacre them, and by representing the English Government as supporting it.*"[17] This way of putting the case differs immensely from Father Cleary's oft repeated charges that Pitt's Policy and the Orangemen did the deadly business. It is simply another case of mistaken identity. The Rev. gentleman is sure that the "goading" came from those whom he regards as his implacable enemies, and it turns out after all, it was the work of those for whom he has no words of condemnation. When the Insurrection assumed an "essentially Popish character" in Munster and Leinster it shook the confidence of the conspirators in Ulster.[18] Further on in the same volume Lecky says, the Northern rebels would probably have risen at the call of Lord Edward Fitzgerald, but "they remained almost passive, when they found the rebellion in Leinster headed by fanatical priests, and by obscure country gentlemen, of whom they had never heard."[19] He adds that the arrest of Lord Fitzgerald saved Ireland from a "Sea of blood." Illustrations of how events were tending, and what might be expected when the Roman Catholics dominated the insurrection, are given by Lecky, for instance:—"Shouts of 'Down with the Orangemen!' and numerous attacks upon Protestants where Catholics were *unmolested*, showed the character the struggle was likely to assume with the Catholic peasantry."[20] Again, "Numbers of panic-stricken Protestants scattered over the districts in rebellion fled for protection to the towns: the Yeomen and Militiamen who *deserted to the rebels appear to have been almost exclusively Catholics*, and the great majority of those who were murdered or plundered by the rebels were *Protestants.*"[21] It is true that whatever grievances the Catholic population really had of a political nature were not only worked upon by a skilful band of agitators, but that every appeal which could be made to their fears or passions was also adroitly presented. I am willing to allow any concession which is based upon truth and reason in considering the ghastly part they took,

---

17 *Ibid*, p. 236.   18 *Ibid*, p. 237.   19 *Ibid*, p. 307.

20 *Ibid*, p. 325. Mr. Lecky also relates:—There were disquieting reports "of disloyalty among the Methodists." The President of that body, however, soon laid the ghosts by saying—"The only foundation for these rumors was the strong reluctance of some Methodist Yeomen to go through military exercises on Sunday."—(*Ireland*, vol. iv. p. 135.)

21 *Ibid*, p. 325.

as a body, in this strife.[22] Apart from the malevolent lies circulated by the United Irishmen as to the Orange Society, Higgins —an informer, who led to the arrest of Lord Fitzgerald, and who, as Lecky says, " was an open, prominent, consistent loyalist, who betrayed no one in this great service to his country "[23]—informed Pelham "that the rumor that the Government designed to reenact the Penal Code was sent by the Dublin conspirators widely through the country, especially by the priests."[24] Mr. Plowden gives the text of a declaration made by the Maynooth Professors, leading Catholic gentry and clergy, and addressed to the " *deluded people*" of their persuasion. It implored them to listen to their bishops and gentry, rather than to a "*set of desperate and profligate men* who are availing themselves of the want of education and experience in those whom they seek to use as instruments for gratifying their own wicked and interested views."[25] The declarants expressed a determination to rescue their names and religion "from the ignominy which each would incur from an *appearance of acquiescence* in such criminal and irreligious conduct."[26] Unfortunately for the good name of the Roman Catholics neither this declaration by their own leading people nor the declaration by the Orange Association, seemed to have had the smallest deterrent effect upon great multitudes of the peasantry. The treachery of many priests[27] did not induce the lower classes to follow wise

---

22 An address was issued by "many respectable Catholics," in which they declared their "loyalty and detestation of the Rebellion." Mr. Lecky says that this elicited a response from one of the largest Orange Associations in Ulster. " We have, with the greatest pleasure, seen declarations of loyalty from many congregations of our Roman Catholic brethren, *in the sincerity of which we declare our firm confidence*, and assure them in the face of the whole world, and of the Being whom we both worship, though under different religious forms, that however the common enemies of all loyal men may misrepresent the Orangemen, we consider *every loyal subject* as our brother and our friend, let his Religious profession be what it may. We associate to suppress Rebellion and Treason, not any mode of worship. We have no enmity but to the enemies of our country." — (Vol. iv. pp. 451, 452.)

23 *Ibid*, p. 307.   24 *Ibid*, p. 293.   25 *Ibid*, p. 294.
26 *Ireland*, vol. iv. p. 294.

27 Lecky mentions in vol. ii. of his work, that as early as "1784 the Irish Government attributed most of the disturbances to French instigation, and a large proportion of the seditious writing to popish priests." (p. 404) The Duke of Rutland's letter to Sydney, Aug. 26, 1784, relates a combination in which Napper Tandy and John Binney appear to act as leaders—" They drink the French King on their knees, and their declared purpose is a separation from England and the establishment of the Roman Catholic religion." (p. 404, Note.) Orde's letter to Nepean, April 30, 1784—" We are now very certain that most of the abominable letters and paragraphs in the public papers are written by popish priests." (p. 405.) Lecky says " there is grave reason to believe that among "

counsels, for Lecky speaks of great numbers of Catholics " headed by their priests" who took the oath of loyalty, "received protection and succeeded in disarming suspicion. Many of these were soon after prominent in the Rebellion."[28] Moreover he says—" The Catholic Rebellion only became *really formidable when the priests touched the one chord to which their people could heartily respond, and turned it into a religious war.*"[29]

THE PRESBYTERIANS DISGUSTED.

The defection of the Presbyterians from the movement of which "they were the main originators," and the great and enduring change which took place in their sentiments "in the last years of the 18th century are facts of the deepest importance in Irish History, and deserve very careful and detailed examination." Mr. Lecky thinks that he can put his finger upon the elements which wrought the change. " Much was due to the growth of the Orange movement which had planted a *new* and rival enthusiasm in the heart of the disaffected province and immensely strengthened the forces opposed to the United Irishmen."[30] In curious corroboration of the much abused Froude is the following passage from Lecky. The Presbyterians " were more and more disinclined to throw in their lot with disorderly Catholic mobs, assembled under nameless chiefs, who were plundering and often murdering Protestants, but who were in most cases scattered like chaff before small bodies of resolute Yeomen. . . . The papers day by day told how the rebels were imprisoning, plundering and murdering the Protestants: how the priests in their vestments were leading them to fight as to a Holy war, which was to end in the extirpation of heresy: how Protestants were thronging the Chapels to be baptised as the sole means of saving their lives." There may have been exaggeration in such reports, but there was undoubtedly " much horrible truth."[31] He notes that at Omagh not less than 6000 Presbyterians "offered their services without expense to the Government, and their example was followed in other places. The ranks of the Orangemen at the same time rapidly filled, and great multitudes of them offered to march to

---

the Government spies and informers " was a man whose literary and social gifts had given him a foremost place among the Irish Catholics, and whose character ranked very high among his contemporaries. Father O'Leary, whose brilliant pen had already been employed to vindicate both the loyalty and faith of the Catholics and to induce them to remain attached to the law, appears to have consented for money to discharge an ignominious office, for a Government which distrusted and despised him." (p. 405.)

28 *Ireland* vol. iv. p. 347. 29 *Ibid*, p 438. 30 *Ibid*, p. 403. 31 *Ibid*, p. 405.

any part of the kingdom to suppress rebellion."[32] Letters from Mr. Cooke and Bishop Percy give graphic pictures of the revulsion of the Presbyterians from a confederacy which was being baptised with the blood of fellow Protestants. Bishop Percy wrote:—"The North is perfectly safe: the Protestants being here in some places murdered by the Irish Papists, has turned all the Dissenters against them."[33] Again—" The murder of the Protestants in the South will prevent them ever joining again with them, much less in the present rebellion."[34] I have now shown Mr. Froude's view of the Catholic element in the rising, at much greater length I have depicted Mr. Lecky's, and in passing from this particular phase of it, I adduce that of *The Annual Register* of even date with the rebellion. " The rancour of the lower classes (Roman Catholics) was particularly violent, and was scandalously encouraged by the Romish clergy, who, with some exceptions, were mortal foes to the Protestants, and excited the mass of the people to hold them in utter abhorrence. It was the sincere desire of the British Ministry to extinguish this religious inveteracy, but it was so strongly connected with political considerations that no remedy appeared fully adequate. The Roman Catholics averred that they were the lawful owners of the property held by the Protestants, whom, for this reason, they hated as plunderers, as much as they detested them for being heretics."[35]

Before passing on to the United Irishmen and the many accusations levelled at the " Orange Yeomanry," I may direct the attention of the reader to the following authorities on

THE FAMOUS LORD MOIRA.

Froude's *History of Ireland*, vol. iii. pp. 317, 335, 337, 338, 339, 342, 343, 344, 346, 328, 512, 513, 516. Wright's *History of Ireland*, vol. ii. pp. 643, 645, 646. Godkin's *Religious History of Ireland*, pp. 259, 260. *The Nineteenth Century*, June, 1890, p. 1023. Wolfe Tone's *Life*, vol. ii. pp. 81, 467. Lecky's *Ireland in the 18th Century*, vol. iv. p. 422 Note. The *Annual Register*, 1798, vol. 40 pp. 160, 161. There was no doubt that Lord Moira's estate, in Fitzgibbon's words, was " a main citadel of treason." Lecky refers to it as " the centre of the rebellion in Ulster." The irony of the occasion was sharpened when the United Irishmen of Down held a county meeting on February 4, 1798, at which " Earl Moira's character was discussed at full

---

32 *Ireland*, vol. iv. p. 415.   33 *Ibid*, p. 414.   34 *Ibid*, p. 415.
35 *Annual Register*, 1798, vol 40 p. 153.

length, to know whether he was a man that could be depended on or not by the people. It was agreed that he was as great a tyrant as the Lord Lieutenant, and *a deeper designing one.*" These are "the words of the secretary's minutes." (Wright's *History of Ireland,* vol. ii. p. 646.) Lecky says that Lord Moira's charges of picketing and half-hanging "resolved themselves into a single well-attested instance." A blacksmith who had manufactured pikes was compelled by "picketing, by the threat of immediate death, and perhaps by half-hanging, to reveal the persons to whom he had given them." There was a conflict of testimony about the half-hanging, though "it was admitted that a rope was put round the culprit's neck."[49] We shall see presently whether this was capricious and persecuting cruelty to goad people into rebellion, or whether it was a stern measure to prevent the illicit arming of a people when it was known that they intended to rise against their loyal fellow subjects. Our sentiments are always against "torture," but our judgment must decide whether the "physical force argument" was, under the circumstances and at that time, a merciless or a merciful act. Personally, I am opposed to submitting any question to the arbitrament of battle; I detest and abhor war; I consider it opposed to the highest sentiment of the Christian religion, but as a matter of expediency I do not see how under some circumstances it can be obviated. When the issue between cutting off a limb or losing a life is unavoidable, I find myself compelled to say—sacrifice the limb. But only when it comes to the unavoidable am I prepared to regard expediency as the determining authority of action. All measures of war are cruel, and the main point is to decide what measures are calculated, all things taken into account, to restrict that cruelty to the smallest possible area. It seems to me that this principle should guide us in forming a judgment on the military methods adopted for the repression and suppression of this insurrection.

THE METHODS OF THE UNITED IRISHMEN.

I extract the following condensed account of this organisation from Mr. Lecky. The society was founded in Belfast in October, 1791. Originally it was a "perfect legal society."[50] It was suppressed in 1794. Subsequently it was reconstructed on a fresh basis "distinctly treasonable." In 1795 it was confined mainly to Dublin and Ulster. In 1796 it spread widely through Leinster. In 1797 it had extended over the greater part of that

---

49 *Ireland,* vol. iv. p. 45.   50 Lecky's *Ireland,* vol. iv. p. 250.

province, was powerful in Munster, and had gained some slight footing in Connaught. "At the close of 1796 and beginning of 1797 a military organisation was grafted on it, and it became a main object to create, arm, and discipline regiments for a rebellion."[51] In February, 1798, before the declaration of martial law and the establishment of free quarters, the executive body computed that 500,000 had been sworn into the Society, and that more than 280,000 of them could be relied on to take the field. Of this number 110,990 were in Ulster, 100,634 in Munster, and 67,272 in Leinster. No returns were to hand from Connaught.[52] Arthur O'Connor, one of the chief leaders, although he was an advocate of Catholic Emancipation, was utterly "without sympathy for the Catholic creed. Few men indeed can have had a greater contempt for priests, and for what they teach, and in his last work he expressed his unmingled detestation of O'Connell, and of the movement which had placed the guidance of popular politics in Ireland under the direction of an ignorant and lowborn priesthood."[53] Wolfe Tone's sentiments* have previously been mentioned, and Dr. McNevin's will be found at the commencement of this chapter. Whatever personal contempt was felt for certain classes of Catholics, the aim of the United Irishmen appears to have been the formation of a confederacy in which religious names would be ignored for the common purpose of setting up a republic similar to that of the American colonists or the French revolutionists. Their purpose may have been merely to make Ireland an independent nation, but unquestionably the reliance upon a French invasion, the aping of French notions, as well as the deistic views of religion[54] which began to prevail, strengthen

---

51 *Ibid*, pp. 250, 251.   52 *Ibid*, p. 252.

Orr told an informant of Government that the United Irishmen "had 200,000 men already officered in regiments; they had pikes and muskets for 150,000, and more were on the way. *The militia were almost to a man United Irishmen."* The informant added that the United Leaders, whose names he mentioned, were "if afraid of nothing else desperately afraid of the Orangemen, who were five times stronger than the people in general believed. . . . The instant the signal was given the whole Orange party were to be assassinated."
—(Froude's *Ireland*, vol. iii. pp. 174-5.)   53 Lecky's *Ireland*, vol. iv. p. 256.

* When in France, Tone reviewed the force to be sent to England to burn and pillage: this force consisted mainly of the " Black or Infernal Brigade," which had done such hideous work in the burning of women and children at La Vendée. The following entry is found in Tone's Journal on the 10th November, 1796 :—
" Saw the 'Legion Noire' reviewed : about 1800 men. They are the banditti intended for England, and sad blackguards they are. They put me strongly in mind of the *Green Boys* of Dublin."—(The *Nineteenth Century*, June, 1890, pp. 1012, 1018.)

54 Lecky, vol. iii p. 489.

the conviction that republicanism was the object of the combination. It would be difficult to conceive "a more dreary or a more ignoble picture than Ireland at this time presented," says Mr. Lecky. The Government was corrupt and bigoted, and in three provinces "almost every county was filled with knots of conspirators and incendiaries who were trying to bring down on their country a foreign invasion, and were stirring up the people to rebellion and to crime."[55] He observes that in 1797 as in later periods "political agitators found it necessary for their purpose to appeal for other than political motives, to agrarian grievances and agrarian cupidity: to religious passion: to the discontent produced by the pressure of poverty in a population which was very poor: to the panic which *skilful falsehood* could easily create in a population which was very ignorant. All these engines were *systematically, unscrupulously* and *successfully employed*, and what in one sphere was politics, in another soon turned into ordinary crime."[56] It can hardly be disputed that among some of the chiefs of the movement, the most brutal measures were either advocated or insinuated, upon the axiom that the end justifies the means. The many persistent rumors of intended massacre were not without foundation. Lord Camden's letter to Pelham towards the close of 1797 has the following passage, disclosing some information by an expert detective. "J. W. (McNally) informs us that the moderate party have carried their point and the intended proscription is given up. O'Connor, Lord Edward Fitzgerald and McNevin are the *advocates for assassinations*, the rest are for moderate measures."[57] In the beginning of 1797 the United Irishmen were strong in Dublin and in Ulster generally, but outside West Meath and Meath their influence seemed inconsiderable. But Defenderism made up for this lack. In King's county the outbreak was fiendish. All the houses over a large area were plundered. They put "several of the honest inhabitants *on the fire* to induce them to deliver up their arms and money."[58] Mr. Bagenal's house was fired: he and his wife were both murdered and shots were fired at their children. The magistrates in February sent a petition to the Lord Lieutenant, to proclaim portions of the county, but two months passed before the request was attended to. Then fifty prisoners were captured, but when the case came before the assizes "the witnesses were so intimidated that they *denied in the witness-box*

---

55 Lecky's *Ireland*, vol. iv. p. 140. 56 *Ibid*, p. 141
57 Lecky, vol iv, p. 85. 58 *Ibid*, p. 127.

everything they had sworn before the magistrates."[59] With this impunity the pleasant occupation became quite a flourishing concern. Outrages went on merrily. Houses were burned, and the owners were threatened with similar treatment to that meted out to the Bagenals unless they surrendered money and arms. "They made it a special object to seize the swords and pistols of the yeomanry."[60] In the County of Kildare there was a "perfect reign of terror."[61] A man named Nicholson gave some help in conducting a prisoner to jail, and he was rewarded for assisting the authorities by having his house burnt : he was afterwards dragged from a farmer's house and stabbed by some 50 pikes to make sure of the ghastly work being properly done. The wretches who had butchered him then deliberately killed his wife. It was thought by the United Irishmen a wise plan to incorporate such brutes as these, and accordingly they had them drafted into the combination. Apart, however, from the policy of incorporating every disaffected individual, they pursued the method of alarming the more peaceful of the Catholic people[62] by representing the Orangemen as coming along to slaughter them, and they skilfully made it appear that a few thousand men in the North belonging to the Orange Society were more than able to exterminate the hundreds of thousands of Catholics scattered over Ireland, and that they had sworn to do it. The most astonishing thing is that they found people willing to believe it, and be scared by this bogey. On one occasion Mr. Lecky tells us that two well-dressed men rode in the dead of night through a village about a mile from Carlow ; they rapped at every door and warned the inmates to fly, as the Orangemen were on the march from Carlow on the famous mission of extermination. The ruse was so successful that the whole population fled for protection to the house of a neighbouring magistrate.[63] At Nenagh in Tipperary a placard was put on the chapel door warning the people about the popular superstition concerning the Orangemen, and pointing out by name a number of persons in the town who were accused of having taken the

---

59 Ibid, p. 128.   60 Ibid, p. 128.   61 Ibid, p. 129.
62 See Lecky, vol. iii. p. 541.
63 Lecky's Ireland, vol. iv. p. 132. Father Cleary refers to a statement reported to be made by Mr. E. Harkness at the Maryborough Orange demonstration of 1887, which ran, "The Orangemen only wanted to be let loose, and they would exterminate them" (the Catholics). I have known Mr. Harkness ever since I was a boy, and I am morally certain that the meaning attached to the term "exterminate" by the Father never even remotely entered into his head. I judge that his idea was merely t· express his faith that in some supposed conflict the Orangemen would come off victorious.—(See Cleary, p. 68)

reputed sanguinary Orange oath. It was an invitation to the people to murder them. Lord Camden wrote the Duke of Portland on November 15, 1797, that the Dublin committee of the United Irishmen had sent a report into a part of Wicklow that the Orangemen were going to march into it and slaughter the Catholics. The result was "those miserable, ignorant, and deluded persons left their houses and lay in the fields and at last assembled in large numbers for their own protection."[64] The same scare was used in other cases " as a pretext for mutiny." The name of Orangeman to the Catholic became as alarming as that phantom of the sea called the Flying Dutchman to the seamen in Marryat's novels : nobody ever saw the thing, but everybody was afraid of it. A good illustration of Catholic superstition concerning Orangemen is given in Cardinal Moran's *History of the Catholic Church in Australia*, p. 52. Lord Shannon regarded the United Irish oath as binding, not because of any intrinsic merit, but because its breach lead to the downfall of the person who broke it. In his letter from Cork he says :—" I am persuaded that there are few, if any, of the lower orders in this county which have not taken the United Irish oath, and though not overscrupulous about breaking every other solemn tie, they are faithful to that, as the *most immediate and barbarous assassination is the certain consequence of having violated it*: shocking instances of which have happened in parts of the County of Waterford on the borders of Cork."[66] Amidst the general corrupting of the people and the debauching of the common classes with republican notions, there was also the plan pursued with great subtilty and varying success of enlisting the sympathies of men accustomed to the use of arms. Lecky speaks of the "incessant efforts to seduce the soldiers, the militiamen, and the yeomen."[67] Indeed, one of the alarming

---

64 Lecky's *Ireland*, vol. iv. p. 132. Lecky records that one man threw the whole country between Arklow and Bray into terror by telling them the French had arrived at Bantry, and that " the Yeomen or Orangemen (who were described as if they were identical) were about to march to encounter them, but that before doing so they had determined to massacre the entire Catholic population around them." He adds that such a report was "skilfully devised " to drive the Catholic population into rebellion.—(Vol. iv. pp. 347.) See also Wright, vol. ii. p. 633.

66 Lecky's *Ireland*, vol. iv. p. 137.

67 Lecky's *Ireland*, vol. iv. p. 230. An United Irishman, under the impression that he was addressing Lord Edward Fitzgerald, gave the following information :—" The militia are all our own, except a black sheep here and there : but you know we can easily dispose of them. We have also gained over most of the Scotch fencible regiments, but we cannot make anything of the English regiments." With regard to Sir Watkin Wynne's company, "it was determined that not a man of that regiment should be in existence in the course of a few

signs of the dangerous condition of Ireland was the corruption of the militia, and the suspicion of disaffection in the yeomanry and regular troops. "The seduction of soldiers was a main object of the United Irishmen."[68] Seventy men of the Monaghan militia admitted that they had taken the oath of the society: and even the Orangemen were suspected of having been tampered with. Gen. Knox intimated in a letter, April, 1797, that the Orangemen "on whose loyalty and firmness I had the most perfect reliance are shaken." But Lord Camden in May of the same year wrote—"The Protestants of the County of Armagh who call themselves Orangemen, and who had for some time been deluded by the United Irishmen, have renounced the societies and are returning to their loyalty."* Among the papers of the United Irishmen seized in April at Belfast was one urging them "to make friends of the Catholics and Orangemen, as *that was doing good* in Armagh."[69] These fragmentary allusions will serve to show the reader what a supple policy possessed the United Irishmen,[70] when it admitted of all these methods of advocacy : the Orange Society was used as a fulcrum upon which they levered into fury and frenzy the Catholics, and though the statements were spurious, and were never *intended* as more than superstitious goads, yet they have passed into a certain class of history as undoubted facts which nobody can deny. Believed at the time by unfortunate Catholic multitudes, they are believed to-day, or at any rate professedly so.

THE YEOMANRY.

In February, 1797, there were 15,000 regular soldiers, 18,000 militia, and 30,000 yeomen (of whom 18,000 were cavalry) available for service in Ireland.[71] We are told that soldiers were habitually employed to discharge police functions, " such as suppressing riots and enforcing revenue laws, and they were now

weeks, as they had done too much mischief in the North."—(Wright's *History of Ireland*, vol. ii. p. 655.

68 Lecky's *Ireland*, vol. iv. p. 76.

*Dean Warburton wrote that a very favorable change had come about, which he ascribed partly to the disappointment of hopes from the French, partly to the proclamation of martial law, and still more to the revival of the Orangemen.— (Lecky's *Ireland*, vol. iv. p. 87.)

69 *Ibid*, p. 77 Note.

70 Froude says—" The conspiracy of the United Irishmen produced perhaps a larger number of deliberate villains than have ever been found arrayed in a movement which has called itself national. From the first moment of its institution the most trusted members of the society were traitors to it.—(*Ireland*, vol. iii. p. 318. Wright's *Ireland*, vol. ii. p. 633.)

71 Mr. Froude's account is as follows :—" Of one kind or another the Govern-

called on to put down innumerable concerted outrages carried on by night over an immense area of wild country, and to disarm a scattered and disloyal population."[72] Some idea of the difficulty experienced by the authorities in forming and maintaining the yeomanry may be gathered from a document drawn up by the magistrates and yeomanry officers of Down and Armagh. Lecky regards it as a "remarkable memorial." Attention is called to the fact that frequently the loyal were disarmed and the rebellious escaped: that numbers of the yeomen in their private houses may be either "disarmed or murdered" as is openly threatened: that already personal injury had been visited on the Yeomen, and they had lost all trade and employment through the fear entertained of the United Irishmen. It was one of the "main objects" of the United Irishmen "to prevent the formation of this new and powerful force and they pursued this object with every kind of outrage, intimidation, abuse and seduction. There had been not a few murders. There were countless instances of attacks on the houses of the Yeomen." Their families were jeopardised and exposed to both insult and peril. A system had sprung up in certain localities of treating Yeomen "as if they were *lepers*," and the policy of boycott and isolation was pursued. In other places the plan of wheedle was substituted for boycott. But on every hand the Yeoman knew that outrage, boycott, or seduction spread their snares for him. Mr. Lecky reflects: "That a powerful Yeomanry force should have been created in spite of all these obstacles, and at a time when Irishmen were pouring into the regular army, the militia and the navy appears to me to be a striking proof both of the military spirit, and of the sturdy independence which then characterised the loyalists of Ireland."[73] Parliament asked

---

ment had under its command nearly 40,000 men. But they were of doubtful quality. Of British regiments there were scarcely any—the Ancient Britons, a Welsh Fencible regiment under Sir Watkin Wynne, a Durham regiment, and a regiment or two of Scotch militia being nearly the whole. The Irish militia, 18,000 strong, were all Catholics, and the utmost uncertainty was felt as to their probable conduct. The rest were Irish yeomanry. most of them, though not all, well disposed, but untrained as soldiers, and no better than armed volunteers. The Orangemen Lord Camden *was still afraid to employ.*"—(*Ireland*, vol. iii. p. 407.)

72 Lecky's *Ireland*, vol. iv. p. 35.

73 Lecky's *Ireland*, vol. iv. p. 39. See also pp. 37-38.

In Lord Castlereagh's letter to the Duke of Portland, dated July 30, 1798, it is said Lord Cornwallis proposed to *except* from pardon the Yeomen who deserted to the rebels—" this description of yeomen *being the active seducers of their own body*, and, in many instances, *having entered into the service expressly for the purpose.*"—Wright's *History of Ireland*, vol. iii. p. 116.)

for 20,000 Yeomen. In six months they had 37,000, and during the Rebellion the force exceeded 50,000, which, if necessary, could have been increased. Father Cleary has commented with great bitterness on the conduct of what he repeatedly calls the " Orange Yeomanry." He accuses them of the grossest cruelties, and licensed barbarities, but he omitted to mention what these yeomen had to endure, and what their families had to suffer when they responded to the claims which loyalty made upon them. Some further light will be shed upon this aspect of the case as we proceed. A magistrate writing from Waringstown on July 23, 1796, urged that a distinction should be drawn between Orangemen organised in loyal societies and the plunderers of the North who sheltered themselves under that honored name. He refers to a company of from 2500 to 3000 Orangemen marching through the town with conduct "perfectly regular and sober," who declared themselves "ready to turn out upon all occasions to assist the civil power." Noticing the spread of the Defenders and United Irishmen he adds—" Within these eight days a general terror prevails among the Protestants in this neighborhood, that their throats are to be cut by the Papists aided by the militia, and they now seem to place their salvation on the Orangemen solely."[74] At a twelfth of July procession in 1797 in which 5000 *unarmed* Orangemen took part some trouble was occasioned. The facts are related to Secretary Pelham in a letter by Mr. Cooke. " When the Orange boys were passing, a party of the Queen's County Militia broke away from their officers, and began taking out the Orange cockades. An Orangeman struck one of the soldiers. The soldier bayoneted him. I fear the militia will be tainted from this religious quarrel, and the United Irishmen in order to seduce the militia and the Catholics promise to join them both against the Orange Boys."[75] With respect to the militia it was a well ascertained fact, that 17,000 of the 20,000 militia of the North " were secretly sworn to go with the people," and that fourteen counties were organised.[76] With his usual vigor Mr. Froude sums up the situation thus:—" The militia were corrupt,

---

74 Lecky, vol. iii. p. 436.

The magistrate also wrote :—" As to the loyalty of the Roman Catholics I differ from you in opinion . . . sorry am I to say that . . . the Militia . . . wherever they have been quartered, disgusted the people beyond measure, and by their actions and declarations have given the strongest proofs of disloyalty."—Letter from H. Waring to Cooke July 23rd, 179). The militia were *mainly* Catholics. - (*Ireland in the 18th Century*, vol. iii., p. 436.)

75 *Ibid*, p. 455. 76 *Ibid*, p. 518.

the army feeble. Of these the United Irishmen had no fear. The Orangemen they made no secret of their fearing most deeply. Samuel Neilson, the most determined and dangerous of the United Irish leaders, told a supposed confederate, who was the spy of the Castle, that he was in far greater dread of the Orangemen than of the soldiers. They were very powerful and very desperate. Had Camden made the Orangemen his allies, treason would have crept back into its den and been heard of no more. Unhappily under constitutional governments *spontaneous loyalty is the last virtue which obtains recognition.*"[77] Mr. Lecky also refers to the prevailing distrust of the militia who were mainly Catholics. " Be assured " wrote Lord Blayney, " the yeomanry of the North are your sheet anchor. Was it not for the confidence the United Irishmen have in the militia, matters would not have gone to the length they have. Therefore *beware of the militia.* I have strong reason for saying so. Among the observations I have made the Roman Catholics alone have universally been guilty of robbery and murder."[78] Elsewhere Mr. Lecky informs us —" Catholics formed the great majority of the Irish militia and *a considerable minority of the Yeomanry.*"[79] On one occasion Yeomanry officers discovered that numbers of Catholics in their corps had been seduced, and they endeavoured to combat the evil by imposing a new test obliging every man " to declare that he was not and would not be either an Orangeman or an United Irishman." Many would not take the declaration and the Government was not favourable to it, but the evil was found to be so serious that a great part of the Yeomanry was disbanded and disarmed. " These precautions, as the Rebellion shows, were certainly far from needless, but the result was that the Yeomanry became almost exclusively Protestant."[80] The Yeomanry, who according to Father Cleary were almost all Orangemen, are not credited by him with more than making a record of melancholy cruelties—cruelties that only Beelzebub,

---

77 Vol. iii. p. 196-197.

" In 1798 . . . Lord Camden, perhaps rightly, refused to employ them (the Orangemen) and thereby give a sectarian character to the Rebellion."—(Cassell's *Dictionary of English History*, p. 783.)

78 *Ireland*, vol. iv. p. 100.   79 *Ibid*, p. 325.   80 *Ibid*, p. 346.

Joseph Holt with outrageous candour wrote the story of his exploits: " My ' Moving Magazine ' (a female spy) brought me intelligence that at the camp of the King's County *Militia*, which consisted of one hundred and sixty men, forty were ready to desert to me, and if I advanced to their neighbourhood, *these men would bayonet forty of their loyal comrades before they deserted*, which would reduce that corps one-half, besides adding forty disciplined men to our strength." —(Wright's *Ireland*, vol. iii. p. 149.)

the Prince of the Devils, could take delight in. On competent authority, however, we are informed that in an era of wholesale fiendishness something else must be due to them, and that something *the root cause of all subsequent odium attaching to the name.* That no reference is made to it in the rev. gentleman's pages is highly significant. Sir George C. Lewis quotes from Lord Cornwallis concerning the Yeomanry "*these men have saved the country.*"[81] A letter from Beresford prophesied when dangers were thickening—" The people called Orangemen (whose principles have been totally misrepresented) keep the country in check, and will overpower the rebels should they stir."[82] It was confessed that " to the zeal, activity, and courage of the yeomanry Dublin is mainly indebted for its tranquillity and the whole country for its salvation."[83] Mr. Lecky says :—"The Irish yeomanry have been much and justly blamed by historians for their want of discipline, for their extreme recklessness in destroying both life and property, and for the violent religious passions they too frequently displayed." This much Father Cleary naturally quoted,[84] but as naturally he omitted the sentence *immediately following,* which runs—" But if their faults were great *their merits were equally conspicuous.* To their patriotic energy, to their ceaseless vigilance, to the courage with which they were always ready to encounter armed bodies five or even ten times as numerous as themselves, *the suppression of the rebellion was mainly due.*"[85] Evidently the Rev. gentleman knows where to leave off and has no need for any one to jog his memory with the old admonition given to the tyro in

---

81 *Administrations of Great Britain,* p. 179. Sir Jonah Barrington speaking against the Union in the Irish House, January, 1799, declared :—" The loyalty of the yeomanry *saved* Ireland : both parties had bled and were weak, and what was called *the lenient* system was adopted : the rebel was pardoned and sent back to rob, to murder and burn : the yeoman and the loyalist were either insulted, oppressed, or degraded, and in some instances executed."—(Wright's *Ireland,* vol. iii. p. 162.) In quoting Barrington against Pitt's policy of the Legislative Union, Father Cleary discreetly overlooked the fact that Sir Jonah was, like Grattan, enamoured of the local Parliament, and prepared to plunge the country into war again to maintain it.

82 *Auckland Correspondence,* iii. p. 442.

83 Lecky's *Ireland,* iv. p. 437.   84 p. 272.

85 *Ireland,* iv. p. 341. On page 67 Father Cleary, working up the evidence of the Orange " oath of blood," quotes a letter of Brigadier Gen. Knox, which ran—" The Orangemen were originally a bigoted set of men, who were ready to destroy the Roman Catholics "—here Father Cleary stopped short, but the letter went on to say—" They now form a political party, and are *the only barrier* we have against the United Irishmen."—(Lecky's *Ireland,* vol. iv. p. 55.)

composition—*mind your stops!* I have still to refer to the accusations of Father Cleary against the policy of Pitt, with which he has connected the Orange Association, and the military excesses perpetrated upon injured innocents, which I find can be better attended to in another chapter. Before passing to it, however, I would simply emphasise what has been made clear during the course of the previous remarks that the apologists for the United Irishman movement have had an interest in defaming the Orangemen, and to this source can be traced the malignant calumnies that survive to this time, and are still urged against the reputation of the Orange Society. Looking back on the troubled period which we have been considering it should be clear to fairminded Roman Catholics that the terror of their co-religionists was created by falsehoods ingeniously plied, appealing both to their ignorance and their fear: and that in combining with the United Irishmen they were made the tools of a faction who, in seeking to bend them to their purposes, encouraged them to act against the formulated declarations of their wisest religious teachers and gentry, and to take up arms against the Government, in fighting the phantom created by shameless lying.[86] I can only express my regret that what appears plain to me has not been equally manifest to Father Cleary.

---

[86] The Duke of Argyll shows that in the beginning of 1792 the Catholic bishops held Tone in suspicion on account of his irreligion, and in August of the same year he wrote his exasperation against them in his journal, by the pithy execration—"Damn all the bishops." Yet with such consummate skill did he pilot his way that he was appointed *secretary* of the Catholic Association. On February 4th, 1793, there is the following entry in his journal—"Will the Catholics be satisfied with this Bill? I believe they will and be damned." On comparing the Government proposals with the Catholic petition it appeared " that every complaint *recited* had been attended to, and every grievance *specified* had been removed." His Grace points out " *The very worst thing* that could be done in the interests of genuine religious toleration was to connect once more the Catholic cause with political treason. Yet *this was the work* to which Wolfe Tone had now devoted himself under the cover of a zeal for the Catholic cause."
—(The *Nineteenth Century*, May, 1890, pp. 751, 753, 754.)

CHAPTER X.

THE REBELLION OF 1798.—THE ORANGE CRUELTIES OF FATHER CLEARY.—BERESFORD'S POLICY AND ITS REASON.—GENERAL DUNDAS ON "GOOD BEHAVIOUR."—THE SOUTHERN RISING.—HOW THE RUSE ACTED ON THE CATHOLICS.—THE PIOUS AND MILITANT PRIESTS.—FLOGGING PROTESTANTS FOR CONFESSIONS OF ORANGEISM.—THE MOST RELIGIOUS, THE MOST MURDEROUS.—FATHER CURRAN IMMORTALISED.—DISTRIBUTING THE BLAME.—CLEARY DISPUTING LECKY.—THE DEGRADATION OF IRISH POLITICAL OPINION.—THE FACTS OF THE REBELLION.

THOSE who have read Father Cleary's work will be well posted up on facts overlaid with fictions, and tragedies plus farces, all inseparably connected with working up or stamping out the Rebellion. Picketing, flogging, torture, the pitchcap and other enormities are familiar terms, and to make them more blood curdling they are large typed or italicised. It may be some relief to learn what may be said upon these topics by those who had to do with crippling the spirit of treason, as well as its body, and the instruments by means of which its object could be effected. That many instances of extreme severity occurred is undeniable; that the Government was not over particular in enquiring closely into these scandalous abuses of military power, is also true: but to represent the worst features of the loyal troops as their normal action, and to remain silent on the savage deeds of the insurgents is not calculated to make a story accepted as "reliable." And to ascribe everything that happened, particularly the vilest, to the Orange Society, is not the way to win a reputation for simple honesty. Sir Richard Musgrave says the enemies of the Orange Lodge fabricated oaths which the Orangemen "abhorred." It was never introduced "into any county or district, till it had *some years* been disturbed or desolated by the Defenders or the United Irishmen."[1] He instances the County Monaghan. From 1792 to 1797 this county was disturbed, but in the latter year the loyalists formed Orange associations, which were discouraged by the local gentry. The result was that the United Irishmen had it all their own way. After an experience of the latter organisation, the very gentry

---
1 *Memoirs*, vol. i. p. 72.

who had succeeded in extinguishing these Orange societies very gladly and actively re-established them.² Musgrave also records Gen. Knox declaring—" He would rest the safety of the North on the fidelity of the Orangemen, who were enrolled in the yeomanry corps."³ It will be remembered that as late as March, 1798, Lord Camden would not, even at the suggestion of the Duke of Portland, the English Minister, avail himself of the proffered assistance of the Orangemen as a body. Mr. Lecky, after referring to the activity of the Dublin yeomanry, which kept the city tranquil amidst so much general turbulence in the country, reports—" The Orangemen would rise *if encouraged by the Government*, and make a crusade if required."⁴ It must, therefore, have been subsequent to March, 1798, that the " Orange yeomanry " became a distinctive entity. Up to that time the term applies to a nebulous force. To connect the Orange Society with atrocities previous to this is simply so much guesswork—an adaptation of the happy hit or miss principle applied in history. But in any event, as Mr. Lecky points out—" It is manifestly *absurd* to describe the severities in Ulster as if they were unprovoked by a *savage outburst of anarchy and crime*, or to deny that in the midst of a great war, and with the extreme probability of a French invasion of Ireland, the disarming of the disaffected province had become urgently necessary."⁵ In saying this he most pronouncedly condemns the Government of the day, and especially on its management of the Catholic question. Its policy was " disastrous not only in what was denied, but also in much that was granted. The Relief Act of 1793 had deluged the county constituencies with an overwhelming multitude of illiterate Catholic forty shilling freehold voters, who were wholly unfit for the exercise of political power . . . and excluded the Catholic gentry from Parliament, and thus deprived them of political influence at the very period when their services were most needed."⁶ While, however, the historian enlarges upon the political heresy of the administration, he recounts events which show that its military policy would require to be both discriminating and powerful, in order to cope with the peculiar exigencies that were continually rising as the rebellion progressed. He is not generally favorable to the treatment which Sir Ralph Abercromby received; but he thinks that Sir Ralph took rather a contemptuous view of things. After an excursion through the

---

2 *Ibid*, pp. 72, 73.   3 *Ibid*, p. 73.   4 *Ireland*, vol. iv. p. 439.
5 *Ibid*, pp. 116, 117.   6 *Ibid*, p. 118.

affected districts, the general said "*he found nothing but tranquillity,* the people cultivating their lands and following their usual avocations." On this Mr. Lecky comments there was little doubt "that he greatly underrated the extent of the conspiracy and the imminence of the danger." Yet Abercromby went so far as to say—"I do not, however, doubt that if an enemy should land the Roman Catholics will rise and cut the throats of the Protestants."[7] In the *Auckland Correspondence* is a letter from Beresford, whom Lecky describes as "the most powerful and most violent" of the loyalists. In this letter the rising is described as "a popish plot" in Munster, Leinster, and Connaught, and as "a Presbyterian plot" in Ulster. Beresford avers that the Roman Catholic clergy "have actually persuaded the people in Munster that their salvation depends upon murdering and massacring every person who stands in their way : and they have established such a system of terror, that it is with the greatest difficulty any magistrate can be got to act or any witness to come forward. They murder every man whom they suspect in the slightest manner to be inclined to give evidence against them."[8] Lord Beresford, who is trenchantly condemned by Father Cleary as a "torturer," reveals the principle upon which he acted. His policy so far from being veiled is frankly avowed. "The rebels show us," he says, "how they think they can carry their point, viz. by *terror,* and that points out how to counteract them, and experience therein confirms the fact. The people are persuaded that everything they have obtained has been given them through fear, and that it is fear of them alone which prevents us from taking the same measures in the other three provinces which were taken in Ulster, that was forcing them to give up the arms they had plundered . . . by threatening to throw down or burn their houses and destroy their property : that stopped them at once, without the necessity of destroying more than a dozen houses.[9] They had destroyed ten times as many and had plundered innumerable others and murdered many persons, and continued to do so until they found retaliation begin, when they stopped directly. They are now

---

7 *Ibid,* pp. 213-214.   8 *Ibid,* p. 232.

9 As an instance of this—the people of Kildare refused to give up their arms. "Gen. Walford at once called the inhabitants together, and announced to them on his honor that if they did not bring in their arms in 24 hours, he would burn every house in the town ; and he at the same time assured them that if they complied with his order they should have complete protection. . . . The measure proved successful and great quantities of arms were brought in."— (Lecky, vol. iv. p. 270.) Sometimes the mere threat was not enough, and measures were taken to prove that it was no idle menace.

in Munster, Leinster, and Connaught, plundering and burning houses, murdering witnesses and magistrates . . . . and in the middle of the noonday in the streets of towns obliging, by force and threats, men to take their oaths and pay contributions for their plans. . . . They murder people merely for the purpose of keeping up this system of terror. . . . . . If in such circumstances . . . we did in some instances exceed the law (it is probable that a dozen acts of severity may have happened on our side), how many hundreds have been performed by the rebels . . . how many of the military have been shot within six months, and not one of their murderers brought to justice?"[10] If this picture be anything like accurate, what a condition of things existed! How far are we to carry our reprobation when payment in kind began, as indicated by Beresford's policy: and if a multitude descend to the committal of brutal actions how far are brutal methods of punishment permissible?[11] The problem is too nice for me to solve. It is within the province of criminologists rather than within the soldier's province, for I understand there is an etiquette in war. Lord Camden gives a grueful account of houses plundered of arms: attacks upon villages at noonday: yeomen disarmed by night: and loyalists driven in multitudes from their homes, which goes far to corroborate Beresford's tale of horror.[12] The stigma which Father Cleary casts upon the yeomanry, whom he persists in calling Orange, is not only undeserved, but the fact that they were Protestants almost exclusively, and Orangemen largely, is due to the tactics of the United Irishmen, for whom he seems to entertain a kindly feel-

---

10 *Ibid*, pp. 232, 233.

11 Taylor relates that in Wexford after the battle of Ross, when the pockets of the dead rebels were searched, the following oath was found in some of them: "I, A.B., do solemnly swear by our Lord Jesus Christ, who suffered for us on the cross, and by the Blessed Virgin Mary. that I will burn, destroy, and murder all heretics up to my knees in blood: So help me God."—(*History Wexford Rebellion*, p. 33.) While Wexford was in the hands of the rebels their test oaths were printed. Taylor gives "the test oath": "the private's oath"; and "the officer's oath." In the midst of the bloodshed the "test oath" ran—"That I will persevere in endeavouring to form a *brotherhood of affection among Irishmen of every religious persuasion.*" This is rather too much after the Scullabogue barn business—for most people to swallow and feel comfortable. But, says Taylor, "there was another oath taken by the Papists which the disaffected Protestants and Presbyterians knew nothing of: this was called the *Black Test*, and was as follows: "Every loyal Irish Protestant heretic I shall murder, and this I swear." The password of those who took this test was composed of the initial letters of the words in the oath—thus "*Eliphismatis.*" (*Ibid*, pp. 42, 43.)

12 Lecky, vol. iv. p. 231.

ing,[18] though it suits his purpose to show that some of the Catholic prelates and gentry denounced them generally. Had it not been for their evil policy in alarming the ignorant Catholic peasantry with forged oaths, and keeping up a separation between loyal and disloyal by inflaming religious feeling, the yeomanry would not have been forced to contain only those who, at risk of life, house, family, and property, and despite continuous and bloody outrage, stood firmly to their allegiance. While the United Irishmen were employing every art, human and demonic, to prevent the formation of a corps of yeomen, Fermanagh, Tyrone, Derry, and Armagh furnished no less than 14,000 men, "*three-fourths of them were Presbyterians, and most of them were Orangemen.*"[14] Notwithstanding the strenuous efforts of the Orange officials to disabuse the public mind of the horrible libels spread concerning the order, Mr. Lecky points out that the venomous reports had completely poisoned the whole Catholic mind to such an extent that "nearly every Protestant was suspected of being an Orangeman, and the belief that Orangemen had sworn to exterminate the Catholics was almost universal."[15] The historian points out that "the Orange Society took *great pains* to repudiate this calumny," and quotes part of the address issued by the organisation—" We solemnly assure you in the presence of Almighty God that the idea of injuring anyone on account of his religious opinion never entered our hearts. We regard every loyal subject as a friend, be his religion what it may : we have no enemy but the enemies of our country."[16] According to the accounts given by Father Cleary, the employ-

---

13 Father Cleary quotes from Lecky's *Leaders of Public Opinion*, the object of the United Irishmen, and implies a contrast between them and the Orangemen, for it is under the paragraph headed " A Union of Hearts." The quotation is :— " To provide a union of friendship between *Irishmen of every religious persuasion*, and to forward *a full, fair, and adequate representation of all the people* in Parliament." The italics are Cleary's. (p. 20.)

14 Lecky, vol. iv. p. 416.   15 *Ibid*, p. 451.

16 *Ibid*, pp. 451, 452. Vide appendix A. Lecky also says—" Such declarations could hardly penetrate to the great masses of the ignorant rebels, and they drank in readily the charges against the Orangemen which were sedulously spread." (Vol. iv. p. 452.) Father Cleary says (pp. 68, 69), "*it is only fair*" to state that at a later date the oath of extermination was denied. " I can find no evidence," he goes on to say, "that this oath has been repudiated by the *first* Orangemen or their leaders." Now (a) Mr. Cleary does not tell us when the Orange Society was *first* accused of subscribing to this oath—the society could not deny until first accused. (b) The allegation was made again and again, and solemnly denied again and again. (c) Justin M'Carthy admits it, and Lecky points it out frequently. I therefore fail to see the coherence of Father Cleary's distinction between a former and a latter period, until he can establish a former and a later accusation.

ment of harsh military measures by the yeomanry, and their sanction by the Government, is made to appear the most atrocious and wanton cruelty, but against this view must be set the fact that the Government knew indubitably, by the aid of its spies and informers, every brutal project that was discussed in the councils of the United Irishmen, and they were in a position to form the clearest judgment of the desperate characters with whom they had to deal, and whose secret machinations were directing the great body of insurgents. I mention a typical instance. Near the end of 1797, Cooke sent Pelham a most circumstantial and frightful account that had been reported by M'Nally. "It was that Lord Edward received some days since, orders from Paris to urge an insurrection here with all speed, in order to draw troops from England. . . . . . They proposed arming a body of 500 with short swords : that this body should repair to all the mass houses at midnight mass on Christmas morning : that *by false attacks they should persuade the people to raise a cry that the Orangemen were murdering the Catholics*, &c. Many priests were anxious for this plan, but Emmet, Chambers, &c., opposed, and in consequence the bishops who were against outrage, put off mass till seven o'clock in the morning."[17] All honor to the Roman Catholic bishops who, when preparing to celebrate amidst the dismal conditions of Ireland the advent of the Prince of Peace, showed themselves sensible of the sanctity of the occasion, by deferring their religious celebrations to a time when daylight would prevent the carrying out of such unholy proposals. Still greater honor would have been theirs, had they denounced from their altars that Christmas morn the men who could calmly make those proposals ; this, however, was too much to expect, seeing they were cognisant of what was being discussed, and how far their own people were involved in the bad business. The Government certainly knew of these proceedings, and thousands of other circumstances of a similar character contemplated, and in actual process of accomplishment. The town of Cahir, in Tipperary, was occupied by a party of armed and mounted rebels, numbering according to the Lord Lieutenant 1000 at noonday, and from the lowest estimates at least 300 men. These proceeded to systematically disarm the inhabitants, and carried off as a result of the sortie more than 100 stand of arms.[18] In the North the eager Protestants called the conspiracy a popish plot, and encouraged the Orangemen to activity ; they avowed themselves

---

17 Lecky, vol. iv. p. 195.   18 *Ibid*, p. 212.

members of the society, and openly declared that until the Penal Laws were again enacted the country would not be safe.[19] Both North and South were seething, to the certain knowledge of the Government, and it could place no reliance upon Roman Catholic assistance. Lecky says one circumstance was felt acutely. "Grants of £25 a year to 200 students at Maynooth had lately been carried by the Government, against the opinion of the Speaker and of several other of their usual supporters: yet it was noticed with some bitterness that when soon after there was a proposal before the Bank of Ireland for a grant of a sum of money for the prosecution of the war, *not one* Roman Catholic among the bank proprietors voted for it, and that the minority who opposed it consisted *almost entirely* of Roman Catholics."[20] It was evidence that the struggle had passed out of the range of politics, pure and simple, and was now a religious one. While, therefore, Mr. Lecky shows that the Government winked at military excesses, he lays before his readers ample information to largely vindicate that policy. Neither the Catholic bishops nor men of means were prepared to place their co-religionists in additional danger; and it could not be expected that the Government would too summarily check its friends. This much is practically conceded by Mr. Lecky in his criticism of the military measures, and he further shows that "such acts of military violence were usually *provoked by great crimes or by serious dangers*, and that their number has been much *exaggerated.*"[21] In a note he relates that one of the Members for the County of West Meath refused to attend the debate in which the military violence was discussed. This Member gave Pelham an account of the condition of his county which "seems to me (Lecky) very impartial." The account ran: "Great enormities, I do confess, were practised by the soldiery at the other side of this county, which I can by no means defend. Were I, therefore, in my place, my silence would be a sanction to the opposition. It may perhaps be some extenuation of these facts to state that the most horrid barbarities had been *previously* practised by the insurgents: that witnesses had been cruelly murdered (one of them in open daylight): and that the minds of the soldiery had been exasperated by the recent fact of attacking twenty-four houses in one night, and almost in the same hour, which seemed to indicate a general rising. Other cruelties might be cited—such as the roasting of three women in one parish to force them to confess where their money was

---

19 *Ibid*, p. 231. 20 Lecky, vol. iv. p. 231. 21 *Ibid*, p. 221

deposited." So that it is apparent, the military violences which are so horrible when done in the interests of law and order, were but severe chastisement for deeds of lawlessness, yet they are represented as exceeding the crimes they were intended to punish. No one, says Mr. Lecky, who will honestly face the situation can doubt that it demanded extreme vigor—a vigor which would inevitably transcend the limits of ordinary law. One of the ablest of the rebels (Miles Byrne) afterwards acknowledged that up to the proclamation of March 30, the process of arming the people for rebellion went smoothly on, and that it was this proclamation and the measures that followed that alone arrested it. " When a half-disciplined yeomanry and militia, demoralised by a long course of outrage, and irritated by many outrages, came to live at free quarters upon a hostile peasantry, who regarded them as Orangemen and who were *taught* that every Orangeman had sworn to exterminate the Catholics, it was not difficult to anticipate the result."[22] Mr. Froude says, in reference to the free quarters, the burnt villages, the pitch cap, the triangle and the lash: "to these outrages it has pleased the Irish to attribute the insurrection. England . . has allowed this legend like so many others to pass unrefuted, and has permitted one more illusion to swell the volume of Ireland's imaginary wrongs. An attention to dates would have sufficed to reduce the charge to modest dimensions. Lake did not take the Commander-in-Chief till the 23rd of April. On the 24th of May the rebellion burst. *The atrocities which are supposed to have caused it were therefore limited to a single month.* . . . For seven years the whole of Ireland had been deliberately preparing for revolt. An invisible authority ruled over the four provinces with a code of laws enforced by dagger, pike, pistol, and houghing knife."[23] He further says the force on which Gen. Lake had to rely " consisted mainly of the loyal Irish Yeomanry, men whose friends had been murdered, who had themselves been marked for murder, whose hands had for years been tied by a law which gave them no protection, while to their enemies it was a convenient shield."[24] The dependence of the Government upon the Protestant, or as Father Cleary terms it the Orange Yeomanry, was emphasised by an occurrence which is recorded by Mr. Froude, but is not mentioned in Father Cleary's " reliable information"—strange to say. " Mr. Clinch, a Catholic gentleman in the district, in apparent loyalty had raised a company of local

---

22 *Ibid*, p. 267-268. 23 *Ireland*. vol. iii. p. 382. 24 Froude, vol. iii. p. 384.

infantry to support "—Captain Ormsby. "These men were all traitors. Their intention was to destroy Ormsby and his Protestants on the appointed day, and then march into Dublin with Clinch at their head. The Catholic Corps attended their own chapels. . . . . To throw Ormsby the more off his guard, the Rathcool priest addressed them on the 20th May (1798) . . . in two eminently loyal sermons in Ormsby's presence, although he discovered afterwards that this priest had been the instigator of the plot." A friend having told Ormsby what awaited him, "the corps was paraded and disarmed. Clinch and the priest were sent to Dublin, where the former was a few days later tried and hanged : the latter was transported to Botany Bay."[25] Father Cleary refers to Gen. Dundas as giving offence to the Orange party by his "lack of ferocity,"[26] and to a similar cause he indicates their distrust of Sir Ralph Abercromby. Of the latter Mr. Froude says—" After having enormously aggravated every element of danger in the country he left Ireland."[27] I have already quoted Mr. Lecky who reports Abercromby's view of the feeling of the Catholics to the Protestants : in which he says that on a French invasion they would cut the throats of the latter. Of Dundas, Mr. Froude declares—" He rode over at the rebels' invitation to parley with them at Kilcullen. He made a speech to them. He took off his hat to them. With their hands red with murder, and their faces grimed with the smoke of the houses which they had been burning, he thanked them for their *good behaviour.*"[28] Lord Camden gives a similar account in his letter to the Duke of Portland, May 31st, 1798. Verily, therefore, is Father Cleary a master in the art of putting on record a famous story ! It may appear outrageous to him that citizens who had risked property, home and life as a Yeomanry Corps to maintain order in the State, should object to an officer of high rank thanking ensanguined ruffians for their " good behaviour ; " but he will find few to support him in that view of the matter. The officers of the Yeomanry were taken from the local gentry, says Mr. Froude, "whom the murder system had not disposed to feel tenderly towards the accomplices of assassins. In some very few instances the innocent may have been confounded with the criminal. When society is disorganised, and peace can only be preserved by the strong hand, such misfortunes occur inevitably, and the responsibility for them rests with those who have

---

25 *Ibid,* p. 408-409.   26 p. 292.
27 *Ireland,* vol. iii. p. 380.   28 *Ibid,* p. 421.

rendered the use of force indispensable."²⁹ Gen. Lake, who became subsequently Lord Lake of Delhi and the conqueror of the Mahrattas, has been liberally bespattered by the mudslinging of party writers. He was an officer of singular moderation and humanity.³⁰ His proclamation at Belfast on 13th March, 1797, declared—"That daring outrages were being perpetrated in many parts of the province with the deliberate purpose of superseding the laws by terror. The Civil power was defied. Loyal subjects who had enrolled themselves as yeomanry under the King's commission were murdered," &c.³¹ All the "reliable" information makes it apparent that the yeomen, who did not live in barracks, became members of their corps on peril of their lives; and that when called to active service they were arrayed against men who thought seduction and assassination fair weapons to use against them. With the experience through which most of them had graduated, their readiness to encounter overwhelming numbers may be accounted for, and to this cause also may be ascribed their occasional resort to extreme measures. These latter were grossly exaggerated. Froude accuses the United Irishmen of pursuing their object "through secret murder and open lying." The Belfast committee issued a manifesto on April 14th, 1797, in which it was stated that their fellow-citizens "were confined in Bastiles: their wives and daughters were made the victims of a licentious *foreign* soldiery." The allegations were enquired into by a Parliamentary committee, which found "that the search for arms had been conducted *with all possible mildness.*"³² Mr. Lecky reports—"There was scarcely a man, it was said in Parliament, on whom corporal punishment had been inflicted to extort confession who did not acknowledge *guilt and discover widely extended accompliceship in treason.* Immense quantities of arms of every kind were discovered, and in consequence cartloads were brought daily into Clonmel from all quarters of the county, and thus by the timely intervention of this spirited magistrate were the lives and properties of the gentlemen and loyal inhabitants preserved on the very brink of destruction."³³ The writer is speaking of Fitzgerald, the High Sheriff of Tipperary. Froude says of this official—He has been rewarded with a

---

29 *Ibid*, p. 273. The Duke of Argyll takes a similar view of 1798. He says— "We are bound to remember which of the two parties set the first example, as well as which of the two parties was representative of the highest interest of society."—(*Irish Nationalism*, p. 259.)
30 Froude, vol. iii. p. 270. 31 *Ibid*, pp. 270, 271. 32 *Ibid*, p. 293.
33 *Ireland*, vol. iv. p. 279-280.

black name in Irish legend, and with the scorn of foolish historians. He was rewarded also by the knowledge that by his general nerve and bravery he had probably saved at least 10,000 lives.[34] According to Lecky his is the figure which stands out in the clearest relief ; though he was bitterly censured, his energy and courage were fully admitted by his critics, and he received, when the Rebellion was over, " a warm and unanimous vote of thanks from the Grand Jury of the county."[35] At the head of 40 men he attacked a large body of armed rebels and carried no less than thirty seven carts full of captured arms into Cashel.[36] A letter from Beresford appears in the *Auckland Correspondence* giving his view of the results of " torture "—as Father Cleary calls it. " So far as I can see, no man has withstood the fear of corporal punishment, and certain I am that without much outrage hundreds would peach."[37] Mr. Lecky, speaking of Beresford's riding school, of which Mr. Cleary has given such a graphic account, but of which while quoting Lecky on it he accidentally or otherwise omitted to add " A plot to seize *Dublin* did unquestionably exist ; great stores of pikes had been accumulated and a great number of them were discovered through the floggings."[38] In judging of the irregular military practices it must be remembered that the authorities were well aware that a secret arming was going on : that all sorts of plots were being hatched: that a multitude of fearful cruelties were enacting : that the means of wholesale butchery were being collected : that ordinary methods were powerless to prevent or discover this collection. These considerations will modify to a very large degree the condemnation which all of us on grounds of pure humanity would naturally accord to such expedients. Those who follow Father Cleary's account of the "tortures" of the Orange yeomanry will unquestionably expend a good deal of honest sympathy upon the victims, but in the light of the facts

---

34 *Ibid*, iii. 387. 35 Vol. iv. p. 277. 36 *Ib.*, p. 279. 37 *Ib.*, p. 280. 38 *Ib.*, p. 276.

Even Gordon admitted that the severity of the measures answered a good end : " In the neighborhood of Gorey, if I am not mistaken. the terror of the whippings was in particular so great that the people would have been extremely glad to renounce for ever all notions of opposition to Government, if they could have been assured a permission to remain in a state of quietness."—(Lecky's *Ireland*, vol. iv. p. 354.)

Gen. Lake in a confidential letter to Pelham said that he had " never heard of any instance either of picketing or half hanging, and did not believe that anything of the kind had happened in Ulster." Lecky adds, " There is little doubt that *enormous falsehoods* and exaggerations were scattered through Ulster," but he condemns the Government for not investigating the charges.—(*Ibid*, p. 45)

Taylor speaks of " murdering weapons " being surrendered through flogging, which he terms a "disagreeable necessity."—(*Rebellion in County of Wexford* p.13.)

I have put together from standard sources, they will see it is a clear waste of good material under the circumstances. Gen. Lake's view of the violence of the troops was stated in this form —" Considering their powers and provocations he believed they had acted so as to deserve the *good opinion* of the public, rather than their reproaches." (Lecky, vol. iv. p. 45.)

THE SOUTHERN RISING.

It was in the South that the most awful scenes of the rebellion of 1798 were enacted. Father Cleary has lightened as much as possible the universal condemnation which is heaped upon that quarter, and has endeavoured to ring in the Orangemen again to take the responsibility for it. Mr. Lecky comments on the part that Wicklow took in the insurrection with some degree of astonishment.[39] In seeking to account for it, he says its "proximity to Dublin, however, made it peculiarly open to the seductions of the United Irishmen, and it is said from an early period of the movement, a party among the Wicklow priests had favored the conspiracy."[40] In the latter part of 1797, the magistrates were made aware that the spirit of sedition was spreading in the county. It was found that secret meetings were held in many districts, and "the *usual rumors* of plots of the Orangemen to murder their Catholic neighbours were being industriously circulated by seditious agents, although, in fact, as an historian who lived in the county observes, there was *no such thing* as an Orange association formed in the County of Wexford until a few months *after* the suppression of the rebellion, nor were there any Orangemen in the county at its breaking out except a few in the towns where detachments of the North Cork militia were stationed."[41] The yeomanry in this county could

---

39 Justin M'Carthy says :—" Something of the character of a religious war was lent to the struggle in Wexford by *the efforts of the Orangemen* (sic), but the movement on the whole was never of a religious complexion." Again—the rebellion " was in no sense a religious war."—(*Ireland since the Union*, p. 53.) Gordon says :—" Whoever denies that the rebellion, from its first eruption, was made a religious war by the lower classes in the South of Ireland *may as well deny the existence of any rebellion at all*—the evidence of facts being as clear in one as in the other case." Father Cleary quotes Gordon saying that "women and children were not put to death by the insurgents, except in the tumultuary and hasty massacre of Scullabogue," and there he stops. Gordon, however, continues, " *but how far they would have been spared* in case of ultimate success, notwithstanding their baptism, is a matter of some doubt. That in this case the Protestant men, baptised by the priests, would have suffered as insincere converts is too probable."—(Wright's *Ireland*, vol. iii. pp. 119, 120. Also Cleary, p. 280, Note 102.)

40 Lecky's *Ireland*, vol. iv. p. 341.

41 Lecky's *Ireland*, vol. iv. p. 346. Also Taylor, p. 8, in Burford's reprint.

therefore not be of the hated colour, but as Mr. Lecky observes, the policy of the United Irishmen prevailed here, and prevented the Catholics from joining it. "The yeomanry force in this county is said to have taken a peculiarly sectarian character," owing to this circumstance. The refusal of the Catholics to be yeomen necessitated the corps being raised of Protestants of "the lowest order." The conspirators having succeeded in thus making the yeomanry non-Catholic, adopted the favorite ruse of whispering "that the Orangemen were about to massacre the Catholics, and were supported and instigated by the Government."[42] These two planks seemed to be the triumphant resort of the United Irishmen; they had all the force of axiomatic truths for working up a rebellion. Father Cleary gives a receipt for making a rebel, but he overlooks this fact attested by multitudinous instances. What always acted with malign magic was —make the yeomen exclusively Protestant, and then yell, or whisper, the Orangemen are coming to murder the Catholics. I have already shown how the people between Arklow and Bray went out at night under such a lying spirit. Wicklow raised the rebel flag. At a place called Boulavogue, between Wexford and Gorey, Father John Murphy planted another standard of insurrection on May 26th. Froude quotes from Father John's journal:—"Began the Republic of Ireland in the County of Wexford, commanded by the Rev. Dr. Murphy . . . . then came to a country village adjoining, where the republic attacked a minister's house for arms, and was denied. Laid seige to it, and killed him and all his forces. The same day burned his house, and all the Orangemen's houses in that and all adjoining parishes in that part of the county."[43] This militant messenger of the Prince of Peace punctuated his cruelties with prayers; and laid the foundations of his republic with a liberal mixture of piety and bloodshed. Hay, Cloney, and Miles Byrne describe Murphy as "an honest and simple minded man, who had been driven to desperation by the burning of his house and chapel,

---

Herr Venedey writes—" The movement of the United Irishmen began with the Presbyterians, and continued to find in their body the firmest support, till the year 1798, when it was confined *almost exclusively* to the Catholics."— (*Ireland and the Irish*, 1843, p. 300.)

42 Lecky's *Ireland*, vol. iv. pp. 341, 342. ·

43 *Ireland*, vol iii. p. 438. The minister's house referred to was that of the Rev. Dr. Burrowes. "Father Murphy assured them that if they would surrender their arms, they should not be injured, but they no sooner left the house than Mr. Burrowes and seven of his parishioners were put to death, and his son, a boy only sixteen years of age, so severely wounded that he dead."
—(Wright's *Ireland*, vol. iii. p. 31. Taylor's *History*, pp. 14, 15.)

and of the houses of some of his parishioners." Musgrave admits that his house was burned, but states, and as Lecky observes "supporting himself by depositions, that *it was not until after that priest had taken arms*, and he asserts that the yeomanry captain prevented his men from burning the chapel."[44] The rebellion in Wexford was wholly of a Catholic nature. "If you will go home and turn Christians, the rebels were accustomed to say, you will be safe enough." Faithful Catholic servants who had been in the service of Protestant households came to their mistresses, imploring them to have the parish priest in to baptise the family as it would be the means of saving them all. The chapels, both in Wexford and the neighborhood and around Vinegar Hill, were crowded with Protestants who sought to secure their lives, property and liberty by obtaining from the priests certificates of conformity.[45] The rebels compelled Protestants to put their prisoners to death in order, as Lecky says, to baffle justice should the culprits not be successful in their insurrection. Mr. Hay depicts massacres said to be committed by Protestants at Gorey[46] in the most lurid colors, but the historian whom I have quoted so frequently deals a deadly blow when he remarks "I have little doubt myself that these charges are at least *immensely exaggerated,*" and he also points out there were only "a few yeomen and militia" collected there.[47] Father Cleary passes strictures on Hunter Gowan and "his black mob," and on Hay's uncertain account accuses them of displaying "all the devices of Orangemen."[48] Mr. Lecky does not share our critic's enthusiasm over this discovery. He terms Gowan "a magistrate of great courage and energy," and says he collected the militia and yeomanry who had abandoned Gorey, and brought them back again to duty in the face of overwhelm-

---

44 *Ireland*, vol. iv. p. 355. Fathers Murphy and Roche headed a night attack on Samuel Wheatley's house, but though they burned the house Wheatley escaped. The rebels during their search for him said:—"He was a bloody Orangeman, though examinant saith he never saw an Orangeman, nor knew what they meant by that appellation, except that examinant has been universally informed that they meant a Protestant by the word Orangeman."—(Wright's *Ireland*, vol. iii. p. 31.)

45 Lecky's *Ireland*, vol. iv. p. 370. Consult the speech made by the Earl of Limerick during the debate in the Lords, May, 1805, on the Catholic petition presented by Lord Grenville. (pp. 311, 312.) Also the letter of the Bishop of Meath to Lord Castlereagh on Maynooth, dated April 27, 1799. (pp. 199-201.) —(Wright's *History of Ireland*, vol iii.)

46 Gordon declares—"The terms Protestant and Orangemen were almost synonymous with the mass of the insurgents, and the Protestants whom they *meant to favor* were generally baptised into the Roman Church."—(Lecky, vol. iv. p. 442.)

47 *Ibid*, p. 373. 48 pp. 266, 267.

ing danger. Gordon praises Gowan, and does not support the rebel statements.[49] There were but few Orangemen in Wexford;[50] and Mr. Lecky says that until shortly before the rebellion religious dissension was very slight, but the usual story had gone the rounds and every Protestant who was not particularly weak about the knees, fell under suspicion. Some of these were shot, others were piked, and others again were flogged in order to extort confessions of Orangeism. There are accounts of the most fearful suffering, and of long drawn out and agonising deaths—" Of the blackness of the tragedy *there can be no question.*" Mr. Lecky further says, " the proceedings on Vinegar Hill were largely directed by priests. Many of them were collected there. The mass was daily celebrated, and fierce sermons sustained the fanaticism of the people. A hot feverish atmosphere of religious excitement prevailed, and there was a ghastly mixture of piety and murder. It was observed that religious hatred, industriously inflamed by accounts of intended massacres of Catholics by Orangemen, played here a much more powerful part than any form of political or civil rancour, and it was often those who were most scrupulously observant of the ceremonials of their religion, who were the most murderous."[51] In the South of Ireland the Catholics were in the vast majority, and it now resounded with the dread music of that " one chord " on which, as Mr. Lecky says, the priests played. Bad as were the wildest stories of the horrors of the North, they never got within speaking distance of the real facts of the South. Father Cleary with commendable prudence touches lightly the agony of Pro-

---

49 Lecky's *Ireland*, vol. iv. p. 374. Taylor joins both Lecky and Gordon in praising the "brave and resolute John Hunter Gowan, Esq."—(*History of Wexford*, p. 19. Lecky's *Ireland*, vol. iv. p. 276.)

50 Gordon relates that when the Wexford rebels burnt the town of Tinnehaly on June 17, which contained " an active Protestant population; who had done good service in keeping the county in order," they put many persons to death " with pikes, under the charge of being Orangemen, and many more would have suffered if they had not been spared at the humane intercession of a Romanist lady, a Mrs. Maher, in that neighbourhood."—(Lecky, vol. iv. p. 443.)

51 *Ibid*, pp. 382, 383. Gordon mentions a contrast to the tolerance of the rebels at Killegny :—" A ruthless mob were collecting the Protestants of *both sexes*, in the adjoining parish of Killan, with the intention to burn them alive in the parish church, or according to their phrase, to make an *ORANGE PIE* of them." They collected the faggots, but a body of yeomanry came on the scene and scattered the cooks.—(Wright's *Ireland*, vol. iii. p. 54.) Taylor supports Lecky's statement of the most religious being the most murderous. - (*History Wexford Rebellion*, p. 50.) Gordon fully corroborates both Lecky and Taylor in these particulars.—(Wright's *Ireland*, vol. iii. p. 120.)

testants under an indubitable Catholic reign of terror.[52] A feather duster could sweep away the handful of cobwebs resting on that fearsome past, and though slight the movement it would reveal a veritable lazar house of abominations. The redeeming feature which Father Cleary makes the most of, was the treatment of women by the southern insurgents. Whilst assenting to that in the main it may be pointed out, that women were forced to look on at the butchery of those most dear to them on earth, and as Froude remarks, "more than one poor woman went mad at what she had witnessed."[53] Here again the alleviating aspect must be taken in connection with the sufferings endured in other repects. The few kindly traits in the character of the rebellion in the south are seized upon and made to do angelic duty, but the scarcity of tender angels only illumines the background the more hideously with its torturing demons.[54] There can be no doubt about the religious nature of the strife—priests praying, blessing, holding holy symbols, led the multitude to ghastly work. The massacre of Wexford Bridge, the Scullabogue Barn horror, the Vinegar Hill atrocities, make the blood run cold. Lecky says respecting the first of these—"So much blood covered the bridge, that it is related that when Dixon and his wife (fancy a woman being there!) endeavoured to ride over it their frightened horses refused to proceed, and they were obliged to dismount, Mrs. Dixon holding up her riding habit lest it should be reddened in the stream."[55] My purpose is not to parade the

[52] James Beaghan, executed on 24th June, 1797 for various murders which he said he was "instigated by popish priests to commit," confessed "every man that was a Protestant was called an Orangeman, and everyone was to be killed from the poorest man in the country. They thought it no more sin to kill a Protestant than a dog."—(Musgrave's *Memoirs*, vol. i. p. 74. See also vol. ii. Appendix. p. 101)

[53] *Ireland*, vol. iii. p. 494.
Mr. Froude mentions that women " were sometimes killed by their own sex." He gives a case which was tried at Naas in 1801. Two boys who had assisted at the murder when asked why they had done so, quietly said " Because she was a Protestant."—(*Ireland*, vol. iii. p. 494-495.) See also the journal of Mrs. Adams in Wright's *Hist. of Ireland*, vol. iii. p. 76 &c. Taylor gives cases in his *History of the Rebellion in Wexford*, pp. 18, 20, 33, 52, &c.

[54] Taylor relates that after the rebels left Gorey and imagined that their rebellion was successful, a proclaimation was issued : "Anyone harboring Protestants and not bringing them to the camp shall be shot and his house burned."—(*Hist. Wexford*, p. 28.)
Father Cleary says, p. 269, Note 52—" Lord Kingsborough was captured by the insurgents in Wexford and was treated by them with *great consideration*." But Lord Kingsborough was the hostage to appease the avengers of blood if the rebels were beaten ; and was used for that purpose, being liberated when the King's troops were closing in upon Wexford. Why keep to half-truths ?

[55] *Ireland*, vol. iv. p. 456.

crimes of which the Roman Catholics were alleged to be guilty in all their naked deformity; as the Hon. Emily Lawless said of 1641, so it may be said of 1798—"let us shut our eyes and pass on." I cannot however take leave of Wexford Bridge without mentioning Father Curran's heroic attempt to prevent the massacre.[56] He, at least, is marked for immortality. Of the kindly deed done by a certain woman, our Lord said that " wherever this Gospel is preached the story will be told as a memorial of her." And on a similar principle when the story of the Rebellion is told, the brave and noble effort made by this clergyman, on the peril of his life, to prevent the inhuman butchery will be recorded. Lecky, Taylor, and Froude agree in placing his name before that of his bishop—Dr. Caulfield. Froude calls attention to the peculiarity that Father Curran knew of the tragedy, and hastened to the scene to protest against it, while the bishop professedly was in his palace quite unconscious of what was going on : yet he was up betimes, and on the spot on the following day when vengeance was in a fair way of overtaking the miscreants who had been to the front in the dismal work.

DISTRIBUTING THE BLAME.

Father Cleary, as we have seen, is very liberal in giving the " Orange yeomanry " the lion's share in provoking, and then in brutally quelling, the insurrection, and also in barbarity *post facto*. Mr. Lecky remarks there is a " remarkable concurrence of both loyal and disloyal writers in attributing the worst excesses to Germans and Welshmen who had never been mixed up in Irish quarrels."[57] This, therefore, is an absolution of the yeomanry from the worst military abuses on agreed testimony by both parties. But what is more remarkable is Lecky's view, that there appears to have been little or no " difference in point of ferocity between the Irish yeomanry, who were *chiefly Protestant*, and the Irish militia, who were *chiefly Catholic*."[58] If

---

56 Taylor, who was one of the Protestant prisoners on the ill-fated bridge, describes the scene.—(*Hist. Wexford Rebellion*, p. 60.)

57 *Ireland*, vol. iv. p. 472.

58 *Ibid*, p. 472. Father Cleary acquiesces in this so far as to say :—" A large body of the Irish militiamen were undoubtedly Catholics." (p. 270, Note 53.) The Bishop of Killala said that when the French were defeated, the loyal regiments, " being *all militia*, seemed to think they had a right to take the property they had been the means of preserving. . . . Their rapacity differed in no other respect from that of the rebels, except that they . . . were incomparably superior to the Irish traitors in dexterity of stealing." A letter, dated August 29th, printed in the *Castlereagh Correspondence*, said that the writer dreaded " the *indiscipline of the Irish militia*—friends or foes are all the same to

we accept this as a fair statement of the spirit which prevailed in the retributive fury provoked by the rebellion, then both loyal Catholics and loyal Protestants are much on the same level: and that such could be the case is a significant comment on the character of the rebels, and the methods by which they carried out their rebellion. Mr. Lecky further remarks:—"As the yeomen were chiefly Protestants, it is perhaps not surprising that they should have been regarded as Orangemen, but it is much more strange that this charge should have especially centred on the North Cork militia. This regiment is accused by historians of both parties of having first publicly introduced the Orange system into the County of Wexford, where it appears previously to have been unknown, and it seems to have excited a stronger popular resentment than any other Irish regiment during the rebellion. . . . It is *probably* true that some of its officers wore Orange badges, and it is *perhaps* true that they had connected themselves with the Orange Society,[59] but it is quite certain that no regiment raised in the South of Ireland, and in an essentially Catholic county, could possibly have consisted largely of Orangemen. . . . . Whatever may have been its demerits no regiment showed a more unflinching loyalty during the rebellion, and it is said to have lost a full third of its members."[60] Newenham, who had been a major in this regiment about two years before the rebellion broke out, mentions that in his time two-thirds of the regiment were Catholics, and he puts it forward as an *example of the loyalty shown by large bodies of Catholics* during the rebellion.[61] Father Cleary has made such capital use of the North Corks, as depicting the ferocity of the Orangemen, that he engages in unseemly conflict

---

them, and they will plunder indiscriminately."—(Wright's *History of Ireland*, vol. iii. p. 135.) Wolfe Tone says that the ranks of the new militia were being *filled* by the Catholics.—(Vide his *Life*, vol. i. p. 111. Also *The Nineteenth Century*, June, 1890, p. 1004.)

59 Compare this with Father Cleary's statement :—"Lecky . . . is prepared to admit that the officers of the regiment were Orangemen:" and also Plowden's statement that in 1810 (*i.e.* twelve years afterwards) a large portion of the Ulster regiments were Orangemen. (p. 270, Note 53.) In this note, Cleary says "Lecky acts as *the apologist* of the North Cork militia." On September 9, 1798, the Commander-in-chief in his general order thanked the yeomanry for their services, "not having tarnished that courage and loyalty which they had displayed in the cause of their king and country *by any act of wanton cruelty* towards their deluded fellow subjects."—Banks' *History Orange Order*, pp. 26, 27. See also Taylor's *History of Wexford*, p. 24.)

60 Lecky's *Ireland*, vol. iv. p. 351. The cold blooded treachery at Prosperous on Sunday night, May 20, 1798, was a legacy to the Cork militia and ancient Britons.—(Wright's *History of Ireland*, vol. iii. p. 11.)

61 Lecky's *Ireland*, vol. iv. p. 351. Newenham's *State of Ireland*, p. 273.)

with Lecky over this passage, and endeavours to weaken its reliability. One can quite understand the chagrin with which he views a conspicuous illustration of Orange iniquity* frustrated by a body largely composed of Catholics. His obstinacy on this point is therefore accountable. Mr. Lecky, as I have shown, has called attention in a hundred passages to the device of the insurgents which drove the Catholics into frenzy, when nameless ruffians here and there yelled the Orangemen are coming to destroy them; it is a singular fact that I have not observed *one solitary reference* to this ruse in Mr. Cleary's pages. The puffed "reliable information" is not quite that which its author's fancy has represented it. But then, as he is careful to point out, "the political creed" of Mr. Lecky, whom he politely terms "the distinguished Unionist writer," is "so much in accord with that of the Orange brethren."[62] The policy of the Government was a desperate one, and it had desperate results. "If regarded purely as a military measure it was certainly successful, but it must be added that it was largely responsible for the ferocity with which the rebellion was waged, and that it contributed enormously to the permanent and deadly evils of Irish life. The hatred and distrust of law and Government, the inveterate proneness to seek redress by secret combination and by barbarous crimes, the savage animosities of class and creed that make Irish Government so difficult, were *not created*, but they were all immensely strengthened by the events which I am relating."[63] Mr. Froude points out—"The common law of England was not calculated for the Irish meridian. The extreme of a country, where juries would not convict, where witnesses were afraid to

---

*Under the heading "The Reign of Terror," the Father refers to Hay's charge of massacre, &c., by the Orange yeomanry, and says:—"The same writer records the massacre and mutilation of *men, women,* and *children* by the Gorey yeomanry on the day that is still remembered in North Wexford as 'Bloody Friday.'" (pp. 296, 297.) It will be a relief to turn from Hay, Stubble, Chaff and Co. to one who is Wright. He says the rebels were heavily defeated at Vinegar Hill on June 21, 1798. Refugee Protestants in Arklow desiring to return to their homes in Gorey disregarded Gen. Needham's order to the contrary, and did so. A body of yeomanry numbering only *seventeen* went with them. Being joined by a few others, the little company searched for rebels "and killed about 50 men whom they found in their houses, or who were *straggling homeward from the rebel army.*" On the next day (June 22) a wing of the defeated army, *numbering about 500,* informed of the affair, swept round on Gorey and slaughtered 37 men. "*No women or children were injured, because the rebels said that their own women had been spared in the massacre of the preceding day.* THIS sanguinary affair was long afterwards remembered among the inhabitants of Gorey under the title of 'Bloody Friday.'" Cleary evidently regards the epithet as a Catholic rather than a Protestant one.—(Wright's *History of Ireland,* vol. iii. pp. 69-71.)

62 p. 53, Note 47.   63 Lecky's *Ireland,* vol. iv. pp. 289, 290.

give evidence, and magistrates to convict, where laws had no terror because the general sentiment combined to shield a criminal, had not been allowed for."[64] In another passage Mr. Lecky says:—"The main problem of Irish history is the fact that Ireland, after a connection with England of no less than seven hundred years, is as *disaffected as a newly conquered province, and that in spite of a long period of national education, of the labors of many able and upright statesmen, of a vast amount of remedial legislation, and of close contact with the free, healthy, and energetic civilisation of Great Britain, Irish popular sentiment on political subjects is, at the present hour, perhaps the most degraded and demoralised in Europe.*"[65] Justin M'Carthy admits that Froude is a writer of "commanding talents,"[66] and Father Cleary affirms that Lecky is "a distinguished Unionist writer." Both these historians agree that Ireland is the home of peculiarities in political and social life, due no doubt to difference in race and religion, and emphasised by the frequent ruptures between their representatives. We shall have occasion to note large bodies of fact which substantiate both Lecky and Froude, and which, irrefragibly, are not due to the Orange Society in Ireland or anywhere else: but which demonstrate to some extent the necessity of such an institution in Ireland, or wherever numbers of the Irish majority are found: for according to Michael Davitt they forget nothing and learn nothing. The *Freeman's Journal* of June 3rd, 1887, has the following from this gentleman—"Our people, however, who so leave Ireland are not lost in the Irish cause, for they will join the ranks of *the Ireland of retribution* beyond the Atlantic: and when the day shall again come, that we have a right to manage our own affairs, the sun may some day shine down upon England, when we here in Ireland will have the opportunity of having *vengeance upon the enemy for its crimes in Ireland.*"[67] This is the way the men, whom the Irish Catholics delight to honor, voice the aspirations of the majority in the "Island of Saints." We must credit them with knowing what they say, and with saying what they mean. Returning, however, to our subject, it will be observed that Mr. Lecky accuses the Government of intensifying the divisions in Irish life by its policy towards the rebels. Lord Cornwallis informed the Duke

---

64 *Ireland*, vol. iii. p. 402. 65 Lecky's *Ireland*, Vol. iii. pp. 546, 547.

66 See Qui Vive's letter *Maryborough Advertiser*, September 7, 1896.

67 Quoted by Prof. Dicey, *A Leap in the Dark*, p. 120. This is the prophecy of a good time for Ireland under Home Rule.

of Portland in a despatch dated July 8, 1798, that the "members of both Houses of Parliament are, in general, averse to all acts of clemency," in which they were supported by "the principal persons" of Ireland. He goes on to say that in "their warmth they lose sight of the real cause of the mischief, of that deep laid conspiracy to revolutionise Ireland on the principles of France."[68] Evidently, therefore, Cornwallis desired to bring back the character of the struggle from its religious development to the original political complexion, and settle its issues upon political grounds. It would have been a good thing, but it was not possible to realise this end, as the Catholic masses were being led by at least some of their priests to the war. The new viceroy admitted that there was a "sanguinary disposition on our side" which he desired to effectually check, but he could see "no prospect of amendment," while the "feeble outrages, burnings, and murders which are still committed by the rebels" were continued.[69] Father Cleary has nothing to say about the latter class of outrages; he is actively concerned to point out that the vindictive spirit survived on the Protestant side, and to fasten the charge of pitiless cruelty on the "Orange yeomanry," when the rebellion was practically quelled.[70] Sir George Cornwall Lewis gives his opinion on the allegations of needless reprisals. Considering the existence of patent rebellion and of martial law for a considerable time, the punishments actually authorised by the Government *appear to have been moderate.*" And again, " Lord Castlereagh appears to . . . have acted cordially with Lord Cornwallis, and never to have been the advocate of a sanguinary policy, notwithstanding the charges of cruelty which have been made against him."[71] Judge Morris in *Ireland from '98 to '98* (p. 32) says—" The conduct of Pitt and the British ministry was

---

68 *Administrations of Great Britain*, Lewis, pp. 178-179.   69 *Ibid*, p. 179.

70 The letter of Lord Cornwallis to the Duke of Portland, dated February 14, 1799, is gruesome reading. After all his "lenient measures," Cornwallis deplores that outrage and disaffection still continue "not less destructive and infinitely more embarrassing than open rebellion." Moreover, "the treasonable disposition exists in its *full force*," outside of Ulster. Holt's letter to the Government, dated February 27, 1799, while he was in jail, says that from the conversation of other rebel prisoners, there were 20,000 rebels organised at Cork : that the southern counties were still secretly organising : that great numbers of the militia have sworn to go with the next rising. The common talk was—"There is not a Catholic who would not kill a Protestant as soon as he would a rat." Holt, though a rebel, was a Protestant.—(Wright's *History of Ireland*, vol iii. pp. 204, 205.)

71 Administrations of Great Britain, p. 181. Gordon tells a grim story of rebel exploits when *open* rebellion was quelled.—(Wright's *Ireland*, vol. iii. p. 117.)

THE USUAL TACTICS.

often feeble and even tortuous . . . but they were hardly to blame for the deeds of violence that were done."

THE FACTS OF THE REBELLION.

Mr. Froude puts these compactly together in his work, the *English in Ireland*, vol. iii. pp. 531-537. I have dwelt at some length upon the various aspects of the Rebellion in order to meet the many allegations which Father Cleary has made against the Orange Society in connection with it. I have shown how the yeomanry were made mainly Protestant and largely Orange: the unquestionable fact that any Protestant became a yeoman on peril of his own life, and at the extreme jeopardy of his home and family: the cruelties practised upon the yeomen by the rebels amongst whom they dwelt: the exercise of seduction and assassination against them : and how the ignorant Catholic peasantry were alarmed and inflamed by the malignant fictions circulated concerning the oath of the Orangemen. I have also shown that the accusations of history against Orangeism during this period rest on Roman Catholic authority or depend upon the testimony of men like Lord Holland, who denied the existence of a conspiracy in Ireland and laughed at the idea of a French invasion. Father Cleary has, perhaps not unnaturally, given credit to every lying statement against the "Orange Yeomanry" and the Orangemen generally, but he must have noticed, during his perusal of Lecky, the numerous references which that historian has made to the efforts of the insurgents to alarm and arouse the Catholics by mendacious inventions respecting the Orange Society. It is certain the Roman Catholic commonalty were not the "injured innocents" which Father Cleary would have the world believe, and though I have not set forth their misdeeds in such colors as the fair-minded Mr. Lecky depicts them, I am satisfied that enough has been stated to disprove the allegations of wholesale cruelty levelled at the Orange Society.

CHAPTER XI.

PITT'S POLICY AND THE GOADING BUSINESS.—THE POLITICAL HERESY OF MR. PITT.—"THE CUMBERLAND PLOT."—THE COMMITTEE APPOINTED.—39 GEORGE 3C. 79.—NOT THE OPINION WANTED.—HOW THE HOUSE DEBATED THE REPORT. —PROCEEDING BY RESOLUTION AND NOT BY ACT OF PARLIAMENT.—THE " SPOOK " FACTORY.

IN order to economise space, I have found it necessary, in this edition, to omit exhaustive argument with respect to the allegations made in Mr. Cleary's book, on the goading policy of Pitt, in which it is said he made use of the Orangemen to rob Ireland of her legislature. I have already shown that the Camden administration would not countenance the Orangemen at as late a date as March, 1798. The rebellion broke out in May. Had there been a sudden change of front on the part of the Ministry, even then there would scarcely be sufficient time for the goading business to be effected. On the other hand, it is well-known that the United Irishmen organisation, around which the rebellion centred, was formed in 1791, and had therefore been steadily working for about *seven years* for its ends. The success of the French Revolution of 1789 gave it both life and direction, and probably a policy as well. This, however, is a matter of no moment to Father Cleary. He gave us previously an illustration of the way to " strain at a gnat and swallow a camel," by parading the story of an infant society expelling more than half the people of a populous county : so his credulity in stating that Pitt and the Orangemen, within a couple of months, goaded the Irish into rebellion, need not excite any special wonder.

The recall of Lord Fitzwilliam is regarded by all sympathisers with Irish grievances as Pitt's masterstroke to rouse the Catholics to boiling point. The Duke of Argyll says—" Wolfe Tone attached not the *smallest importance* to the mission of Lord Fitzwilliam."[1] Judge Morris admits that Fitzwilliam's " Whig colleagues *threw him over*."[2] Wright, referring to the many accusations made during this period, says—" The revolutionary party, furious at the disappointment of their hopes, employed every means of throwing odium upon the Government. It was

---

1 *The Nineteenth Century*, June, 1890, p. 1006. 2 *Ireland from '98 to '98*, p. 24.

said before, with some truth, that the severities employed against the United Irishmen had goaded the Irish into insurrection, but they *now* said that ministers had promoted the rebellion in a more direct manner, and there were not wanting men to assert and pretend that the horrible massacre in the barn of Scullabogue had been perpetrated by Government Agents in order to throw odium on the Catholics."³ . Mr. Lecky, commenting on Grattan's attitude, observed : " Peace he believed to be vitally necessary, and he shared the belief *which was then very prevalent*, though the publication of confidential documents *has now shown it to be unfounded*, that Pitt did not sincerely desire it." I would refer the reader who desires to pursue this matter further, to the following authorities, viz.: Sir Geo. C. Lewis' *Administrations of Great Britain*, pp. 175, 176, 183, 187, 190, 196, 197, 143, 142, 203. Lecky's *Ireland in the 18th Century*, vol. iv. pp. 24, 25, 57, 75, 241 ; vol. ii. pp. 518, 459, 461, 344, 347 ; vol. iii. pp. 371, 372. The Duke of Argyll in the *Nineteenth Century*, June 1890, pp. 1005, 1006. *Irish Nationalism*, pp. 260, 263. Mr. Martin's *Ireland Before and After the Union*, pp. 21, 26, 30, 29. Walpole's *Short History of Ireland*, pp. 404, 405. The Hon. Emily Lawless' *Ireland*, pp. 351, 352. Green's *History of the English People*, pp. 783, 787, 789, 792, 793. (The essential difference between Mr. Green's treatment and that of Mr. Cleary is that one believes in the Empire, the other is a Nationalist. The reader who follows Green through the pages I have indicated, will scarcely understand and will barely credit Father Cleary when he says :—" Toleration was better understood in Ireland in 1793 and 1795—before the formation of the Orange lodges—than it was in 1829 and 1869."⁴ In 1829 the Duke of Wellington " emancipated " the Catholics by admitting them to Parliament. In 1869 the Episcopal Church of Ireland was disestablished and disendowed by the Gladstone Ministry.⁵) Wright's *History of Ireland*, vol. iii. pp. 197, 153, 157. Pitt's great speeches on the Union will be found on pp. 176-184.

On the question of robbing Ireland of her legislature, and bringing about the Union, Mr. Green says : " *It was agreed on all sides* that their (the Catholics') opposition would have secured its defeat : *but no Catholic opposition showed itself.*"⁶ Lord Castlereagh wrote Pitt on January 1st, 1801, describing the difficulties he had to meet on the question of the Union, and in this letter he said :—" The Protestant body was divided on the

---

3 *Ireland*, vol. iii. p. 153.   4 p. 22.
5 Green's *History of English People*, pp. 814, 819.   6 *Ibid*, p. 793.

question, with the disadvantage of Dublin and the Orange societies against us."⁷ Father Cleary, evidently forgetting the goading job, makes an obscure reference in his appendices (p. 403, Note 18) to the attitude of the Orange Society, on the authority of a Mr. Bouverie-Pusey. The Father quotes—" The majority of the Orangemen were *opposed* to the Legislative Union." But if this means anything at all, it means that they were opposed to robbing Ireland of her legislature, and this contradicts his former allegation that the Orangemen were a party to Pitt's policy. This is a rather awkward and unlooked for complication in his work. His Orangemen are a people that were never known upon the earth previous to the issue of his book, but even such extraordinary creatures cannot be both *for* and *against* a certain policy *at one and the same time*. Mr. Wright relates that on December 11, 1798 :—" A meeting of the Masters of the Orange lodges was held in Dublin, but they came to a resolution that having associated merely *to resist insurrection*, it did not become them to interfere with respect to any other political matter : and that though they did not individually pledge themselves *to any side on the question of Union*, and should hold themselves at liberty to come forward on the subject in their towns and counties as citizens and freeholders: yet that as *Orangemen* they should remain neuter." This writer adds—" Nevertheless, the Orangemen in general *were opposed* to the Union."⁸ Mr. Cleary gleans chiefly from Lecky's writings in 1871.⁹ My quotations are wholly taken from the more mature Lecky of 1892. Mr. W. T. Stead, writing on "The Centenary of 1798," says that he blushes, hangs his head, has confusion of face, and other distressing symptoms at the thought of it; then in an outburst of cheap penitence he confesses the sins of England against Ireland in step-motherly accents, and according to the stock-in-trade of Irish Nationalists. We have heard of the leaning tower of Pisa, but in the way of "*leaning*" this article puts the famous tower out of sight altogether. Yet Stead admits that Lecky, in his *Ireland in the 18th Century*, "repels the charge brought against the British Government, that they provoked the rebellion in order to bring about the Union."¹⁰ Father Cleary plays on broken strings when he repeats accusations long ago refuted. It would efface many of his cherished political prejudices were he to frankly adopt the view delineated by Mr. Lecky when tracing the difference between a Government

---

7 Wright's *Ireland*, vol. iii. p. 255. 8 *Ibid*, p. 155.   9 pp. 261, 262.
10 *Review of Reviews*, August, 1898, p. 215.

peculiarly English, and one peculiarly Irish. Ireland is the country, so the distinguished Unionist writer says, " where *large classes of crime are commonly looked upon as acts of war: where jurymen will acquit in the face of the clearest evidence: and where known criminals may live in security under the shelter of popular connivance or popular intimidation.*"[11] This is uncommonly like the sentiment of Mr. Froude, which I have previously recorded (p. 182) and it makes the similarity of view the more remarkable. Mr. Lecky forwarded a letter to *The Times* in January, 1886, when the Home Rule commotion was exciting public attention, in which he said : " Read for only three months *United Ireland*, the most accredited organ of the party . . . I will venture to say that any statesman who reads that paper, and then proposes to hand over the property and the virtual government of Ireland to the men whose ideas it represents, must be either *a traitor or a fool.*" In this letter he also adds, " At the present time there is far more of the liberty of the individual in Russia and in Turkey than in Ireland," through what *The Times* calls the " hateful tyranny"[12] of the Land League. Bubble-blowing is a pleasant occupation when a child has plenty of soapy water and a new pipe, but inflated " suds " collapse when touched. I add to the already broken bubbles that of

THE CUMBERLAND PLOT.[13]

Father Cleary has been very circumstantial on the question of this alleged conspiracy on the part of the Orange Society, but his inductive methods have not made out a stable case, and as I will show, he has overlooked certain facts which quash his theory. It will be observed that his prudence in omitting these facts is of a piece with the discretion seen to be paramount throughout his story. The Parliamentary history of the appointment of the committee to enquire into the character and tendencies of Orange Lodges is given in the *Annual Register*, and from that record I shall extract the circumstances which put the historic " snuffer " on Father Cleary's ingenious " Cumberland Plot." The opening paragraph is ominous:—" The influence which the Irish Opposition had acquired by its union with the ousted Cabinet manifested itself early in the session by the commencement of a series of Parliamentary attacks directed against the

---
11 Lecky's *Ireland*, vol. ii. pp. 516-517.
12 *Times Articles and Correspondence*, pp. 458-459.
13 See Sir Chas. Russell's treatment of the way to put a conspiracy case.— (*Ireland's Vindication*, p. 9.)

Orange Lodges."[14] The way that the Orange Lodge was assailed—or the pretext for the attack—was that it had presented loyal addresses to the King. On the 6th of March, 1835, Mr. Shiel[15] moved for the " production of addresses presented to the King from certain Orange societies, and the answers which had been returned to them." The papers were immediately produced, and though there was nothing in either the addresses, or the replies, which could furnish cause for grievance, yet the discussion was " distinguished principally by the unbounded and rabid abuse which the Irish opposition poured out upon the Orangemen,[16] and the rational advice given by Sir Robert Peel to the House." The matter was not allowed to drop, for the member for County Kilkenny (Mr Finn), on the 23rd of March, moved :—" That a select committee be appointed to enquire into the nature, character, extent, and tendencies of Orange lodges, associations, or societies *in Ireland*, and to *report their opinion* thereon to the House." This was seconded by Mr. Maxwell, member for County Cavan, an avowed Orangeman,

---

14 *The Annual Register*, 1835, vol. 77 p. 324.
Molesworth, in common with others, quite understood how the defeat of the Orangemen came about. " The Irish Catholic party which, though not very numerous, was sufficiently large *to hold the balance of power between the Government and the Opposition*, and to give the majority to one or the other as it suited the purpose of its leader. O'Connell used the *enormous power* which this state of things placed in his hands very skilfully."—(*History of England*, vol. i. p. 379.)

15 This is the Right Hon. Lalor Shiel, who said that the Rev. Dr. Robinson, in 1826, at an Orange meeting in Omagh, longed ''*for a general massacre*'' of the Roman Catholics. One would like to read Dr. Robinson's words, because Mr. Shiel's account smacks strongly of the apocryphal. Father Cleary gives Shiel's words, but not Robinson's. (pp. 67, 63.) Lord John Russell's Government made Mr. Shiel, in 1847, "the Master of the Mint, with a salary of £2000 a year." He " distinguished his advent to office by *omitting on the very first coin that he struck the usual legend that declared the supremacy of the Queen in church and State:* an insult to Her Majesty and the country, which was instantly remedied by the officers of the Crown, on the immediate and indignant denunciation of the people." Notwithstanding, Mr Shiel was *subsequently* sent as Ambassador to the Roman Chtholic state of Tuscany.—(Wright's *History of Ireland*, vol. iii. p. 563.) See Duffy's caustic letter to Shiel—" the Catholic champion "—who was a member of the Ministry that put Duffy on his trial. The writer hints that, as a minister, Shiel's interest in Irish patriots had pretty well evaporated.—(*Four Years of Irish History*, pp. 735, 736.)

16 The discussion first assumed that the Orange Society was an illegal organisation, and the Government was accused of encouraging it by " appointing to offices persons known to be members." O'Connell, however was too good a lawyer, and too able a tactician, to keep this false issue before Parliament, and he speedily corrected the Irish furiosos by declaring—"*there was no law which declared Orange lodges illegal.*"—(*Annual Register*, 1835, vol. 77 p. 324.) Sir R. Peel also said : "The society was legal." He intimated that Shiel's motion "*was an attempt to narrow the right and privilege of the subject to address the Crown.*"—(*Ibid.*)

who declared that he "*courted the fullest enquiry*, with a hope that the committee would be constituted in the most impartial manner."[17] At a later period of the year—August 4th—while this committee was going on -with its labors, Mr. Joseph Hume (who had a complete Irish policy of his own) brought a portion of its proceedings under the notice of the House. He had seen in the newspapers that Orange lodges had been introduced into the army, and he moved a resolution containing eleven clauses on the matter, which concluded by requesting the appointment of another committee to take evidence on Orange lodges "*in Great Britain and the colonies.*" In support of his resolution he showed how impartial he was on this subject by saying— "The members of the Orange lodges had ventured to act illegally because they knew they had hitherto had the support of the Government. If the Whig ministers had done their duty during the four years they had been in office, there would not have been an Orangeman in existence at the present moment. They had been positively afraid of attacking them, but *he would have put his heel upon their necks and trampled them to death.*"[18] Father Cleary informs us of the well-merited and thoroughgoing condemnation which the society received at the hands of a "committee of English gentlemen." One is in no quandary as to which way "the cat jumped" with Mr. Hume.[19] The Orangemen are tried and hanged before the Committee is appointed, and the proposer does not scruple to declare his own attitude to the society which he is nevertheless proposing to *try*. Mr. Patten, chairman of the Sitting Committee, was indignant that Mr. Hume should introduce the subject in the way which he did.[20] He complained that such a proceeding "must necessarily pre-judge the whole question." In the course of his remarks he said " to have been impartial, it should have been stated that there were other secret societies in the army, whose proceedings were so enveloped in mystery that it was almost impossible to arrive at

---

17 *Ibid*, p. 326.   18 *Ibid*, p. 328.

19 Mr. Hume's advanced opinions on "religious toleration" recommended him powerfully to O'Connell for political ends. Hume, who sat for Middlesex from 1830 to 1837, was rejected by that constituency in the last named year, but he found his way into Parliament for *Kilkenny*, "*which O'Connell placed at his disposal.*" It cannot be said that the Irish party was ungrateful to Hume for his services to it.—(Maunder's *Biographical Treasury*, 1873, p. 492.)

. 20 Mr. Patten declared—" It was a farce to appoint a committee to enquire into a subject if, when a portion of the evidence was printed—not half of the whole— and the enquiry was still pending a member was to be permitted to bring the subject forward in such a manner. . . . and at the same time make *attacks on the character of individuals.*"—(*Annual Register*, 1835, vol. 77 p. 329.)

the discovery of them; he meant Riband Lodges. So secret were the proceedings of the Riband Societies that although the committee examined two Lords Lieutenant, several magistrates, and Sir Frederick Stovin, the superintendent of Irish police, upon the subject, they could obtain no trace of the existence of Riband Lodges." They began to doubt whether there was any foundation for the rumours, when "subsequently the committee obtained a clue to evidence which proved that Riband Lodges existed under the very eyes of Sir F. Stovin, who nevertheless was ignorant of the fact, so secretly were their proceedings carried on."[21] This is the Sir Frederick Stovin whom Father Cleary triumphantly produces in evidence alleging that the Orangemen banging drums and playing fifes gave offence to the Roman Catholics. How stupid! Why did they not "lay low and say nuffin?" If they had done so Sir Frederick would never have discovered them. The chairman of the sitting committee declared he could not discover a Riband Society which was under his " very eyes." Colonel Perceval, member for County Sligo, in speaking to Hume's motion, contended: "In itself the Orange Institution was proved by *the evidence of every witness who had been examined to be exclusively of a defensive character.* They all admitted that Orange Lodges were a mere defence against the operations of Riband Societies, and other secret societies, existing in Ireland. . . . It did not prove much that Orange Lodges were secret societies when not only had they produced before the committee *their books and documents in the public investigation which had taken place, but even the signs and passwords by which Orangemen were known to each other.*"[22] After discussion on the 11th August, Hume withdrew two of the clauses of the motion,[23] and Lord John Russell

---

21 *Ibid*, p. 329. Patten is here replying to that portion of Hume's resolution dealing with Orange Lodges in the army.

22 *Ibid*, p. 330.
Perceval, the Grand Treasurer of the Lodge also said that both the Duke of Cumberland and himself were ignorant of Lodges being in the army ; and that everyone who had read the evidence must know that a man professing hostility to the Roman Catholic portion of the community was ineligible to admission as an Orangeman. He also added that " the Orange Societies of Ireland were ready to dissolve themselves providing other societies were put down."—(*Annual Register*, vol. 77 p. 330.

23 The clauses which Hume withdrew were Nos. 5 and 6. These had reference to the " general interference " of Orange Societies in political matters : those retained related to their existence in the army. The excised clause aimed at the Duke of Cumberland, was that which accused him of signing " warrants in his capacity as Grand Master of the Grand Orange Lodge of Ireland, which warrants had been used for constituting Orange Lodges in Ireland." All words after " which warrants " were, at Lord John Russell's instance, omitted.—(*Ibid.*)

demurring to a paragraph aimed at the Duke of Cumberland, this was also excised. The motion was then passed. The committee was appointed to "enquire into the origin, nature, extent and tendency of the Orange Institution in Great Britain and the colonies, and to report the evidence and *their opinion thereon.*" Mr. Hume was made chairman, Mr. Shiel and Mr. Finn were also upon the Committee. These were known and openly confessed enemies to Orangeism.[24] The reader will bear in mind : —1st. That an "opinion" expressed by a Parliamentary committee is privileged : it is not as a corporate body, or in its several capacity, liable to an action at law for libel. 2nd. That this committee was directed by the House to return "*the evidence and their opinion thereon.*" 3rd. That the chairman, and at least two members of this committee, were pronouncedly hostile to the cause they were intended to try. If, therefore, the evidence disclosed the faintest vestige of a conspiracy, it was to be expected that the committee would not be slow to express an "opinion" to that effect. As a matter of fact, every phrase used in the Orange Correspondence, which was capable of having more than one construction placed upon it, was noted in the report. For example, the phrase, "*the next to the Throne,*" appeared in a *draft* circular letter, intended to be sent out for the purpose merely of showing the extent of the Orange Institution : the draft was amended and another phrase substituted, but the committee put the circumstance in ; and it furnishes one of the pegs upon which Father Cleary hangs "the Cumberland Plot." Nothing is more apparent than that if the evidence had disclosed the features of a *plausible* conspiracy, the committee would have delivered an opinion to that effect, in accordance with their instructions. Strange to say, that although the Committee recorded every circumstance which was regarded as being suspicious, or which might form a contributory item to a plot builder, it stopped short of expressing the opinion that the evidence disclosed a plot. It, indeed, hinted at a conspiracy in the following words :—"Your committee think it right to place before the House the words of the statute, the 39 George 3c. 79, regarding *Corresponding Societies,* sec. 9—

---

24 See Note 30 present chapter. Hall prides himself on having made enquiry from the *enemies* of the Orange Society, as well as from its friends, and he comes to the conclusion that he will not pronounce any opinion on Orangeism, apart from the Rules and Qualifications, for which he has the highest admiration. "It is also but fair to add," he says, "that the society *stood the test of two most scrutinising* Parliamentary committees. One of the Lords in 1825, and the other of the Commons, 1836, *without the slightest imputation being cast upon it which has any weight with rational men.*"—(*Ireland,* vol. ii. pp. 466, 467.)

'Any society composed of different divisions or branches, or of different parts acting in any manner separately or distinct from each other, or of which any part shall have any distinct president, secretary, treasurer, delegate, or other officer,' &c. And in conclusion your committee submit that it will be for the *House to consider whether the present organisation of Orange lodges*, in connection with the Imperial Grand Lodge, *comes within the words of that statute* : and, if so, whether the law officers of the Crown should not be directed to institute legal proceedings, without delay, against the Grand Officers of all Orange Lodges." Why is this passage not quoted to show the conspiracy of which the Orange Lodge was guilty, at least speculatively, according to the committee's report? I will explain the reason. The enemies of the organisation accuse it of endeavouring *to alter the succession*; to prevent the Princess Victoria being called to the Throne; and to place the Duke of Cumberland there. If this were true, it would be naked treason, but the committee dared not render such an opinion. And hence they brought up the George statute about "corresponding societies"—one of those convenient pieces of legislation which can be used against any combination it is thought desirable to crush. Under this statute the Broken Hill labor leaders were sentenced. This was the precious law which the committee sought to bring in operation against the Orange Society. But if, as Father Cleary argues, the case was transparent, and the general features of a plot were disclosed, why did not the committee express an "*opinion*" to that effect? They were not asked to prove anything—merely to give their *opinion on the evidence*. When everything is so clear to others, why this significant refusal; this marked silence on the part of the committee? Why the roundabout and paltry quotation of a statute, which made even a labor combination a conspiracy within the meaning of the Act, when a straight out opinion of treason would have brought the matter to a definite issue?[25] There must be some reason for

---

25 In 1844 O'Connell and Co. appeared before a judicial tribunal charged with having conspired and confederated together to excite discontent and disaffection *in the army* : to *corrupt justice* : to *intimidate the individual* and EVEN PARLIAMENT ITSELF : and in the words of the indictment to " assume and usurp the prerogative of the Crown *in the establishment of courts for the administration of law.*" These charges were not only made, they were also substantially *proved*. O'Connell's sentence was imprisonment for 12 months, a fine of £500, and security of £2000 for future good behaviour. The penalty was subsequently remitted on an appeal to the House of Lords. But the charm was broken. The Irish Achilles was shown to be vulnerable, and the competency of the British Government to deal with him was established. That was enough.—(Wright's *History of Ireland*, vol. iii. pp. 555-6.)

this, and I will endeavour to unravel the skein which Father Cleary has tangled. He has made much of the fact that Col. Fairman refused to produce a book said to contain copies of a correspondence maintained by him as officer of the lodge. This is regarded as a darkly suspicious circumstance by the Father. I find, however, that Fairman's refusal was "on the ground that it was a *private book and contained private documents.*" The Orangemen in the House urged Fairman to concede the point and produce the book, but he was obstinate on the subject, and would neither yield to friend or foe. It never occurred to the critic of the Orange Society to mention that the Grand Secretary was publicly invited by leading Orangemen in the House of Commons to comply with the request of the committee.[26] It would be rather discouraging to the dark suspicions which he was affixing to the Grand Secretary's refusal. But I observe that Lord John Russell cuts the ground from under Father Cleary's feet on this matter. He asked the House: "Was the enquiry at all thwarted by the non-production of the book? If the book affected any great interest, something might be said in favor of the hon. member's intended motion,[27] but *nobody asserted this* or *even suggested it.*"[28] Let us now see how the report of Hume's committee was received by the British House. The authority is the *Annual Register,* as before—only vol. 78 and year 1836. It opens in the same ominous strain. "Mr. O'Connell[29] and his friends lost no time in returning to the attack on the Orange Societies, which had been begun during the preceding session. On the 11th February

---

26 I observe that Father Cleary says, when a motion was passed calling upon Fairman to produce the book—"*The Orange party in the House opposed the motion.*" According to *The Annual Register,* his statement is a random guess, and as he gives no authority for his accusation, it is manifestly a stroke off his own bat.

27 Hume gave notice of motion that he would ask the House to use force and seize the book, as well as take Fairman into custody for contempt of Parliament in refusing to do as requested. 28 *The Annual Register,* p. 334.

29 Sir Charles G. Duffy shows O'Connell's political omnipotence. The Lord Mayor of Dublin quoted the words of Lord Bessborough : "If the Government wished to conciliate Ireland, and to promote her prosperity, *all the patronage of the country should be placed in the hands of Daniel O'Connell.*"—(*Four Years of Irish History,* p. 319.)

Duffy sent £1000 from Melbourne for O'Connell's monument, which was "a larger sum than any county in Ireland contributed."—(*Ibid,* p. 326.)

Canning declared in 1824 : "Much as I wish to serve the Catholic cause, I have seen that the service of the Catholic leaders is no easy service. They are hard taskmasters, and the advocate who would satisfy them must deliver himself up to them *bound hand and foot.*"—(Godkin's *Religious History of Ireland,* p. 246.) See also Wright's *Hist. of Ireland,* vol. iii. p. 529.

Mr. Finn moved a resolution—'That Orangeism has been productive of the most baneful effects upon the character and administration of public justice in Ireland: that its prevalence in the constabulary and peace-preservation force and Yeomanry in that country has led individual members as well as large bodies of the above description of force to the gross neglect and violation of their public duty, and to open, daring, and lawless resistance to the authority of the magistracy, and of the execution of government on various occasions. That the systematic and surreptitious introduction of Orangeism into every branch of the military service, in almost every part of the Empire, in direct violation of orders issued in 1822 and 1829 by the Commander-in-Chief of his Majesty's forces; and the absolute power and control vested by its governing body, the Grand Orange Lodge of England and Ireland, in his Royal Highness the Duke of Cumberland, together with the rank, station, influence, and numbers of that formidable and *secret conspiracy*, are well calculated to excite serious apprehensions in all his Majesty's loyal subjects, and imperatively call for the most energetic expression on the part of the representatives of the people of the Empire to secure the safe, peaceable, legal, and rightful succession to the throne of these realms."[30] This is a resolution framed with conspicuous ability and care, in which the scare of conspiracy is raised, and an adroit hint is introduced about endangering the regal succession. The *Register* is somewhat caustic in its comment on Finn's motion, for it remarks that "some parts of this resolution betrayed as much of the blindness and incredulity of party spirit as could be ascribed to the most bigoted Orangeman. As the Orange Societies were founded in the interests or the ascendency of Protestantism in a country where Popery was the religion of the great majority in numbers, and as they furnished means for concentrating and regulating the influence of those Protestants, it might be very true that they were viewed with great apprehension by his Majesty's popish subjects in Ireland. But assuredly the people of England and Scotland had neither felt nor expressed any fears regarding them: and when Mr. Finn by his resolution declared

---

30 *Annual Register*, vol. 78 (1836), pp. 8-9.

I find that the committee appointed on the motion of Mr. Finn consisted of five Roman Catholics (Daniel O'Connell was one), 9 adherents of the Ministry, 11 Tories, and 2 Orangemen. The great majority of these were known to be hostile to the Orange Institution. The Grand Lodge of Ireland issued an address at the conclusion of its labors, the full text of which is printed in the Melbourne *Argus*, July 28th, 1846.—(See Chapter xii. on this.)

these societies to be engaged in a conspiracy, and *insinuated*, at least, that the object of this conspiracy was no less than to alter the succession to the throne, and for that purpose to corrupt the army, he fell into one of those outrageous absurdities, the belief in which betrays that a man's mind is too much under the influence of party animosity to judge calmly of any political question."[31] I am afraid that the rev. gentleman, who has followed Mr. Finn's Roman Catholic idea of the Orange Society, will hardly relish the force of this comment upon the nature of it : it is not to be expected that its exterminating sentences will find a congenial resting place in his bosom. The significance of the debate which followed Mr. Finn's resolution is phenomenal. His resolution laid before the House all the issues which Father Cleary has been laying before the public in his book, including such topics as *corrupting justice; resistance to constituted authority;* invading the *police, yeomanry,* and *army forces,* and degrading them : and the *disloyalty of the Cumberland plot.* All these points are covered by Finn's resolution, and should be abundantly evident in the reports of both the English and Irish committees. The treatment his motion received is sufficient, I think, to indicate what little importance the British Parliament of that day, when the subject was fresh, attached to the wild allegations contained in it. It also illustrates the discovery of a "mare's nest" by the Father.[32] The debate was postponed to allow the redoubtable chairman of the committee, Mr Hume, to make his speech and frame his resolution. That gentleman reviewed the evidence which had been published, and stated that "almost the whole of the evidence had been derived from the officers of the institution—*a fearlessness of disclosure which betrayed no consciousness of either moral or of legal guilt.*"[33] Mr. Hume also, "although he did not assert, like Mr. Finn, that the Orange lodges were in a conspiracy to alter the succession, yet maintained that the Duke of Cumberland, as their official Master, was a dangerous man."[34] This, of course, must be taken in connection with the known variance of political creeds and feeling between Hume and Cumberland at the time. The speaker also made reference to an individual who had gone through the Kingdom under warrant from the Grand Master,

---

31 *The Annual Register*, p. 9.

32 Consult the *Register* for fuller information than is given here.

33 *Ibid*, p. 10. I have given this passage as it appeared in the *Register*, but I am disposed to think that the clause in italics is the comment of the writer of the account, rather than the statement of Mr. Hume.

34 *Ibid*, p. 11.

and who "had hazarded speculations on the possibility of the King being deposed, and a Regency, at least, being established under the Duke of Cumberland during the minority of the heir apparent."[35] The *Register* explains that this allusion was made to a person of the name of Haywood, who after being *dismissed from a lodge*, addressed to Lord Kenyon in October, 1835, a letter in which he asked—" Did not his Royal Highness, as Grand Master, and Lord Kenyon, as Deputy Grand Master, know what their missionary, Col. Fairman, had done in 1832 : or rather, did he not act under the directions of his Royal Highness or Lord Kenyon, and was he not, under their directions, intrusted to sound the brethren how they would be disposed in the event of King William IV. being deposed, which was not improbable on account of his sanctioning reform in Parliament; and if so, it would become the duty of every Orangeman to support his Royal Highness, who would then in all probability be called to the Throne." There was "something very suspicious," adds the *Register*, "in this revelation of supposed designs entertained by a body, to which the maker of the revelation had nevertheless continued to belong for three years. Col. Fairman immediately published a letter declaring the whole statement to be a falsehood, and adopted judicial proceedings against Haywood, which dropped, however, in consequence of the death of the latter."[36] It is unfortunate that this pretty bit of scandal was never properly investigated. His prosecution at the instance of Fairman, and the fact that he was expelled from the lodge with his known dangerous secret (if he had any) go a long way to discredit his statements, and render him unworthy of any serious attention. Mr. Hume's resolution was—that the House, having received the evidence of both committees on Orange Societies, was convinced that " Orange Societies, and all other

---

35 *Ibid*, p. 11.
36 *Ibid*, pp. 11, 12, Note. Father Cleary, playing to the gallery, misrepresents the incident of Haywood's prosecution by Col. Fairman, by saying :— "The public were on the tiptoe of expectation of seeing the King's brother and his associates of the Imperial Grand Lodge placed in the dock *on a charge of high treason.*" He quotes Killen to allege that Haywood was "*the chief witness* against the conspirators," and that "*the peculiarly dangerous position in which he stood*" so excited him that he "burst a blood-vessel and died." Now, how could Haywood's position be *dangerous?* According to Cleary's account—(1.) The committee's report bore out his statements. (2.) The committee took him under their protecting wing. (3.) The committee retained eminent counsel for his defence. And (4.) The documents and letters to vindicate him were all prepared and in order. With a clear conscience, Haywood was so hedged in that to talk of danger is ridiculous.—(Vide Cleary, p. 380.)

political societies which have secret forms of initiation, and are bound together by any religious ceremony, are particularly deserving of the severest reprobation of the House, and should no longer be permitted to continue," and that "an humble address should be presented to his Majesty, that his Majesty will be graciously pleased to direct measures to be taken to remove from the public service every judge, &c., who shall attend the meetings of any Orange lodge, of any Riband lodge, or of any other political club, institution, or association wherever or whenever assembled," &c.[37] Sir Wm. Molesworth, trusty henchman and swashbuckler of Hume, tried to prove that the Orange societies were illegal as a matter of fact, and quoted the section of the George statute referred to by the committee's report. He contended that the Statutes were "in full force, and had been vigorously executed against the ignorant and simple. It was not long since certain laborers had been convicted under them at Dorchester, and were now suffering the sentence of transportation. These men had combined to raise their wages, which was not in itself an illegal proceeding: but they had formed themselves into an association pledged by an oath, or what was construed to be an oath. Let the leaders of the Orangemen be dealt with in the same way. . . . Many members of the institution, now aware of its noxious tendencies, *would gladly bear such testimony* as would infallibly convict the chiefs of a misdemeanor," &c.† The orator proceeded to indicate how much he was in accord with Mr. Hume, who would have "put his heel on the necks of the Orangemen and trampled them to death." Sir William Molesworth was in favor of Hume's motion for expelling members of the order from civil occupations, and would willingly have shipped "the titled criminals" to the Antartic Circle. As the *Register* said, he "claimed for the Commons in his hot zeal for the people's rights, the power of depriving every functionary in the Empire of his office at their pleasure."[38] Lord John Russell, in speaking to the legal aspect of the question, cooled the ardour and enlightened the intelligence of the enemies of Orangeism, by informing the House that "he had discussed this question (suppression of the Orange Society) in all its bearings with the Attorney General, and the impression on his mind was that the question whether these societies were

---

37 *The Annual Register*, p. 12.

†This is the proposal to prosecute the Orangemen so grandly referred to by the Father on p. 380, Note 73.

38 *The Annual Register*, pp. 13, 14.

legal was one of great doubt. The Attorney General had said that without looking most carefully at the whole subject he could not venture absolutely to pronounce an opinion as to their legality or illegality: and the Solicitor General took a similar view of the case. .... It appeared from the *opinion of eminent lawyers, of whom Lord Gifford was one, that in 1822 the Orange Societies were not held to come within the meaning of the law,* and therefore if they came at present within the terms of any Act it must be in consequence of some recent change in their constitution."[39] Though personally hostile to the Orange Society, Lord · Russell pricked the bubble of Hume and his committee, as also Sir Wm. Molesworth's inflation. Russell moved—"That an humble address be presented to his Majesty praying that his Majesty would be graciously pleased to take such measures as to his Majesty seemed advisable for the effectual discouragement of Orange Lodges and generally of all political societies excluding persons of different faith, using signs and symbols and acting by associated branches."[40] It was seen that neither Finn's motion nor Hume's stood a chance of passing the House, and as it was essential that Irish support should be purchased,[41] some modification was necessary. Russell's motion, therefore, appeared to be the most likely one to obtain the support of Parliament. Mr. Maxwell of Cavan, Col. Perceval of Sligo, and Col. Verner of Armagh—all Irish Orangemen—declared their refusal " to be tried by the report of the Committee, for its proceedings, they said, had been partial and biassed, and there had been nothing like a full and impartial investigation." So little did the Orange Society dread inquiry, that they had placed their books, etc., at the disposal of the Committee. " They treated with *deserved* contempt the insinuation that the Orange body wished to alter the succession to the Throne. ..... The principles of Orangemen were those of uncompromising loyalty to the Crown,

---

39 *Ibid*, p. 15.   40 *Ibid*, p. 16.

41 The Rev. Nassau Molesworth, who is not enamoured of the Orangemen, says on p. 379 of his work :—" It was alleged that there was a conspiracy on the part of the Orangemen to set aside the Princess Victoria, the next heir to the throne, in favor of the Duke of Cumberland, and though all *well informed persons* saw that these suspicions were *destitute of foundation,* they were nevertheless extensively believed by the *very ignorant."* On p. 383 he returns to the matter, saying that the Duke of Cumberland was *"absurdly supposed to be aspiring to the English throne."* In 1833, according to Barry O'Brien, O'Connell had said :—"The Orange party have thrown down the gauntlet at the Winchelsea dinner and *the Catholics must take it up.* The struggle against ascendency must be persevered in to the end."—(*History of England*, 1830-74, vol. i.)—(*Fifty Years' Concessions,* vol. i.)—(*Letters of O'Connell,* vols. i. ii.)

the Constitution and the Church, and by these they would be found to stand, whatever might be their circumstances—of prosperity or adversity. They had been strictly defensive, and had been called into existence by the exigencies of the times, and the dangers arising from Associations of a very different character. They would not oppose the resolution: the Orangemen would at once acquiesce in the wish of the House and yield obedience to the expressed will of his Majesty. . . . . But they objected to the specific mention of the Orange Lodges by name in the address, while those formed only part of the secret societies which existed in Ireland. This was to stigmatise those who were ready at the call of his Majesty to relinquish all secret association, but who still would feel the sting of being chiefly aimed at, as the only Society named. The influence of those individuals who took the lead in Orange Lodges, and who were most willing to act upon the spirit of the resolution, would be greatly weakened, and their power of inducing others to imitate their example would be much diminished, if they believed (and they would believe it if they saw that they only were mentioned) that the chief aim of the resolution was to put down Orange Associations exclusively."[42] Lord Stanley complimented the "Irish Orange members on the frank and manly conduct with which they had met the conciliatory views of the Government," and he "strongly urged the omission of the obnoxious words." The Orange leaders in Parliament had promised to yield submissively to the spirit of the resolution, and "it was important for the purpose of the resolution itself, that this power should not be diminished, nor any stigma be thrown on those who were ready to exert it. . . . He was sure it was not meant by the use of these words to cast any *imputation. The resolution was so understood by the Opposition side of the House.*"[43] Sir Robert Peel said that "although he was prepared to agree in the resolution, it was not without a great sacrifice of opinion."[44] His objection was to "proceeding by resolution: he thought they ought to indicate the will of the Legislature *by a law*, rather than by a *resolution of one branch of it.* They ought studiously to avoid a course *by which a dominant majority of that House could denounce any party.*[45] . . The resolutions of that House had no force,

---
42 The *Annual Register*, p. 17.   43 *Ibid*, p. 17.   44 *Ibid*, p. 18.

45 In 1829 a *Whig* Ministry passed the Party Processions Act as a sop to the Irish party, but it was so worded that O'Connell's great demonstrations went down under it. In 1833 Earl Grey "bitterly lamented the disappointment h had experienced at finding that the Emancipation Act *had not produced th*

except such as the prerogative of the Crown might give them : they had not the force of law, and this was the first time that he had heard of establishing the precedent of a resolution of that House, *disqualifying for office on the alleged ground of conduct, the legality of which, at least, was questionable."* He also urged the excision of the objectionable words, in favor of a motion intended to be proposed by Mr. Patten, the chairman of the first committee. On this head he argued—" the Orange members had expressed themselves disposed to make sacrifices for this purpose, and it would be prudent and politic in the House not to weaken the influence of those from whom they had reason to expect much useful co-operation."[46] Lord John Russell having declared that *" there was no opinion pronounced as to the legality of these Societies, but merely that they as well as other secret Societies should meet the disapprobation of the Crown,"* and the friends of the Orange Society not pressing for a division, the motion was agreed to. The *Register* said :—" The Orange Societies immediately acquiesced, some of them with more cheerfulness, others of them with less, and all of them with regret.[47] People asked would a similar regard to expression of opinion by the Commons, and the Crown, have been manifested by those mischievous associations which the Popish demagogues employed to extend their own political power and the influence of their Church, and which set *even Acts of Parliament at defiance."*[48] Both Finn's resolution and that of Hume were

---

tranquillity which all who had supported it so strongly anticipated." A Protestant writer says—" *As long as O'Connell lived agitation in Ireland did not cease.*"— (Wright's *Ireland,* pp. 528-530. See also Stanley's speech.—(*Hansard,* 3rd series, vol. xv. and xvi.)

46 The *Annual Register,* p. 19.

47 Hall says that immediately the resolution was carried, the Grand Lodge met and discussed the situation, and ultimately agreed to dissolve by 92 votes to 62.—(*Ireland : its Scenery, Character,* etc., vol. ii. p. 467.) Molesworth corroborates the *Register.*—(*Hist. England,* vol. i. p. 383.)

48 The *Annual Register,* p. 19.

The Roman Catholic organ, the *Tablet,* July 26, 1851, gave the following lusty defiance to the Ecclesiastical Titles Bill :—" Neither in England nor in Ireland will the Roman Catholics obey the law, that is the law of the Imperial Parliament. They have or are likely to have before them two things called laws which unhappily (or happily) contradict each other. Both cannot be obeyed and both cannot be disobeyed. *One of them is the law of God ; the other is no law at all.* It pretends to be an Act of Parliament : but in the ethics of legislation it has no more force or value than a solemn enactment that the moon is made of green cheese. It is not a law, but a lie—a parliamentary lie—which its very utterers know to be false, and which they deliberately put forward as a falsehood, careless of contempt and ignominy, so that they can retain their hold of office. Of these two things we need hardly say which will be obeyed and which disobeyed. *The law of God,* that is, *the pope's command,* will be, or rather has been and is being, carried

scouted by the Commons, and the suspicion of a plot of the nature insisted upon by Father Cleary was not, so far as I can find, even entertained by the chief statesmen who were deadly opponents of the Orange Society. Hume himself, it appears, did not credit Mr. Finn's malignant insinuation, and Father Cleary was ashamed to put forward prominently this "distinguished" statesman from Kilkenny in support of his famous conspiracy. The debate was conducted on other lines absolutely, in which Lord John Russell, the mover of the resolution that was carried, quoted Lord Gifford as to the legality of Orangeism. The Government dared not proceed, as asked by Sir Robert Peel, by Act of Parliament to suppress the Society : its proposal was in the form of a resolution, and that resolution was only put when the head of the Government had first declared that his motion expressed no opinion on the *legality* of the Orange Society. Judge Morris, I believe a Roman Catholic, in *Ireland from '98 to '98*, mentions the allegation of the Cumberland Conspiracy, but disposes of it by saying:—" The charge, if not above suspicion, was *without real proof*." (p. 121) The Father's book is a veritable " spook " factory, but his historic shams only pass muster in party gloom.

---

into effect: the Parliamentary lie will be spit upon and trampled under foot and treated as all honest men treat a lie, that is, rigorously disobeyed." What becomes of the declaration repeatedly made " *that the pope hath no jurisdiction in this realm* " ?—(Wylie's *Rome and Civil Liberty*, pp. 91-92.)

CHAPTER XII.

A SAMPLE COLLECTION.—CROSS AND DENWORTH.—RIBANDISM. —"THE BOTTLE RIOT."—AN "ORANGE BIBLE" INCIDENT. —THE HATTER'S STORY.—ORANGEISM DISGUISED PROTESTANT JESUITISM.—LORD GOSFORD, MR. SINCLAIR, AND SIR FRED. STOVIN CROSS-EXAMINED.—WHY THE SOCIETY AROSE IN VICTORIA.—"ORANGE ORATORY."—OFFICIAL BLUE BOOKS. DOLLY'S BRAE.—"THE WORST OF ALL CAESARISMS."—HOW TO EXTINGUISH ORANGEISM.

THE book by Father Cleary abounds with incidents, which, if true, are highly discreditable to the Orange Society. I have not been able to test the accuracy of every alleged case, but of some I have found the related circumstances. The original plan of this work having been abridged so as to keep within certain space limits, I will here briefly deal with *specimen* matters, from which the reader will be enabled to form a shrewd conclusion on the "mess of pottage" served up to explain "certain broad features" confidently supposed to exist in Orangeism. The advocate who trades on ignorance in the jury need not be very skilful to obtain a verdict, but the verdict so obtained does not carry with it any value as to the merits of the case. To be of lasting consequence, a verdict must be based upon a thorough knowledge of facts : if not thus based, public opinion will re-act against it, and the reaction will be all the more forceful from the sense of injustice added to injury. The Father himself has laid down the principle that—"the essence of persecution is *injustice*—not cruelty."[1] We shall now see how it acts.

THE LAD CROSS AND THE MAN DENWORTH.

The Rev. J. Gilbertson, of East Melbourne, sends me the following account of these cases: "Father Cleary refers on page 7 to the Orange Society as having '*tasted blood*' in the death of the boy Cross in November, 1882. The Father seems pretty precise in the date. An alteration in the date of this sad event, I assume, has been made to throw his readers off the scent, and so lead them to suppose Cross was a Roman Catholic martyr.

---
1 p. 309.

The real date is November, 1867. The boy Cross was a Protestant, and a very good, quiet boy—*even at that*. He was a St. Peter's boy with no popish leanings or longings : he was near the Protestant Hall on the occasion of the first visit of the Duke of Edinburgh to Melbourne, when an attack was made on the building, or at the least on the transparency of William III., which was exhibited there in honor of the occasion. A shot was fired, presumably in defence, or by accident. Cross had nothing to do with the rising riot, nor had he any alliance with the disturbers of the peace, who, probably being 'out for the day,' were bent on mischief 'in honor of their religion' *a la* the Brunswick mob. I know all this. The boy had been under my care for some time, and I was on the scene when an angry lot of young fellows went after every man who seemed in a hurry. Unfortunately for Father Cleary's addition to the Roman Martyrology, the facts are too recent for its success. I was in Melbourne in December, 1882, but I did not hear that Cross had been killed *that year.*" Mr. Gilbertson has evidently been reading the *First* Edition of Father Cleary's book. In the *Fourth* Edition no mention is made of the Orange Society having "tasted blood"; nor of the name of the "poor boy"; and the date is corrected. An extract is quietly substituted from a work called *The Cruise of H.M.S. Galatea* (see p. 6). This silent withdrawal is worthy of notice. The readers of the *First* Edition of his book are doubtless treasuring up the view on his authority that the Orange Society in Victoria "TASTED BLOOD" in 1882, all the time utterly unconscious that the Father has without apology, explanation, or even notice of any kind, withdrawn the statement, and inserted an account of a different complexion. He also went far afield for his later authority. Were there no Melbourne papers at the Public Library accessible to him ? Why were they not quoted and put in as evidence ? In the preface to the *Fourth* Edition of his book the author smoothly says—" Several typographical and *other* MINOR *errors*, which were inadvertently passed over in several editions have been corrected." (p. xi.). This is all. Let it be remembered that the Father asserts—" The essence of persecution is injustice, not cruelty." On his own principle, therefore, the accusation of having " tasted blood " is a piece of essential *persecution* of the Orange Society.

With respect to the case of Mr. Jeremiah Denworth (who is not said to be a Roman Catholic) the account shows that this person was accidentally hit by a bullet, on July 12th, 1846, near the hotel of Mr. J. T. Smith, while removing some furniture (p. 6). The Rev. J. Gilbertson, quoted previously, remarks on this:—" According to Father Cleary, his informant—a Mr. Mansfield—asserts that one Jeremiah Denworth was struck by a bullet on the *12th of July*, 1846, from the effects of which he died some three years afterwards. Now, the 12th July in the given year fell on a *Sunday*, whilst the 'popish riot,' as it was called in the *Argus* of that time, occurred on *Monday*, the 13th. By the blessing of the saints, it is on Romish grounds supposable, that a bullet fired on the *Sunday might not have reached its mark until the Monday*. But it is not in the power of all the Saints put together to make an injury inflicted on the *Sunday*, to have been caused by a weapon used *on a day after the injury was received.*" Here is food for profound thought. (See also *Appendix B.*)

THE NATURE OF FATHER CLEARY'S EVIDENCE.

He assures his readers that the "*overwhelming majority* of the statements . . . are drawn from the reports of parliamentary committees, royal commissions, &c."[2] By drawing on similar sources what a story could be told of Roman Catholic influence in Ireland from the year 1640! It has occupied the the attention of Parliament and been condemned by it over and over again: and the "priest in politics" has been the subject of crushing censure from countless statesmen, commissions, and Parliaments. If, therefore, the rev. gentleman pins his faith to the infallibility of a parliamentary debate or, the text of a royal commission report in condemnation of the Orange Society, how will he escape the accumulating force of similar condemnations levelled at the priesthood: and how will he consistently maintain his accusations against Orangeism of having slandered Roman Catholics *in globo ?* Catholic associations have been suppressed : Catholic petitions, on stated grounds, have been repeatedly refused : secret societies in Ireland, exclusively Catholic, have been handled severely by successive Governments : juries, police force,[3] and justice corrupted in Catholic interests,

---

2 p. x.

3 "It is curious that just when disunionists are proposing to make Ireland happy with Home Rule, the Legislature of Massachusetts finds itself obliged to take the police out of the hands of the city of Boston on account of the growth of the Irish element and *the consequent disorder and corruption.*"—(Professor Goldwin Smith's letter quoted in the *Times*' *Articles and Letters*, p. 57.) A letter by Unionist (p. 61) speaks of "the growing disinclination of the police to place themselves in opposition to those who, they have reason to believe, will soon become their masters."

have been proved and denounced until it has become proverbial by exactly the same kind of agency as he quotes against Orangeism. It is the custom to plead that these persistent and prevalent condemnations are simply evidence of " Protestant bigotry " and part of England's " foreign despotism." It is open to demonstration, however, that the Orange Society was only denounced in this way when a Roman Catholic political party held the balance of power in the House of Commons.[4] This fact is indisputable, and I have furnished abundant evidence of it But it cannot be pleaded that Orangeism was in the ascendent when Roman Catholic influence, agitation, and corruption were thus denounced. Such denunciation had taken place a hundred years before the origin of Orangeism, and was made subsequent to 1835, when, the Father tells us, " English Orangeism fell like another temple of Dagon. Since that fateful year the olden glories of the Society have never returned."[5] From his side of the question, therefore, this is proof that Orange ascendency does not account for the condemnations referred to. Mr. Shaw called the attention of Parliament to the state of crime in Ireland in 1839 and roundly accused Normanby's administration of winking at the enormities of the Riband innocents. Thomas Drummond, of anti-Orange memory, was then under-secretary and from all accounts (Barry O'Brien and Judge Morris for instance) was an exemplary officer—at any rate from the Roman Catholic standpoint. Mr. Shaw said " he would show that the outrages continued under the practical encouragement of the Government." " They have encouraged agitation and are now reaping its inevitable fruits." " They have slighted the judges : they have insulted the magistracy." " They have selected from the ranks of (O'Connell's) precursor society the legal adviser of the Crown, and have made Lord Lieutenant a nobleman who had avowed his interest in the war which was going on against the Church in Ireland."[6] In 1835 the attacks on the Orange Society, which can be dated from O'Connell's declaration in 1833 concerning the " Winchelsea dinner," culminated in the dissolution of the lodge as shown elsewhere. Note the alleged result of this on crime in Ireland. Mr. Shaw contended that from 1835 to 1839 there was a marked increase in criminal practices. The returns presented had been " illusory as well as inaccurate."

---

4 One Protestant writer testifies that in 1831 O'Connell " had a power at his back in the priesthood of Ireland which no earthly influence could gainsay. His might was omnipotent. . . . That autumn laid the foundation of Irish power in the British Parliament."—(Wright's *History of Ireland*, vol. iii. p 520.)

5 p. 4.   6 *Annual Register*, 1839, p. 43.

Out of several instances I merely mention one. While in actual fact in Tipperary " 63 cases had been committed for murder and homicide, only 16 cases of these crimes had been *reported*."[7] The same speaker also quoted parts of a deposition made by a member of the Riband Society. A Ribandman " was bound by oath to keep secret whatever he might see or hear, to be true and loyal to each brother, to fight for him to the death, and to hold himself ready on all occasions to rise in defence *of his religion.*" At their meetings instructions were given for the " carding or maltreating" of persons who by " vote or evidence" or other means were obnoxious to the Ribandmen. A member from a distance was usually selected to do the job, while a local member pointed out the victim.[8] Father Cleary says that the oath of the Riband confederacy 1820-71, read by Mr. Monk in the House of Commons, March 8th, 1871, and quoted in an Orange tract, is a " bogus" one. He remarks—" The oath in question bears no resemblance whatever to the *genuine* Fenian oath, which is given in A. M. Sullivan's *New Ireland.*"[9] Has his reverence some intuitive gift, some infallible faculty by which he detects the false from the true that he is able *at sight* to tell the difference ? Sir Henry James points out that among the Fenians " the power of death was given to the supreme council. The power of causing death and putting to death was exercised."[10] In the debate which followed Mr. Shaw's speech in 1839, Mr. Colquhoun " was at a loss for the reason why the title 'Ribandism' had been omitted from the police returns since 1834, when the existence of that conspiracy was a notorious fact and admitted by Lord Morpeth."[11] Mr. Sergeant Jackson said that the Government in its exercises of patronage " had favored for its own ends the cause of agitation."[12] In the Lords a motion for inquiring into outrages in Ireland was carried at the instance of Lord Roden. The Duke of Wellington supported the resolution. Lord Melbourne, in the course of the debate, referred wearily to Irish crime, and thought the inquiry was a useless thing as it would merely reveal what they all knew. In curious agreement with Prof. Stokes, as quoted on page 62 of this work, Melbourne said—" there was in Ireland, unfortunately, from causes of long existence a disregard for human life, and a comparative indisposition to discover the murderer. In that unhappy country a notion of right was connected with murder, which secured to

---

7 *Ibid*, p. 41.   8 *Ibid* pp. 42, 43.   9 p. 166.
10 *The Work of the Irish Leagues*, pp. 308, 309.
11 *Annual Register*, 1839, p. 49.   12 *Ibid*, p. 51.

the criminal the sympathy of the people." His Lordship looked upon this characteristic as a "disease most difficult of extirpation."[13] Uproar and confusion were created by Orange Lodges' over the question of the disestablishment of the Irish State Church, at least Father Cleary says such was the case. But on looking up the matter I find that the trouble was occasioned by the Fenian Conspiracy. Mr. Gladstone's Church Bill and his Land Bill were the concessions made to Irish agitation. While these measures were stewing in the political pot, the suspension of the *Habeas Corpus* Act was having an extended run in Ireland. In 1866, 1867, 1868, 1869, ordinary law was found inadequate to govern the Fenian elements.[14] Where Orangeism is concerned Fenian atrocities are not worth mentioning. Readers have suffered much from accounts of alleged riots and violence connected with the Orange Society, while the virtues of Defenderism, Ribandism, Fenianism, Land Leagueism, Nationalism, and other isms peculiar to the Roman Catholics of Ireland have been left in well-merited but unnatural obscurity. On page 209 we are informed that Mr. Johnson was imprisoned for a month for violating the Party Processions Act, and at the next elections the Orangemen returned him to Parliament. Yet we have seen stranger things done in Ireland than this. *Convicts* have been returned to Parliament. O'Donovan Rossa was elected.[15]

A section of Roman Catholic writers regard Orangeism as being their peculiar bane, but overlook the fact that even their Protestant champions have had to condemn continuous excesses on the part of the Catholics. I will give a notable instance of it here, because it will lead to a matter which Father Cleary has garbled. In 1812, when the Catholic claims were being debated in the House of Lords, the Marquis of Wellesley, replying to a very strong speech by Lord Sidmouth, spoke strenuously in their favor, and yet, to the dismay of his party, objected to enter into Committee, "for the purpose of instantaneously removing the disabilities under which the Catholics labored. The reasons for his conduct he drew from *the menacing attitude* which the Catholics had assumed, *the numerous outrages* committed by members of that body in violation of the laws of the land, the then *present trials of offenders*, and the absolute necessity that existed of a return to tranquillity on the part of the

---

13 *Ibid*, p. 57. See also Lecky and Froude, pp. 189, 182, 183 in this work.
14 The *Annual Register*, 1868, pp. 1-4. See Note 41 present chapter.
15 See also p. 19, Note 24 of this work.

delinquents, before any hearing could reasonably be given to the body of whom they formed so important a part."[16] This is merely a specimen fact of a multitude which Irish History furnishes. Father Cleary has spoken of Orangemen calling the Marquis "Papist Wellesley," for "having dared to entertain opinions favorable to Catholic Emancipation."[17] He also accuses them, on Roman Catholic authority of course (M.P.'s *History of Orangeism*), of having "violently assaulted" the Marquis in

"THE BOTTLE RIOT."

What are the facts? Lord Wellesley, when in the Irish Office, "vigorously prosecuted the system of what was called *conciliation*." One of his peculiar methods was to fleece the Magisterial Bench. No less than 200 noblemen and gentry received writs of "*supersedeas*," and were thus displaced. It had been the usual custom to decorate the statue of William III. on November 4th: this Wellesley forbade out of deference to the Catholics, or, as an historian puts it "to humor their feelings," and he placed a police guard around the statue. The Dublin Corporation, whom O'Connell stigmatised as a "beggarly body," met and censured the Mayor who had been a party to this transaction, and some rather plain allusions were made to the Lord Lieutenant. The Guild of Merchants was also indignant at this high-handed authority, and in its meeting recorded its feeling by a strongly worded resolution. On December 14, 1822, Wellesley attended the theatre, when the general displeasure was expressed by "a universal burst of hisses" on his entrance. A bottle and the fragment of a watchman's rattle were flung *in the direction* of the Vice-regal box. The Attorney General attempted to make political capital out of this display of popular censure. He called it "high treason," and commenced proceedings for "attempted murder," but they came to nothing. "Lord Wellesley had in fact placed himself in a false position; for friendly himself to the Catholic claims, he had engaged to govern Ireland according to anti-Catholic laws, and under an anti-Catholic Cabinet."[18] The matter did not end here, for when Mr. Plunkett, the Attorney-General, withdrew the accusations of attempted murder, he preferred a charge of "riot and conspiracy" against ten of the accused. The Grand Jury found a true Bill against only *two*, and as the law does not con-

16 Wright's *Hist. of Ireland*, vol. iii. p. 373.
17 p. 98.
18 Wright's *Ireland*, vol. iii. p. 465.

sider that two persons can create a riot, it amounted to a virtual acquittal. Mr. Plunkett thereupon intimated that the Grand Jury had been "packed," which drew a spirited remonstrance from Sir George Whiteford, the foreman. Parliament was appealed to. The High Sheriff and Grand Jurors prayed for an inquiry into the charges made against them by Mr. Plunkett. After the usual bickering, there was a majority of 34 in favor of granting the inquiry. On May 2nd the House resolved itself into Committee to take evidence, and the inquiry was continued on the 5th, 6th, 7th, 23rd and 24th of the month, when the finding of the Committee was that the Attorney General's charges were *not proved* and the High Sheriff was "*completely exculpated.*"[19] Wright says the whole affair had "resolved itself into a contest between the Irish Government and the Orange party," and the latter came out on top because its hands were clean. The riot of Maghera is one of the many Orange massacres in Father Cleary's book, but he omitted to tell us that on the 12th of June, when both parties were properly worked up by the "conciliation" policy of the Marquis of Wellesley, the Ribandmen attacked the Orangemen at a fair, and drove them to the barracks, where the latter made a stand : and in protecting themselves rendered the assault disastrous to their assailants.[20] During 1823, under the benign reign of Wellesley, Ireland was favored with a return of "the good old times," and the Catholic reign of terror returned as fresh and frisky as ever. Crime, midnight outrage, and destruction held carnival. On a jury there were eleven Protestants and one Catholic. The murderer in the dock was a Catholic.[21] But the one man held out against a verdict and the murderer subsequently escaped, and in this way Ireland kept up its record of crime and its reputation for shielding criminals.[22] "It is but justice to the Protestants," remarks the

---

19 *Ibid*, pp. 466, 467.
The attentive reader will observe how Father Cleary has garbled the proceedings of this inquiry on page 108. He says—"The Orange assailants of the Protestant Viceroy, 'Papist' Wellesley, were placed on their trial." Evidently he is at sea on the matter. It was Mr. Plunkett's *accusations* that were placed " on trial " and *upset*.

20 Wright's *History of Ireland*, vol. iii. p. 468.

21 Mr. E. M. Richards says : " Anyone who has ever attended an Irish court of justice, and seen how little the sanctity of an oath upon the Bible is regarded by certain classes, will have no difficulty in understanding that official oaths of impartiality will turn out to be mere forms to be disregarded at will."—(*Times Articles and Letters*, p. 319.)

22 What can be done in Ireland is illustrated by the proceedings of O'Connell's Catholic Association. "The committee of the association assumed to themselves the power of adjudicating upon the conduct of every man in Ireland. All the

writer from whom I quote, "to say that *none of them* were found to be concerned in any of these proceedings." Under the pressure of these symptoms, even Lord Wellesley required, and the ministry readily obtained, a renewal of the Insurrection Act from Parliament.[23]

With reference to the Marquis of Anglesey, whom Father Cleary accuses the Orangemen of dubbing "papist" in common with Wellesley, it is sufficient to say that after a *three months'* *term* as the Irish viceroy he had to be *recalled*. Moreover, it is a highly significant fact that when Lord Anglesey retired from office he carried away "an ardent vote of thanks from the Roman Catholic Association." The Association was not the body to ardently give thanks for *nothing*. Certain it was that in his "official capacity" he took not the slightest notice of the tone which characterised the speeches of the members of the Catholic Association. Anglesey had permitted the attendance of members of his own family at their meetings "when the most seditious language was used by the speakers."[24] As a matter of fact he had indulged in what was thought to be indirect patronage of O'Connell's tall talk.

THE HATTER'S STORY.

Father Cleary tells this with variations on pp. 41, 302, 303, 315, 316, 313. Another writer, however, gives us the sequel. O'Neill belonged to Dungannon, and he alleged that the Orangemen burned his shop, and tried to sacrifice him as a burnt offering to appease their wrath. He bewailed in all the moods and tenses of Irish garrulity his hard fate, and declared that no magistrate in Ulster would see his persecutors punished. Mr. Richard Wilson (whom the Father elevates to the magistracy, while Mr. Banks says he was a *disappointed seeker* after that

---

machinery possessed by the Romish Church was used with a most facile unscrupulousness. If testimony was wanted to convict a man, plenty of witnesses were found ready to swear to his guilt. If an offender was to be liberated evidence was never wanting to prove an *alibi* or swear to the prisoner's innocence. No extent of perjury was too great to be committed." One case is that of a man sworn to be murdered. Witness after witness declared on oath that they saw the prisoner jump on the throat of the deceased, kick him about the throat, &c., in the most barbarous manner. The doctors, however, could find *no trace of the alleged violence*, and it was shown afterwards that the deceased met his death by an accidental fall over a short post. Peculiar expedients were tried against the military and police. The idea was to work up the Catholics against the Protestants by every sort of pretext.—(Wright's *Ireland*, vol. iii. p. 474-5.)

23 *Ibid*, p. 468-9.

24 The Duke of Wellington's letter to Anglesey is given in Wright, vol. iii. p. 507.

office), wrote various letters accusing the magistrates of scandalous neglect and criminal partiality. Feeling became so acute in consequence, that several magistrates were arraigned before Mr. Justice McClelland; the charges were investigated, and, as usual, fell to the ground.[25] Mr. Cleary repeats the exploded accusations over and over again, but is silent as the grave concerning Judge McClelland's inquiry in 1806. I have already dealt with Baron Fletcher's much flourished address. If the Father desires information of what the judges say, let him read up the remarks of Lord Norbury and Judge Day on the McDonnell incident in 1815-1816. The story is told in Wright's *History of Ireland*, vol. iii. p. 442. Read also what Mr. Recorder Shaw said of the Marquis of Normanby and the Irish Judges in the *Annual Register*, 1839, p. 74. Father Cleary's mountain of "corrupted justice" in an agony of travail gives birth to a few stillborn mice.

The Romance of an Orange Warrant.

Warrant of Lodge No. 11 travelled far from Ireland, and has a history attaching to it which is worthy of being re-told. This warrant was either issued to a military member or subsequently became the military one of the 17th Light Dragoons. This regiment was in service on the field of Waterloo, and strange to say "every Orangemen in the regiment but one was killed." The survivor brought the piece of paper back to Ireland from the scene of carnage. It was recognised by the Grand Lodge when eventually submitted and renewed on August 24th, 1824.[26] Another warrant, No. 859, also had a military career. It went to the Crimea. The master of the lodge in whose possession it was fell a victim to the enemy. A Turk, rifling the pockets of the dead, found the warrant and was apparently wondering what value it represented when a member of the ambulance corps passing by recognised the document, and speedily captured it. The warrant and its story are now in the archives of the Armagh Orange Hall.[27] Those who have read Mr. Cleary's book will remember his pleasantry about the Orangemen being challenged to show their loyalty at the time of the Crimean war. They did not send, so he says, "so much as a corporal's secretary." (pp. 330, 331) Yet his last chapter is full of hints, opinions, and insinuations about Orangemen being "on a vast

---

25 *Hist. Orange Order*, p. 33.   26 Bank's *History Orange Order*, p. 29.
27 *Ibid*, p. 29.

scale" in the army for a sinister purpose. The Father evidently places his trust in the unique veracity of Nationalist and Catholic newspapers. With a simplicity "childlike and bland" he rehashes their fairy tales of Orangeism.

On p. 124 Father Cleary is dying to know what the "Orange secret" is. In superstitious awe he declares: "It is manifestly something which it is neither safe nor politic to openly avow." And yet *Catholics have been admitted to the Lodge*—men that came to spy and lied most foully in order to fathom this mystery. Why have not these Catholics told the secret? They told all they knew, but it was too tame for belief. The Grand Lodge met on Jan. 10, 1820 for the purpose of revising the rules, &c., of the Order and of issuing a fresh code of ritual, signs, and passwords. This was the *second* time such a course was rendered necessary. Some Roman Catholics had crept in unawares and the Orange system was paraded in the press. "The secret signs and passwords were made public in *Carrick's Journal*—a Roman Catholic paper."[28] What with the Parliamentary committees' reports of 1835 which the Father says "laid bare the secrets of the well tiled Orange Society," and the publication of its inner mysteries by Roman Catholic spies, the "Orange secret" should be pretty well known by now. And yet Mr. Cleary seems to think that the half has not been told. Perhaps, however, the Rev. Dr. James Doyle, R.C. Bishop of Kildare and Loughlin, may be regarded as a worthy witness by our critic. That prelate in 1822 issued an address to his gentle flock enjoining them to live in peace with their neighbors, and pointed out to them as a suitable example to follow the law-abiding character of the Orangemen. As Mr. Banks says, this is a compliment "from a strange quarter."[29]

LINKS OF HISTORY.

In 1813 O'Connell told the Catholics if they resorted to unconstitutional means of enforcing their demands: "*you will find me against you.*"[30] The Catholic prelates in the same year

---

28 *Ibid*, p. 35.

29 *Ibid*, p. 37.

Sir Chas. G. Duffy relates some instances of Orange tolerance in *Four Years of Irish History*, pp. 440, 679, 746. He says an Orangeman named Stephenson Dobbyn wormed himself into the confidence of the Young Irelanders in order to betray them; but he adds: "It is only proper to state that the Orange Society *expelled* Dobbyn for his deliberate treachery."—(*Ibid*, pp. 714, 715.) Father Cleary will rejoice to learn from such respectable authority that Orangemen do occasionally expel for offences other than "marrying a papist."

30 Wright's *Ireland*, vol. iii. p. 423.

issued an address in which they were prepared to swear that they would not appoint any bishop unless he were of "unimpeachable loyalty," and they declared that they would not hold any communication "with the chief pastor of the Church" for the purpose of "overthrowing the Protestant Government or the Protestant Church."[31] The historian drily says "these declarations and the parallels of their conduct in after times are the commentaries of each other." The Father speaks of a lady that "doth protest too much." (p. 243.) He does not say, but it is suspected that her gown was *green.* The reference in the bishops' address is to "Canning's Clauses." Mr. Grattan brought in a Bill for Catholic relief. Canning moved a significant amendment requiring (1) Every priest to swear not to vote for a disloyal cleric, (2) A veto board, to which the name of every person proposed for the Episcopacy should be submitted before being forwarded to Rome.[32] "The chief pastor of the Church" was under a cloud at the time, but in 1814 Napoleon was defeated and Pius VII. was at liberty once more. On May 5th he advertised himself to the world as "God's vicar upon earth." One of his first measures was to restore the Jesuits, who had been expelled from every country in Europe, and abolished *for ever* by a previous pontiff. Fancy one "infallible" reversing the act of another "infallible"! As the Roman clock struck the old time note its effects in Great Britain were electrical. On June 23, 1814, Peel had to bring in a measure "for the better execution of the laws in Ireland." Lord Holland—"the distinguished contemporary Protestant statesman," as Mr. Cleary felicitously terms him—opposed it, but it was speedily carried.[33] Mr. Stapleton refers to "the dread of the pope" in England when Canning took office in 1816. In 1825 and again in 1827, this was still apparent. Even the *Edinburgh Review,* June, 1827, said the difficulty was with "*the people* of England." As Sir Geo. Lewis tells us this is the "admission of an *unwilling* witness." In indicating England's position towards the Catholics of Ireland, this same writer observes "the spirit of the English people rose *against threats.*"[34] Two letters are preserved which indicate Irish feeling under O'Connell. (1) Lord Anglesey's letter, July, 2, 1828 : "Such is the extraordinary power of the Association, or rather of the agitators . . . that I am quite certain they could lead on the people to open rebellion *at a moment's notice.*" This is from the friendly viceroy whom the

---

31 *Ibid*, p. 424.　32 *Ibid*, p. 418.　33 *Ibid*, p. 430.
34 *Administrations of Great Britain*, pp. 433, 435.

Association effusively thanked when leaving Ireland. (2) His successor, Lord Leveson's letter, December 2, 1828: "1 have little doubt that the peasantry of the South at present look forward to the period of O'Connell's expulsion from the House of Commons *as the time of rising*, but any occurrence in the interval which should appear to be adverse to the interests of the Roman Catholic body might precipitate the result."[35] The reader will look in vain for historic incidents of this character in Mr. Cleary's work. Had space permitted, some interesting paragraphs could also be given from a review of the Rev. Mortimer O'Sullivan's *Case of the Protestants in Ireland*, which is published in the *Dublin University Magazine*, 1836, vol. viii. pp. 3-15.

AN " ORANGE BIBLE " INCIDENT.

Herr J. Venedey, writing of the Roman Catholics of the north of Ireland, mentions that their feelings are too often "concentrated in a settled hatred against the Protestants amongst whom they live." As a sample fact he recounts the following incident. " Upon the 23rd July (1843) two Protestant girls about twelve years of age in returning home from Sunday School met with a number of Roman Catholics coming from a funeral. One of the Catholic women called out : ' Look at that one, she has a Protestant—an Orange Bible: take it from her !' As the child ventured to resist the spoliation, she was set upon by four or five women, who struck her down with stones, and wounded her so severely that she was for several weeks confined to her bed. *The mob stood around and looked on*."[36] Venedey was then, or had been, a Continental Roman Catholic, and speaks against the Orange Society as Father Cleary's next of kin : but the virulence of the Catholic feeling in the north impressed itself upon his mind. O'Connell was a hero in Venedey's eyes. He quoted from a speech made by Sir Robert Peel on the Arms Bill, Aug. 9, 1843, to show what O'Connell had done. " The results of the Emancipation Act, of the Reform and Corporation Bill were these : that they had given the Parliamentary repre-

---
35 *Ibid*, p. 454.
36 *Ireland and the Irish*, 1843 (McCabe's translation), p. 297.
Venedey also says that Catholic professional men rendered the injured child every assistance. A Catholic doctor proffered his services : a Catholic lawyer offered his, and when the case came on for trial the defendant's solicitor helped instead of hindered the course of justice. Notwithstanding these mitigating circumstances, Venedey severely says : " That frightful deed was committed, and it remains as a proof that amongst the mass of the population there is combined barbarism in manners with deep angry passions fermenting in the heart."
— (*Ibid*, p. 297)

sentation of the counties of Ireland, which had formerly been in the hands of the Protestants, to the Catholics : that the representation of the boroughs which had been held by the Protestants was now in the possession of the Catholics : that the municipal corporations which had formerly been exclusively Protestant were now Catholic. These mighty changes had taken place in thirteen years, and none of them were mere nominal speculative changes, because in the carrying them out *large masses of property had passed from the Protestants to the Catholics.*"[37] It is evident, therefore, from this summary that the " proscribed creed" had been winning all along the line, and if it could be satisfied with anything less than a Rome-ruled Ireland it might have rested on its oars. Before illustrating this aspect let me refer to a quotation that Venedey makes from the Rev. Mr. Moriarty. This clergyman, who had formerly been a " transfugee " Catholic, displayed a singular insight into political truckling for the Catholic vote. Moriarty has his eye, trained by experience doubtless, upon political hucksters who " make super-excellent speeches on the platform, when they stand in need of political support, and will then give their hundred pounds for a Catholic chapel whilst they refuse to give a penny to a Protestant Church."[38] Father Cleary speaks of the " selling price " of Orange loyalty, of " loyalty in the market," and such like; but of course he is in a state of virgin innocence with respect to donations of the nature mentioned by Mr. Moriarty. Herr Venedey, having the firm antipathy one expects towards the Orange Society, declares that Orangeism always received new vigor " whenever Ireland was on the point

TO BULLY ENGLAND

out of some additional particle of a right hitherto refused."[39] During his sojourn in Ireland he had caught up the anti-English

---

37 *Ibid*, p. 339.   38 *Ibid*, p. 331.

The tolerance of Protestants towards Roman Catholic ceremonials was illustrated at the St. Patrick Cathedral consecration (Melbourne) when leading Protestant citizens were present. How many prominent Catholic citizens would have been present at a Protestant celebration of a similar character? It would be interesting to know how much Catholic money goes to support Protestant religious institutions.

39 *Ibid*, p. 320.

Venedey, like some other sympathisers with Irish Catholics, regards them as excusable in their resort to violent methods to enforce their demands. While the Marquis of Anglesey was viceroy, O'Connell was elected to Parliament and refused to take the oaths tendered to him. On his return to Ireland the frenzy was seven-fold hotter than usual. "The Protestants, seeing that *no aid was to be rendered to them by the authorities*, found themselves compelled to take some

feeling; but neither Venedey nor any other authority has ever yet told us what really will satisfy the Irish Catholic. The Dublin correspondent of the *New York Nation*, "a journal of the highest character, lately told the story of a conversation with a Roman Catholic priest on the cause of the (Home Rule) strife: 'I'll tell you what,' said the priest, 'there's no use in your talking of moderation or reconcilement with England. They hate us and we hate them. So long as I have the power I'll work and I'll work for Home Rule: and then I'd work and I'd work for separation: and then I'd strive and I'd work for *the destruction of the British Empire.*'"[40] This gentleman has proposed for himself a pretty complete programme, but we may hope that by the time he has got Home Rule, he will be either exhausted, or else converted to more pacific intentions. If he is not mollified then "the British Empire" must be resigned to its fate. Professor Dicey, however, notices the difficulty of. reaching satisfaction point in Irish politics. He states the facts thus: "The treaty of union missed its mark because not combined with Catholic emancipation. The Catholics were emancipated, but emancipation instead of producing loyalty brought forth the cry of repeal. The Repeal movement ended in failure, but its death gave birth to the attempted rebellion of 1848. Suppressed rebellion begot Fenianism, to be followed in its turn by the agitation for Home Rule."[41] What an epitome of a people's history for ninety years! It was under the Duke of Wellington's cabinet that Catholic emancipation was granted. Yet the

measures to avert or reduce the common danger." The magistrates led the way, Public meetings of Protestants were held, and "the old Protestant Orange lodges were revived with all their strictness of Union." Brunswick clubs were also formed in England as well as in Ireland. This is the way Venedey's statement is supported. Why will not Roman Catholic advocates look facts in the face?— (Wright's *Ireland*, vol. iii. p. 485.)

40 *The Times Articles, &c.*, p. 477.

41 *England's Case against Home Rule*, p. 73.

Father Cleary says the Orange Society "systematically and on a vast scale tampered with the loyalty of the nation's last resource—its army." (p. 4.) Let us hear what a priest boastfully said of Fenianism in the "nation's last resource." The Rev Father McCrae, C.C., 29th Aug, 1886, in his speech wished to "recall to Sir Redvers Buller a little incident of the year '67, during the Fenian times. We have it on the authority of those who enrolled them. and had charge of the Fenians in the army. There were 25,000 Irish soldiers in the army of England, and 13,000 of these were in Ireland. *One whole regiment* (the 3rd Buffs) *were Fenians to a man*, so much so that at the Curragh, where they were stationed, the colonel commanding used to have *a threatening letter forced under his own door every morning;* and I say yet there are Irishmen in the army and Buller will find that the Irish soldiers will not carry out the work for Buller the Knight Commander of the Queen's Garter."—(*The Work of the Irish Leagues*, pp 724-5. See also pp. 308, 309, 347, 348. For boycotting turn to pp. 285, 288, 289, &c.)

Duke took the precaution of having iron bars or shutters placed as a protection in front of his windows. None knew the temper of the Catholics better. The Hon. Maurice Fitzgerald—the Knight of Kerry—wrote his Grace on December 6, 1832, saying that he had always calculated on the question of repeal being raised in connection with emancipation. The Duke replied: "You are quite right in what you say about the repeal of the union. The Protestants of all classes will soon discover that, like the rebellion of 1798, it must become a *religious affair*. They must draw away from it or be destroyed in another Scullabogue."[42] The date of this letter is December 16, 1832. Ten days later the Duke wrote Lord Roden: "We must expect that the repeal of the union will be the great field *upon which the battle will be fought*, and I draw your attention more particularly to this question, as it appears to me that it is a rallying point upon which you might collect your party."[43] In 1829 Wellington had passed the Emancipation Act, and yet in 1832, according to his correspondence, these are his forebodings. His letter to Lord Roden is a virtual request for the support of the Orange Association, and it was to be used once more as a buffer between the Catholic party and the English Government. Mr. Fowles made a happy hit in the Home Rule debates by saying that "the English Empire is for all the world like a bewildered hen perpetually clucking to one forlorn and tiresome chick."[44] As Professor Dicey remarks, " Ireland, or part of the Irish people, has been divided from England by a feud of centuries, and it would be difficult among Irish Nationalists to obtain even *the show* of loyalty to the Crown."[45] These matters will supply certain " missing links " in Father Cleary's peculiar analysis of Orange history in the former part of this century.

GUARDING THE SECRET.

Father Cleary displays the usual extravagance over what he calls " guarding the secret." To read his story one would

---

42 *The Times Articles, &c.*, p. 347.

Mr. Goulburn in supporting the Bill for Catholic Emancipation, 1829, reviewed the state of Ireland and said : " No power could reach it without *the risk of a general massacre*, for the priesthood, the people, and their leaders were all comprised in one universal combination." Mr. Bankes ridiculed the view of the Chancellor on the disturbed state of Ireland. " According to the doctrine professed by Mr. Goulburn, the security against that disturbance could only be obtained by throwing the Church of Ireland into the power of Rome."—(Wright's *History of Ireland*, vol. iii. pp. 490, 491.)

43 *Times Articles, &c.*, pp. 348, 349.   44 *Ibid*, p. 211.

45 *A Leap in the Dark*, p. 164.

imagine that Orangeism contained some ghastly mystery, and we are correspondingly surprised to note his exultation over "the disclosures" of 1835, which he says came principally from *Orangemen*. This is a singular way of guarding secrets. Drowsy guardians! What happened to them? The reverend gentleman deemed it highly inexpedient to inform the readers of his book that the Grand Lodge of Ireland, so far from shrouding the Society, opened to the Parliamentary committee every avenue to knowledge at their disposal, and the Father knew this perfectly well. The first witness examined was Colonel Verner, who in commencing his evidence read the following resolutions from the Grand Lodge. (1) "That an authority be granted under the grand seal of the Institution, to those brethren who may be examined before the Committee of the House of Commons now appointed to investigate the nature, tendency, &c., of the Institution: *to disclose all signs, passwords, and secrets of the Institution* WITHOUT ANY CONCEALMENT WHATEVER, and that the proper officer be instructed to prepare the same." (2) "That in furtherance of the above resolution the brethren therein alluded to shall have the power of laying before the House of Commons *all books and documents connected with the Institution, and all such further information as may be required of them without any reservation whatsoever.*" (3) "That we hereby give full power to the committee appointed by us to carry on our affairs in London to act in every way that they may deem necessary for the good of the Orange Institution, and the public vindication of its principles and the general character of that Association."[46] Father Cleary, conning over rules and regulations, observes: "The natural and presumably intended effect of this part of the 'obligation' is as follows: Unless the Grand Lodge accords an Orange witness, under seal, written permission to give evidence on lodge proceedings he must, by reason of his solemn promise or oath, either (a) refuse to give evidence and thus commit contempt of court or (b) give false evidence and thereby be guilty of perjury."[47] It has been shown

---

46 *Minutes of Evidence*, p. 1.   47 p. 114.

Father Cleary in this connection also says that "this solemn promise (or oath) extends by *force of its wording* to *courts of justice*, and Parliamentary or other forms of official inquiry, no exception being made in their favor." (p. 114.) Yet note the "force of its wording" in the following portion of the same declaration: "That I am not, nor ever was, nor ever will become, a member of any treasonable society or body of men who are enemies to the lawful sovereign, or the Protestant religion, and that I never took an oath of secrecy to any treasonable society: that I will as far as in me lies *assist magistrates and civil authorities* of the colonies in *the lawful execution of their duties when called upon to do so.*" (p. 405.) The obligation should be treated in its wholeness: it loses coherence otherwise.

that when the subject of inquiry is the Orange Society the Grand Lodge is frank enough in all conscience, and to its utmost prepared to assist the inquiry. This fact is worth surely a hundred pages of "cheap and nasty" forensic inferences on possibilities never likely to occur. Father Cleary naturally makes no mention of the foregoing resolutions in his book. It is quite conceivable that when the cause of justice is not assisted, and the proceedings of the Orange Society are remote from, or not connected with, an issue being tried, that a witness who happens to be an Orangeman would resent a purely *fishing* method of interlocution. Probably instances of this sort are relied upon by the reverend gentleman to sustain his position.

ORANGEISM DISGUISED PROTESTANT JESUITISM.

The Father's idea of the Orange Society appears to be that Orangeism is in essence a rough model of "popery," and that it has a pope, a college of cardinals, and the equivalent of "spiritual direction at the hustings," with some exclusive notion of Protestantism. This idea of it colours almost every page of his book. If, therefore, his conception of Orangeism leads him to regard the Society as a Romanised and secret Protestant system, the subtile analyses in chapters vi. and vii. of his book will readily be understood, and the underlying fallacy on which they are based is explained. Nobody is more astonished at the wonderful powers inherent in the laws and constitution of the Orange Society as set out and commented on by Father Cleary than the Orangemen themselves. What luminous legal lore: what profound penetration : what powers of sympathetic interpretation the reverend gentleman is blessed with ! One is reminded of Goldsmith's schoolmaster of whom it is said :

> And still they gazed, and still the wonder grew
> That one small head could carry all he knew.

I do not take the chapters mentioned seriously.[48] Certainly they are a laboured and even clever production, but for practical purposes only "much ado about nothing." For instance he inveighs against the powers vested in the Grand Lodge officials, but as he shows, himself, the Grand Lodge is constituted from the minor lodges as an elective and representative form of

---

[48] I do not regard the Father as *original* in this part of his work, for I have read a similar exposition of "lodge law" in the *Maryborough Advertiser* from the pen of *Qui Vive* (Letters dated Aug. 7th and 13th, 1896). There is not the slightest doubt in my mind that both writers have been suckled at the same breast on this theme. Such exposition has a flavor found in wig and gown rather than in surplice.

government and its privileges must be commensurate with its responsibilities. The safeguarding rules of which he complains are merely rules adopted in every organisation, which, while affording certain liberty to the lower courts, cause the supremacy of the highest court to be acknowledged, and afford the means for enforcing its authority. The existence of such rules is the federal bond. They are not a menace to the lodges-in-ordinary, but simply a pledge and token of their inferiority. It is the old question in organisation of *how best to secure local liberty in the minor courts consistently with supremacy in the major.* The Orange Society, I should judge, has found a settlement of that question in these rules, and they are maintained, presumably, on the principle that they are found to work well. If they had been found oppressive or harsh in their action no doubt they would have been amended. The powers of the Grand Master, as I read the rules published in Father Cleary's book, are not "autocratic." He is not the virtual "pope" of the order, nor yet a Jesuit "general." His disciplinary acts are not despotic. Authority does not reach its climax in him. His acts are subject to review by a higher tribunal of the lodge, viz., *the power which created his office.* Provision also is made for appeal against his decisions, and they may be either reversed, revised, or altogether set aside. Compare the following rules. " 26. All warrants, seals, and rituals issued to lodges are the property of the Grand Lodge, which has the power of cancelling, suspending, or withdrawing any warrant as it may see fit and of again issuing the same to any other lodge . . . and the Grand Master shall have full power to suspend, take, or authorise possession to be taken of, any warrant, *subject to appeal to the Grand Lodge,*" &c.[49] " 37. At each meeting of the Grand Lodge the Grand Secretary shall first read, and then place on record, the credentials of all delegates entitled to take their seats in the Grand Lodge. They shall *then hear and determine all appeals,*" &c.[50] " 46. The Grand Lodge shall within *one month* after its November meeting issue a *Report of all its proceedings* and furnish copies to *the members* of the Institution through the secretaries of the private lodges, such report to specify the name and numbers of the lodges, and names of all persons who may have resigned, been rejected, suspended, or expelled, giving the reason for such rejection, suspension, or expulsion, and period of such suspension as the case may be."[51]

We have therefore, in rule 26, provision for appeal from " the

---

49 pp. 413, 414.   50. p. 416.   51 p. 417.

autocrat of the lodges ": in rule 37 arrangement for decision on appeals in the business of the Grand Lodge: and in rule 46 a direction for information of Grand Lodge proceedings to be conveyed to the members of the Society. In this light the Grand Lodge is not the "Star Chamber" of Orangeism nor its College of Cardinals[52] since it is under necessity to issue "within one month after their November meeting . . . *a report of all their proceedings, and* FURNISH COPIES TO THE MEMBERS OF THE INSTITUTION."

As in this chapter I am giving, for lack of space, sample facts, the foregoing must suffice as an illustration of Father Cleary's delusions on "lodge law." Let us now glance in a similar way at the chief witnesses before the Irish Parliamentary committee of 1835 relied on by him against the Orange Society.

LORD GOSFORD IN THE BOX.

The Australian critic of the Society has leaned heavily on Gosford's testimony. I give the following specimens of this nobleman's evidence under question by the Orange counsel. Q. 3985. "Does not Orangeism prevail most in the province of Ulster? A. Yes. 3986. Consequently it is to be taken for granted that there is more opportunity at least of collision between the Protestants and Roman Catholics in Ulster than in other parts of Ireland? A. Yes, I should think there was. 3987. Does not your Lordship know that learned judges in their charges to grand juries have constantly observed that *as they proceeded northward the calendar has diminished in point of atrocity?* A. *Yes, and I believe it.*" Gosford in another part of his evidence gives frank expression to his hostile attitude to all secret combinations. In answer to Q. 3936 he stated " I am not against the Orangemen of the country for I think they are *a very fine race of men as can be: a set of people that would do credit to any country,* but when they band themselves

---

[52] Prof. Mivart says: "The Congregation of the Index *does not assign reasons for its acts.*" (p. 987.) He quotes Father Clarke, S.J., as saying judgment is "issued in the name of the congregation, *not in that of the pope,* and remains, therefore, altogether outside the sphere of infallibility." (p. 989.) Yet the professor oddly says that he bows to the judgment of the congregation out of consideration for "our supreme pontiff Leo xiii.," and has "almost a gladness to go out and meet *his correction and accept it with alacrity and filial submission,*" (pp. 989, 990.) The professor bolts the whole papal claim. "The Church of Rome does assert itself to possess not only ABSOLUTE but also INFALLIBLE *authority,* and that without being inspired it is nevertheless so assisted by the Divine Spirit that its supreme head, the pope, when teaching *ex cathedra cannot fall into error* as regards either faith or morals." (p. 982.)—(The *Nineteenth Century,* December, 1893.

into political associations, *it is these associations I am opposed to, &c.* 3937.* It is not against the men but against their principles as Orangemen? A. I am against the principles on which they act. 3937. As Orangemén? A. We had the rules yesterday : if they are to be considered as the rules by which they are governed, *in several instances* their practice varies from their rules. 3938. Your Lordship is of opinion that the rules are good? A. There appears a great deal in these rules which is good Christian charity, but they are *not always* adhered to in practice. 3939. Your Lordship is of opinion that the principles and rules are good, and that the men are good, and it is only when these men deviate from the principles that there is mischief in the Orange Association? A. I before said that I think that *all Associations* whether Ribandmen or Orangemen *are bad in themselves and dangerous to the State.*"[53]

Manifestly when a man swears to his hostility to *all* such associations in these uncompromising terms, it is impossible to expect he should give evidence *in their favor*. Of course nothing is said by Father Cleary of the self-confessed bias of this witness or of the preconception of Orange mischievousness in the mind of the deponent. Having made the above admissions on the character of Orangemen, apart from the Society, Gosford was further questioned. Q. 3946. " Your Lordship is understood to state—that you had an impression upon your mind that Orange lodges led to dissipation and idleness and to the demoralisation of the people ? A. I think the answer I gave to that question was not directly as it is stated, but that I think it tends positively to idleness, and in many instances to dissipation." Lord Gosford was tied to this point, and having admitted that many noblemen (his personal acquaintances) who had joined the organisation were not men against whom this charge could be sustained ; he said it had reference to " *the lower orders.*" This is how he proved it. Q. 3974. " Have you known any instance where it has existed among your own people (tenantry), either in the County Armagh or in the County Cavan, where they have been demoralised by being connected with the Orange Institution, or that they have become drunkards ? A. *No, I don't know that I have.* 3975. Is your Lordship aware of any

---

53 Protestant writers and speakers who take up a non-partisan position in religion and politics are the authorities relied upon by Father Cleary for condemnation of the Orange Society. The Father carefully refrains from revealing this fact. Those who assume that a Protestant party is bad *per se* necessarily condemn it apart from its actions. Lord Gosford, Sinclair, the *Edinburgh Review*, &c., take up this position and suffer from periodic attacks of Orangephobia.

instance, among your own people, where a number of those persons have been demoralised by reason of their connection with Orange Lodges? A. *I cannot charge my memory with any at this moment.* 3976. Your Lordship cannot refer to any instances either in Cavan or Armagh, where a man of good moral habits has been converted into a man of bad habits by his attendance on Orange lodges? A. *I cannot mention a man who has become so in consequence of his connection with an Orange Lodge,"* &c. Gosford then explained that he "spoke in the abstract." 3977. " Can your Lordship say that *any* of your tenantry have got into habits of idleness and dissipation in consequence of their attendance on Orange lodges? A. *I cannot for the reason mentioned."* This looks remarkably like a breakdown of testimony when *actual instances* are demanded of the witness. Our friend Cleary speaks of the "mysterious paralysis of memory" which attacks an "Orange witness." Such seizures do afflict persons when giving testimony *against* the Orange Society. The Father has occasionally come to an abrupt halt in his quotations as I have shown, and the lapses of memory in Lord Gosford are painful.[54] Q. 4031. " Does not your Lordship think there already exists in Ireland a very serious organisation among the Roman Catholic community? A. *I have heard so.* 4032 Mr. Wyse, in his book, states that in Ireland on one occasion there were convened together at simultaneous meetings 1,500,000 Roman Catholics, and the writer states that can be done *at any time* that circumstances may require it. Is not that a very formidable organisation in the country if such an assemblage can be simultaneously assembled as 1,500,000? A. *I believe there are societies of Ribandmen and societies of Orangemen."* The inaptness of this reply shows that Gosford is not prepared to venture an opinion on Catholic questions. On that subject the pump is dry. 4034. " Did not your Lordship convene a meeting at Ballybot of the magistrates in the County of Armagh, in consequence of Ribandmen parading about the country for two or three days and nights? A. I recollect convening at meeting at Ballybot respecting something which took place at a fair at a place called Omeath. 4035. Is it not in your Lordship's recollection that there were great bodies

---

[54] Sir Henry James addressing the *Times*—Parnell commission referred to the "distinguished" Mr. Biggar, who had the mysterious paralysis mentioned by Father Cleary and had it badly. Counsel said : " Mr. Biggar informed me exactly 144 times that he either did not know or did not remember most important matters connected with the League." Yet Mr. Biggar was the League's treasurer.—(*The Work of the Irish Leagues*, p. 117.)

P

of Ribandmen who continued together, to the great terror of the country, for two or three days and nights, and that your Lordship as Lieutenant of the county thought it your duty to convene the magistrates? A. I do: three or four meetings at Ballybot, chiefly on parochial matters connected with tithes and so on. Lord Charlemont came over and attended it. I recollect a meeting, but *whether it was about 3000 or 4000 Roman Catholics* being assembled in a body—I do not recollect anything to that extent. 4039. The question did not refer to the *specific number* of 3000 or 4000 but a large body parading the country for three or four days and nights: it is a remarkable circumstance? A. It is, but I do not recollect anything so formidable at that."

This is an interesting case of aberration of memory. It is like the famous case of the man who forgot his own name. Yet Gosford had a memory like a book when the subject was Orangeism: every paltry detail stood out as if in capital letters then. This peculiarity evidently occurred to the examining counsel, for the matter was further investigated. 4040. " Has your Lordship on your recollection the having convened several meetings of magistrates in the county of Armagh by reason of threatening notices and other circumstances of an alarming nature on *the part of the Catholics?* A. I do not recollect it. I may have gone into Armagh and spoken to the magistrates respecting circumstances I had heard, but I do not recollect convening magistrates for such a purpose. 4041. Do you recollect that the magistrates being together you called their attention to such circumstances as threatening notices and burnings and things of that kind by the Roman Catholics? A. I may have called the attention of the magistrates to any circumstances I had heard at petty sessions. I have gone over to petty sessions and called their attention to circumstances which had occurred. I do not know that there have been circumstances particularly respecting Ribandmen: if the cases were referred to *more particularly* they might bring to my mind the recollection of them."

John Chinaman would have looked vacuous and merely said: " *No savee!* " but Gosford, more elaborately wise, relied on his faulty memory. Let us, however, continue. Q. 4044. " Is there any doubt upon your mind that simultaneous meetings of the Roman Catholics were held in January, 1828, throughout the greater part of Ireland? A. I believe that there were a great many meetings of Roman Catholics held in that year, but I should suppose that the greater proportion was on the subject of Catholic Emancipation. 4045. Has your Lordship any doubt that in point of fact simultaneous meetings of Roman Catholics were held throughout Ireland in January, 1828 ? A. Whether they were simultaneous or not I cannot take upon me to say, but that meetings did take place that year I am certain. 4046. Has your Lordship any—the slightest—doubt upon your mind that the Roman Catholic association directed that simultaneous meetings should be held ? A. I do not recollect that circumstance. I have a recollection that something of the kind did pass, but whether it was true or what followed from it I cannot say."

This is a specimen of Lord Gosford under cross-examination, and it sheds abundant light on the feats of memory he was able to perform on the Catholic question contrasted with his glib utterances on Orangeism. But he distinctly testified to his hostility on principle to the Orange Society, and is therefore not an admissible witness on this count, in addition to his starved recollection.

Mr. Sinclair's Testimony.

This is another Protestant said to have a long acquaintance with the performances of Orangeism. Father Cleary has extracted certain statements from Sinclair's evidence which he relates with great gusto. I will indicate a few others to which the reverend gentleman did not conceive it prudent to call attention. In examination Mr. Sinclair was asked: Q. 4973. "One of their (the Orangemen) rules is that they will not admit anyone into their brotherhood not well-known to be incapable of persecuting or upbraiding anyone on account of his religious opinion ? A. That is ridiculous. 4974. Is that the practice ? A. No; the upbraiding is very common. 4975. What terms have come to your knowledge as being used ? A. The term 'papist' is a common expression. 4976. 'To hell with the pope'? A. That is not common in my part."

The silly fellow would not assent though the phrase was put in his mouth. One is reminded of the lugubrious complaint of Dr. Carr because Dr. Rentoul referred to his flock as "Romanists," on which the Presbyterian minister in his reply demonstrated that the prelate himself *had formerly used what was said to be the* "*offensive*" *designation and applied it to the Roman Catholics.*[55]

---

[55] *The Early Church and the Roman Claim*, p. 219.

Under cross-examination Sinclair made some striking admissions which, like the broken drum of advertising fame, "*can't be beat.*" Q. 5002. "Is there a strong feeling of hatred among those men who take a conspicuous part among the Orangemen displayed by their language and conduct, towards the Catholics? A. I declare I think *that some of the most warm and zealous Orangemen I know are exceedingly kind to their Catholic neighbors:* but generally speaking the thing must be calculated to create mischief among them no doubt." Mr. Sinclair in reply to Q. 5181 said, "I never knew the Orangemen in the North of Ireland or any portion of them, as Orangemen, assist in the preservation of the peace or in the execution of the laws; that is my opinion. 5182. Do not you consider that Orange Magistrates are a part of the population of the North of Ireland? A. I do: *a very bad part,*" Father Cleary quoted this much to swell the "reliable information," but knew precisely where to stop. Counsel did not stop just here, however 5183. "You state, notwithstanding, that Orange Magistrates have acted with *great impartiality,* and inflicted as severe punishments as they could? A. Uniformly they are men of *education, men of honor, and men of justice,* but I think it very unlucky after all that they are Orangemen. 5184. If they are men of education, and men of honor, and men of justice uniformly, how can they be considered a bad part of the population? A. *It is only with reference to their being Orangemen as Magistrates."* The critic knows how to take the photograph of the Orange Society, so much light must pass into the camera and no more, too much light would spoil the picture. 5097. "Can you name any Judge who is an Orangeman? A. No I cannot. I will not at all events; but *I have never seen Orangeism interfere with the duty of either Magistrate or Judge in my life.* 5098. You apply that expression to the whole of the North of Ireland? A. As far as I have seen."

Sinclair, like Gosford, is opposed to the Orange Society on some grounds, and is, therefore, a quotable authority, but Father Cleary does not show that their testimony is a capital illustration of the head eating the tail, and in this way neutralising itself. Sir Fred. Stovin is another witness relied upon, especially with reference to Orange Demonstrations. He was Superintendent of the Irish Police, and in his examination-in-chief he wanted Orangeism "put down." Under cross-examination his ardour abated and he explained his meaning. Q. 4728 . . . . " What I mean by putting down Orangeism is the outward display of it:

that is the offensive thing in my mind. 4729. You mean that an Act should be passed for putting down all Orange processions? A. The emblems, drums, and fifes, and outward display, *that is all I go to*. 4730. Then you do not so much object to the circumstance that the Protestants of the North of Ireland should be united in a political organisation, as to the mere circumstance of the occasional and annual display of party banners, and the playing of party tunes? A. Certainly."

From the Policeman's point of view, not Orangeism in essence but Orangeism in accident or scarf; not in principle, but in display; not in reality, but in circumstance; in short the mere *parade* of Orangeism is the objectionable feature. To do Father Cleary justice, while he has made liberal use of that which is said to be incidental to the Orange Society, he does not overlook what is fundamental. He does not make the egregious blunder of supposing that when a man is robbed of his clothes he has been deprived of his manhood. He has a very distinct idea that the *essential* in Orangeism is not, and cannot be, affected by suppressing its processions, and denuding it of bands, banners and badges. He, at least, is much ahead of his many contemporaries in recognising that the colour of a movement is not the movement itself. If the Orange Society subsisted on demonstrations, then it would die of atrophy. There would be no need to destroy it for it would perish from within.

ORANGE DEMONSTRATIONS.

Father Cleary refers to Orange processions as "unnecessary displays which are, which are known to be, and which as we have likewise seen *are intended to be*, highly offensive to the most cherished feelings of a large section of the community." (p. 211). I was under the impression that the Orangemen merely demanded *equality of treatment with the Roman Catholics on this question of parading*. The Father tells us that Green is the "National colour," and I may be mistaken, but my opinion has always been that *only* Roman Catholics celebrated St. Patrick's Day, that, indeed, it was peculiarly an Irish sectarian display, and, therefore, properly speaking a *party* demonstration; its tunes, emblems, and sentiments utterly discordant with the convictions of Protestants. Instead, however, of taking offence or regarding the parade as intended to be offensive, it has been looked upon with the utmost toleration. Orangemen only claim an equality of treatment—not partiality—in the eye of the law and of the public. But to stop a procession on July 12th, and allow a procession on March 17th, are regarded, I understand, as *moral*, if not political, victories by the Hibernian party. It is news to me that Orange demonstrations are "*intended* to be highly offensive" to anybody: and I have yet to learn that Orangemen care two straws about a procession in itself: their objection is to a Protestant Government decreeing a loyal Protestant display an illegality and permitting an Irish national one as legitimate and lawful. On every single occasion, so far as I am able to discover, the uproar in connection with Orange processions' has been occasioned by the savage attacks of persons professing the Roman Catholic faith—especially is this the case in Victoria[56] A reference to *Appendix B* will show how they acted in 1846. The press accounts in the second chapter of this work will indicate their proceedings fifty years later. Whilst the Orange Society is strenuously presented as the promoter of disturbance on these occasions, it is remarkable that *no single instance is produced in Father Cleary's work* wherein the bigoted (?) Orangemen have attacked a procession on St. Patrick's Day. This fact ought to brush away the unmerited stigma so often laid on "the Twelfth July" celebrations, for it incontestably shows which is the belligerent party.[57] Father Cleary on "Orange Demonstrations" illustrates Young's couplet:

"Ocean's waves by tempest toss'd
To waft a *feather* or to drown a *fly*."

Herr Venedey, writing in 1843 of the Catholics of the north of Ireland, depicted them as having a "*settled hatred*" of the Protestants amongst whom they lived. Sir Geo. Lewis, reviewing a long period, but speaking in this case of the year 1828, says: "The Irish Protestants, a high-spirited body, accustomed to command and ignorant of fear, had been roused by the *violence of their opponents*: they had converted their Orange Lodges into Bruns_

---

[56] The Roman Catholics of New Zealand indulged in the usual raving because their Governor, Lord Ranfurly, replying to an address of welcome presented by Orangemen, said: "The Queen owns no more law-abiding or industrious citizens than the Orangemen of Ulster." The Roman Catholics did not offer any address of welcome, I understand.—(The *Belfast Weekly News*, June 11, 1898.)

[57] At the Brunswick police court, when the legality of Orange processions was being tested, Senior Constable Nolan deposed that his feelings were hurt "by the *wearing* of Orange symbols." He was asked: "*Who told you* that the display of certain colours had a disturbing effect on the feelings of Catholics?" The reply was: "*I refuse to say.*" The question was pressed, but the bench over-ruled it. This witness admitted that he was *color blind.*—(The *Argus*, Feb. 12, 1898.)

At the same court the Rev. G. Tregear deposed: "The processionists *did not desire* to flaunt their emblems before the eyes of certain people for the sake of insulting them or their religion."—(The *Age*, Feb. 11, 1898.)

wick Clubs, and were ready at a moment's notice to take the field against their Catholic countrymen."[58] Ever since 1640 such had been, more or less, the feeling of the northern Protestants, and it accounts for the prevalence and persistence in Irish life of the sentiment which maintains Orangeism as a living organisation. Whenever matters reached a tolerable level and the Orange Society became a mere tradition rather than a piece of utility, there arose some symptomatic disorder which made it a living centre again.[59] Lecky notices, in connection with the yeomanry of 1798, the sturdy spirit of self-reliance which characterised the men of the north. The Protestant organisation mentioned by Sir Geo. Lewis which transformed the Orange Lodge into a Brunswick Club was "*not likely* to be long confined to Ireland. The Protestants of England soon began to express their sympathies with their Irish brethren, and a great county meeting for Kent was held on Penenden Heath in October for the purpose of supporting the Irish Brunswickers."[60] These are two features in connection with Orangeism which I have observed in its history. Its independency of spirit, which refuses to be intimidated by local events of a threatening nature though vastly outnumbered, and the quick, responsive sympathy of the bulk of the English and Scotch Protestants in its conflicts.[61] I can only mention them in passing ; to dwell on them would divert me from my purpose at this stage. Mr. Lecky tells us there was nothing " particularly novel " in the Orange Society annually celebrating the Battle of the Boyne. Protestant associations for the purpose of commemorating the events and maintaining the principles of the Revolution had

---

58 *Administrations of Great Britain*, p. 455.

59 Venedey, calling attention to the characteristics of the Catholics of the north, says : " Every 50 or 55 years there has been repeated over and over again the same scenes . . the Catholics and Protestants placed in battle-array against one another. . . . The spirit of the Catholics in the north is that of a very excitable, deeply injured, and strongly passioned, infirm man."—(*Ireland and the Irish*, 1843, pp. 295-6.)

60 *Administrations, &c.*, p. 456.

61 A notable instance of this in recent years is the declaration of the Ulster Convention, June 17, 1892, on Home Rule. The declaration was carried by a meeting of 20,000 Ulstermen, over 11,000 of whom attended in the capacity of delegates, and each, therefore, represented more than the opinion of a unit. The resolution of the Convention is published in the *Illustrated London News*, Aust. Ed., Aug. 20, 1892. The Nationalists refer to it as " Ulsteria," the " Orange Bogey," &c. It is the privilege of an outrivalled party to be abusive : it seems compensatory, at any rate it relieves the feelings. See Prof. Dowden on "Irish Opinion on the Home Rule Bill," *Fortnightly Review*, 1893, vol. lix. p. 593, and Prof. Dicey on "The Protest of Irish Protestantism," *Contemporary Review*, vol. lxii., 1892.

long been known. The battles of the Boyne and Aghrim with the relief of Londonderry " were annually celebrated *long before* the Orange Society existed."[62] At these celebrations ladies wore orange ribands and soldiers orange cockades. Wolfe Tone noticed that in 1792 for the first time since the Institution of the volunteers the ceremony around the statue of William III. was objected to and omitted. *Three* years, therefore, before the birth of the Orange Society the volunteers were dominated by a sentiment clearly hostile to the principles established by the Revolution and centring in William III. Father Cleary all through his book has made it appear that the Orange Society is an organisation opposed to *individuals*, and has quietly diverted the reader's mind from the essential fact that it is opposed to *a religious system which has consistently exhibited in Ireland and elsewhere a remarkable capacity for dominating political movements and combinations to promote sectional and sectarian interests exclusively:* and that Orangeism only became a forceful body when such political movements were more than usually outrageous and violent.

WHY ORANGEISM CAME TO VICTORIA.

One who reads extensively is well aware of the intemperate manner in which most Irish advocates refer to Irish grievances, and the frantic attempts commonly made to represent movements intended to checkmate sectarian and party designs in Ireland as gratuitous persecutions of an injured people. It is also noticeable how some trifling occurrence is exaggerated into a burning injustice crying aloud for redress. This literary style has been imported into Victoria. The *Advocate* has given a small sample of it as shown in the second chapter. Father Cleary deprecates the Orange procession as inimical to peace. If the Orangemen demonstrate, it is stated to be provocation: if they do not, there is at times insulting and irritating exultation over it; when collision is disastrous to the opponents of the Orangemen—the world is invited to sympathise with "the oppressed." (See Dolly's Brae.) Canada appears to be the only spot where Irish Protestants and Irish Catholics can parade without coming into collision. Bryce in his *Short History of the Canadian People*, p. 488, remarks that in most parts of Canada they "look upon the rival processions of one another without bitterness." Prof. Goldwin Smith in *Canada and the Canadian Question*, does not express a very large amount of confidence in

---

62 *Ireland*, vol. iii. p. 427.

the tolerance of the Irish majority. (p. 188.) He refers to the corrupt political influence of the hierarchy in relation to education. (p. 229.) On the same page he says: "The abasement of American politicians and the American press before the Irish vote is one of the most ignominious and disheartening passages in the history of our Institutions." In cutting terms he refers to "the Irish groggeries of New York." Bryce, in the *American Commonwealth*, vol. iii. p. 481, says the Roman Catholic bishops are accused of using secret influence in regard to public instruction, and he admits they "press warmly their claims of denominational education." Why is it that Orangeism arises in those lands where the "Irish majority" are found in large numbers, and is unheard of under other circumstances? As I have no personal knowledge of the conditions under which the Orange Society was introduced into Victoria,[63] I am obliged to fall back upon a publication which I have quoted previously. The Melbourne correspondent of the *Stawell Times* appears to be well informed on the subject, and in his account of the belligerent display by persons wearing green at the Brunswick "Orange Outrage" (*sic*) he expresses himself as follows:—

Sensible people naturally inquire why should these things be? Why should we, who enjoy national and individual freedom in its broadest and most comprehensive sense, be swayed by the strifes and struggles of centuries ago, and driven to take sides in quarrels with which we can have little sympathy? So far as Victoria is concerned, it is accounted for in this way:—In the early settlement of the colony the Irish Catholic element largely predominated. Many of the leading statesmen were of that persuasion, including Sir John O'Shannassy, Chas. Gavan Duffy, who described himself as a rebel to the backbone and spinal marrow; and many others whose names need not be mentioned. The Irish, most of whom belonged to the denomination indicated, were appointed to billets in the Government service, the gaols, police and corporations scattered around the metropolis. As time rolled on the effects became manifest. A spirit of exclusiveness and favoritism was rampant in the department. Then counteracting principles were gradually asserted, and the opponents of the' older system bettered to some extent their instruction. *In plain language the Orangemen became the natural defenders of the common right of all to participate in the privileges and advantages of citizenship, and their efforts in this direction became, in time, successful;* hence those tears.

---

63 In June, 1843, during the first elections in Victoria, Dr. Lang defeated Mr. Curr—a Roman Catholic. "Sectarian feeling unhappily imparted a keen and acrimonious character to the contest, which issued in riots and *awakened slumbering enmities which should never have survived the passage of the seas.*"—(*Colonization and Church Work in Victoria*, Rev. C. S. Ross, p. 133.)

It is a delicate subject to deal with, but of this fact all who know anything of the inner workings of the Government service will tell you that every branch is dominated by one sect or another, and in some cases the officers are divided into distinct camps, each working for the good of its own order.[64]

Here we have a candid statement, and I assume that the writer would not publicly communicate it unless the facts used were notorious, or else he was possessed of evidence so strong as to remove his account from the region of mere probability. The opposition of Victorian Orangeism to Roman Catholic influence on this explanation is as distinct in its nature from that which Father Cleary represents it to be as chalk is from cheese. He sets forth that the Orange Society is based on inveterate opposition to any and every individual who makes a *profession* of the Roman faith, whereas it turns out that a compact portion of the population was unduly in possession of "the emoluments of the public service" because of a political patronage which operated for the almost exclusive advantage of members of the favored creed. Moreover, while they enjoyed this monopoly, persons of a different religious belief were regarded as intruders. There appears to be little doubt that intolerance and exclusion on religious grounds were rampant, but unluckily for Father Cleary's cherished fiction the intolerant and exclusive party were of his own faith, and the "helots" in this colony were *the Protestants*. Graphic pictures of Orangeism need to be disconnected in order to have effect, for when their related circumstances are looked up it is often observed that the public scandals said to be of an orange color change their pigment and turn to *green*. Such men as the writer in the *Stawell Times* and the Rev. J. Gilbertson have inconvenient memories and wield awkward pens, and in this way a curious light is shed upon the inner mysteries of Orange history compiled by Roman Catholic scribes.[65]

---

64 *Stawell Times*, July 26, 1897.
65 Cleary says of Orangemen : "Their system of exclusive dealing loads the dice to some extent against Catholics engaged in business pursuits." (pp. 191-2.) On those matters in which Catholics are notoriously infirm the Father complains most loudly of the Orange Society. Has he forgotten O'Connell's plan of "exclusive dealing," the Land League's terrible "boycott." &c ? The Rev. F. Lynch, B.A., writes, concerning Catholic beliefs : "To enter a Protestant church during worship therein and to die thereafter unshriven would be to incur *the fires of Hell for ever*. To deal with an Orangeman to the neglect of a fellow-religionist would be in some countries to meet *the same dreadful fate.*" —(*Why I left the Church of Rome.* 1895, p. 5.) Information of the way Roman Catholics load the dice may be obtained from the publisher of this work.

"ORANGE ORATORY."

I will now relate some specimen matters to illustrate the subjects discussed at Orange celebrations. They are taken from the Irish press reports of 1897. Mr. J. W. D. Barron, referring to the Diamond Jubilee festivities, remarked: "Nothing could justify the discordant note which had been struck in the House of Commons by the disloyal conduct of the Irish Home Rulers. Such conduct had its reflection in the childish behaviour of their followers in certain portions of Ireland, in parading the streets with black flags and in other ways seeking to dishonor the aged monarch whose reign had been marked by such sympathy towards the Irish people."[66]

The *Catholic Vindicator* in one of its issues asked its readers : —" How does *the Church* regard Queen Victoria and other heretical sovereigns ? Has her name much prominence in her services—nay, is it there at all ? . . . Queen Victoria *is not a member of the Christian Church*. . . . Let us never forget that, whatever her boasted authority may be, it is as nothing, and *less than nothing*, compared to that of the Vicar of Christ."[67] Years ago Lord Russell said the Ultramontane Party "cannot be satisfied unless the sovereignty of Ireland be transferred from our Queen to the Pope."[68] Yet we are to believe that the Orange Society is the quintessence of malignity, for presuming to credit Catholic loyalty as expressed in the terms of its own exponents and from the lips of prominent British statesmen.

Col. Saunderson in 1897 remarked that the Orangemen had assumed " a position of reality and power in the eyes of the world we never occupied before," and he intimated that the Orange Society did not stand " before the Irish people as *a sign of menace to anyone, but as a reassuring element in the country.*" The Rev. Dr. O'Loughlin called attention to the condition of Trinity College, Dublin, which "had been stripped by the Roman Catholic party, and the radicals of England of every distinctive mark of the ascendency of the National Church. The fellow-

---

66 Father Cleary, on pp. 99, 100, quotes instances of extreme statements said to be made by some Orangemen respecting the Queen. He then refers to Her Majesty accepting and reciprocating the pope's congratulations on her jubilee. Alas for the Father ! Michael Davitt has sounded the praise of the " priest in politics," and says that the pope is small potatoes "in Irish national or secular affairs " with both priest and prelate. Then he shatters those pleasing salutations between pope and Queen by representing them as mere *political trickery.*— (*Nineteenth Century*, Jan., 1893. pp. 147-8.)

67 Wylie's *Rome and Civil Liberty*, pp. 94, 95, 96.

68 Godkin's *Religious Hist. of Ireland*, p. 313.

ships, and scholarships, and every position of emolument were thrown open to every man, *independent of creed*, who was able to take them. There was no question as to religious convictions. There was a Roman Catholic Fellów at the present moment. The President of the Philosophical Society was a Roman Catholic. But, because it was not under the heel of Archbishop Walsh, and the Roman Catholic Bishops of Ireland, it was said to be a Protestant University. They wanted 'equality,' and *they had it.* Archbishop Walsh summed up *what they really wanted*, when he asked for an University that was under the absolute control of Roman Catholic authority, and free entirely from an un-Catholic supervision. That would mean *at least half a million of money to go from the pockets, mainly of Protestants, to erect Roman Catholic ascendency.*"[69] Oliver Twist with his plate and Mr. Bumble's " *What!* MORE ? " pale into insignificance beside the characteristic modesty of Archbishop Walsh's request. The Rev. Dr. Kane pointed out a different feature : " We have had a notable instance of the bigotry of spirit which characterises the dominant religion in this country. A Roman Catholic Bishop was asked to allow prayers for Queen Victoria in his diocese on Jubilee Sunday, and he said he would not allow them—*he would forbid them.* He was not an Irish Bishop, but the Irish bishops, of the Roman Catholic body, have displayed a spirit towards the Queen's Jubilee not very different from the right Rev. gentleman, who forbade prayers to be offered for the Queen ; and their representatives in Parliament and their disciples in Dublin have manifested a feeling of the utmost disrespect and disloyalty for our beloved Sovereign. Then we have the dogged bigotry of the Nationalists of Dublin who refuse, year after year, to allow the most eminent citizen to be elected Lord Mayor if he be a *Unionist and a Protestant.*" The Rev. Geo. Moriarty dealt with the Educational question. He asked—" Has not Maynooth College been richly and permanently endowed in 1785 with State money, and in 1869 was handed over a capitalised sum of over £465,000 by the Irish Church Act ? And I find upon most reliable authority that the Romish Church receives nearly £40,000 a year for University education ; and for elementary

---

69 As far back as 1812 Lord Redesdale, opposing Lord Donoughmore's motion on the relief of Catholic disabilities, tabled on April 21st, predicted : " Whoever made up his mind then to vote for the present motion must make up his mind also to give up the Protestant Church in Ireland to make way for a Roman Catholic Establishment in that country." He also recalled Lord Clare's prophecy in 1793 : " You will go on step by step until at last you establish a Roman Catholic Church in Ireland."(—Wright's *Hist. of Ireland*, vol. iii. p. 378.)

industrial education about £830,000 per annum."[70] With respect to the Roman Church in Canada, Mr. Moriarty said that where it was endowed "by the state of Quebec, the population is 600,000. The British have all the wealth and commerce in their own hands, and the Roman Church receives annually the enormous sum of £1,500,000; that is to say—each parish receives £1600 for maintenance and there are about 900 parishes. The Roman Church is said to be endowed with over £12,400,000." Under these conditions the parish priest is pretty sure of his daily bread. These, however, were not the only notes struck. The Rev. E. A. Cooper panegyrised Orangeism by saying: "It has done good work in the past at times when the lives and liberties and properties of Protestants were in danger, and has been a source of strength to the Throne and Empire, and on different occasions *votes of thanks have been passed to the Orange Society in Parliament.* [Father Cleary, in 400 pages of reading matter devoted to the Society never *once* puts before his readers the slightest inkling of this; yet his bantling has a crow over its "reliable information."] On the *third* occasion the vote was proposed by Sir Robert Peel, which gained for him the title of 'Orange Peel.' In more recent times this Society has done incalculable service by being the foremost to stay the tide of the Home Rule movement." The same speaker put into the coin of speech the sentiment of the Orange Society the world over: "We do not want Protestant ascendency, but Roman Catholic ascendency we will not have. We demand simply complete religious freedom and equality, and insist that no advantages shall be given to one section of Christians that are not enjoyed by all. When any attempt is made at unequal or unfair treatment the Orange Society is ever the first to raise the note of alarm."[71] Sir Henry

---

70 Through Maynooth the Roman Catholics by the liberality of state endowment can give their clergy a *gratuitous* education. No Protestant denomination in Ireland can do this, and as Godkin puts it, "the Protestant state *manufactures priests*, but it does not manufacture Protestant ministers."—(*Religious History of Ireland*, p. 312.)

The synod of Thurles, September, 1850, had for its objects a condemnation of the system of instruction adopted in the Queen's colleges and an intention to erect a Roman Catholic University in Ireland on the model of one founded by the Belgian bishops at Louvain.—(*Rome and Civil Liberty*, p. 125.)

The tenacity with which the Irish prelates maintain their policy is indicated by the proposal recently made by Mr. Balfour for a Roman Catholic university in Ireland.

71 In 1834 "the combined efforts of the Irish members proved, as O'Connell had predicted, far too much for the ministry to control. The Catholics had by pertinacious perseverance gained almost everything they had desired to obtain, and had lost nothing. The Protestants had sought for nothing but had lost everything but the uncertain tenure of a State Church. . . . The religious

Lawrence echoed the same sentiment: "All they demanded was true equality of treatment in every respect—religious, political, and social." The Protestant succession to the Crown, said one of the speakers, "is the best guarantee for civil and religious equality."

A writer in the *Belfast Weekly*, commenting on the demonstrations from a civic point of view, observed: "By degrees the most reckless slanderers of Orange Lodges must be shamed into better ways," and that "those most sensitively jealous for the Orange name may well be proud of them." He says that the authorities did not import a single extra policeman and refers to the "folly of flooding the city with strange police, many of them *hot-headed partisans* too, who know nothing of the people of the north." See also Mr. Sinclair's evidence on the "peaceable" character of those who live in the "black" north. (Q's 5087, 5088, 5089) *Irish Parliamentary Committee's Report*, 1835. He describes them as better conducted than either the people of the South of Ireland or the people of England. In the same enquiry it was elicited that for thirty years previous to 1835 Armagh, the most Orange part of Ulster, had not been under the operation of an Insurrection Act, whilst in many of the Green parts of the island during that period this instrument of Government had been frequently introduced. A notable case was given in which the Insurrection Act had a career from 1807 to 1810.—(Q's 4687-4690.)

The two chief resolutions in the 1897 demonstrations were as follow: Prof. Macklin at Glasgow moved: "That we thank God for the scriptural, and *therefore* Protestant Constitution, devised, secured, and established by our patriotic forefathers under William III., the Prince of Orange, and to the principles embedded in this Constitution we ascribe all that gratifying progress in every department of our social and commercial life which has so much distinguished the long reign of our most illustrious and beloved Queen, and which Constitution we pledge ourselves to defend and maintain to the last of our blood and our breath." At Belfast the first resolution was one of congratulation to her Majesty. It was expounded by the Rev. Dr. Kane, G.M. of the county, who said it "speaks the heart language of every Orangeman." This was amply corroborated by the G.M. of Canada, by two delegates from Toronto

---

ascendency in the island in numbers, position, and power had been successfully contended for, had been won, and was for the time, at least, firmly grasped by the Roman Catholics."—(Wright's *History of Ireland*, vol. iii. p. 535. See also Godkin's *Religious History of Ireland*, p. 309.)

by Mr. Beresford of New Zealand, and by an English statesman, Mr. Richardson. This is a rapid analysis of the principal topics engaging the old land Orangeism in 1897, and the reader will see whether it is the ghastly carnival of muddleheadedness, blood-spilling, intolerance, and abuse which it is supposed to be from the type described in the work of the Australian critic. (See "*The Dance of Death,*" p. 220; "*An Ulster Holiday,*" p. 229, &c.) I need only add that the moneys contributed were, as usual, devoted to charitable objects, principal amongst which are the Protestant Orphan Societies of Antrim, Down, Enniskillen, Armagh, Londonderry, and the Presbyterian Orphan Society.[72]

OFFICIAL BLUE BOOKS.

I have already referred to the Parliamentary Committees of Inquiry in 1835, without which Mr. Cleary's work would be emasculated. The report of the English Committee is a master-piece of insinuation against English Orangeism based on the text that every movement of the lodge "*had some political end in view.*" In order to drive this into the public mind the Committee adroitly uses every shred of evidence which can be plausibly urged in favor of its text. The Irish Committee had a peculiar method of procedure in elucidating the truth about Orangeism in Ireland. The *Edinburgh Review* of 1835-36, vol. 62, divides the Committee on its political names, because, as it says, the Grand Lodge accused it (the Committee) of scandalous

---

[72] Father Cleary does not, as he supposes, know all about Orangeism, for he says—"In all its records I have failed to find *a single instance* in which—even at the height of its wealth and power—the Orange Society ever turned aside from the cherished task of fomenting sectarian strife, to found or endow even one solitary hospital, one home for the aged, one *orphanage*, one free school, one college, one university, or that it ever sent a missionary to the heathen, or a voice to speak of Christ to the dwellers in the slums." (p. 103.) I have not thought it necessary to defend the Orange name against such an attack as this, because—1. I understand that one of its principles has ever been to look after its own poor. 2. The Institutions of its benevolence have been steadily growing up in the North and in Canada. 3. The usual Colonial practice has been to devote its public celebration offerings to local hospitals or to other charitable institutions. As to the charge of not sending a missionary to the heathen the Father must see that such a trumpery appeal to bathos is a mis-hit. *Orangeism is not a separate sect.* He complains that the Orange Society libels the good works of Roman Catholicism. What does he say to the following? "The Roman Catholic Church points with pride to her charitable institutions, and the world too often taking such statements at their own valuation, looks on and applauds, and envies this magnificent organisation. But *how little of the truth is known*? The crushing hand of ecclesiastical despotism stifles every cry of suffering or complaint." The writer is approved by Papal Briefs, and is known favorably amongst the Roman Catholics in Ireland, America, and Australia. Does she lie?—(*The Nun of Kenmare*, p. 404.)

partiality, but the *Review* does not contradict the charges made with respect to the unfair means adopted to gag the Orangemen. In the *Dublin University Magazine* we are informed that the Irish Committee " although a party *opposed to the Orangemen possessed a decided majority of its members*, contented themselves with merely laying the minutes of evidence before the House, a line of proceeding which from the character of the tribunal might fairly be interpreted as a VERDICT OF ACQUITTAL."[73] The same magazine, reflecting on Mr. Hume's resolution, says that "upon the most vague, and we may also add ludicrous grounds, *drawn from the English evidence*, he proceeded to bring certain charges against the Irish Orangemen, among others the most absurd and audacious one of a design to alter the succession."[74] With respect to the procedure, we are informed Mr. Finn " appeared throughout as the conductor of the prosecution." At the beginning he was not " ready to adduce any witnesses and called on the opposite party to bring forward those for the defence."[75] After the chief Orange *officials* had been subjected to a *hostile* examination, the calling of Orange witnesses was interrupted. The lodge vigorously objected to this practice, and a definite arrangement was come to that when the case for the prosecution was closed the defence would then be continued. But when Finn's witnesses were exhausted the Commitee *closed its inquiry* and laid the " incomplete and, may we not say, *ex parte* evidence before the House."[76] Neither Cleary nor the *Edinburgh Review* hints at this peculiarity. Gagging Orangeism appears a highly estimable expedient. The *Review* quotes largely from the evidence of Kernan, a Roman Catholic barrister, and all *his* samples of Orange iniquity are faithfully repeated by the Father. They are not answered in the minutes of evidence. But this is not surprising when it is remembered that the replies were *suppressed* by the rising of the Committee. The *University Magazine* declares " Never was there a more honestly unreserved surrender of all their documents made by any public body " than was made by the Irish Orange Order.[77] Speaking of English as compared with Irish Orangeism it is said : " The constitutions of the two bodies were perfectly different—indeed opposite. And the Irish lodges were no more compromised by the insane vagaries of Col. Fairman than by those of Sir. Wm.

---

73 *Dublin University Magazine*, 1836, vol. 7, p. 400.
74 *Ibid*, p. 400.   75 *Ibid*, p. 401.   76 *Ibid*, p. 401.
77 *Ibid*, p. 401.

Molesworth or Mr. Hume."[78] This journal disagreed with the Orange members in Parliament on some points. It says they should have divided the House over retaining the word "Orange" in Lord Russell's motion, and moved a resolution expressive of the objects and utility of the Orange Institution and had it recorded on the journals of Parliament as their protest against the unfair action of the committee.[79] See its issue, p. 687, for an account of the dissolution of the Lodge in loyal obedience to the resolution of ONE BRANCH of the Legislature supported by the expression from the throne. It records Orange sympathy with the peculiar embarrassment of the Sovereign, who had at the time as his cabinet a party with whom he was notoriously on anything but good terms.[80] The *Edinburgh Review* in its bitter prejudice sneers at the "oldest, best, and most sacred of institutions," but admits that the Orangemen "have had a firm and fierce faith in the truth and righteousness and utility of their pernicious institution." Yet it reveals the cloven hoof of political partisanship when it remarks at the conclusion of its tirade :— "We have shown who both can and wish to put it (Orangeism) down: also who neither can nor whose interest it is that it should be put down. All, therefore, who desire the continuance of Orangeism and the raising of the 'no popery' cry will band together against *the present Government*. ITS EXISTENCE AND THAT OF ORANGEISM ARE IN AN INVERSE RATIO TO ONE ANOTHER."[81] Is any further proof needed to show that this article was penned in the interests of the existing ministry and that its support was advocated by the sacrifice of the Orangemen? The *Review* very honestly apologised for some errors respecting the Orange Institution made in this article in a subsequent edition.[82] In a critique of a French author's work on the Reformation the same journal said Phillip II. "held out offers of gold and distinction to any man who was able to accomplish the murder of the Prince of Orange."[83] The object of the infamous Catholic League is said to have been "to exterminate or expel from France all who had embraced a different faith from the Catholic."[84] In its malignity the *Review* draws a parallel between this confederation for the extermination or expulsion of Protestants in which Roman Catholic nobles, bishops and classes were banded, and the Orange Society, but even its hardened literary conscience failed and it virtually gave the advantage *to the latter*.[85]

---

78 *Ibid*, p. 401.   79 *Ibid*, p. 402.   80 *Ibid*, p. 402.
81 *Edinburgh Review*, 1835-6, vol. 62, p. 522.   82 *Ibid*, 1836, vol. 63, p. 275.
83 *Ibid*, p. 7.   84 *Ibid*, p. 9, 23.   85 *Ibid*, pp. 24-5.

I may mention one or two samples of the evidence extracted by the English committee. Mr. Chetwoode, the first witness examined, said that he invited the Duke of York, Commander-in-Chief of the British army, to join the Lodge. The Duke desired to do so provided the Society was indisputably legal. In order to satisfy his mind the rules were submitted to eminent counsel, viz., Sir R. Gifford, Sir Wm. House, Sergeant Lens, Mr. Gurney, Mr. Gaselee, and Mr. Adolphus. On the advice of these jurists new rules were formed and its legality indefeasibly established. (Q's 67-79.) By the passing of the Irish Associations Bill, 1825, such Societies as the Orange Lodges were generally forbidden, and "in deference to the law they (the Irish Society) discontinued their proceedings and dissolved their Grand Lodge." There was also an interruption of lodge existence in England during the Catholic Emancipation agitation but it was only temporary. (Q's 261-2.) Lord Kenyon, having stated that the Irish Orangemen joined the English Society while the Irish Associations Bill lasted (it lived three years), was asked whether he did not think this was an *evasion* of the law. The nobleman replied that he did not, inasmuch as the Irish Institution was in fact given up absolutely during the continuance of the Act. Mr. Innes humorously illustrated the evils of Orange demonstrations in Scotland when he testified that a body of Orangemen held a procession at Airdrie. A number of Irish Catholics from Glasgow came down to oppose it. This militant company missed the men in the gay colors through being strange to Glasgow streets, and positively refused to have their trouble for nothing. As they could not assault the Orangemen, they brawled promiscuously, and "proceeded to acts of considerable violence." (Q's 2904-2916.) This Scotch witness mentioned a second occasion when an Orange procession was proposed to be held. For some reason or other the parade did not take place. But the blood of the anti-Orange party was up, and though the cause of offence was *non est*, somebody had to suffer. The usual "assaults and wounds" were served out. This occurred at Port Glasgow. (Q's 2934 - 2938.) Happy illustrations of the visionary character of Catholic grievances with respect to Orangeism abound in these reports, and at some future day I may return to their more extended recital.

The Report of the Lords on Crime in Ireland, 1839. The reader may compare Father Cleary's selections of the evidence with the following brief extracts. Mr. Plunkett, S.M., bore evidence that Orange processions were peaceable and free from outrage or crime. (Q's 4692, 4700.) Mr. Faucett, J.P., Provost of Sligo, revealed how Government had encouraged the Orange Societies in previous years, and Parliament had thanked them. (Q's 2462-2466.) Mr. Kelly, a magistrate, referred to the prejudice excited against them under the then existing administration, and said that all persons who opposed the late or present ministry were called Orangemen. (Q's 6234-6236.) Capt. Despard, S.M., related the story of one Campbell, an Orangeman, done to death by violence, at Summer Hill. (Q's 3421, 3424.) That the objects of Orangeism were to uphold the Constitution was admitted by Mr. Hamilton, Crown Solicitor. (Q's 9232, 9233), and by Father Cleary's much lauded Under Secretary Drummond. (Q's 13,324-13,327.) No less than three magistrates avowed that Orangeism did not conduce to outrages, neither was it the cause of crime. Mr. Rowan (Q's 1986, 1997.) Mr. Warburton (Q's 803-807.) Mr. Tracey (Q's 4539, 4533.) The following abridged catalogue of evidence was tendered on Ribandism. Mr. Brown, Police Commissioner, said it was bound to commit murders if required. (Q's 4990-4994.) To assemble on pain of death at two hours' notice, said Mr. Rowan, a magistrate. (Q's 1732-1739, 1950.) It had the power to raise the country in a few days, was the verdict of another magistrate, Mr. Despard. (Q's 4869-4075.) Mr. Rowan mentioned that they assembled by order of the Roman Catholic priests. (Q's 1977, 1980-1985.) To exterminate the Protestant religion was represented as an object of Ribandism by Mr. Plunkett. (Q's 4570-4573), and by Mr. O'Ferrall, Police Commissioner. (Q's 4945-4966.) That it was directed against Protestants, was maintained by Mr. Uniacke (Q. 6512), and Asst. Crown Solicitor Seed (Q's 10,238-10,241).

Report of Lords on Outrages in Ireland, 1852-3. Mr. Kirk, in speaking of the party spirit, reflected on Orangeism. Q. 4737. "Has not the legislature of England dealt with party processions and with Orangeism by law ? A. Decidedly, of late. 4738. Has it not put down processions? A. Yes. 4739. Has not the law, generally speaking, been obeyed in the North of Ireland by Orangemen ? A. There was an Orange procession in which a man was killed about a fortnight ago. 4740. Did not the jury find in that case that the policeman who fired at the Orangeman fired imprudently ? Yes. 4741. Generally over the North of Ireland has that law been obeyed ? It has." With regard to Ribandism being but a counterblast to Orangeism, the following evidence was tendered : Hamilton, Crown Solicitor for the North-East Circuit, said that Ribandism was not caused by Orangeism, that, in fact, where there were no Orangemen, the Riband Society was seen at its worst, and the district was full of crime (Q's 1571-1577). Mr. O'Callaghan, a Roman Catholic J.P., declared that Ribandism did not arise in consequence of Orangeism (Q's 5014-5018). This witness spoke of the system of mock trials by Riband tribunals, and alleged that sentences of either severe beating or death were passed upon the offenders against Riband law. "Then they draw lots to see who is to execute the death warrant, and the man who is drawn if he does not go and do it will surely be killed." (Q's 5178-5184.) Brownrigg, Deputy Sup. General of Constabulary, said that witnesses against Riband prisoners, especially informers, had to be protected after giving their evidence (Q's 1939, 1940). This witness put in documents from Ribandmen, all of them with coffins scrawled upon them, and one with a pistol and coffin both. (Q's 1932, 1933, 1934.) Warburton, a magistrate, said he had never heard of anyone but Roman Catholics belonging to the Riband Associations (Q's 63, 64). Hamilton stated that the denunciations of the R.C. clergy had produced "no beneficial change." (Q's 1908, 1909.) Father McMeel admitted that Ribandism was essentially of the Roman Catholic people (Q's 2814, 2815). Add to the foregoing on Ribandism what has been previously mentioned, and the following from Lord Hartington in 1871. "All these acts of violence are, we have reason to believe, the work of the Riband Society. The reports which we receive show that such a state of terrorism prevails that the society has only to issue an edict to secure obedience, nor has it even to issue its edict, its laws are so well-known, and infringement of them is followed so regularly by *murder and outrage* that few indeed can treat them with defiance. Riband law, and not the law of the land, appears to be that which is obeyed," &c.[86] Sir Henry James remarking on this reference by the counsel for Mr. Parnell, said : "*Every word* that my friend Sir Chas. Russell quoted to you as applying to the condition of Ireland in 1870 and 1871, now applies to the condition of Ireland in 1881."[87] The new signboard was the Land League. Father Cleary accuses the Orange Society of being the prime cause of these secret societies in Ireland among Catholics that are so renowned for crime, but their atrocities are not confined to any special season of the year, while his

---

[86] *Ireland's Vindication,* pp. 33-34.
[87] *The Work of the Irish Leagues,* pp. 595, 596.

allegations respecting Orange outrages centre round the 12th July, and then only as the Orangemen were attacked by Roman Catholics.

INCIDENTS OF 1883.

The rev. gentleman has been indebted to party papers for the Rosslea disturbances. I can only quote from non-party sources. With respect to Lord Rossmore's dismissal, in consequence of "resisting the authorities" at an Orange demonstration, Lord Crichton contended in the Commons that while Rossmore "might technically have been in error in refusing to obey the resident magistrate," yet his action had saved a contest between the Home Rulers and the party for the Empire, or, as Crichton put it, he led his people "past the Nationalists without collision." Lord Randolph Churchill said the Orangemen had learnt lessons of violent agitation from the Nationalists, and pronounced the dismissal of Lord Rossmore "as a mere bait thrown out by the Government to catch the Irish vote, and additional evidence that the Kilmainham treaty was still in force."[88] Trevelyan's defence of the Administration was that the Orange Party had not trusted the Executive, " but had taken a way of their own to stop the Nationalist meetings."[89] Mr. Gibson said the action of Government with regard to the Ulster meetings was "uncertain and irregular." He asked why the Orange Lord Rossmore was singled out and other magistrates passed over? With respect to the Dromore business, if the Lord Lieutenant had proclaimed the Nationalist meeting instead of bringing up an army to keep the peace, it might have ended without loss of life.[90] A selection disjointed from surroundings makes effective reading against Orangeism, but it is a perilous expedient for a writer who desires to be trusted by his readers. In 1886 two bottles filled with powder, to which were attached lighted fuses, were thrown into an Orange procession in the month of August.[91] Have we not by such events indicated to us the party of outrage? In 1869 the rights of free speech were assailed at North Shields. A "no popery" lecturer was attacked by an Irish mob 400 strong, who fired into the hall, smashed the windows, and rioted outrageously. In fact, the military had to be called out to cool the heated pulses of those who identified themselves with " popery."[92]

---

[88] *Annual Register*, 1884, p. 21.
[89] *Ibid*, p. 25. [90] *Ibid*, p. 25. [91] *Ibid*, 1886 Chronicle, p. 37. [92] *Ibid*, 1869 Chronicle, page 22.

DOLLY'S BRAE.[93]

The Father has framed his account partially on the lines of Berwick's *Report* and the *Edinburgh Review*, but he is not faithful to either. The latter makes a specious and laboured attack on Orange processions, going back some 20 years. Under cover of assailing Orangeism, a political assault is made upon public individuals who are opposed to Lord John Russell's Government. (pp. 109-118.) It rather grandly intimates that its "sympathies are with the oppressed," and this doubtless accounts for its ingenious undercurrent of apology for Roman Catholics who are presumptively "the oppressed." In the course of its article it is conceded that the Orange leaders "yielded a manly and dignified obedience to the will of the nation," with regard to the resolution of the Commons 1836, for we are told that the Grand Lodge of Ireland dissolved in April of that year. Old Sir Harcourt Lees was said to be the only one who resisted to the death. (p. 92.) Pervaded through and through with Father Cleary's notion that Orange processions provoke the innocent and peaceable Ribandmen, the *Review* does not consider any other aspect worth mentioning. There are variations, however, in its account, from the story related by his reverence. For instance, it is said that 34 years before a contest had taken place at the Brae and a Catholic was killed. The mother of the departed man "left her dying injunctions—so the story goes—that no Orange procession should ever be allowed to pass that way." (p. 99.)[94] Berwick, in his *Report*, says it was a point of honor with the Catholics not to permit Orangemen to pass over Dolly's Brae.[95] According to Berwick, the Orange Institution was reorganised in 1848. This was the year of the Young Ireland conspiracy. In the early part of that year the Orangemen "determined to make a show of their strength, partly at least as a counter-demonstration to the revolutionary party."[96] The Orange procession marched along the new road of Dolly's Brae, and now will appear the many serious gaps in Father Cleary's story as compared with Mr. Berwick's *Report*. The Government Commissioner remarked that the "forbearance shown by the

---

93 Cleary's account will be found on pp. 222-24.
94 *The Edinburgh Review*, 1849-50, Vol. 91.
95 *Official Report*, p. 4.
The Edinburgh Review reveals its bias by mendaciously adding to this statement of Mr Berwick that it was "a point of honor" with the Orangemen to go over Dolly's Brae in spite of their opponents.
96 *Ibid*, p. 4.

Orange Party in not marching by the old road was *claimed as a triumph* by the Riband party, and very gross and insulting songs were printed and sung publicly in the market towns to celebrate the victory."[97] Subsequently to these irritating tactics, an Orangeman was wounded by some of the Riband boys which resulted in his death. In consequence, local feeling was rendered acute, and after his funeral, some of the dead man's friends wrecked the houses belonging to persons they believed had a hand in his murder. Berwick reported that when it was known that the Orange procession meant to follow the old route, the Ribandmen sent a letter, challenging the police, magistrates, and soldiers to meet them at Dolly's Brae. This letter breathed the utmost defiance to the civil and military power, and to Her Majesty's authority, and said it was the last twelfth the Orangemen would ever walk.[98] Naturally, such methods of intimidation roused the spirit of a people, and they refused to be browbeaten. Berwick observes, with some degree of astonishment, that no information was laid before any magistrate, nor any step taken to prevent the procession, nor to warn the parties preparing to join in it of the probable consequences of such conduct.[99] Where were the Catholic objectors who, as a rule, are well acquainted with the forms of law? The Father asserts the Orangemen meant to provoke a breach of the peace, but Berwick's *Report*, the *Edinburgh Review*, the *Annual Register,* 1849, and Wright's *History of Ireland*, all agree that the procession was a perfectly legal one, and the first-named expressly states that no steps were taken by the parties who were hostile to the demonstration to lay their views before the magistrates except in the form of vaporing threats. Berwick refers to the absence of all irritating demeanour by the Orangemen as they marched.[100] The Riband Party crowded on the heights armed, and disported themselves during the whole of the day firing their guns, and performing similar exploits to show their military fitness; and yet, as the commissioner points out, with all the apprehensions entertained about a collision between the parties, no steps were taken to *arrest or disband them.*[101] Nothing occurred on the return through Dolly's Brae, except that some women tauntingly told the Orangemen, many of whom had their wives and families with them, that they "were prisoners and would catch it before

---

97 *Ibid*, p. 5. Naturally, this part of the Commissioner's Report is conspicuous by its *absence*, in the narratives of Dolly's Brae in *The Edinburgh Review* and Father Cleary's book.

98 *Ibid*, p. 6. 99 *Ibid*, p. 6. 100 *Ibid*, p. 7. 101 *Ibid*, pp. 7, 8.

they passed Magheramayo Hill."[102] Evidently therefore it was the well-known design of those Ribandmen, who had been prowling about all day, to slaughter the Orangemen at a certain point. After the squib exploded, Berwick says two shots were fired from the Riband party, followed almost immediately by a volley from the same quarter. With respect to the burning of houses and alleged violence by the Orangemen in the village of Magheramayo, it was said that shots had been fired at the head of the procession, under cover of or from the houses.[103] Beers, against whom the Father is so bitter, saved the life of one Catholic,[104] and, as Berwick observes, the banquet (which his reverence misrepresents as given to "the hero of the day," in speedy celebration of Dolly's Brae), was arranged *long before* the occurrence, elaborate preparations having been made, and tickets of invitation issued in view of it. In concluding his report, the commissioner declared that he did not accuse Lord Roden or Mr. Beers of "using their authority as magistrates with intentional injustice or partiality to either party, nor did he mean to pass any opinion on the legality or character of the Orange Institution or members."[105] Major Wilkinson, in his evidence, said that the leaders of the procession admonished the Orangemen not to fire as they marched—"Mind, boys, not a shot, even in fun."[106] This witness further observed if the Orange party had been told to disperse they would have done so.[107] Major White stated that some of the houses which were burned may have been lighted by stragglers.[108] Capt. Fitzmaurice testified that he never saw the Orangemen use force against the authorities, and never heard an expression from them which would lead him to think they would have resisted changing the route of their procession.[108*] A fair reading of Berwick's report and of the evidence will show the following: (1) That the Orangemen were induced by the intimidating and provoking tactics of the Ribandmen to follow the old route. (2) That had it been reasonably represented to them that bloodshed would probably result from such a course, it would have been abandoned. (3) That the hostile party made no attempt to dissuade the Orangemen from acting within their legal rights, neither did they appeal to the Magistrates, to show cause for their forebodings. (4) That the faction of violence, armed with murder weapons, were allowed to mobilise in the neighbourhood during the whole of the day without any attempt being made by the authorities to disperse them. (5) That this

---

102 *Ibid*, p. 8. 103 *Ibid*, p. 9. 104 *Ibid*, p. 11. 105 *Ibid*, pp. 11, 12.
106 *Ibid*, p. 13. 107 *Ibid*. p. 14. 108 *Ibid*, p. 15. 108* *Ibid*, p. 26.

faction intended to do murderous work when a favourable moment arrived. (6) That they deliberately carried this intention into practice when they were not molested. (7) That only when maddened by the volley poured in upon them and their families did the Orangemen resort to their weapons. (8) That the Magheramayo destruction was the result of alleged shooting at the Orangemen from the shelter of the houses. Berwick, in Cleary's quotation, terms it "the work of *retaliation*" (p. 223).

A political attack was made upon the Orange party in consequence of Dolly's Brae by the Government. Lord Roden (on whom, see Venedey's *Ireland and the Irish*, p. 280), and several magistrates were dismissed from official positions. This was indignantly resented, and Parliament was appealed to. Lord Stanley and the opposition stated the case with great power. The matter was made so serious that the Viceroy of Ireland, Lord Clarendon (on whom, see Duffy, p. 711), was compelled to return to England to meet charges of injustice in connection with this political move. But Irish politics were in such a confused state at the time, that the "no party" cry of Lord Russell prevailed. The episode of 1848 was still warm, and the melancholy " cabbage garden " fiasco was yet fresh in the Irish heart. England's soothing and placatory treatment to ruffled Ireland had to be applied once more. The following quotations from Sir Chas. Gavan Duffy will indicate what had been passing through the minds of Irishmen during this period. Speaking for the Young Irelanders, Mr. Duffy said :—" We knew that the Irish heart *was not dead* under the scarlet jacket. *Nearly half the British army was Irish*, and if we held our ground it was reasonably probable that *they would fly to the national flag*."[109] " *The constabulary and the Irish soldiers* would remember that they and their families *must live in the country* when the contest was over, and that the obligation of subjects and sovereigns was *reciprocal.*"[110] " Loyalty, in the sense of devotion to the person of the Sovereign, *was little known in Ireland.*"[111] Duffy also mentions that after a visit made in the interests of health, subsequent to his trial, he came back to Dublin and found it " in a flutter of factitious enthusiasm welcoming a visit from the Queen." A young Dublin priest came to him " in a fever of excitement to announce that the secret societies *were about to seize the Queen's person* and hold her as a hostage for the State prisoners." The

---

[109] *Four Years of Irish History*, pp. 540-1.
[110] *Ibid*, p. 581.   [111] *Ibid*, p. 554.

proposal was to carry her Majesty to Holt's quarters, the "Dublin Mountains." Duffy, however, says he assured the pious cleric that the project was "folly."[112] The same writer preserves some samples of the poetry of the period. A verse which "was a *prodigious* favorite " ran:

> Ah, my heart is weary waiting,
> *Waiting for the fray—*
> Waiting for the sunlight dancing.
> Where the bristling pikeheads glancing,
> With the rifles alternating,
> Ranks in green and gray.
> Ah my heart is weary waiting,
> WAITING FOR THE FRAY.[113]

Cleary says in connection with Dolly's Brae that the country was reeling from the great famine. But amidst the many injustices Ireland suffered at the hands of England, there is not much prominence given to the addition of £10,000,000 to England's debt to relieve Irish need apart from the private charity of the Protestants at that time. (See what a priest said and how it led to the Six Mile bridge affray.—Wright's *History of Ireland*, vol. iii. pp. 572-3.) For the attitude of the Orangemen towards the insurrectionary movement of 1848 consult Duffy's *Four Years of Irish History*, p. 557. The reason of Father Cleary's effusive compliment to Dr. McKnight is indicated by the same writer. McKnight was the spokesman of the Ulster Presbyterians. "They were willing to join the south, but *on the land question only*," and says Duffy, Dr. McKnight "*believed he could not carry his party with him.*" In other words his personal preferences were not shared by the Presbyterians generally, and McKnight as an honest man was careful to point this out. (p. 437.) Observe also a letter from "the man who exercised the widest influence over Protestant opinion at the time," in which it is stated that Duffy could "not find *ten men of his own creed* in Ireland who would be as tolerant as himself." (p. 580.)

"THE WORST OF CÆSARISMS."

In closing these chapters, it will be manifest to the reader that I have not occupied myself with repeating old songs and party watchwords to depict the glories of Orangeism. Nor yet have I aimed to represent Orangemen as ridiculously ideal creatures in sinless garments. Most people know to-day that—Roman Catholicism excepted—there is no perfect thing on earth ; and

---

112 *Ibid*, p. 762.   113 *Ibid*, p. 622.

we are even told that there are "spots" on the sun. My object has been to show that through a long period of time, and by a whole series of events, Roman Catholic influence, socially and politically, has naturally expressed itself. These acts and movements have created and sustained the Orange Society. Anyone hitherto unacquainted with Orangeism, reading Father Cleary's work, would inevitably come to the conclusion that Orangemen, from the beginning even until now, have been *fiends* or *fools*, or BOTH, masquerading under Christian and humane sentiments, without one inherent qualification to match their outward professions. I cannot conceive it possible that an intelligent reader could arrive at any different verdict in substance. It was imperative that this should be called to book, seeing that the attack came from a Roman Catholic priest, who cannot plead now, as he did before, that he wrote in a spirit of self-defence. All through the work bearing Father Cleary's name, his mind appears to be weighted with the view that, because he has a Pope, the Orangemen must have one too ; and that as his Church is co-ordinated by a crushing despotism, this must be the principle which holds Orangeism together. Let us hear two eminent Continental scholars, whose acquaintance with the policy of the Vatican is unquestionable. The former is in " Holy Orders," whose genuineness is not disputed by the Holy See, while the latter is in the front rank of German theological thinkers.

Pére Hyacinthe Loyson, writing from Paris, Whit Sunday, 1893, gave what he called "*My Testament*,"[114] at the age of 66 years. In that writing he says :—" I closed, in the very meridian of its splendour, my career as a preacher, and deliberately descended from the pulpit of Notre Dame, to enter on a hand to hand conflict with *the worst of Cæsarisms*—that of the Papacy." Speaking of the Roman Church, he asks—" What has she done ?' She has never ceased dreaming of the temporal power, and promoting clerical reactions, including that which she is concealing —not very clearly just now—under the mask of the Catholic Republic, and of Christian Socialism. She has stifled in the soul that worship of the Father in spirit and in truth, which her Divine Founder bequeathed to her as the very essence of His Religion, and she has taxed her ingenuity to fill its place with puerile performances, with grotesque legends, and with pilgrimages, popular, alas, in proportion as they are *pagan*." Father Hyacinthe has been looking for a Pope who would take

---

[114] The *Contemporary Review*, July, 1893.

in hand *the reformation of the Papacy,* but his hope is small, for he despairingly says—" it would be *a miracle,* I admit." Dr. Döllinger has an even more strenuous tone in his statements. " The fulness of power to which the Popes, from the time of Gregory VII., have laid claim, is quite BOUNDLESS and UNDENIABLE ; it can penetrate over all, wherever, as Innocent III. says—*there is sin,* and call everyone to account with Sovereign caprice ; it tolerates no appeal, as the Pope, according to the utterance of Boniface VIII. carries all rights in the shrine of his breast; in other words *the tribunal of God and of the Pope* IS ONE AND THE SAME." The doctor is a Roman Catholic, and is said by Prof. Rentoul to be " the most learned man the Roman Church possessed."[115] Döllinger further says:—" Yes, indeed ! Protestantism must be conquered, or where possible, annihilated and extirpated, and the idea of *toleration, equality of religions, or freedom of conscience,* is to be condemned to the lowest hell."[116] These words are pretty plain.

Father Cleary's loaded blunderbuss is apparently aimed, in Father O'Doherty's phrase, to *"seal the doom"* of Orangeism in Victoria. His production is calculated, it seems to me, to inflame the feelings of Roman Catholic readers, and induce them and others to imagine that the members of the Orange Society cherish, with malignant zeal, an intention to trample upon them. It is more likely and better adapted to do this than to form a public opinion, leavened by fairmindedness adverse to Orangeism. His work ignores every historical incident, narrative, and circumstance which is favourable to the Society made the subject of his pen. Some of its quotations are scandalously clipped, samples of which I have given. It suppresses in many instances all local connections with regard to episodes used to illustrate the supposed native and essential evils of Orangeism. It is querulous always—at times bordering on the hysterical—towards every form of speech adopted on Orange platforms to express the nature, methods, and dogmas of the Church of Rome. On page 170 occurs the following : " In the last chapter I have tested the sincerity of the ' Qualifications of an Orangeman,' by the touchstone of a single fact, namely, the *language* habitually used by the brethren regarding Catholic persons," &c. If the Roman Church were tested by the same " touchstone " to find out its true feeling towards Protes-

---

[115] *The Early Church,* &c., p. 189.
[116] *History of the Jesuits*—Griesinger (Scott's translation, 3rd edition), 1892, p. 778.

tants—what then? Possibly the reverend gentleman sees nothing ominous or offensive to Protestants in the term *heretic*, which is notoriously the habitual epithet in the Catholic vocabulary to describe them. Ignoring all such matters his "muckrake" is employed gathering up particles of rubbish, doubtless on the principle that every "mickle makes a muckle" against the Orange Society.

To accomplish his object of rendering the Society innocuous to Catholics, I commend to him, and to those of his co-religionists who are in agreement with him, the following from a weekly journal: "If any considerable number of Catholic Irishmen wish to put down Orangeism let them say straight out what their policy is and they will be admired for their frankness.[117] . . . There is but one effective method of suppressing political and militant Orangeism in Victoria. The way to do it is for the Hibernian Hall politicians to discontinue the practices which have provoked Orangemen into forming themselves into political organisations. Orange Societies exist because Home Rule Societies exist. . . . . What is objected of many Irishmen in Australia is that they permit Home Rule considerations to enter into and form part of their political action in these colonies. They vote at Australian elections for candidates who take a Home Rule view of Irish grievances. They acclimatise, ventilate, and live upon grievances (mainly sentimental) which in no way concern Australia. They think they are showing loyalty to Ireland by brooding over Irish troubles in Australia,[118] and by

---

117 Andrew Kennedy, the informant in the Brunswick case, to test the legality of Orange processions, stated that he was fined £10 for an assault on the processionists in 1897. "Mr. Purves :—Where did you get the money to pay the fine? Where do you think? Was it from the Roman Catholic Hibernian Lodge?' I don't know. How much money did you give Mr. Gaunson when you instructed him? *I had nothing to do with the money.* Witness continuing, said that he did not know where the money came from unless it was from the 'Test Fund.' He *did not know* what the 'Test Fund' was. Mr. Purves :—Come now! Did you come down by the last shower? Don't you know that it is a fund subscribed by Roman Catholics to prosecute these people because they are Orangemen? Witness continuing, said that he went to Brunswick *to have a hand in breaking up the procession.*"—(*The Age*, Feb. 11, 1898.)

118 See similar views from America, *Times Articles, &c.*, pp. 423-425.

In the Melbourne *Argus*, May 23, 1891, appears an article on "Irish Australians," by "One of Them," in which the writer asserts : "The Irish in Australia are on the down grade to helotage." He gives as the inducing cause : "Briefly, separate Roman Catholic education. This contains in itself another cause—*the usual ascendency of a priesthood* when comparative prosperity follows indigence in their flocks. For *the people themselves* would not have refused the advantages of education and communion with their fellow men, which the Education Acts gave. Their present opposition *is solely due to the action of their priests*, and on their heads of course, any evil results will, in the long run, rebound."

allowing such troubles to influence them in the attitude they assume towards their fellow Australians. . . . Such being the case the so-called Defence League instead of getting Orangeism wiped out will only succeed in intensifying the zeal of the Orangemen, who, whenever issues of a semi-religious character are raised in Australia, always find themselves on the winning side. Whenever there is a coalition against the Irish party, as there was at the elections in 1883, the party almost disappears from the Legislative Assembly."[119]

We are assured by the book under notice that the Orange question is "looming up," and that "for several years past a distinctly *forward movement* has been manifest among the Orange Lodges in the colony of Victoria." Does the author know that "for several years past" writers—most likely priests—have been using the press, in the month of July, to make attacks on the Orange body? Has it escaped him that these fighting letters have skilfully bidden for Protestant sympathy against alleged Orange intolerance? Then what of the recent violent attacks made on Orange processions: the formation of a Catholic Defence (*sic*) League: the prosecution of Orange processionists: the raising of a "Test Fund": and to crown all the appearance of a work—and such a work—as *The Orange Society*: what does it all mean? Possibly the Father's "sixth sense" enables him to proclaim that on the *subject* of Orangeism there is a "forward movement"; and yet its functions may be so defective as to prevent him locating the precise point from whence the movement starts, or identifying the hand that gave it stimulus. However this may be, it appears very certain from the circumstances mentioned that a section, at least, of Roman Catholics is bent on discrediting the Society in Victoria. I withhold my opinion as to the result of the efforts. But I venture to affirm that the Protestant feeling which Orangeism represents is not a vanishing quantity, and it will exist in the form of the Orange Society or some other until the causes which created and keep it alive have ceased to be. Mr. Cleary refers to Orangeism as being "little known": these brief chapters may therefore contribute towards that "comprehension" which the late Professor Huxley declared "is more than half way to sympathy."

---

[119] The *Australasian*, Sept. 17, 1897.

Sir Chas. Dilke records the circumstance, and gives an interesting account of the brief period of power, succeeded by a crushing and unequivocal defeat.—(*Problems of Greater Britain*, pp. 129, 130).

CHAPTER XIII.

The Roman Church and its Priesthood.—Earl Aberdeen's Commission on Maynooth.—Suppression of Orangeism in 1825.

This chapter is omitted in this edition in order to economise space.

APPENDIX A.

The following is what Wright calls one of the Orange Society's "*earliest* public declarations, that of the Orangemen of Dublin, which was addressed ' to the Loyal Subjects of Ireland '":—

"From the various attempts that have been made to poison the public mind, and slander those who have had the spirit to adhere to their King and Constitution, and to maintain the laws, we, the Protestants of Dublin, assuming the name of Orangemen, feel ourselves called upon, *not to vindicate* our principles, for we know that our honor and loyalty bid defiance to the shafts of malevolence and disaffection, but openly to *avow* those principles, and to declare to the world the objects of our Institution. We have long observed with indignation, the efforts that have been made to foment rebellion in this Kingdom, by the seditious, who have formed themselves into Societies, under the specious name of United Irishmen. We have seen with pain the lower orders of our fellow citizens forced, or seduced, from their allegiance by the threats and machinations of traitors; and we have viewed with horror the successful exertions of miscreants to encourage a foreign enemy to invade this happy land, in hopes of rising into consequence on the downfall of their country. 'We, therefore, thought it high time to rally round the Constitution, and there pledge ourselves to each other to maintain the laws, and support our good King against all his enemies, whether rebels to their God or their country; and, by so doing, show to the world that there is a body of men in the Island, who are ready in the hour of danger to stand forward in defence of that grand palladium of our liberties, the Constitution of Great Britain and Ireland, obtained and established by the courage and loyalty of our ancestors under the great King William. Fellow subjects,—we are accused with being an Institution founded on principles *too shocking to repeat, and bound together by oaths at which human nature would shudder*; but we caution you not to be led away by such malevolent falsehoods, for we solemnly assure you in the presence of Almighty God, that the idea of injuring anyone, on account of his religious opinions, never entered our hearts. We regard every loyal subject as our friend, be his religion what it may. We have no enmity but to the enemies of our country. We further declare that we are ready, at all times, to submit ourselves to the orders of those in authority under his Majesty, and that we will cheerfully undertake any duty which they shall think proper to point out to us, in case either a foreign enemy shall dare to invade our coasts, or that a domestic foe shall presume to raise the standard of rebellion in the land. To these principles we are pledged, and in support of them we are ready to shed the last drop of our blood."—(Wright's *Ireland*, vol. ii. p. 593.)

Sir R. Musgrave, in his *Memoirs*, says this declaration was published in the newspapers of the North, at "an early period" of the Society's existence.—(Vol. i. p. 71.) In his appendix, the following signatures are given as attached to the declaration.

THOMAS VERNER.   WILLIAM JAMES.
EDWARD BALL.   ISAAC DE JONCOURT.
JOHN CLAUDIUS BERESFORD.

APPENDIX B.

I was informed that I would find an account of the first attack made upon the Orangemen in this colony in the *Argus* files for 1846. (Father Cleary devotes a few lines to it on p. 6 of his work.) In looking up the volume in the Melbourne Public Library, I noticed that the date and probably the report of the proceedings had been torn out of the paper. On account of this mutilation I am unable to give the date of the *Argus* in which the account first appeared; but the following minute of the Orange Lodge passed July 16th, 1846, was advertised:—

"The Grand Lodge having taken into consideration the position in which the Order is placed by the violent outrage committed on a few of the brethren on the afternoon of the 13th inst., and the unjust and unconstitutional proceedings of the civil authorities thereupon, it was unanimously resolved that the members of the Loyal Orange Institution, having from the beginning made it their study to maintain their opinions without intermeddling with, or giving unnecessary offence to others, and having adhered to this principle on this occasion, the display of their banners being sanctioned by immemorial usage, and being moreover in perfect accordance with the practice even of the St. Patrick's Society, the Grand Lodge considers the outrage which has been committed on a few of their members by an armed Popish rabble as wholly unprovoked and unjustifiable; and regards the conduct of the magistrates, in aiding and abetting a lawless mob, in accomplishing the object of their rioting, as well as in withdrawing protection from the Orangemen when violently assaulted in the quiet and peaceable discharge of their duties (having thereto the *sanction of the magistrates themselves*) as in the highest degree unworthy, unjust, and unconstitutional. The Grand Lodge cannot, therefore, in future repose any faith in magistrates who have shown themselves culpable of so gross a dereliction of their duty, and feeling that with the unlimited powers these magistrates possess in the regulation of public houses, longer dependence on their will is highly unwise and inexpedient, the Grand Lodge enjoins upon all private lodges to proceed immediately with the raising of a fund, by subscriptions or otherwise as may seem meet, for the erection of a building to serve the double purpose of a school to be established in connection with the Institution, and a hall where the anniversary banquets and other festivals of the Order can be held, free from all interference but such as the members of the Institution are able to repel.—By order," &c.

As indicating the aroused feeling of the Protestant section, a piece of poetry was inserted by "Cromwell's Ghost," and it seems to me that the publication of such poetry in the public press could only be justified by the wanton and bloodthirsty character of the attack made on the Orangemen. I do not give the lines at length but only a sample.

> Ye Orangemen of Melbourne, who fondly dreamed the laws
> Were strong enough, at least, to clip the papist rabble's claws,
> No longer on the broken reed of Government rely,
> But "put your trust in God, my boys, and keep your powder dry."
> Sharp ground be every sabre which hangs against your wall,
> Well furnished every loyal house with powder and with ball.
> For of those Ribbon braggarts naught so soon the courage chills
> As a dose of good steel lozenges, when followed by lead pills, &c.

Contrast with this significant poetry the following portion of a series of resolutions carried by a public meeting of the congregation of Scots' Church, Sydney, published in the same issue of the *Argus* and appearing also in that of July 21st and again in July 24th, 1846.

1st Resolution: "That the rapid extension and extraordinary prevalence of Popery in this colony and hemisphere within the last few years, arising on the one hand from an extensive immigration into this territory, at the public expense, from the south and west of Ireland, and from French influence and exertions among the South Sea Islands on the other: combined with the *unequivocal manifestations of the same intolerant, usurping and domineering spirit, which Popery has universally exhibited*, wherever it has hitherto obtained a footing, constitutes a reasonable ground of apprehension and alarm to all the friends of Scriptural Protestantism, and of civil and religious liberty, throughout these important dependencies of the British Empire."

Take, therefore, the Orange resolution, the poem, and the Scots' Church resolution, and an idea will be gained that the "Proscribed Creed" was signalising its existence in a way that Protestants did not exactly relish in 1846.

On July 21, *The Argus* commented : " The Popish riots of the past week are at end, but they have left behind them remembrances which will not be easily obliterated. Of these, utter contempt for the injustice and pusillanimity of the authorities, though the uppermost, is not the worst. It is the effect which their conduct has produced which will tell most fearfully hereafter. Had the magistrates, when they interfered in the disturbance—as it was their duty to do,—acted with sufficient promptness and decision, had they shown they were there merely to preserve the public peace, and *not to aid and assist a lawless mob in violating the law;* the effect of their presence would undoubtedly have been beneficial, and might have tended to the prevention of bloodshed then, as well as in future. As it is, their conduct has produced on the savage minds of the Papists (as well it might), the baneful impression that they have *the countenance and* ASSISTANCE *of the authorities* in their bloodthirsty designs against the Orangemen."

For this outspokenness on the part of the *Argus*, its premises and editor were threatened with mob violence, and being abundantly warned by threats of this character, a letter was forwarded to the Mayor of Melbourne, desiring adequate protection " from the armed rabble of Ribbonmen," but the courtesy of a reply was denied, and no protection given, doubtless as the paper said because it was not of the "*favored color or creed,*" and had criticised the mayoral action severely, which it repeated subsequently, as we shall see.

In the issue for July 24, the *Argus* again deals with current phases of the party feeling which had been stirred by the earlier disturbances of the month. It appears that an effort had been made to issue a Catholic paper, like the *Chronicle*, at Sydney " under the surveillance of the resident clergyman of the Roman Catholic Church." The attempt was a dismal failure, but it was induced because the organ which protected them would not " 'go to the whole hog ' *in justification of the Popish murderers* who assailed the Pastoral Hotel on the afternoon of the 13th inst." A further comment was made in the following passage : " The Popish rabble who *began the battle* seem determined that no step shall be wanting to reduce Melbourne to a par with the most unsettled districts of the south and west of Ireland, the nest from which these birds of ill omen were set loose on the province." Letters were being written to Protestant clergymen under the cognomen of " Captain Rock," threatening them if certain matters were not duly attended to. The chief object of these letters appeared to be the Protestant Sunday schools which were objectionable. I was glad to find in the issue of this date (July 24th, 1846) a full account of the origin and nature of the trouble which agitated Melbourne. It is introduced thus: "Many of our readers having expressed an anxious desire for the publication of a full, true, and particular account of the late Popish riots in time for transmission to the mother country by the mail of the *Glenbervie*, we gladly comply with their wish."

I cannot afford space for all the particulars, but will briefly indicate the leading features. The Orangemen determined to celebrate the 12th July, which fell on a Sunday, by a dinner at the Pastoral Hotel on the following day. The Hibernians called a hurling match at Batman's Hill, which was a ruse to collect their party and invent a plan for spoiling the Orange celebration.* There were thirteen Orangemen in the hotel in the afternoon, seven of whom were furnished with the means of defence. Their chivalrous opponents, having observed the departure of the main body of Orangemen, thought that it was a safe thing to put these thirteen to flight, and then "spoil the Egyptians!" The rioters came prepared for "hurling," and were armed with muskets, fowling pieces, and bludgeons. The initial assault was with stones and other missiles. A man named Leary, a cooper, of Bourke-street, was said to be the first to use a firearm. The Mayor came to put a stop to the rioting, and he was observed in company with Mr. Michael McNamara, Mr. Cr. O'Shaughnessy, and Mr. Patrick Kennedy, " three notorious ringleaders of the Irish rabble on such occasions as municipal elections." On the demand of the Mayor, the Orangemen in the Pastoral Hotel opened the door, when a rush was made, which imprisoned the Mayor in the building, *where he had to remain,* during the bombardment it sustained of bullets and

---

* It is a singular coincidence that an advertisement was inserted in the press calling together a meeting "*to discuss the Irish question,*" on the same date and at much the same place, where it was thought a body of Protestants intended to march in procession at Brunswick in 1896. Mr. Chomley, Chief Commissioner of Police, at the case in Brunswick, when the legality of Orange processions was being tested, testified as follows, under examination by Mr. Purves.

"Do you attribute any effect to that advertisment calling the Irishmen to discuss the Irish question? Yes, I think it was to get them together.

" What was the Irish question? I don't know. I'm too long away from Ireland to say.

" Have you any doubt as to that 'Irish question'? I have very little doubt: but I'm not going to say.

" What was the reason for men carrying sticks do you think? To be ready for an emergency.

" Is 'emergency' your national way for describing a fight? Yes. (Laughter.)

" Do you think if the Orangemen had marched *without* regalia the crowd would have dispersed? No. I don't think so. (Laughter.)"—(The *Herald*, Feb. 10, 1898.)

stones,† but as the Orangemen vigorously returned the compliment, and as the outsiders were not making a successful thing of the campaign, one of the ringleaders called out—"go away! as it was no use attempting to dislodge the Orangemen then, but to return at night and pop the b—— b——-s off one by one as they came from dinner."

When quietude was restored "the poor Orangemen who had been guilty of the serious crime of defending their own lives, had not yet got over their troubles; for though watch-house room was not found for *one out of the many hundreds of armed ruffians* who assailed the Pastoral Hotel, and who were patrolling the streets with their loaded muskets under the very noses of their worships, not fewer than four of the defenders of the house were lodged in durance vile for the offence of having firearms in their possession. One, on the warrant of his Worship the Mayor, three by order of Messrs. Moor and Westby, and bail was refused for their appearance on the following morning at the police office."

One pleasing feature the *Argus* records; the Rev. Mr. Geoghegan, a Roman Catholic clergyman, was early on the scene of the conflict, earnestly persuading his co-religionists to abstain from their hostile proceedings, but as his efforts were futile, he retreated, with the observation that if he were injured by some stray missile, " the fury of the rioters would not stop short of laying Melbourne in ashes."

On the following day the carriage of the resident judge was fired at and he had to return to Melbourne. This occurrence has been minimised by a statement from the judge himself, but the editor makes a special note on the judge's version. Mr. O'Shaughnessy, who had knocked down a youth attached to the Post Office because he was proceeding to the Orange festival, was fined *sixpence* for the assault. In addition to incidents of this nature an interesting account of the methods adopted for pacifying the Irish mob on the one hand and the Orangemen on the other is given in this narrative of the disturbance.

On July 28th, the *Argus* again referred to the matter as follows: " It is a sad mistake in the organs of the popish faction to imagine that any effort at blackening the Orange Institution will have the effect of blinding the Protestant inhabitants of this community, to the extreme atrocity of the late Ribbon attempt at *a general massacre;* or that it

---

† Father Cleary states the matter very coolly in this way:—" A number of armed Orangemen, assembled in the Pastoral Hotel in that city (Melbourne), illegally hung out ' offensive ' party emblems, and, *while the authorities were proceeding to remove the banners and arrest the brethren, fired through an open window a volley* which wounded an inoffensive spectator named David Hurley, led to the death of a chance passer by (Jeremiah Denworth), and narrowly missed taking the valued life of one of the most distinguished statesmen of the colony, Sir John (then Mr.) O'Shanassy." (p. 6.)

will even have the effect of making men who are in the habit of thinking for themselves and allowing other people to do the same, consider the outrage as in any degree excusable."

The famous Parliamentary Committee's Reports of 1835, descanted upon by Father Cleary, were doubtless used, for the *Argus* dissects the Irish committee, and quotes the address of the Grand Lodge in full at the conclusion of its inquiry. On the 31st of July the paper mentioned that the *Sydney Morning Herald* had published the various accounts given of the occurrence in the Melbourne papers, viz., the *Herald*, the *Patriot*, and the *Argus*. The *Sydney Herald* condemned the "Romanists" and the "Melbourne magistrates who mistook their duty in this matter." A letter from "An English Protestant" declares: "It is a well-known fact that the members of the Orange Institution *refrained from walking in procession that no just cause of offence might be given to the Roman Catholics.*" It would appear, however, that whether the Orangemen parade or not the objection still lies to the 12th July coming round in the course of the calendar: the only method of removing offence is to expunge it from the almanac; but that would not annihilate the historic significance of 1690.

In the August 4th number, the *Argus* publishes the mayor's defence of his conduct to the council, and replies to it. In the course of its strictures occurs the following passage: " The *downright falsehood* of which we complain is his Worship's representation 'that about one o'clock on the following day (Tuesday) the opposite factions again arranged themselves into parties and presented an armed appearance, so as to render it again necessary to call out the military, and to read the Riot Act twice.' This is true enough as regards the popish rioters, but *a more palpable falsehood as regards the Orangemen was never given utterance to.* However peaceable the Mayor's own intentions were (and God knows nobody hereafter will suspect him of an inclination for war), they were not more peaceable than those of the Orangemen, nor was their 'armed appearance,' sitting quietly in the upper chamber of an inn, half so warlike as his own." The paper laughs at the Mayor reading the riot act to his own troops, with no rioters in the street, and more than hints that not a desire to preserve the public peace, but pure fright inspired him.

On the Hibernian Organisation the *Argus* delivers the following criticism : " It is perfectly true that the St. Patrick's Society assumes to be a *National* Institution, and professes to repudiate all idea of sectarianism, but of the banners of the Society, one openly pourtrays Popish ascendency, and the others are the banners of the Irish Repealers ; the colors of the Society are those of the Irish Ribbonmen ; and the tunes they play in their public processions are the party tunes of the Croppies. If these, the outward signs and symbols of the Society, are not sufficiently indicative of the real nature of the Society, they ought to be, and it only needs that we should bring to the recollection of our Protestant readers, the protests of the more liberal members of the Society in 1835, and the disclosures of the views of its present leaders during the discussion which was consequent thereupon, to satisfy everybody who is open to conviction, that these outward signs and symbols are to all intents and purposes *the true indication of the state of things within.*" There was some mention made of a public enquiry into the causes of the outbreak, which the *Argus* hailed with delight, but apparently nothing came of the proposal, for I can find no account of it. It would be a useful thing if the Orange Society collected the articles, paragraphs, letters and extracts appearing in the *Argus* during 1846, in connection with the matter, and issued them complete; they would furnish a chapter of Victorian history not very widely or intimately known to-day, and be a commentary on the Brunswick episode of 1896.*

APPENDIX C.

I have regretfully been compelled to omit this schedule of facts and figures, but the following authorities may be indicated :—Mr. Gladstone in the *Annual Register*, 1870, p. 25. Mr. Sinclair in the *Contemporary Review*, July, 1893, " Ulster: Facts and Figures." Consult also Lord Brabourne's *Facts and Fictions of Irish History*, and Dr. Ingram's *History of the Irish Union*. See also Father Cleary, p. 245, Note 9.

APPENDIX D.

Father Cleary uses the proceedings of the " Melbourne Post Office Inquiry Board in 1896 " as a starting point for his long story. These proceedings are supposed to supply very apt illustrations of Orangemen

---

* A short account of the 1846 disturbances is given in *Colonization and Church Work in Victoria*, by the Rev. C. S. Ross, 1891 (pp. 163, 164, 165). Mr. Ross says: "The riotous spirit wandered far afield, and broke the peace of the quiet hamlet of Kilmore; and away out on the Werribee plains one unobtrusive settler nearly fell a martyr to his taste for gorgeous colors." His peril was occasioned through having a handkerchief of " yellow and blue, which without any deep or dark political or partizan design, he had *purchased at John O'Shanassy's shop !!!*" The author mentions that feeling was excited by public attention being directed to " the undue proportion of Roman Catholic immigrants."

and their methods. The inquiry, being a deparmental one, brought into prominence certain statements which, from the selected extracts in the Father's book, suggest the view that some of the speakers were shielding the Orange Society. The Board, because of its limitations, could not —at any rate it did not—pursue its investigations into the connection of the Orange Order with these allegations, but the reverend critic of Orangemen has founded upon them an indictment against the Society of a formidable character. 1st, That "the main features of the evidence" given before the Board, "go to indicate a menacing condition of things for one portion of the population of the colony." Father O'Doherty put it: "The Post Office inquiry reveals what is in store for Catholics if Orangeism be allowed to work its own sweet will." These statements clearly show that the Orange Society is regarded upon *the strength of the evidence* given before the Board as seeking to injure individuals because they are Catholics. But this is not all. Father Cleary proceeds to state two points in connection with the conduct of a witness, viz. (a) "It furnishes evidence of *the iron grip* in which Orangemen are held by their oath or solemn protestation of secrecy." (b) "Our witness's hedging, memory-paralysis, and defiance of the Board of Inquiry are *thoroughly typical* of the attitude of ' loyal' Orangemen all over the world when questioned as to the ' proceedings of the brethren in lodge assembled.'" These, then, are what the Post Office Inquiry of 1896 are to prove.

I wrote to Mr. Macleod, whose name was referred to in the course of the proceedings as W.M. of the Queen's Own Lodge, for information concerning the letter which was said to have come into his possession and which is frequently the subject of remark in close association with the Orange Lodge. (*Vide* Q's 1164, 1166, 1168, 1169, 1170, 1176, 1181, &c.) Mr. Macleod's reply, which is dated "Law Courts, Melbourne, 10/2/98," answers my queries categorically. 1st. He explicitly states: "*The letter referred to in evidence before the Board never came into my possession, nor was it ever seen by me.*" 2nd. Asked to explain the probable grounds of his name being referred to in connection with the said letter, Mr. Macleod states : " At the time of the letter referred to, I was W.M. of the Queen's Own Orange Lodge. One day, three or four men came to my office, and desired to see me. Being strangers to me I enquired what their business was, and they informed me they were Post Office employes, and members of the Queen's Own Lodge." Mr. Macleod then relates the substance of a complaint his visitors desired to make against a servant of the department which was of a very serious nature. "I told them that *this was a matter that the Lodge could not deal with*, and that if their statements were correct, it should be reported to the police. They said that they would be guided by me, and I told them to put their statements into writing and I would deal with it. A day or two later, Mr. Wood, Secretary of the Queen's Own Lodge, told me that he had received their statements, and agreed with me that the police were the proper persons to deal with the matter, and I told him to forward the statement and the names of the men to the Post Office police." 3rd. In reply to a further question Mr. Macleod wrote: "To my knowledge *the question was never mentioned in any way in the Lodge.*" 4th. In concluding his letter the writer stated: "When I heard of my name being mentioned I was quite willing to give evidence before the Board, if called, and to state then what I state now. I would further add that *the Lodge had no knowledge of this matter at all*, as I acted on my own responsibility as W.M. in connection with it", Mr. Wood amply corroborates Mr. Macleod, and was anxious to appear before the Board in order to refute officially the statements which at least implied that the Lodge as such was a party to the letter so often referred to. The Father has overloaded his gun with this charge and the weapon "kicks." As it is very evident that the Orange Lodge did not discuss the matters contained in this letter, it is hardly to be wondered at that the witnesses said to be Orangemen were unable to assist the Board with any revelations of what transpired in the Lodge-room. And because they could not tell anything, the circumstance furnishes Father Cleary with an illustration of the "iron grip," "memory paralysis," &c. &c. "thoroughly typical" of Orangemen. The treatment of the Post Office Inquiry 1896 in the reverend gentleman's book indicates the character and characteristic of the whole work. There is a little plausible something as a nucleus and then it develops into a miracle of outrage or injustice.

www.ingramcontent.com/pod-product-compliance
Lightning Source LLC
Chambersburg PA
CBHW032144230426
43672CB00011B/2450